The United Nations

The United Nations

An Introduction

Second Edition

Sven Bernhard Gareis

Editorial Consultant: Trudy Fraser

First edition authored by Sven Bernhard Gareis
and Johannes Varwick and translated from the German
by Lindsay P. Cohn

Originally published in German by Verlag Barbara Budrich

This is an adapted and updated translation of the 4th German edition.

This edition published 2012 by PALGRAVE MACMILLAN

Palgrave Macmillan in the UK is an imprint of Macmillan Publishers Limited,
registered in England, company number 785998, of Houndmills, Basingstoke,
Hampshire RG21 6XS.

Palgrave Macmillan in the US is a division of St Martin's Press LLC,
175 Fifth Avenue, New York, NY 10010.

Palgrave Macmillan is the global academic imprint of the above companies
and has companies and representatives throughout the world.

Palgrave® and Macmillan® are registered trademarks in the United States,
the United Kingdom, Europe and other countries

ISBN 978-0-230-20889-6   hardback
ISBN 978-0-230-20890-2   paperback

This book is printed on paper suitable for recycling and made from fully
managed and sustained forest sources. Logging, pulping and manufacturing
processes are expected to conform to the environmental regulations of the
country of origin.

A catalogue record for this book is available from the British Library.

A catalog record for this book is available from the Library of Congress.

10 9 8 7 6 5 4 3 2 1
21 20 19 18 17 16 15 14 13 12

Printed and bound in Great Britain by
CPI Antony Rowe, Chippenham and Eastbourne

Contents

List of Figures and Tables

Figures

Tables

Preface to the Second Edition

Almost seven years after the publication of the first edition of *The United Nations: An Introduction*, a revised and updated second edition is overdue. Dynamic developments in all areas of global politics have strongly impacted the structures and working procedures of the United Nations, which in turn has required new institutions and new mechanisms to meet these new challenges and tasks.

In September 2005 more than 150 heads of states and governments convened at the World Summit to celebrate the United Nations' sixtieth anniversary and to herald a number of substantial reform steps intended to make the organisation fit for the challenges of the twenty-first century. In the end, expectations for the 2005 World Summit usurped achievement, but the Summit's outcome document still represents the most comprehensive initiative for reform in the history of the United Nations, and some significant steps have subsequently been achieved in the organisation's core areas of responsibility. The creation of the UN Peacebuilding Commission opened new paths to more consistent international efforts for the sustainable re-establishment of peace and order in war-torn states. Growing confidence in the UN's capacity to conduct increasingly complex peace missions found expression in an ever-increasing number of peacekeepers (there are now fifteen peacekeeping deployments worldwide.) A permanent Human Rights Council was established to replace the discredited Commission on Human Rights. The 'Responsibility to Protect' – the idea that the international community must take measures, including the use of Security Council-mandated force, to protect populations when their own governments are unable or unwilling to do so – has been accepted as an emerging norm.

On the other hand, a number of crucial problems remained unsolved. Little progress has been made towards accomplishing the Millennium Development Goals that aim to significantly reduce global poverty and under-development. The 2009 Copenhagen Conference on climate change failed to reach an agreement on a follow-up of the Kyoto-Protocol. Significant institutional reform of key UN bodies, such as the long overdue reform of the Security Council, remains caught in a time-loop of endless debate.

Seven years of UN achievements and shortcomings called for a comprehensive revision of the first edition of this book. Though this second edition largely sticks to the well-proven structure of the first edition, considerable change and update had to be done in all chapters. As a result, this second edition similarly claims to provide a broad-ranging and state of the art introduction to the UN, reliable information and concise analyses of the UN's structure and work, and the prospects for the UN in the twenty-first century.

As with the first edition, I would be eager to receive any suggestions for improvement or for any information that could be useful in preparing the next edition – and particularly for any feedback arising from the use of this book on university and other courses.

Over the course of preparation of this new edition, a change in the book's authorship took place. Due to new obligations and a massive workload resulting from the takeover of a new professorship at the University of Erlangen-Nuremberg, Johannes Varwick decided to withdraw from our common project. I am grateful for his dedicated work on the first edition and I sincerely hope that he will be rejoining forthcoming versions. I also want to thank Trudy Fraser for her excellent editing and indexing which has contributed so much to the clarity and readability of this book and for her other helpful suggestions.

SVEN BERNHARD GAREIS

Preface to the First Edition

The United Nations (UN) plays a singular role in the discussion regarding the future of international politics. Although founded in 1945 and thus at the time of writing, some six decades old, the organization sometimes gives the impression that it is still in need of a foundation. Whether it be peacekeeping, strengthening human rights, dealing with problems of the global environment or the struggle against international terrorism and its manifold causes, there hardly seems to be a global problem in the world today in which the United Nations is not expected to play a key role. On the other hand, it is always pointed out in the very same breath that, for the UN to play its role adequately, it stands in need of reform and renewal. Moreover, a fundamental change in perspective – especially on the part of the more powerful member states – is necessary for the UN's success. A further complaint often heard is that on especially important issues – such as the recent war in Iraq – the UN is frequently avoided or even deliberately shoved aside. It is obvious that a great gulf still exists between the UN's actual capabilities and the strong organization that many desire it to be.

That the United Nations is sought-after in its capacities as an agent and as a forum in such a wide spectrum of political issues is attributable primarily to the fact that the organization can boast almost perfect universality (with 191 states as members). Also important, however, is the UN's self-understanding as a broad global forum for international co-operation. The United Nations was created to be a comprehensive organization not only in terms of its membership, but also in terms of the breadth of its competencies. Each aspect of its work – peacekeeping, human rights, development co-operation, environmental protection and so on – will be emphasized in turn by the people for whom those tasks take precedence. Since the very beginning, the work of the United Nations has been based on a broad concept of peace; one that goes beyond the mere prevention of war to include the improvement of the humanitarian and social condition of humankind, the strengthening of international law, and concerns regarding sustainable development. In this sense, at least, the UN has been astonishingly modern.

It is because of this broader concept of peace that the goals of the UN Charter comprise a much broader field of responsibility than the mere possibility of using military force against an aggressor. Other areas include the resolution of disputes by peaceful means, the search for co-operative solutions for economic, social, cultural and humanitarian problems, and the encouragement of behaviour that accords with the principles of international law. This ambitious catalogue of goals makes it quite clear that the UN does not understand itself as a mere means to the fulfilment of a specific task, but rather envisions a qualitative change in international relations in general. The UN's concrete fields of activity have broadened considerably since the founding, without requiring changes to the Charter. In the words of the current Secretary-General, Kofi Annan, for the first forty-five years of its existence, the UN stood in the shadow of the Cold War, which prevented the organization from fulfilling some of its core responsibilities, but also led to the discovery of other essential tasks. But now, even the core tasks have undergone some changes of their own. For example, at the time of its founding, inter-state warfare was the greatest threat to international peace and security, but at the start of the twenty-first century, internal conflicts and a fundamentally different concept of war are on the agenda.

It is also impossible to overlook the fact that the UN in its present form is unable to play its role adequately as motor and agent of a comprehensive politics of world order. It is thus no coincidence that reform of the UN has a prominent position on the international agenda. Within the reform debate, a distinction can be made between reforms of organizational law, which can be made without any changes to the Charter, and constitutional reforms, which require the Charter to be amended. While numerous important projects falling under the first heading have been implemented during Kofi Annan's tenure, the hurdles facing changes of the second kind remain extremely high. Thus, with reliable regularity, some portion of the list of reform proposals is to be found on the agendas of diverse working groups of the General Assembly and Security Council without there ever being a consensus in sight. Although there exist plentiful fundamental disagreements over the organization's precise future form and function, there is a general consensus that the UN stands in need of comprehensive reform. Both the Charter and the organization itself require a basic overhaul, and what all the reform exigencies have in common is that the measures necessary to implement them can be decided upon and put into practice only by the member states themselves. In such a situation as this, it is almost impossible to make predictions about the chances for success of central projects such as Security Council reform.

The world organization's persistent need for reform should not, however, distract anyone from the fact that the United Nations is indispensable for the stability of the international system. Political practice unfortunately does not usually keep pace with the demands of an ever more complex listing of international problems. Sustainable solutions to humanity's chief challenges in the twenty-first century are most likely to be found multilaterally, and the UN plays a prominent role in the warp and woof of international regimes and organizations. However, it is also true that if the existing institutions do not succeed in solving the problems of international politics, states will seek other types of solutions. Thus it is necessary for the UN to deliver realistic contributions to the solution of problems if the organization does not wish to sacrifice its significance. If the member states fail to support the organization more strongly and consistently, however, success will not be possible.

This book approaches its subject in nine steps, each presented in a separate chapter. The individual chapters may be seen as self-contained pedagogic units, but they do, of course, build on one another, and a truly substantiated picture of the UN's potentialities emerges only when the book is taken as a whole.

The first chapter presents a basic introduction to the structure of the UN. Along with an overview of the organization's historical development, the UN charter and the principal organs, programmes, funds and specialized agencies will be introduced, and their functions and decision-making processes explained. How the UN is financed will also be explained.

In the second chapter, the theoretical perspective takes precedence. Here we ask how an international organization's work can be classified and explained conceptually, and address the challenges that arise from increasing globalization and its impact on the main tasks and functions of the UN.

The third chapter focuses on the principle of collective security – one of the key elements of the UN in the area of securing international peace and security. Both the limitations and possibilities of this principle are explained, as well as the development of the general prohibition on the use of force and the way in which that principle is anchored in the Charter itself.

The fourth chapter assesses the practical side of UN peacekeeping. We provide an overview of all UN peacekeeping operations to date, as well as of the strengths and weaknesses of peacekeeping generally. We also address the role of the UN in relation to disarmament, arms control and prevention. Finally, two short case studies (the impact of international terrorism and the Iraq War) will be used to illustrate current challenges in the area of peacekeeping.

Chapter 5 is about the protection of human rights in the framework of the UN. As in Chapter 3, with peacekeeping, we here discuss the basic questions of the normative development, codification and definition of human rights.

In the sixth chapter, the practice of human rights protection and the relevant treaty bodies take centre stage. Newer approaches to the protection of human rights are discussed, along with so-called humanitarian interventions and international criminal jurisdiction.

Chapter 7 addresses an area of the UN that is often neglected because of the far higher profile (at least in the western world) of peacekeeping and human rights. None the less, we argue, development work and efforts on environmental issues has also become a core task of the United Nations.

Chapter 8 moves on to consider the issue of reform, and in particular the necessity and prospects for change in relation to the areas described in the preceding chapters. Along with conceptual questions of the extent and limitations of the reformability of the various UN organizations, this chapter will introduce and analyse several concrete reform proposals.

In the final chapter, we attempt to pull all these strands together to produce a balance sheet of the work of the UN. This chapter raises the fundamental question of how possible it is to steer and direct international politics, introduces new concepts of global governance and multilateral co-operation; and assesses the prospects and outlook for the UN in the twenty-first century.

Overall, our central purpose is to provide an introduction to the UN's central fields of activities, to evaluate the chances of reform in these fields, and to discuss the role of the organization in international politics. The book is addressed primarily to students of the political and social sciences, but also to teachers and lecturers involved in political education as well as a broader circle of interested readers in politics, journalism and society at large. It is conceptualized in such a way that the most important organs, committees and mechanisms of the United Nations will be described in terms of their legal and institutional composition, but will also be subjected to a political science treatment of their strengths and weaknesses. Thus the book should be useful even to readers who are not yet well acquainted with the United Nations organization.

A review of the original German-language version of this book in the periodical *Vereinte Nationen* ('United Nations') concluded that the book 'conveys a clear and readable synopsis of the potentialities, advantages, weaknesses, and problems of the UN, and it is to be presumed that anyone who has read this book is now in possession of a well-founded understanding of the United Nations'. If this is in fact the case, then we, the authors, have achieved our goal: to produce a challenging but readable, comprehensive but not too detail-obsessed, critical but not unfair, political science analysis of the organization with all its potential and limitations.

In 2004, this book went into its third edition in the German language, and has enjoyed a widespread and positive reception in the German-speaking world. For this English version, the book has been further revised and substantially recast in line with the rather different style and approach of Anglo-American textbooks. We very much hope that the book is as well received in the English-speaking world! We shall, of course, be grateful for any suggestions for improvement or for any information that could be useful in preparing the next edition – and particularly for any feedback arising from the use of this book on university and other courses.

The English edition has a companion website at www.palgrave.com/politics/gareis-varwick, which includes links to other relevant websites: the complete text of the UN charter; a full list of member states with their accession dates and current budget contributions; and more detailed information on the United Nations system and its constituent organizations. We also plan to provide updated material reflecting substantial changes in the organization and functioning of the UN since completion of the book.

We would like to express our heartfelt thanks to Lindsay Cohn, who not only transformed the German manuscript into idiomatic English with great dedication and competence, but whose understanding of political science has also contributed to the clarity and readability of the content.

Sven Bernhard Gareis
Johannes Varwick

List of Abbreviations

ACABQ	Advisory Committee for Administrative and Budgetary Questions
APLC	Anti-Personnel Landmines Convention
AU	African Union
BTWC	Biological and Toxin Weapons Convention
CAT	Convention against Torture
CCM	Convention on Cluster Munitions
CD	Conference on Disarmament
CEDAW	Convention on the Elimination of all Forms of Discrimination against Women
CERD	Convention on the Elimination of all Forms of Racism
CHR	Commission on Human Rights
CPC	Committee on Planning and Coordination
CRC	Convention on the Rights of the Child
CSD	Commission on Sustainable Development
CTBT	Comprehensive Test Ban Treaty
CTBTO	Comprehensive Test Ban Treaty Organization (preparatory commission)
CTC	Counter-Terrorism Committee (of the Security Council)
CTITF	Counter-terrorism Implementation Task Force
CWC	Chemical Weapons Convention
DC	Disarmament Commission
DDR	Disarmament, Demobilization and Reintegration (of former soldiers or warriors)
DESA	Department for Economic and Social Affairs
DFS	Department of Field Support
DGACM	Department for General Assembly and Conference Management
DM	Department of Management
DPA	Department of Political Affairs
DPI	Department of Public Information
DPKO	Department of Peacekeeping Operations
DSS	Department of Safety and Security
ECA	Economic Commission for Africa
ECE	Economic Commission for Europe
ECLAC	Economic Commission for Latin America and the Caribbean
ECOSOC	Economic and Social Council
ECOWAS	Economic Community of West African States
ECPS	Executive Committee on Peace and Security
EOSG	Executive Office of the Secretary-General
ESCAP	Economic and Social Commission for Asia and the Pacific
ESCWA	Economic and Social Commission for Western Asia
EU	European Union
EUFOR	European Union Force
FAO	Food and Agriculture Organization
GNI	Gross National Income
HDI	Human Development Index

HLP	High-Level Panel
HRC	Human Rights Council
IAEA	International Atomic Energy Agency
IBRD	International Bank for Reconstruction and Development
ICAO	International Civil Aviation Organization
ICC	International Criminal Court
ICCPR	International Covenant on Civil and Political Rights
ICESCR	International Covenant on Economic, Social and Cultural Rights
ICISS	International Commission on Intervention and State Sovereignty
ICJ	International Court of Justice
ICSID	International Centre for Settlement of Investment Disputes
ICTR	International Criminal Tribunal for Rwanda
ICTY	International Criminal Tribunal for the Former Yugoslavia
IDA	International Development Agency
IFAD	International Fund for Agricultural Development
IFC	International Finance Corporation
IFOR	Implementation Force
IGO	International Governmental Organization
ILC	International Law Commission
ILO	International Labour Organization
IMF	International Monetary Fund
IMO	International Maritime Organization
INGO	International Non-Governmental Organization
INSTRAW	International Research and Training Institute for the Advancement of Women
IRO	International Refugee Organization
ISAF	International Security Assistance Force
ITU	International Telecommunication Union
KFOR	Kosovo Force (NATO)
LAF	Lebanese Armed Forces
LDCs	Least Developed Countries
MDG	Millennium Development Goals
MIGA	Multilateral Investment Guarantee Agency
MINUCI	United Nations Mission in Côte d'Ivoire
MINURCAT	United Nations Mission in the Central African Republic and Chad
MINURSO	United Nations Mission for the Referendum in Western Sahara
MINUSTAH	United Nations Stabilization Mission in Haiti
MONUC	United Nations Organization Mission in the Democratic Republic of Congo
MONUSCO	United Nations Organization Stabilization Mission in the Democratic Republic of the Congo
NAM	Non-Aligned Movement
NATO	North Atlantic Treaty Organization
NGO	Non-Governmental Organization
NRF	NATO Response Force
OAS	Organization of American States
OAU	Organization of African Unity
OCHA	Office for the Coordination of Humanitarian Affairs
ODA	Official Development Assistance
OECD	Organisation for Economic Co-operation and Development
OHCHR	Office of the High Commissioner for Human Rights

OIOS	Office of Internal Oversight Services
OLA	Office of Legal Affairs
ONUC	United Nations Operation in the Congo
OPCW	Organization for the Prohibition of Chemical Weapons
OSAA	Office for the Special Adviser on Africa
OSCE	Organization for Security and Co-operation
OSG	Office of the Secretary-General
P5	Permanent Five
PBC	Peacebuilding Commission
PBF	Peacebuilding Fund
PBSO	Peacebuilding Support Office
PKO	Peacekeeping Operation
SC	Security Council
SFOR	Stabilization Force
SHIRBRIG	Standby High Readiness Brigade
SRSG	Special Representative of the Secretary General
UN	United Nations
UNAIDS	Joint United Nations Programme on HIV/AIDS
UNAMA	UN Assistance Mission in Afghanistan
UNAMET	United Nations Mission in East Timor
UNAMID	African Union/United Nations Hybrid Operation in Darfur
UNAMIR	United Nations Assistance Mission for Rwanda
UNAMIS	UN Advance Mission in Sudan
UNAMSIL	United Nations Mission in Sierra Leone
UNAVEM	United Nations Angola Verification Mission
UNCRO	United Nations Confidence Restoration Operation in Croatia
UNCTAD	United Nations Conference on Trade and Development
UNDC	United Nations Disarmament Commission
UNDCP	United Nations International Drug Control Programme
UNDESA	United Nations Department of Economic and Social Affairs
UNDG	United Nations Development Group
UNDOF	United Nations Disengagement Observer Force
UNDP	United Nations Development Programme
UNEF	United Nations Emergency Force
UNEP	United Nations Environmental Programme
UNESCO	United Nations Educational, Scientific and Cultural Organization
UNFCCC	United Nations Framework Convention on Climate Change
UNFICYP	United Nations Peacekeeping Force in Cyprus
UNFPA	United Nations Fund for Population Activities
UN-HABIT	United Nations Human Settlement Programme
UNHCHR	United Nations High Commissioner for Human Rights
UNHCR	United Nations High Commissioner for Refugees
UNICEF	United Nations Children's Fund
UNICRI	United Nations Interregional Crime and Justice Research Institute
UNIDIR	United Nations Institute for Disarmament Research
UNIDO	United Nations Industrial Development Organization
UNIFEM	United Nations Development Fund for Women
UNIFIL	United Nations Interim Force in Lebanon
UNIKOM	United Nations Iraq–Kuwait Observation Mission
UNISDR	United Nations International Strategy for Disaster Reduction
UNISFA	United Nations Interim Security Mission to Abyei/Sudan

UNITAR	United Nations Institute for Training and Research
UNLB	UN Logistics Base (in Brindisi)
UNMEE	United Nations Mission in Ethiopia and Eritrea
UNMIBH	United Nations Mission in Bosnia and Herzegovina
UNMIK	United Nations Interim Administration Mission in Kosovo
UNMIL	UN Mission in Liberia
UNMIS	United Nations Mission in the Sudan
UNMISS	United Nations Mission in the Republic of South Sudan
UNMIT	United Nations Integrated Mission in Timor-Leste
UNMOGIP	United Nations Military Observer Group in India and Pakistan
UNMOP	United Nations Mission of Observers in Prevlaka
UNMOVIC	United Nations Monitoring, Verification and Inspection Commission (Iraq)
UNO	United Nations Organization
UNODA	United Nations Office for Disarmament Affairs
UNODC	United Nations Office on Drugs and Crime
UNOHRLLS	UN Office of the High Representative for Least Developed Countries, Landlocked Developing Countries and Small Islands Developing Countries
UNOMIG	United Nations Observer Mission in Georgia
UNOPS	United Nations Office for Project Services
UNPREDEP	United Nations Preventive Deployment Force
UNPROFOR	United Nations Protection Force in the Former Yugoslavia
UNRISD	United Nations Research Institute for Social Development
UNRWA	United Nations Relief and Works Agency for Palestine Refugees in the Near East
UNSAS	United Nations Standby Arrangement System
UNSCOM	United Nations Special Commission (Iraq)
UNSSC	United Nations System Staff College
UNTAC	United Nations Transitional Authority in Cambodia
UPU	Universal Postal Union
USA	United States of America
UNSECOORD	Office of the United Nations Security Coordinator
UNTAES	United Nations Transitional Administration for Eastern Slavonia, Baranja and Western Smyrnum
UNTAET	United Nations Transitional Administration in East Timor
UNTAG	United Nations Transition Assistance Group
UNTSO	United Nations Truce Supervision Organization
UNU	United Nations University
UNWTO	World Tourism Organization
USG	Under Secretary-General
WFP	World Food Programme
WHO	World Health Organization
WIPO	World Intellectual Property Organization
WMD	Weapons of Mass Destruction
WMO	World Meteorological Organization
WTO	World Trade Organization

1

The United Nations System

The United Nations (UN) is an international organization of 193 member states – since July 2011 with the accession of South Sudan (see Table 1.1) – that have voluntarily committed themselves to a mutual obligation to safeguard peace and humane living conditions for the peoples of the world. In addition to the current 193 member states the UN includes one non-member state and one non-member entity – The Holy See and Palestine respectively – who participate as observers to UN sessions and activities. Various other intergovernmental organizations also have standing invitations to participate as permanent observers. The UN's unusually large membership and breadth of participation are some of the elements that help the organization to realize its claims of universality for its goals, norms and principles.

The UN Charter was signed in June 1945 by fifty founding member states. (Poland, which had not been able to participate in the founding conference, later entered as the fifty-first founding member state). Since the UN's foundation, a further 142 states have joined and this expansion has had fundamental effects on the work of the organization (see Table 1.1). New issues such as development have been drawn into the UN's remit, new organs, organizations, and programmes have been created, and developing countries have acquired a two-thirds majority in the General Assembly. The dramatic increase in membership has been the result of the creation of newly independent states following decolonisation throughout the 1970s, and the establishment of a new international order following the end of the Cold War in the 1990s. (During the East–West conflict of the Cold War there were often political disputes over the accession of any given state, so that many applications for admission came to grief on the alternating vetoes of the USA and the USSR and such states often only obtained admission during phases of eased political tension.) UN membership can never be considered 'complete' or 'capped' – the enduring possibility of state disintegration and the creation of new states means that UN membership will almost certainly evolve from its current 193 members.

Acquisition and loss of membership are covered in Articles 3 to 6 of the Charter. According to these articles, 'all peace-loving states' may become members. The content of the concept of 'peace-loving' is not, however, defined with any measure of specificity and is thus only minimally useful as far as political practice goes. States may become members as long as they 'accept the obligations

TABLE 1.1
UN membership since 1945

Founding members	51 states
Joined 1945 to 1954	9 states
Joined 1955 to 1974	78 states
Joined 1975 to 1984	21 states
Joined 1985 to 2011	34 states
Total members	**193 states**

Source: Information compiled from UN website, www.un.org.

contained in the present Charter, and, in the judgement of the organization, are able and willing to carry out these obligations'. No right of exit or withdrawal is provided for in the Charter. (To date, Indonesia is the only member state to have withdrawn from the UN, which it did from March 1965 to September 1966.) The General Assembly has the option – upon the recommendation of the Security Council and if certain conditions have been met – to withdraw a member state's right to exercise the rights of membership for a certain period of time. The General Assembly additionally has the option to foreclose a state's chances of membership, although this has never happened in practice.

State admission into the UN follows formally on a decision of the General Assembly based on the recommendation of the Security Council. Only sovereign states may become members – thus it is that newly emerged states often consider admission to the UN as the most visible symbol of their new statehood. Almost unavoidably, however, disputes have arisen about what qualifies a state for admission, or what form a state must take to be entitled to the right to enter the UN. One example is the representation of China, which took place for quite some time through the Republic of China (Taiwan), but which – following a decision of the General Assembly in 1971 – has since been administered through the People's Republic of China. Furthermore, between 1974 and 1994 the General Assembly refused to recognize the government of South Africa as the legitimate representative of that country on the grounds of its policies of racial discrimination (apartheid). In the case of Germany, it took until September 1973 for the then two German states – the Federal Republic of Germany (FRG) and the German Democratic Republic (GDR) – to be admitted to the UN, and the GDR's membership then lapsed when it was unified with the Federal Republic in October 1990.

Further problems arise out of the dissolution of states or through secession, when 'pieces of states' demand sovereignty under international law. The example of Kosovo highlights the difficulties a new state may face when trying to join the UN. Kosovo declared its independence from Serbia on 17 February 2008, but despite an advisory opinion by the International Court of Justice (22 July 2010) confirming independent Kosovo's compliance with international law, its status as a sovereign state is still being contested by a number of states including Russia and China. These two permanent members of the Security Council cannot agree to a Security Council recommendation for admission, which is necessary for a decision of admission by the General Assembly. So it remains unclear whether and when the new state of Kosovo will become a UN member. In remains to be seen how long Palestine, which applied for full membership in September 2011, will face similar accession problems due to US opposition in the Security Council. The modalities of state accession to the UN are inadequately regulated in the Charter. However, legal commentaries and decisions of the International Court of Justice and other international treaties and agreements offer assistance in the interpretation of the regulations that do exist. Nonetheless, it is in the nature of international law that recognition is primarily a political right, the practical implementation of which often runs into limitations. The international system has nothing at its disposal comparable to the binding legal instruments of a national political system.

The work of the UN is based on a broad conceptualization of the notion of peace, which goes beyond the mere prevention of war to the improvement of the humanitarian and social conditions of mankind, the strengthening of international law, and extensive concerns of development. The UN Charter articulates a number of opportunities for the principal organs to create appropriate secondary or special organs or to work with other organizations and actors for the accomplishment of their goals. The result of these actions is the so-called 'UN system' – a densely interwoven fabric of institutions and co-operative relationships. The elements of this system, which differentiates itself according to various functional and regional criteria, can be subdivided into two categories:

(i)   the special organs, programmes and regional arrangements created by the UN itself and assigned to the authority of the General Assembly, the Social and Economic Council, or the Secretariat; and

(ii) the specialized agencies: independent bodies that have bound themselves to the UN through agreements, which enjoy legal standing and which fall into a 'family of organizations'.

This system is rounded out by manifold, more-or-less formalized connections to other areas and actors, such as international civil society, the world of business, and the world of science. Thus there are approximately 3,200 NGOs registered with the Economic and Social Council (ECOSOC) with consultative status, and the UN's special organs and programmes maintain fully independent co-operative relationships with committees of experts and state as well as non-state institutions worldwide. The system of the UN is a dynamic image, difficult to define precisely and defying even experts to maintain an overview of the whole.

Along with their differing legal natures, the participating institutions also have different competencies. This variety of form and function makes both the vertical steering and horizontal co-operation of their work anything but easy. Complexity, redundancy and at least partial inefficiency are among the most common accusations laid at the UN's door. These accusations, however, tend to overlook two things:

(i)   This convoluted structure did not emerge independently, but was the product of member states. It is member states' responsibility to adjust the system according to contemporary political circumstances and challenges, even if such action means closing significant interest gaps – for example, between industrial and developing countries.

(ii)   Over the course of nearly six decades, the UN has produced a unique system for the common analysis of problems and the development of solution options for ever-more-global challenges. It is less the deficiencies of the system that prevent its decisive use by the member states than it is their relatively weak will to engage in multilateral co-operation.

Thus, when one sees the terms 'UN system' or 'UN family' in technical literature, this is correct in reference to the description of the extensive network of institutions that the UN has cultivated over the course of its history. Such a description, however, obscures the lack of co-ordination within and among these networks, as well as the real power structures through which the member states play a decisive role. The UN system is therefore best characterized as a 'complicated-diffuse structure', which 'is characterized more as a network of very loosely-coupled institutions which act autonomously – some *de jure,* some *de facto*' (Hüfner, 2002, p. 636).

A Short History of the United Nations

In 2012, the UN looked back on more than sixty-five years of history in a world full of turbulent change. The emergence of the UN during the end-phase of the Second World War meant that the organization was inextricably connected with the experiences of that conflict. However, the mounting East–West conflict of the Cold War made it largely impossible for the organization to be engaged effectively in its original core task of maintaining international peace because its primary decision-making body, the Security Council, was trapped in de facto permanent gridlock because of the antagonism between the East–West superpowers. As a result, processes such as decolonization, and their associated conflicts stood in the shadow of the Cold War. It was also during this time that the UN experienced a continuous increase in its membership, institutional expansion, differentiation in its fields of activity, and the development of new political instruments in the realms of, for example, peace maintenance and the protection of human rights.

It was not until the USA–USSR détente and the Cold War's eventual end that the UN was better able to realize its claims to universality for its norms and values, and achieved the status of a true world organization. The destruction of the USSR and the socialist bloc created a new wave of applicants for UN membership, the Security Council experienced unprecedented freedom of action, and the UN's spheres of responsibility and regulation expanded dynamically until they included numerous domestic affairs of member states. This explosive increase in the number and types of tasks, taking place in the context of globalization, pushed the

UN to the very limits of its capabilities. Following the failures of a few of the larger peacekeeping missions, phases of marginalization alternated with phases of brief renaissance. Since 9/11 and the subsequent Iraq War, the UN has stood at a decisive point in its development: it must, with the support of member states, master the institutional and normative reforms necessary for its continual functioning in a complex world.

The following short history of the UN will present an overview of the major phases of the organization's development. It should be noted that such generalizations are never exact, and that the various phases often overlap in some ways. This historical summary will avoid comprehensive analysis and discussion, as Chapters 2 to 8 discuss the genesis and historical context of the UN's various areas of responsibility in much more detail.

Phase I: The Founding (1941–45)

The idea of founding a world organization existed long before the Second World War. The looming threat and unabated aggression of the German Reich, Italy, and Japan convinced US President Franklin D. Roosevelt as early as 1937 that another world war was unavoidable, and that the USA would have to be involved in it. However, the isolationist mood of large segments of the American population required the creation of a political framework in which American involvement – and the likelihood of great sacrifice – might find widespread acceptance. The lessons emerging from the fate of the League of Nations proved to be an important point of contact. That organization, founded at the end of the First World War as an attempt to gradually eliminate war and violence from international relations, had been defunct for many years. Furthermore, given the inadequacies of the League – from normative provisions, through a lack of sufficient authority, to the unhappy linkage of peacekeeping tasks with the implementation of the Treaties of Versailles, Trianon, St Germain and Neuilly – it would have been in no position to oppose the impending catastrophe of the Second World War. The decisive element, however, was that the League was never able to bring all the great powers into its Permanent Council to take responsibility for world peace. Germany and Japan – permanent members of the Council – left the League in the 1930s, and the USSR was expelled in 1939 after its attack on Finland. Despite the fact that the League had been largely initiated by US President Woodrow Wilson, the USA had never become a member. In forming the UN, US President Roosevelt wanted to ensure that the USA did not repeat this mistake. In the summer of 1941, Roosevelt proposed to British Prime Minister Winston Churchill that a security organization for monitoring the conquered enemy states should be set up, and that this organization should not belong to the USA alone, but should be led in concert with the UK. Churchill anticipated problems in having an organization led by only two powers and instead supported strengthened representation from other regions and powers. Roosevelt and Churchill presented the functional tasks of a future order of world peace in their Atlantic Charter of 14 October 1941, but the organization that was to be responsible for this world order was only mentioned indirectly in its eighth point:

> Since no future peace can be maintained if land, sea or air armaments continue to be employed by nations which threaten, or may threaten, aggression outside of their frontiers, they believe, pending the establishment of a wider and permanent system of general security, that the disarmament of such nations is essential.

After the entry of the USA into the Second World War twenty-six countries, including the USA, UK, USSR and China, took the pledge – via the 'Declaration by United Nations' of 1 January 1942 – to support the Atlantic alliance against Germany, Italy and Japan. This declaration, too, avoided a concrete announcement of a new institution but the self-definition of the group as the 'United Nations' was to become the name of the as-yet-unborn institution.

In 1941 Roosevelt believed firmly in a post-war order led by the USA and the UK, but by 1942 he was willing to include the USSR and China to the circle of powers responsible for world peace (Russell, 1958, p. 96). Roosevelt still believed that the greatest threat came from the enemy states of the Second World War, and that these states could be controlled by the cooperation of the 'Four Policemen'. Churchill objected that future co-operation with the Soviet Union would prove very difficult, and that a China weakened by civil war and Japanese occupation would not be able to meet its responsibilities (Luard, 1982, vol. 1, p. 19). Churchill instead proposed the creation of a more strongly regionalized organization (he suggested regional councils for Europe and Asia under the leadership of a common organization) but these ideas were not well received and were not implemented. Instead, in October 1943, at the conference of foreign ministers in Moscow, China was co-opted into the circle of responsible powers. In their concluding declaration, the four powers – the USA, the UK, the USSR and China – stated:

> [t]hat they recognize the necessity of establishing at the earliest practicable date a general international organization, based on the principle of the sovereign equality of all peace-loving states, and open to membership by all such states, large and small, for the maintenance of international peace and security. (Joint Four Nation Declaration, 1943, Point 4)

The Moscow Conference was a breakthrough point in the creation of the UN. As the lead-state at the Teheran Conference of November 1943, the USA drafted an Outline Plan for the world organization. The Outline Plan placed the creation of an executive council – later to be called the Security Council – at the centre of the organization's decision-making mechanisms. During the following months of 1943 the US State Department developed further Tentative Proposals for a General Organization. Among the most important of these Tentative Proposals was the expansion of the permanent members' circle to include France, and the inclusion of regional arrangements in the collective security system. These 'Tentative Proposals' were the subject of the Dumbarton Oaks Conference of 21

August to 9 October 1944, where experts produced the first draft of a statute and were able to reach agreement on a large number of the proposed provisions that were later incorporated into the UN Charter. (For a comprehensive treatment, see Hilderbrand, 1990.)

The Dumbarton Oaks conference left open a few controversial points, which had to then be personally negotiated by the heads of state of the US, the UK and the USSR, Roosevelt, Churchill and Stalin at Yalta in February 1945, as follows:

- Given the increasingly evident dominance of the Americans in the organization, the USSR sought to rebalance the membership in their direction with the inclusion of its sixteen unified Republics as individual, equal members. A compromise was reached in which Ukraine and Byelorussia (now Belarus) received independent memberships.
- The voting procedure in the Security Council was arranged so that, for non-procedural questions, a quorum of seven out of ten votes, including all five permanent members, was necessary. This formula formed the basis of the Permanent Five's right of veto.
- The USSR was also able to insist that the decision on whether the question at hand was procedural or not was also subject to the veto.
- Roosevelt and Churchill sought to prevent the use of veto in situations where the permanent member is directly affected by the decision, but they were unsuccessful. Only in processes of peaceful dispute resolution under Chapter VI are permanent members expected to withhold their votes in matters pertaining to their own affairs.
- Finally, the American initiative to anchor human rights in the Charter was rejected by Stalin who refused to recognize any connection between human rights and world peace.

After the Yalta agreements, the US, UK, USSR and China (although it would eventually become a permanent member, France was insulted at its non-inclusion in Yalta) invited the forty-five allied states that had opposed Germany and Japan in the war to the founding conference of the UN in San Francisco. Poland was allowed to enter as the fifty-first founding member once its political representation was resolved to the satisfaction of the USSR. At this historic meeting in San Francisco, lasting from 25 April to 26 June 1945, the double privilege of the Big Five through permanent representation and right of veto came under particular criticism. The great powers made it very clear from the beginning, however, that this was the price of their participation in the responsibility for world peace. With such a choice set before them – either to accept the elevated position of the Permanent Five or to give up the project of a world organization for peace – the founding states resolved to accept the lesser evil. The Charter, with nineteen chapters and 111 articles of detailed provisions, came into force on 24 October 1945 with the deposition of the Soviet Union's instruments of ratification.

The UN Charter represents the success of a remarkable compromise, achieved in the exceptional context of the Second World War. The UN thus exhibits much stronger egalitarian tendencies and characteristics borrowed from the League of Nations than Roosevelt had intended. However, the idea of the UN evolved from being an efficiently-run security institution to an inter-state organization with a broad spectrum of tasks. This evolution was necessitated by the growing recognition – expressed early by Churchill – that the level of agreement necessary among the Permanent Five for the sake of taking responsibility for world peace would in fact be nearly impossible to achieve. The looming contradiction between democratic and socialist camps threw a heavy shadow over the negotiations for the UN. Rather than burdening themselves with such responsibility, the great powers concentrated on making it impossible for the rules of the collective security system to be used against them (as later evidenced by Security Council stagnation during the East–West conflict of the Cold War). On the other hand, however, this state of affairs also ensured that the UN could not be put to direct use in the East–West conflict. Had the organization been put to such a test, it would surely have collapsed. Thus the UN was in many ways prevented from meaningful action, but was at the same time and as a direct result of this stagnation able to develop initiatives and instruments that would otherwise never have come to pass.

Phase II: Start-up and Stagnation in the Cold War (1945–54)

Before the Charter came into force a preparatory committee of all prospective member states began work on the organizational and institutional formation of the new organization. An executive committee of fourteen states, including those that would become the Permanent Five, undertook the important conceptual work. The structure of the General Assembly was quickly agreed upon (it was relatively simple to fall back on the model of the League of Nations) and six main committees were created. Against the wishes of the USSR, which was in favour of a decentralized secretariat structure for each of the main bodies, a single centralized UN Secretariat was created. After a few East–West skirmishes, the Norwegian foreign minister Trygve Lie was installed as the first UN Secretary-General on 1 February 1946. In the course of choosing the first Secretary-General, it was also agreed that no representative of any of the Permanent Five should occupy the office of Secretary-General. Following the dissolution of the League of Nations on 18 April 1946, the UN took over not only its offices in Geneva, but also its social and economic working panels. Special agreements were made with pre-existing specialized agencies such as the International Labour Organization (ILO), while others, such as the Food and Agriculture Organization (FAO), were newly created. The 'first-aid' organizations, such as UNICEF (1946) and the Economic Commission for Europe (ECE) (1947), were also founded. The UN Human Rights Commission (1946) was tasked with developing an International Bill of Human Rights independent of the Charter. The first milestone was reached on 10 December 1948 with the passing of the General Declaration on Human Rights was as Resolution 217 A (m).

The maiden session of the General Assembly took place on 10 January 1946 in London, before the question of where the organization would have its main base had been decided. Most of the European states wanted the new organization to be anchored in Europe. Secretary-General Lie, however, pointing to the tragic fate of the League of Nations, supported a completely new start in the USA. This would also, he hoped, tie the Americans into the organization more tightly:

> The challenging question of the future was how to secure the fullest possible US participation in whatever international organization might emerge. A repetition of the tragedy of the League of Nations, stemming not least from the US's refusal to join, could not be permitted. (Lie, 1954, p. 54)

After a discussion lasting more than a month and sometimes becoming very dramatic indeed, the decision was made following a gift of US$8.5 million – for the purchase of real estate on New York's East River – from US business leader and philanthropist John D. Rockefeller, Jr. Rockefeller's offer was accepted, and until their first session in the new buildings, in October 1952, the General Assembly and Secretariat were housed temporarily at Lake Success in New York State.

Several of the organizational decisions made during the initial phase of UN activity showed signs of being influenced by the growing East–West conflict. Given that the majority of member states in the General Assembly were western – and there is, of course, no veto in the General Assembly – the Western bloc was able to push through many of its programmes. The situation was different, however, in the Security Council where vetoes and threats of vetoes were and are a constant presence in every discussion (Patil, 1992). In the Security Council, it became very clear, very early, just how limited the justification for Roosevelt's optimism about the responsibilities of the 'Global Policemen' had really been.

The first major conflict emerged in the debate over the admission of new members. Article 4(1) provides that 'Membership in the United Nations is open to all other peace-loving states which accept the obligations contained in the present Charter and, in the judgement of the Organization are able and willing to carry out these obligations.' The decision based on these conditions is, according to Article 4(2), to be made by the General Assembly on the recommendation of the Security Council. Therefore every permanent member of the Security Council also possesses a practical veto right over the admission of new members. In the years following the organization's founding, the East–West superpowers watched particularly closely to make sure that the other camp did not enjoy any major increases in member numbers. Thus only a small group of states – each of which was considered neutral – was admitted, including Afghanistan, Iceland, Sweden and Thailand (1946); Yemen and Pakistan (1947); and Burma (1948). Several other states failed repeatedly in their attempts to join the organization. Israel was admitted in 1949, but was to be the last state allowed in for a period of six years. The blockade was only overcome in 1955 after which the way was opened for a stream of new members.

Conflicts also developed very quickly over the zones around the fault lines between the two blocs. The USSR attempted to extend its sphere of influence in Iran, Greece and Czechoslovakia, and in the Berlin crisis of 1948–9, the USSR challenged the western powers directly. The UN offered mediation services, started its own initiatives and played an altogether constructive role, but without exercising any decisive influence on the course of the political process between the two superpowers. During the conflict in Palestine, the UN created ceasefire and observer commissions. Indeed, the UN Truce Supervision Organization – the oldest UN peace mission still functioning – evolved out of the ceasefire commission created in 1948. These accomplishments, together with the UN Military Observer Group in India and Pakistan (UNMOGIP) created in 1949 in Kashmir, constituted the foundation for a concept of peacekeeping on the edges of the superpowers' spheres of interest that respected their sovereignty, but was also relatively successful in achieving their objectives.

The young collective security system faced a major challenge on 25 June 1950, when North Korea invaded South Korea. The Security Council met immediately and was able on that same day to pass Resolution 82, which demanded the immediate cessation of hostilities and the withdrawal of the North Korean armed forces behind the 38th parallel. Crucially, Section III of the Resolution also required all member states 'to render every assistance to the United Nations in the execution of this resolution and to refrain from giving assistance to the North Korean authorities' (S/RES/82, 25 June 1950). The Resolution was passed with nine 'yes' votes and one abstention (from non-permanent member Yugoslavia). The USSR was not present to cast a vote because the USSR was boycotting the organization in protest at the General Assembly's decision to recognize the nationalist Republic of China government – which had fled to Taiwan after the Chinese Civil War – over the communist People's Republic of China as the legitimate representative of China. Disregarding the Soviet absence, the Security Council determined two days later to use force against North Korea. Under Resolution 83, the Security Council recommended 'that the Members of the United Nations furnish such assistance to the Republic of Korea as may be necessary to repel the armed attack and to restore international peace and security in the area' (S/RES/83, 27 June 1950).

Under Resolution 83, the collective security mechanism of the UN was set in motion for the first time. The Resolution, however, was not passed according to the provisions of Chapter VII (Action with Respect to Threats to the Peace, Breaches of the Peace and Acts of Aggression) but rather in the form of a Security Council recommendation legitimizing the use of military force. So when the USSR assumed the rotating presidency of the Security Council on 1 August 1950, they used the presidency to hinder progress on the Korean issue through the creative use of the rules of procedures, and in September 1950, the USSR began to use its veto on all Korea resolutions. The issue was only overcome following the passage of the American-initiated Uniting for Peace resolution (A/RES/377 (V)) of 3 November 1950 in the General Assembly which stated in the very first paragraph that:

[I]f the Security Council, because of lack of unanimity of the permanent members, fails to exercise its primary responsibility for the maintenance of international peace and security in any case where there appears to be a threat to the peace, breach of the peace, or act of aggression, the General Assembly shall consider the matter immediately with a view to making appropriate recommendations to Members for collective measures, including in the case of a breach of the peace or act of aggression the use of armed force when necessary, to maintain or restore international peace and security.

As a result of the Uniting for Peace resolution, a commission was established that eventually contributed to the ending of a three-year bloody war (on the role of the UN in the Korean War, see Luard, 1982, vol. I, pp. 229 *et seq.*). This action, however, heralded a power struggle between the General Assembly and the Security Council. After all, according to Article 12(1) of the Charter, the General Assembly enjoys only a subsidiary competence to address issues of international conflict with which the Security Council is already occupied. The Uniting for Peace resolution threw serious doubt on the validity of this rule, and it has in fact over the years lost all significance. The General Assembly's right to give recommendations is now essentially uncontested, and has been confirmed in ten Emergency Special Sessions called on the basis of General Assembly Resolution 377. On the other hand, the hopes nurtured by the USA, that the General Assembly might be established as an alternative decision-making forum for those times when the Security Council was gridlocked, have not been fulfilled. The authority of the General Assembly has never gone beyond the making of recommendations. Even in times when the General Assembly has assumed an authority – such as the General Assembly decision that peacekeeping troops should be immediately deployed to the Suez Crisis (1956) or to Irian Jaya (1962) – each eventually became the purview of the Security Council. For a time at least, however, the General Assembly was in fact able to act as a corrective for the Security Council under the auspices of a US-friendly majority. The Western bloc's interest in such a function for the General Assembly was lost when the decolonization process began to cause a shift in the balance of power.

Phase III: Decolonization and the Emergence of the 'Third World' (1955–74)

The death of Joseph Stalin in March 1953 led to a détente (of sorts) between the two Cold War superpowers. Improved co-operation led also to the dissipation of the stagnation caused by their animosity at the UN. The USSR began to co-operate in a number of UN organizations, such as the ILO and UNESCO, but maintained its distance with respect to others such as the World Bank Group. A series of international conferences led to a far more relaxed international climate, and agreement over the status of Austria, along with the 1955 Geneva Summit Conference of the USA, the USSR, the UK and France, brought the great powers into even closer dialogue. This new willingness to co-operate found its most important expression in the acceptance of numerous states for UN membership. By the beginning of the 1960s, the number of member states at the UN had climbed to 118, necessitating an increase in the number of non-permanent members on the Security Council from six to ten. This was achieved through a General Assembly resolution (A/RES 1991A (XVIII)) of 17 December 1963, which came into force in 1965.

The decisive movement of the UN's second decade was heralded by the independence of numerous colonies, particularly those in the southern hemisphere. As a consequence, the affairs of these new member states began to assume central importance in the work of the UN. The changing balance of majorities in the General Assembly ensured that the interests of the developing countries would be taken into account appropriately in the organizational and institutional development of the UN. The establishment of a number of subsidiary organs focused in particular on development issues (for example, the World Food Programme (WFP, 1961); the UN Conference on Trade and Development (UNCTAD, 1965); and the UN Industrial Development Organization (UNIDO, 1966)). The political organization of developing countries also progressed significantly during this period. Representatives from a group of twenty-nine states met in Bandung, Indonesia, in April 1955, and subsequently became the platform for the Non-aligned Movement (NAM) that was officially established six years later at the Belgrade Conference. At the time of writing NAM has 113 members and is numerically the strongest group of member states within the UN, and its support is required to pass majority decisions. The Bandung Conference was also the starting point for the emergence of the so-called 'Third World' of developing countries, which joined the 'First World' Western bloc and the 'Second World' Eastern bloc. Beginning in 1961, the UN initiated its first 'Development Decade', which was followed immediately by a second, starting in 1971. The General Assembly's recognition of the communist People's Republic of China on 25 October 1971 can be seen as an important step in this context. With that decision, the permanent seat in the Security Council was passed to the mainland-based People's Republic of China, from the Taiwan-based Republic of China.

The role and function of the UN in the countless conflicts plaguing this period was extremely dependent on the constellations of superpower interests. During the Suez Crisis of October and November 1956, France, the UK and Israel employed armed force against Egypt following Egyptian President Nasser's nationalization of the Suez Canal, even though the Security Council had declined to label Egypt's actions a threat to peace. After draft resolutions to end the conflict failed on the French and British vetoes, Yugoslavia proposed calling the first Emergency Special Session of the General Assembly based on the Uniting for Peace resolution. This session produced demands for an immediate ceasefire and the withdrawal of the British, French and Israeli forces. The day after this agreement was reached, Secretary-General Dag Hammarskjöld proposed the creation of a peacekeeping force to monitor the ceasefire. On 4 November 1956, the General Assembly determined to send the United Nations Emergency Force (UNEF I) to act as a buffer between the conflicting parties. Thus the most important peacekeeping instrument of the United Nations, the 'blue-helmet missions', was called into being. For eleven years, UNEF I succeeded in maintaining relative stability in Sinai. When Nasser demanded the withdrawal of the blue-helmets in 1967, the Six Day War followed on their heels.

A second spectacular blue-helmet mission was not far behind. In the summer of 1960, a province (Katanga) of the recently independent former Belgian colony of Congo declared itself independent. Belgium supported Katanga, and Congolese President Patrice Lumumba called on the UN for help. Secretary-General Hammarskjöld recommended the undertaking of an *Opération des Nations Unies pour le Congo* (ONUC). This operation succeeded in negotiating the withdrawal of Belgian forces, but was then drawn into the maze of Congolese domestic politics, which was sliding quickly towards civil war. It was only after serious loss of life and with massive intervention on the part of the USA that the Congo was eventually unified. Secretary-General Hammarskjöld, who had supported this controversial mission in the Security Council and in the third Emergency Special Session of the General Assembly, and had engaged himself actively in its implementation, was killed when his plane crashed in the Congo on 12 September 1961. Although ONUC was considered an overall success, the mission had in fact thrown not only the idea of blue-helmet missions but also the entire UN into a serious crisis. On the basis of ONUC, the USSR and a large number of other states refused to pay their regular contributions and as a consequence the UN was threatened with financial ruin.

During this entire period the UN proved to be largely powerless in dealing with issues directly related to the Cold War superpowers. In 1956, in Hungary, the USSR crushed a civil uprising and then used the Soviet position as a permanent member of the Security Council to veto any action on the issue from that body. The General Assembly consequently called a second Emergency Special Session, and produced a number of declarations and recommendations, but the power of the General Assembly was severely limited and it could do little to influence the course of events It was a similar story during the Cuban Missile Crisis of 1962 when Secretary-General U Thant sought to facilitate discussions between the USA and the USSR without either of them being forced to 'lose face' – but it soon became clear that it would be impossible for the UN to act as an effective mediator between the superpowers. This limited influence also evinced itself in the many-faceted disarmament and arms control efforts with which the UN was constantly occupied through General Assembly panels. The breakthroughs (for example, the Non-proliferation Treaty of 1968–70) and the important talks on strategic arms limitations (for example, SALT I and II) were all affairs of the superpowers.

Phase IV: The Dominance of the North–South Conflict (1975–84)

For a long time, the East–West opposition of the Cold War constituted the central world conflict. The numerical increase in member states from the 'Third World' resulted in that group approaching a two-thirds majority in the General Assembly and as a result, the 'Third World' developed a much stronger self-consciousness. The conflict between the developed North and the developing South, which largely concerned questions of a just world economic order and the balancing of industrialized and developing countries' interests, began to have phases where it overshadowed even the East–West conflict of the Cold War. Besides basic demands for a New International Economic Order, these states' efforts found their most potent expression in the Charter of Economic Rights and Duties of States, adopted by the General Assembly in 1974 (A/RES/39/163). Article 1 of this Charter states that the General Assembly:

> [D]ecides to undertake a thorough and systematic review of the implementation of the Charter of Economic Rights and Duties of States, taking into account the evolution of all the economic, social, legal and other factors related to the principles upon which the Charter is based and to its purpose, in order to identify the most appropriate actions for the implementation of the Charter that would lead to lasting solutions to the grave economic problems of developing countries within the framework of the United Nations.

The dominance attributed to the Group of 77 – a sort of labour union for developing countries – in both the General Assembly and in several of the UN's funds, programmes, and specialized agencies was met with serious criticism from western member states. Some such member states, particularly the USA in its function as both the leading western member state, and as the leading economic state, reacted by withholding payments and contributions and by withdrawing from certain specialized agencies such as the ILO and UNESCO. During this time, the UN was involved in a number of long-term conflicts in the Middle East. In 1973, following the 1967 Six Day War, Israel was attacked for the third time and new blue-helmet missions were begun in the Golan Heights (UNDOF, 1974) and in the Sinai Peninsula (UNEF, II, 1974–9). The partition of Cyprus also required a peacekeeping mission (UNFICYP, 1974), and in Lebanon in 1978, the UNIFIL was added to the list.

At the end of 1979, however, the USSR's invasion of Afghanistan made it once again clear to the world just how narrow the limits of the UN's collective security system really were. The Security Council was gridlocked, and while the urgently-called Emergency Special Session of the General Assembly condemned the aggression, the organization was essentially powerless. The UN's fourth decade had begun with a hopeful explosion of multilateralism and co-operation, but as both sides of the North–South conflict continued to intensify their political–ideological opposition, and as NATO decided to catch up on nuclear armaments leading to a dramatic worsening of relations between East and West, the UN was left with very little room for manoeuvre. It was not until 1985 that a fundamental change in this situation took place, when Mikhail Gorbachev became Secretary-General of the Communist Party in the Soviet Union and there began a lasting thaw between the two blocs that led eventually to the end of the Cold War and the opening up of a UN playing field wider than any it had ever known.

Phase V: Renaissance, Crisis and Attempts at Reform (1985 to Present)

The final phase of UN history will be dealt with in very cursory fashion here, since its developments are the central topics of the following chapters of this book. The superpowers' mutual approach to one another led to a strengthening of the Security Council. The nearly habitual use of the veto became a thing of the past, although the veto by no means disappeared from the stage. The number of new peacekeeping missions matched the number of newly emerging forms of conflict that began to appear all over the world following the end of the all-encompassing Cold War. Within the space of approximately twenty years, the number of peace-keeping missions rose from fourteen to sixty-six (as of October 2011). New tasks in the areas of post-conflict management or transitional situations (for example, in Namibia and Cambodia) required new concepts, but attempts at peace enforce-ment such as those in Somalia and Yugoslavia proved more difficult. The 1990–01 Gulf War for the liberation of Kuwait, conducted on the basis of a Security Coun-cil mandate, fuelled hopes for a new world order built on UN foundations. World Conferences on every imaginable global issue followed one another in rapid succession, from the rights of the child (New York, 1991), sustainable develop-ment and protection of the global environment (Rio de Janeiro, 1992), human rights (Vienna, 1993), women's rights (Beijing, 1995), world population (Cairo, 1999), financing of development in Monterrey (2002) and Doha (2008), and world climate (Copenhagen 2009 and Cancún 2010).

Against the hopes of a more strongly multilateral world, however, stood a number of setbacks and crises. During the Kosovo conflict in 1999, a lack of will-ingness to co-operate in the Security Council led to the first lasting marginalization of the UN through NATO's non-mandated action against the former Yugoslavia. Not least, the attacks of 9/11 and the 2003 Iraq War demonstrated that the United Nations was in need of a fundamental reform of its decision-making structures, as well as both its normative and operational apparatus. Secretary-General Boutros Boutros-Ghali undertook the first steps toward reform in these areas. His successor, Secretary-General Kofi Annan, made decisive progress with reforms of the Secre-tariat and peacekeeping In preparation for the 60th anniversary of the UN, Annan launched a comprehensive reform initiative, including normative and structural changes to the UN System but at the 2005 World Summit the heads of state and government showed only a limited willingness to accept substantial reforms of the world organization. Some progress – such as the creation of a new Peacebuilding Commission (see Chapter 4) or the replacement of the UN Human Rights Commis-sion by the Human Rights Council (see Chapter 6) – was achieved, obsolete passages in the Charter, concerning the enemy state clauses or the Chapter on the Trusteeship Council were also deleted. In crucial policy fields like development, climate change, ecology, or disarmament, however, the heads of state and govern-ment failed to produce more than non-binding declarations of intent. As was the case ten years ago, decisions on the future shape and structure of the UN remain postponed and reform of the UN's main bodies remains at the top of the waiting list of world politics (see World Summit, 2005). The current Secretary-General, Ban Ki-Moon who inherited an uncompleted reform project from his predecessor, has had to focus instead on gradual amendments to the internal organization of the UN rather than on pushing forward decisive renewals.

This short look at the history of the UN has demonstrated that the organization is, and always has been, totally dependent on external conditions. For instance, both the East–West conflict of the Cold War and the North–South conflicts between the developed and the developing worlds have defined the UN's scope of action and left structural impressions on the organization's work:

> The major industrialized countries tend to be interested in promoting order in the international system and managerial and financial efficiency in multilateral institutions like the UN. The developing countries tend to be more concerned with promoting justice, that is, achieving greater economic and political equity through redistribution of resources and enhanced participation in key decision-making. (Mingst and Karns, 2000, p. 44)

The second important circumstance influencing the UN's work was the considerable difference among the various member states' expectations for the organization, and in particular the divergent understandings of the scope of actions to be allowed by international organizations (see Chapter 2). Organizations such as the UN

> have been created largely to promote and protect the interests of states. They enhance the opportunities for participation and influence by small states, coalitions of states, and NGOs. They have also facilitated their own emergence as actors in the international system. (Ibid.)

Since the end of the Cold War, the UN has found itself in the most demanding phase of its development to date. The chances and opportunities, but also the problems and challenges, facing the UN will be subjected to a deep and comprehensive analysis in the following pages. A look at the UN's history, however, makes it very clear that phases of marginalization have alternated consistently with phases of renaissance. In fact, this history can be formulated very simply: crisis is always followed by renewal, until the next crisis comes along.

The UN Charter: Purposes and Principles

The Charter of the UN is the founding document of the world organization. It emerged as an answer to the failure of the League of Nations, which had earned very little respect from its member states and had consequently not been in a position to prevent the Second World War. This catastrophe, the dimensions of which overshadowed all previous wars, led necessarily to the contemplation of a new world order, one that would attempt to altogether prevent further war.

The Charter is often regarded as an odd compromise, and one that could only have been accomplished in the exceptional circumstances that followed the Second World War. The USA, the UK, and the USSR each accepted their respective (and very different) views on the form and purpose of a new world organization, and consequently they came to an agreement on a concert of the great powers. They also agreed that they would co-opt into this concert two more participant states that were more the victims of the war than its victors. The overwhelming majority of the fifty-one founding member states were forced to recognize that an effective world organization was achievable only at the cost of a dramatic lowering of expectations regarding the ideal of equal rights of sovereign states. The UN system that emerged thus carried with it as a birth defect an internal contradiction: on the one hand, the aspiration was to subject states to a universal regime for securing peace, but on the other, the great powers were unwilling to accept the rules of that regime for themselves. Notwithstanding, the Charter of the UN represents a sort of 'constitution of the world community' (Ress, 2002) which has proven itself to be robust and flexible to not only survive the political processes and changes of the second half of the twentieth century, but also to provide it with a generally accepted foundation of international law and an organizational framework. That said, the Charter's legal classification of the UN's goals and principles remains in many ways unclear. Neither the degree to which the Charter is binding – nor the consequences for violations of its terms – are precisely articulated. No unambiguous prioritization of goals can be inferred, and even the assignment of competencies to individual organs and the regulation of responsibilities, remain open to interpretation. The 111 articles of the Charter are divided into nineteen chapters and a Preamble. The Charter serves as follows:

- to bind the behaviour of states in their intercourse with one another, and to an increasing degree in their internal politics, to norms and rules;
- as the organization's statute, to clarify all legal questions relating to the organization, from the conditions of membership to the process of emendation;
- to define the competencies and modes of operation of the primary organs; and
- to limit the responsibilities of the organization with respect to the member states and other international bodies.

In the Preamble, which was first drafted and included with the Charter at the San Francisco Conference, general avowals of the future form of international relations are articulated in very lofty terms: 'We, the peoples of the United Nations' are determined to 'save succeeding generations from the scourge of war', to 'reaffirm faith in fundamental human rights, in the dignity and worth of the human person, in the equal rights of men and women and of nations large and small'. Furthermore, the Charter aims 'to establish conditions under which justice and respect for the obligations arising from treaties and other sources of international law can be maintained', as well as to 'promote social progress and better standards of life in larger freedom'. For these purposes, member states should 'practice tolerance and live together in peace with one another as good neighbours', 'unite our strength to maintain international peace and security', 'ensure, by the acceptance of principles and the institution of methods, that armed force shall not be used, save in the common interest', and 'employ international machinery for the promotion of the economic and social advancement of all peoples'. The purposes of the UN are codified in Article 1 of the Charter in the form of normative obligations for the organization as well as for the member states that comprise it. The basic instruments and guidelines for enactment of these goals are also named. Article 1 reads:

The purposes of the United Nations are:

(1)   To maintain international peace and security, and to that end: to take effective collective measures for the prevention and removal of threats to the peace, and for the suppression of acts of aggression or other breaches of the peace, and to bring about by peaceful means, and in conformity with the principles of justice and international law, adjustment or settlement of international disputes or situations which might lead to a breach of the peace.
(2)   To develop friendly relations among nations based on respect for the principle of equal rights and self-determination of peoples, and to take other appropriate measures to strengthen universal peace.
(3)   To achieve international co-operation in solving international problems of an economic, social, cultural, or humanitarian character, and in promoting and encouraging respect for human rights and for fundamental freedoms for all without distinction as to race, sex, language, or religion.
(4)   To be a centre for harmonizing the actions of nations in the attainment of these common ends.

The primary goal of the UN is the maintenance of international peace and security. All other goals are to serve this primary purpose, which in the sole justification for the existence of the organization (Cede, 2001). Although the concept of 'peace' is of central importance to the work of the UN – and the word is used fifty-two times in the Charter, thirty-two times in reference to 'world' or 'international' peace (Dicke and Rengeling, 1975, p. 15) – there is no precise definition of the concept of peace. The discussion about how to interpret the term has been conducted with predictable controversy, not least because differing views of 'peace' affect the interpretation of the entire Charter and have the potential to impact how various areas of UN competency are evaluated. A narrow interpretation of 'peace' would severely constrict the spectrum of possible actions for the prevention of war and the use of force in the international arena. However, Article 1 seems to suggest a very broad interpretation of 'positive peace' with human dignity and human rights, as well as the creation of social justice, as central components of this position. Thus, the UN – unlike the League of Nations – consciously closely connects the idea of maintenance of international peace and security with several other areas. UN practice also accords with this wider concept of peace in that it has constantly exerted itself in an attempt to remove the structural causes of war and violence, not only through the creation of new special organs, but also through a large number of specific programmes and actions. Furthermore, and in increasing measure, the UN sees its future tasks to be of this kind (Annan, 2000). The development of the UN into a central forum of interaction for the formation of global governance processes would hardly have been possible had it been working from a narrow, or 'negative' concept of peace.

A positive conception of peace, however, raises questions concerning the precise parameters of that concept, and that specific rights and duties to be inferred from it by both the organization and member states. In the history of the UN – and in particular during the 1990s – questions of humanitarianism and self-determination of peoples have come into conflict with the principle of sovereignty and the prohibition on intervention enshrined in Article 2 of the Charter. During the early 1990s some authors suggested that the mere existence of the principles articulated in Article 2 indicated that the purposes of the UN were not to be pursued at *any* price. However, the emergence of twenty-first century humanitarian intervention initiated an intense debate concerning whether or not the protection of human rights and the right of self-determination of peoples should be regarded as having equal weight with the principles of sovereignty and non-intervention. In light of this debate, the Preamble of the Charter has received renewed attention. The Preamble articulates the general purposes of the organization but does not assign specific duties to member states for undertaking these purposes. As a consequence, the Preamble has in practice been considered an aid to the interpretation of the rest of the Charter. The millennium activities of the UN, however, were carried out under the leitmotiv of the first three words of the Preamble: 'We the Peoples', which was intended to express that the UN was not simply dedicated to the interests and concerns of member states, but that the activities of member states is bound up in a responsibility towards the people who inhabit them. This return to the original *raison d'être* of the organization emphasizes an orientation on a positive concept of peace, which not only legitimizes, but practically demands UN operation in areas of economic and social development as well as in the protection of human rights and humanitarianism.

Article 2 of the Charter articulates the UN's basic principles and clarifies the rights and duties of both the organization and its member states. To this end, the position of member states is clarified, and their respective rights and duties specified; the basic structure of the organization is defined; and the competencies of the UN in relation to member states are limited. The principles are described as follows in the seven paragraphs of Article 2:

(1)   sovereign equality of all members of the organization;
(2)   good-faith fulfilment of all obligations assumed in accordance with the Charter;
(3)   the duty to settle international disputes by peaceful means in such a manner that international peace and security, and justice, are not endangered;
(4)   the duty to refrain from the threat or use of force against the territorial integrity or political independence of any state, or in any other manner inconsistent with the purposes of the United Nations;
(5)   the duty to assist in any action taken by the organization, and to refrain from giving assistance to any states against which the organization is implementing preventive or enforcement measures;
(6)   the duty of the organization to ensure that states which are not members act in accordance with the principles in the Charter so far as may be necessary for the maintenance of international peace and security;

(7)   the exclusion of any right of the organization to interfere in matters which are essentially within the domestic jurisdiction of a state except of cases of measures under Chapter VII.

The seven principles – some of which are clarified more precisely later in the Charter – are not equally relevant in UN practice. Paragraph 2, for example, is merely a declamatory emphasis of the old legal principle of *pacta sunt servanda* ('treaties must be fulfilled'). This was intended to express the importance of the general international legal principle of 'good faith', and the expectation that member states would take seriously their Charter obligations. The obligation articulated in Paragraph 5 for member states to assist the UN contains no new obligations beyond those already established in Paragraph 2. This duty relates to enforcement measures that may be undertaken by the Security Council under Chapter VII of the Charter, and is further specified to that effect in Article 25: the member states are bound to accept and implement the decisions of the Security Council. However, no duty to provide troops in the case of military actions is contained in this paragraph, as this obligation could arise only from a special agreement under Article 43. In practice, every use of national personnel for UN actions has been based on the principle of voluntary participation. The entirety of Paragraph 6 is now somewhat redundant given that UN membership is now essentially universal.

On the other hand, the obligation contained in Paragraph 3 to settle disputes using peaceful means, which is further specified in Chapter VI and is constantly reemphasized in one UN declaration after another (see in particular the Manila Declaration on the Peaceful Settlement of Disputes Among States, of 15 November 1982, and the Declaration on the Prevention and Elimination of Conflicts and Situations which might threaten World Peace and International Security, of 5 December 1988), is one of the main pillars of the UN. The peaceful settlement of disputes aims at a comprehensive and lasting end to conflict as a necessary prerequisite to peaceful coexistence. The instruments made available for the peaceful settlement of disputes are more far-reaching and differentiated than traditional military instruments. For example, consensus, confidence-building, co-operation, increasing interdependence and legalization of relations are given as long-term effective instruments for the peaceful settlement of disputes. On the basis of this principle, and following Chapter VI of the Charter, the UN has developed some of their most successful instruments for a sustainable peace of which peace missions (or so-called 'blue-helmet' missions based on the consensus of the belligerent parties) have acquired particular significance. The duty of the peaceful resolution of disputes is intimately connected to the general prohibition on the use of force (Paragraph 4), which has become a central compulsory norm of international law and is often called the heart of the Charter (Cede, 2001).

The general prohibition on the use of force is the UN's attempt to avoid the failures of the League of Nations, which contained only a partial prohibition. Attempts to prohibit the use of force date back to the Briand-Kellogg Pact of 27 August 1928, but that document's attempt to prohibit war allowed the threat and use of military force. The Charter's general prohibition on the use of force is a negative right for all states, whose comprehensive form and clarity of meaning are above all an attempt to prevent the victimization of smaller or weaker states in the service of an 'overarching interest of peace' (as, for example, in the case of Czechoslovakia in the Munich Agreements of 1938). According to this paragraph, violence is fundamentally impermissible – but should it be used, it requires exceptional legitimization. Justification for the use of force can be predicated only on two circumstances: under the right to individual and collective self-defence (Article 51) and on the authority of the Security Council in the case of a threat to or breach of the peace, or an act of aggression (Chapter VII). The exact parameters of member states' right to self-defence has been hotly contested. For example, in the case of intervention to protect a state's citizens (Israel in Uganda, 1976; and the USA in Iran, 1980); of pre-emptive measures (Israel in Egypt, 1967); of retaliatory measures (USA against Libya, 1986; and the USA against Afghanistan and Sudan, 1998); of attempts to recover 'lost territories' (Argentina in the Falklands, 1982); and most recently concerning the US's claim to the right of pre-emptive self-defence, such as in the cases of terrorism and terrorist use of weapons of mass destruction where the US must be able to defend itself through early military action (see Chapters 4 and 8).

With the new capacity for action that the Security Council began to enjoy in the 1990s, the number of interventions mandated on the basis of Chapter VII increased dramatically. The Kosovo crisis of 1999 highlighted the grey zones between the prohibition on the use of force, military intervention in the case of humanitarian catastrophes such as genocide or ethnic cleansing, and the use of military force according to member states' own definitions of interest external to any established international law. Furthermore, the 2003 Iraq War was conducted against the expressed will of the Security Council and consequently presented a serious test to the Charter based system of international peace and security maintenance. These conflicts have drawn both the general prohibition on the use of force and the ostensible monopoly of the Security Council over the legitimization of the use of force in non-self-defence cases into crisis. The general prohibition on the use of force claimed to be a compulsory norm of international law, but the threshold for breaching it legitimately has been lowered (see Chapter 4).

Paragraphs 1 and 7 of Article 2 are closely related, together forming the decisive constitutional principle of the Charter. Paragraph 1 makes clear that states in no way abrogate their sovereignty by joining the UN. This is precisely because they are, of their own free will, assuming certain limitations upon themselves over their sovereign rights associated with particular regulations. These limitations do not encroach on the core of member states' constitutional sovereignty. Additionally, they emphasize the principle of sovereign equality of all UN member states, which corresponds to a fundamental principle of international law. The prohibition on intervention contained in Paragraph 7 arises out of the principle of sovereignty. It creates a negative right for states against the possibility of interference by the organization in matters that 'are essentially within the domestic jurisdiction of a state'. The only limitation on this negative right to be left alone is found in

Chapter VII, in the power to take enforcement measures for the sake of protecting world peace. At that point, the principle of sovereignty and the prohibition on intervention give way to the collective interest in peace. Questions concerning the extent of the constraints on state sovereignty that arise from entry into the UN, as well as that of the competencies of the organization's active organs, constitute the most controversial issues in the UN relationship with its member states. This is particularly the case insofar as the UN is not a type of world government or world court under the rule of world law, but rather a political union whose decisions are dominated by considerations of political opportunity.

In practice, it would appear that the UN has always considered its recommendations to member states to be compatible with the prohibition on intervention. For example, the Security Council delivered two emphatic illustrations of the legitimacy of such actions when it sanctioned then Southern Rhodesia and South Africa in the 1960s and 1970s. In both instances, the Security Council based its interference on the fact that internal human rights situations in both countries were endangering world peace. Beginning with the so-called 'Kurd Resolution' (Res. 688, 5 April 1991), the Security Council expanded its competence systematically over the course of the 1990s to carry out or authorize interventions for humanitarian purposes or in cases of civil war. These interventions have included a gamut of newly created instruments, from criminal tribunals to transitional governments, and also included the use of military force to implement agreed-upon measures. This expansion of the concept of security in general and the understanding of 'international security' in particular caused the dynamic development – possibly even the redefinition – of some of the Charter's central principles:

> The difficulty of precisely delimiting in individual cases the scope of what, in the current status of international relations, belongs exclusively to the realm of an individual state's sovereignty, in which neither the UN nor other states may involve themselves, arises from the fact that the relevant political understandings have changed fundamentally over the past 50 years. (Cede, 2001)

At its core, the principle of state sovereignty remains, but the *domaines réservés* of member states have grown noticeably smaller. The UN Security Council has become more sensitive and active, especially in the field of civil wars and large-scale human rights violations, in recognizing the potential for internal conflicts to become threats to international peace and security. At the 2005 World Summit the heads of state and government accepted a 'responsibility to protect' in cases of genocide, ethnic cleansing, war crimes or crimes against humanity. Although states continue to insist upon the right to defend their sovereignty, the threshold for international intervention into formerly domestic affairs has been systematically lowered (World Summit, 2005, para. 138; 139). However, it still remains an open question as to whether this development should be regarded as a real change in the principle; or whether there now exists some sort of global domestic politics. At any rate, the broad interpretation – especially of Paragraph 7 – points to a progressive erosion of state sovereignty, especially in the areas of humanitarianism and internal conflict.

The Principal Organs: Competencies, Functions and Decision-Making Processes

The UN system – as already mentioned – consists of various and sometimes independent decentralized organizations and programmes, each with its own by-laws, membership, structure and budget. According to Article 7 of the Charter, the UN encompasses six principal organs, the composition, competencies and decision-making processes of which are regulated in later chapters of the Charter. The functioning and policies of these organs are also codified in their respective by-laws. The six principal organs are:

- the General Assembly (Chapter IV of the Charter);
- the Security Council (Chapter V);
- the Economic and Social Council (Chapter X);
- the Trusteeship Council (Chapter XIII);
- the International Court of Justice (Chapter XIV); and
- the Secretariat (Chapter XV).

With the exception of the International Court of Justice in The Hague, Netherlands, all principal organs (also referred to in this text as 'main bodies') of the UN are based in New York. Article 7(2) makes it possible for these organs to create secondary and assistant bodies as they consider it necessary for the fulfilment of their tasks. The Trusteeship Council suspended its work in November 1994; eleven years later member states decided to abolish the Council in the course of a comprehensive reform of the Charter. The main bodies have made frequent and multifarious use of this right, to the extent that there are now hundreds of secondary organs at work worldwide in the form of commissions, boards, standing conferences, funds, offices, high commissioners and missions. These derivational structures have grown organically, and have freed themselves over the course of time in varying degrees from the organizational structure foreseen in the statutes. They thus exhibit various peculiarities, in particular with respect to their configuration, their degree of independence from the main bodies, and their financing (Trauttmansdorff, 2001).

The character of the UN as an inter-state entity finds clear expression in the configuration of its principal organs. The General Assembly, the Security Council, and the Economic and Social Council are comprised of Member State delegations that are bound by instructions from their respective governments. The Secretariat and International Court of Justice are staffed by UN employees and independent judges in the case of the International Court of Justice. The Charter fundamentally regulates both the position of the various organs and their relationships to one another. That being said, certain changes in the role and meaning of certain of the main bodies have taken place in UN practice so that the current constellation is also at least partially the result of the organization's historical development. The main bodies and overall structure of the UN are set out in Figure 1.1. For our purposes it will suffice to limit the treatment here to a brief sketch of their functions within the organization and their relationships with one another.

The General Assembly

The General Assembly is the organizational centre of the UN. It is the only main body in which all member states of the organization are represented equally on the principle of 'one state, one vote'. Representation of the members is accomplished through delegations of up to five representatives of the respective governments. A number of observers also participate in the work of the General Assembly (but do so without voting powers). Observers are primarily states that do not belong to the UN, or special organizations on the basis of special agreements, as well as other international organizations and national relief organizations resulting from special decisions of the General Assembly. In spite of the frequent use of the term, the General Assembly is not a 'world parliament', but rather an inter-governmental forum for consultation and cooperation. The work of the General Assembly takes place primarily in its six main committees, in which the decisions are prepared in plenum. In these committees, as in the General Assembly itself, all member states are represented. The committees are currently responsible for dealing with:

- disarmament and international security (First Committee);
- economic and financial issues (Second Committee);
- social, humanitarian and cultural affairs (Third Committee);
- special political questions and issues of decolonization (Fourth Committee);
- administrative and budgetary affairs internal to the organization (Fifth Committee); and
- legal issues (Sixth Committee).

Every issue of international significance can find a home in at least one of these committees. This basic structure of the General Assembly is also supplemented by a number of secondary and assistant organs that can be activated as necessary.

The General Assembly begins its yearly sessions in September with the election of its leading councils and the general debate (which is usually led by the foreign ministers, or secretaries of state of the member states). In the past, sessions were generally finished by the third week of December, but for some time now the General Assembly has continued to hold meetings throughout the year. Decisions of the General Assembly usually require a simple majority. For important questions (those listed in Article 18(2)), however, such as the selection of non-permanent members of the Security Council or the acceptance or rejection of member states, a two-thirds voting majority is required. The number of resolutions adopted by consensus or acclamation has increased dramatically since the 1990s, so that an overwhelming number of decisions are now reached through consensus proceedings rather than through a formal vote.

With respect to the political work of the General Assembly it is possible to make a distinction between internal and external competencies. The General Assembly functions something like a legislature within the organization itself – it can impose binding decisions on the other main bodies (such as the Secretariat) and the subsidiary bodies (such as those pertaining to the budget) – but it enjoys no such authority in its external relations. Recommendations of the General Assembly are not binding under international law and thus have no claim on the obedience of member states. The Assembly's right to discuss any issue does not have any corresponding authority to constitute binding resolutions. According to the Charter, the General Assembly merely enjoys the privilege of issuing recommendations on all issues falling under its purview (Trauttmansdorff, 2001). However, Article 10 of the Charter empowers the General Assembly to concern itself with practically every question of international relevance, as specified in a number of later articles. The once-significant constraint in Article 12, according to which the General Assembly may not issue any recommendations on a problem that is still being discussed in the Security Council, has in practice lost all meaning.

Although the General Assembly may lack hard instruments such as sanctions, its decisions and declarations are not utterly without effect. Public pressure, together with the political and moral authority of the world community, has helped countless General Assembly declarations and recommendations to reach nearly universal acceptance, and have promoted the development of political and legal standards worldwide. The General Assembly may also create public awareness of world peace and international security issues via their emergency sessions. Emergency sessions are convened when the Security Council is unable to effectively respond to situations of acute crisis or conflict – based on the aforementioned Uniting for Peace Resolution of 3 November 1950 – but what constituted a dangerous raising of tensions in 1950 has now developed into an accepted mode of co-existence between the General Assembly and the Security Council. This finds expression in particular in the fact that the Security Council has called six of the ten emergency special sessions that have so far taken place in the General Assembly. This special form of meeting remains reserved for situations where Security Council action under Chapter VII is impossible because of a veto by a permanent member. Even in the case of emergency sessions, however, the decisions of the General Assembly are restricted to recommendations, and no enforcement measures are available. The first emergency session, called in November 1956 to deal with the Suez Crisis, produced the United Nations Emergency Force (UNEF I) on the basis of the General Assembly's recommendation and the agreement of the parties to the conflict. This was not only the first UN peacekeeping force, but was also the embodiment of the standards for a new instrument for keeping the peace that would prove successful over the long term (see Chapter 4). Thus, at the request of the General Assembly, special meetings may be called to handle current and urgent problems. The tenth – and so far last – of these emergency special sessions was convened for the first time in April 1997 at the request of Qatar, following a number of Security Council meetings on the Israeli decision to build housing areas in Har Homa in an area of East Jerusalem. This special session on 'Illegal Israeli actions in occupied East Jerusalem and the rest of the Occupied Palestinian Territory' is still active and was last resumed in January 2009 in order to consider the situation in the Gaza strip.

26

FIGURE 1.1 The UN system

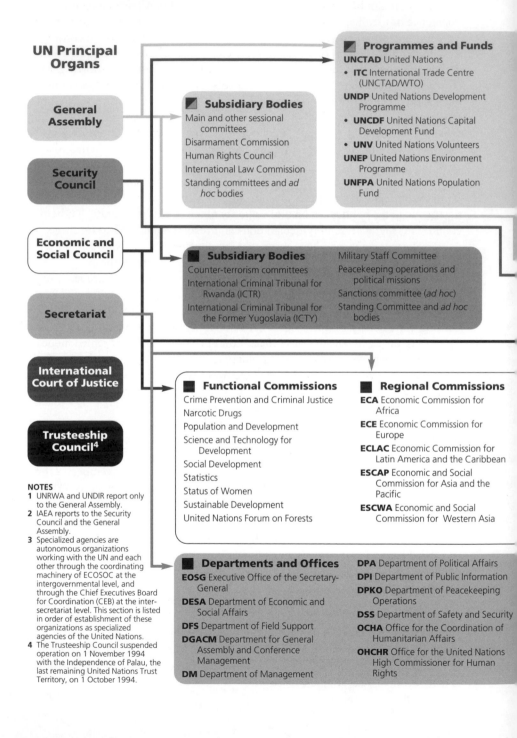

NOTES
1 UNRWA and UNDIR report only to the General Assembly.
2 IAEA reports to the Security Council and the General Assembly.
3 Specialized agencies are autonomous organizations working with the UN and each other through the coordinating machinery of ECOSOC at the intergovernmental level, and through the Chief Executives Board for Coordination (CEB) at the inter-secretariat level. This section is listed in order of establishment of these organizations as specialized agencies of the United Nations.
4 The Trusteeship Council suspended operation on 1 November 1994 with the Independence of Palau, the last remaining United Nations Trust Territory, on 1 October 1994.

UN-HABIT United Nations Human Settlements
Programme

UNHCR Office of the United Nations High
Commissioner for Refugees

UNICEF United Nations Childrens Fund

UNODC United Nations Office on Drugs and Crime

UNRWA[1] United Nations Relief and Works Agency
for

UN-Women United Nations Entity for Gender
Equality and the Empowerment of Women

WFP World Food Programme

Research and Training Institutes

UNICRI United Nations Interregional Crime and
Justice Research Institute

UNIDIR[1] United Nations Institute for Disarmament
Research

UNITAR United Nations Institute for Training
and Research

UNRISD United Nations Research Institute for
Social Development

UNSSC United Nations System Staff College

UNU United Nations University

Other entities

UNAIDS Joint United Nations Programme on
HIV/AIDS

UNISDR United Nations Internatonal Strategy
for Disaster Reduction

UNOPS United Nations Office for Project Services

Related Organizations

CTBTO Preparatory Commission for the
Comprehensive Nuclear-Test-Ban Treaty
Organization

IAEA[2] International Atomic Energy Agency

OPCW Organization for the Prohibition of
Chemical Weapons

WTO World Trade Organization

Advisory
Subsidiary
Body

UN Peacebuilding
Commission

Specialized Agencies[3]

ILO International Labour
Organization

FAO Food and Agriculture
Organization of the United
Nations

UNESCO United Nations Educational,
Scientific and Cultural
Organization

WHO World Health Organization

World Bank Group

- **IBRD** International Bank for
Reconstruction and Development
- **IDA** International Development
Association
- **IFC** International Finance
Corporation
- **MIGA** Multilateral Investment
Guarantee Agency

- **ICSID** International Centre for
Settlement of Investment Disputes
- **IMF** International Monetary Fund
- **ICAO** International Civil Aviation
Organization
- **IMO** International Maritime
Organization
- **ITU** International
Telecommunication Union
- **UPU** Universal Postal Union
- **WMO** World Meterological
Organization
- **WIPO** World Intellectual Property
Organization
- **IFAD** International Fund for
Agricultural Development
- **UNIDO** United Nations Industrial
Development Organization
- **UNWTO** World Tourism
Organization

Other Bodies

Committee for Development Policy

Committee of Experts on Public
Administration

Committee on Non-Governmental
Organizations

Permanent Forum on Indigenous
Issues

United Nations Group of Experts
on Geographical Names

Other sessional and standing
committees and expert, ad hoc
and related bodies

OIOS Office of Internal Oversight Services

OLA Office of Legal Affairs

OSAA Office of the Special Adviser on
Africa

SRSG/CAAC Office of the Special
Representative of the Secretary-General
for Children and Armed Conflict

UNSECOORD Office of the United Nations
Security Coordinator

UNODA Office for Disarmament Affairs

UNOG UN Office at Geneva

UN-OHRLLS Office of the High
Representative for the Least Developed
Countries, Landlocked Developing
Countries and Small Island
Developing States

UNON UN Office at Nairobi

UNOV UN Office at Vienna

Source: Reproduced
from UN website
(www.un.org);
version DPI/2470 –
10-00133 – April
2011 (with the
permission of the UN
Department of Public
Information).

The Security Council

The Security Council consists of fifteen UN member states, of which the USA, the UK, France, Russia and the People's Republic of China are permanent members (the People's Republic of China replaced the debarred Republic of China (Taiwan) in 1971, and Russia succeeded the USSR in 1991). The ten non-permanent members are elected by the General Assembly for two-year terms but may not serve two consecutive terms. Five non-permanent seats are up for election every year and as a result the Security Council's composition changes annually. In January 1966, the number of non-permanent members was increased from six to ten, bringing with it a need for an appropriate geographic distribution of the seats (Art. 23(2)). In practice, a rough system has been established whereby there are always three African, two Asian, two Latin American, one Eastern European and two Western European or Other states represented on the Security Council.

The Security Council's mode of operation is regulated in its rules of procedure – which are still provisional. It is organized to be able to perform its functions at any time, meaning that all its members must be represented at all times at the organization's headquarters. The president of the Security Council calls a session whenever the situation requires, or when a meeting is requested by a Security Council member, the General Assembly, a UN member state, or if the Secretary-General directs the president's attention to an issue. By-laws require that two sessions must not be separated by a period of longer than fourteen days and in practice the Security Council meets nearly every day, and frequently more than once a day. The presidency of the Security Council changes every month, following alphabetical order according to the English version of the countries' names. The Security Council reaches a decision when nine of the fifteen members are in agreement. The Charter, however, provides a special category of issues that requires nine of the fifteen members to be in agreement, including the concurring votes of the permanent members. The article in question – Article 27 – differentiates between procedural questions and all other types of questions and articulates that the agreement of all the permanent members is required for the latter. Indeed, Article 27(3)) provides the basis of the permanent members' veto power. Abstention by a permanent member, however, does not carry the same relevance as an active veto and does not hinder the taking of a decision. For the realization of its duties, the Security Council may create subsidiary organs (Art. 29), which may be classified under three headings:

(i)   committees (Military Staff Committee, Committee of Experts on Rules of Procedure, Committee on Admission of New Members, and ad hoc committees for the execution of sanctions and other measures imposed by the Security Council);
(ii)   peace missions; and
(iii)   the International Criminal Tribunals for the Former Yugoslavia and for Rwanda.

On 20 December 2005 the Security Council (under resolution S/RES/1645) and the General Assembly (under resolution A/RES/60/180) established the UN Peace-building Commission as the first subsidiary organ reporting to two main bodies.

The Security Council is by far the most powerful of the UN's main bodies and is a unique instrument in international politics. The Charter assigns its primary responsibility for world peace and international security (Article 24), and bestows upon it far-reaching powers for the administration of this responsibility. Within the framework of peaceful settlement of disputes (Chapter VI), the Security Council has the power to investigate any situation (Article 34), and to give recommendations for the peaceful settlement of any dispute determined to have implications for international peace and security (Article 36 *et seq.*). The Security Council's role – according to the Charter – remains merely advisory or moderative; and its use of coercive power is regulated under Chapter VII of the Charter. According to Article 39, it is the responsibility of the Security Council to determine whether or not a situation constitutes a threat to the peace, a breach of the peace, or an act of aggression. Should the Security Council come to such a determination, it may then recommend appropriate measures to address that situation. The Security Council may also take measures for the forceful execution of its decisions. According to Article 41, such measures may consist of gradations of non-military (primarily economic) sanctions; Article 42 allows the use of military measures. The Charter also allows – under Article 53 – that the Security Council may call on regional organizations such as the Organization for Security and Co-operation in Europe (OSCE) for the execution of enforcement measures under its own authority. According to Article 25, all member states must accept and implement the decisions of the Security Council. The special position of the Security Council is also apparent in its competencies within the organization. For example, a number of important decisions – especially those of the General Assembly – are contingent on an antecedent vote of the Security Council. This affects primarily the acceptance or rejection of new members, as well as the choice of Secretary-General and the judges of the International Court of Justice.

The double privilege of permanent membership and veto rights for five permanent members is doubly problematic – first with respect to the principle of sovereign equality of all UN member states, second with respect to the decades-long period of *practical* impotence that the use of the veto has caused in the Security Council. For a time, this even led to conflicts of competence with, and even a partial shifting of gravity towards, the General Assembly. Only with the beginning of the subsidence of the East–West conflict in the late 1980s did the Security Council begin to regain its capacity to act. Formal vetoes became rare exceptions. Although the threat of a veto still belongs to the normal proceedings of consultations, the Security Council has been able to reach decisions and to develop its instruments further even in new and difficult situations such as civil wars. At the end of the 1990s, and again in 2003, the Security Council experienced a crisis of authority and ran the risk of losing its monopoly on the legitimization of the use of force. Although all problems of international peace and security were treated rhetorically as being within the competency of the Security Council, it remained clear that, in a number of cases, such problems were not in fact being handled under that authority. In the case of the former Yugoslavia, a group of states wrote draft resolutions that the Security Council then implemented. In the 2002–03 Iraq crisis, there was a concentrated attempt to find a solution within the framework of the Security Council. When this failed, however, the central organ of the UN was simply bypassed by two permanent members (the USA and the UK) and even declared irrelevant by the then US administration (see Chapter 4). The decisive factor will be whether or not the Security Council can overcome its divisions and find its way back to a mode of trusting co-operation among its members. The future of the Security Council as the centre of an effective Charter-based system of collective security will depend primarily on its reform and the support of its work by member states (Teixeira, 2003).

The Economic and Social Council

The Economic and Social Council (ECOSOC) currently encompasses fifty-four members, elected by the General Assembly. ECOSOC's main task is to take responsibility, together with the General Assembly, for the economic and social issues enumerated in Chapter IX of the Charter. According to Article 63, ECOSOC may be active in issues of economics, social entities, culture, education, health and related areas. In accordance with this task, ECOSOC's system of regional representation is weighted towards developing countries. Fourteen members come from the African continent, eleven from Asia, ten from Central and South America, and six from Eastern Europe. Thirteen members come from the Western European and Other States group. Every year, a third of the members are selected for a three-year term. Since there is no bar to serving consecutive terms some states have served for a long time and have become semi-permanent members. Since 1997, ECOSOC has met once a year for a four-week session to which non-members and representatives of special organizations or relief organizations recognized by the General Assembly may also be invited as observers – observer entities are entitled to make suggestions and recommendations but have no voting power.

A large part of ECOSOC's work is accomplished through its subsidiary bodies, which has led to the accusation that ECOSOC is a sort of 'organizational jungle' (Trauttmansdorff, 2001). These bodies comprise nine functional commissions, among which are the Commission on the Status of Women; the Commission on Crime Prevention and Criminal Justice; the Commission on Sustainable Development; Social Development; and Population and Development. The long-time most famous of these subsidiary bodies, the UN Commission on Human Rights, was dissolved in 2006 and replaced by the Human Rights Council (see Chapters 5 and 6). Five regional economic commissions, three standing committees (which handle the on- going work between sessions), and a constantly fluctuating number of ad hoc bodies, working groups and expert commissions complete the complex appearance of the ECOSOC's subsidiary organs. Of particular importance are the five regional economic commissions. Furthermore, ECOSOC co-operates constantly with a large number of subsidiary organs, and maintains consultative relations with more than 3,200 non-governmental organizations. In accordance with the goals of the UN as expressed in Article 1(3) and the concerns listed in Article 55, ECOSOC concerns itself primarily with questions of development in poorer countries (see Chapter 7). Its capacities, however, are limited and subject to the authority of the General Assembly to the degree that it has been observed that ECOSOC is evolving increasingly into a mere helper-organization for the General Assembly (Verdross and Simma, 1984, p. 110). Furthermore, the General Assembly has withdrawn a number of areas of competence from ECOSOC through the creation of special bodies such as the UNDP (UN Development Programme) and the UNCTAD (Conference on Trade and Development) to the extent that hardly any issue outside human rights remains within its purview.

The Trusteeship Council

The Trusteeship Council is the only principal organ of the UN to have suspended its work; this occurred following the transition of the last trustee territory to independence (Palau on 1 October 1994). The roots of the trusteeship system (Chapter XII) and the construction of the Trusteeship Council (Chapter XIII) go all the way back to the Mandate system of the League of Nations, through which the colonial possessions of the German and Ottoman Empires were given to mandate states to administer after the end of the First World War. While the mandate system confined itself exclusively to territory that had belonged to the 'enemy' states, the UN trusteeship system expanded the scope of the types of territory coming into question. According to Article 77 possible candidates for trusteeship status were those that were mandate territories at the time the Charter came into force, those territories separated from 'enemy' states during the Second World War, and any territories placed voluntarily under the trusteeship system by the governments currently responsible for them. For the last category, there is no historical example. The basis for trusteeship status was a trusteeship treaty, the execution of which was to be overseen by the Trusteeship Council. The Council was made up of those states that were administering trusteeship territories, plus the permanent members of the Security Council, as well as enough other UN member states to make the numbers of trusteeship-holders and non-trusteeship-holders equal (Article 86). With the gradual release of the eleven trusteeship territories, the number of members of the Council also shrank, such that by the end of its work it was composed of only the permanent members of the Security Council and the Council was not entrusted with any new duties, such as the administration of failed states, despite serious considerations of this option (Caplan, 2002). At the 2005 World Summit it was decided to delete Chapter XIII as well as all references to the Trusteeship Council in Chapter XII (World Summit, 2005, para. 176).

The International Court of Justice

The International Court of Justice (ICJ) is the primary juridical organ of the UN (Article 92). The ICJ is comprised of fifteen independent judges who are appointed through a procedure involving both the Security Council and the General Assembly. The Court's competencies and duties are enumerated in Chapter XIV of the Charter as well as in its own statute. This statute, which is essentially the same as that which had governed the Permanent Court of International Justice of the League of Nations, is an integral part of the UN Charter. As such, every UN member state is automatically party to the ICJ. Furthermore, non-members of the UN may become parties to the ICJ, as Switzerland did in 1948, or they may place themselves under ICJ jurisdiction in specific cases.

The ICJ deals only with disputes between states – it does not consider disputes between persons, or between persons and any other entity (ICJ Statute, Article 34(1)). Individuals may be called to account in the International Criminal Tribunals – such as the International Criminal Tribunal for the Former Yugoslavia, called into being in 1993 as a subsidiary organ by the Security Council or the International Criminal Court (ICC), which, came into existence in July 2002 following a 1998 statute and possesses jurisdiction over the prosecution of crimes against humanity (for the work of the ICC and its limiting factors, such as complementarity and so on, see Chapter 6).

The role of the ICJ cannot be compared to that of a domestic court. There is no international legal rule from which an obligatory international jurisdiction could be inferred. Indeed, the co-operative nature of international law would seem to require agreement among all the parties and if even one state-party to a dispute is unwilling to submit itself to the Court, the ICJ cannot take action in a dispute. Furthermore, the judgements of the ICJ are binding only on the parties to the dispute; its decisions do not have a general juridical effect. With the so-called facultative clause in Article 36(1), states may subject themselves voluntarily to the jurisdiction of the court, either unrestrictedly or subject to certain conditions, for the purposes of determining questions related to the interpretation of treaties, or international law, or the violation of international obligations, as well as of compensation for such violations. In practice, however, only a small number of states (66 as of October 2011) have lodged declarations on the basis of this clause with the Secretary-General, so the development of an exercise of obligatory international jurisdiction through the ICJ remains unlikely. With only 102 decisions (as of October 2011) in over six decades, the ICJ has not played a very active role in international politics, but it has certainly – through its decisions and its twenty-six advisory opinions – performed considerable service in the further development of international law in the areas for which it is responsible. Its significance lies in its special position as the 'universal juridical organ, and the resulting authority of its jurisprudence' (Trauttmansdorff, 2001). Furthermore, the ICJ remains the only international juridical instrument that can interpret international law without being restricted to a particular treaty system.

The Secretariat

The secretariat is the main administrative organ of the UN. In accordance with Article 97 the Secretariat is composed of the Secretary-General and any other public servants the organization requires. The Secretary-General is selected by the General Assembly on the recommendation of the Security Council to ensure that neither organ has full control of naming a candidate. Since 1946, following a General Assembly decision on the issue, the Secretary General has served a five year term of office, with the possibility of one second term. With the exception of Secretary-General Boutros Boutros-Ghali, whose re-election was prevented by a US veto in November 1996, all Secretaries-General have been elected for a second term (see Table 1.2).

Ban Ki-Moon of the Republic of Korea (South Korea) has presently stood at the head of the Secretariat hierarchy since January 2007 being re-elected for a five-year term in 2011. The Secretariat is organized into branches or divisions and departments, the latter of which are headed by Under-Secretaries-General (USG) or Assistant Secretaries-General (ASG). The office of Deputy Secretary-General was created in March 1998 and has since been held by three people: Louise Fréchette of Canada, Mark Malloch Brown of the UK, and Asha-Rose Migiro of Tanzania (Migiro took office on 1 February 2007). As with all public servant positions in the Secretariat, the post of Deputy Secretary-General is appointed by the Secretary-General (Article 101).

As of 2010, 44,134 personnel from 187 countries were working in the Secretariat – 20,141 in the category of non-field operations (departments and offices, regional commissions, international tribunals) and 23,993 in field operations like UNAMA or UNAMID. Of this total number, 6,587 staff are employed at UN headquarters in New York. Secretariat staff owes their occupational loyalty not to their citizenship states, but to the UN itself, and they must not 'seek or receive instructions from any government or from any other authority external to the Organisation' (Article 100). In addition to its headquarters in New York, the UN has three subsidiary offices in Geneva, Nairobi and Vienna. Employees of the Secretariat are also active in a large number of other offices worldwide, administering the UN policies. In addition to the aforementioned Secretariat staff the UN employs tens of thousands of other non-Secretariat staff across its related entities such as UNICEF, UNDP, UNRWA or the ICJ. In total, the UN employs about 74,800 people (for details see Ban, 2010).

TABLE 1.2
Secretaries-General of the UN

Term of office	Name	Country of origin
1946–53	Trygve Lie	Norway
1953–61	Dag Hammarskjöld	Sweden
1961–71	U Thant	Myanmar (Burma)
1972–81	Kurt Waldheim	Austria
1982–91	Javier Perez de Cuéllar	Peru
1992–96	Boutros Boutros-Ghali	Egypt
1997–2006	Kofi Annan	Ghana
2007–present	Ban-Ki-Moon	Republic of Korea

The Secretary-General, in conjunction with the Secretariat, carries out both political and administrative responsibilities. The Secretary-General must also co-ordinate the work of the other main bodies (with the exception of the ICJ) and is responsible for the construction of the budgetary plan and the execution of the financial administration. The Secretary-General registers and publicizes the treaties and notifications deposited to them by UN member states, and represents the organization as a whole both in the international realm and with respect to each of the member states. One of the Secretary-General's main original political tasks, according to Article 99, was to steer the attention of the Security Council to all matters considered to be possible threats to the peace.

Various Secretaries-General have made very different uses of their rather non-specific duty. With the exception of Dag Hammarskjöld, who actively exercised personal diplomacy and interference into international crisis management, the first five Secretaries-General acted as head administrative officers rather than as world diplomats. Boutros Boutros-Ghali undertook to define the political position of the Secretary-General more clearly, and did not shrink from reminding member states emphatically of their responsibilities towards the peace of the world. After Boutros-Ghali's tenure as Secretary-General was shipwrecked on the US veto in November 1996, Kofi Annan managed to walk the thin line between his different roles as supreme administrative official and moderator or catalyst of international politics with comparative success. The mandate given to him by the General Assembly and Security Council granted him and his staff of experts more room to manoeuvre and a greater opportunity to influence the decisions of the main bodies than any previous Secretary-General before him. In December 2001, Kofi Annan and the UN were jointly awarded the Nobel Peace Prize. In his first four years as Secretary-General Ban Ki-Moon has concentrated on internal management reform projects that had been launched but not completed by his predecessor, and has preferred silent diplomacy over public advice to member states and govern-ments. The need to manage the delicate interplay between the collective concerns of the organization and consideration for the individual or group interests of the member states ensures that the office of Secretary-General remains 'the toughest job in the world' (on the role of the Secretary-General in world politics see Chesterman, 2007).

The secretariat – considered by some to be a static, ponderous and over-manned administration body – has been in a permanent process of renewal since the 1990s. Immediately upon taking office in 1997, Kofi Annan enacted the most far-reaching reform agenda that the Secretariat had ever experienced – far-reach-ing not only in its structural reforms, but also, and above all, in reforming its modes of work and communication. A completely new management culture was introduced to ensure that the capacities of the various offices were used to maxi-mum efficiency and to eliminate redundancy. In addition to the aforementioned introduction of the office of Deputy Secretary-General, a high-level management group, now consisting of thirty-six top officials (Heads of Departments and Offices, Programmes and Funds), was also created to support the work of the Secretary-General in the realization of his operative and administrative tasks. The

Office of the Secretary-General (OSG) now also includes a strategic planning unit whose task is to evaluate changes in global trends and then to give appropriate recommendations on them to the Secretary-General. Additionally, four executive committees were called into being for the purpose of co-ordinating the work of the departments of the Secretariat with that of the special organs and programmes. These committees are concerned with the central interest areas of the UN: peace and security; economic and social issues; development co-operation; and humanitarian issues. The question of human rights was made into a cross-cutting responsibility of all the core interest areas.

In preparing for the 2005 World Summit Kofi Annan undertook a comprehensive reform initiative proposing more efficiency and accountability in the work of the Secretariat in return for larger freedom of action for the Secretary-General in the fields of internal management, personnel policy, procurement and budget (see Annan, 2005, para. 184 *et seq.*). At the World Summit, however, no decision was made and at the beginning of 2006, the member states requested a new report from Annan. In this subsequent report of 2006 'Investing in the United Nations', Annan proposed a 'radical overhaul of the United Nations Secretariat – its rules, structure, systems and culture' (Annan, 2006, p. 1). Annan highlighted seven major areas of investment: people, leadership, information and communication technology, new delivering systems (procurement), budget and finance, governance (internal audit and oversight) and change management. Member states' willingness, however, to confer extended responsibilities on the Secretary-General remains limited and the creation of the UN Ethics Office was the only visible success in this area during Annan's term. In particular, the G77 – a group of member states from the developing South – are suspicious of a powerful Secretary-General who might seek to serve the interests and demands of the wealthy developed North at the expense of their own interests. Secretary-General Ban Ki-Moon tried to address these concerns of the developing South by appointing staff from the region to positions of influence within the organization. In addition to aforementioned Deputy Secretary-General Migiro (of Tanzania), Ban also appointed Alicia Marcena Ibarra (of Mexico) as head of the Department of Management (DM). Under Ban's authority some further minor changes have been realized, such as: The Office of the High Commissioner for Human Rights (OHCHR) has been upgraded into a department of the Secretariat, and the creation of a new Department for Field Support (DFS) as a spin-off of Department of Peacekeeping Operations. But such renewals – each of which require the approval of member states – are proceeding slowly, in small steps, and a comprehensive management reform agenda re-organization and restructuring remains on the UN reform agenda (see below Chapter 8).

The Secretariat, whose workforce has been reduced by approximately 20 per cent in the space of only a few years, is clearly on the way to becoming a more streamlined and powerful administrative organ, better able to fulfil its many administrative tasks and delegated political functions in a modernized way. Admittedly, however, the number of challenges in the realm of peace maintenance, which has been rising since 1999 and reached an all-time high in 2011 with about 123,000 peacekeepers in sixteen missions (as of October 2011), is highlighting serious personnel deficits, especially in the Department of Peacekeeping Operations. Despite pressure for lean management practices – especially in the area of peace maintenance – the UN will not be able to avoid at least a sectoral enlargement of personnel resources (on the Secretariat see detailed Thant and Scott, 2007).

Programmes, Funds and Specialized Agencies

In the UN system, a number of functional institutions concerned with the accomplishment of specific tasks are integrated around the core organization. As has been indicated already, these institutions may be differentiated into two categories:

(i)   programmes and funds, (also referred to in this text as 'subsidiary organs') created by the organization itself; and
(ii)   specialized agencies, international organizations with their own legal personalities with which the United Nations co-operates on the basis of contractual ties.

The subsidiary organs are constituted by the General Assembly and regulated by it, sometimes directly, and sometimes through ECOSOC. In contrast to specialized agencies, these programmes and funds enjoy no international legal personalities and are bound only to the recommendations they receive from the General Assembly. They have no budgetary authority, even though most of them enjoy their own income from voluntary, earmarked allocations by member states or from private donations. Subsidiary organs are often described as quasi-autonomous institutions because they appear to be autonomous in comparison with their partners outside the UN and have a differentiated internal structure and their own political steering organs. The subsidiary organs' areas of responsibility fall primarily into three categories:

(i)   development aid programmes (for example, the UNDP, the UN Environmental Programme (UNEP), the UN Children's Fund (UNICEF), the UN Conference on Trade and Development (UNCTAD);
(ii)   humanitarian issues (for example, the United Nations Relief and Works Agency for Palestine Refugees in the Near East (UNRWA), the High Commissioner for Refugees (UNHCR), or the World Food Programme (WFP)); and
(iii) educational and research activities (for example, the UN University (UNU), or the Institute for Training and Research (UNITAR)).

Most of the programmes and funds emerged in the period of decolonization during which the member states of the 'Third World' achieved a majority in the General Assembly and consequently engaged that body primarily with the economic and social problems of developing countries. The General Assembly – with its principle of formal sovereign equality for all member states – became the central forum for the expression of newly-formed states' interests, Furthermore, the General Assembly remained capable of action – at least in the area of issues affecting the organization itself – while the Cold War rendered the Security Council largely impotent. The formidable number of subsidiary organs created in the first forty years of the UN's existence is an expression of the desire of developing countries to defend themselves against a world economic order they considered to be unjust and working only to the advantage of the industrialized countries. Although developing countries were thus able to ensure the place of the North–South conflict on the UN agenda, they were unable to effect any structural improvements in the positions of developing countries (see Chapter 7). Indeed, the operative subsidiary organs of the UN continue to largely bear the character of fire-fighting programmes, providing punctual assistance in latent and acute emergency situations, rather than being instruments of sustained improvement for the lands and groups of people for whose sake they were originally created.

Specialized agencies (some of which work in the same areas of operation as a number of the subsidiary organs) are inter-state institutions, resting on the basis of their own international law treaties with their own membership and organizational structure, and their own budgets. The specialized agencies' scope of action reaches across almost all areas of technical, economic, social, educational and environmental issues that are looked after and acted on under global auspices. A few of these organizations are significantly older even than the League of Nations. Others have been created by their member states at the instigation of the UN. Their status as specialized agencies is based on special agreements under Article 63, for the purposes of contributing to the achievement of the economic and social goals laid out in Article 55 – the maintenance of peaceful co-existence among states. These special agreements, which are all substantively similar, are made by ECOSOC with the permission of the General Assembly, and regulate the forms of co-operation as well as the rights and duties of both parties. These organizations are commonly divided into three categories:

(i)   technical bodies (for example, the Universal Postal Union (UPU), the World Meteorology Organization (WMO), or the International Labour Organization (ILO));
(ii) specialized agencies in social, cultural, and humanitarian areas (for example, the World Health Organization (WHO), the United Nations Educational, Scientific, and Cultural Organization (UNESCO), the UN Industrial Development Organization (UNIDO), or the Food and Agriculture Organization (FAO)); and
(iii) financial organizations (for example, the International Monetary Fund (IMF), the World Bank, and the International Fund for Agricultural Development (IFAD)).

There are currently fifteen specialized agencies in operation, one of which, the World Bank Group, consists of four different institutions.

Further important institutions, such as the World Trade Organization (WTO) and the International Atomic Energy Agency (IAEA) co-operate extensively with the UN, but without Article 63 agreements with the UN they do not count as specialized agencies. Instead they exist as autonomous organizations within the UN system. As is the case with the subsidiary organs, the conflict of interests between industrialized and developing countries is reflected in the field of the specialized agencies. The wealthier developed states are more likely to view the financial bodies – where they dominate because of the voting weighted according to contribution size – as effective. In contrast, the poorer developing countries put more weight on institutions for multilateral development co-operation (which are equally dependent on the support of industrialized countries)]. Even the powerful specialized agencies have been scarcely able to overcome this difficulty. Effective co-operation among the specialized agencies is made even more difficult by the fact that the responsibility for the activities of the various members of the organi-zations lies primarily with the respective functional departments, so that the inter-state co-ordination problems are compounded by intrastate difficulties. What is true for the UN as a whole is also true for the specialized agencies: the success of their work depends largely on the will of the member states to engage in multilat-eral co-operation. Hence, system-wide coherence is one of the major issues on the UN-reform agenda (see below Chapter 8).

Financing the United Nations

The work of the UN is financed primarily through contributions by member states. These contributions fall into three categories:

(i)   obligatory dues for the maintenance of a regular budget;
(ii)   obligatory dues for UN peace missions and for the International Criminal Tribunals for the Former Yugoslavia and Rwanda; and
(iii)   voluntary contributions to funds and programmes of the UN.

The regular budget pays primarily for the personnel, administrative and property expenses of the UN. To a lesser extent, monies are expended from this budget for the work of the subsidiary organs and programmes. At the time of writing, two observation missions are being funded (as exceptions) out of this budget: UNTSO and UNMOGIP. The budget procedure involves the submission of a budget plan by the Secretary-General to the Coordination and Programming Committee (CPC) for examination, from where it proceeds to the Advisory Committee for Adminis-trative and Budgetary Questions (ACABQ) for further examination. When finally approved by the Fifth Committee, the budget goes to the General Assembly where it must be approved by a two-thirds majority. For the two-year period covering 2010 and 2011, the regular budget has been fixed at US\$5.16 billion (A/RES/64/244) – a figure that, considering the complex tasks involved, appears relatively modest. (In this book all references to billions and trillions are according to US style; see Table 1.3). In fact, this budget covers only a small portion of the total expenses of the UN (see Table 1.4). Member states pay their dues into this budget on the basis of a scale of assessments that is subject to readjustment every three years. The standard for measuring the extent of a member state's dues is the state's economic capacity, computed on the basis of the average per capita GNP during a given reference period of (usually) three to six years. Both the level of the state's debt and the variance in actual distribution of income are taken into account and these may lower the expected contribution. Detailed technical determinations of all financial aspects are contained in the 'Financial Regulations and Rules of the United Nations', the latest version of which came into effect in January 2003. According to the scale of assessments 2010–12 from 24 December 2009 (A/RES/64/248), the upper limit of obligatory dues was set at 22 per cent and the lower limit at 0.001 per cent of the regular budget. According to this schedule, the poorest states would have payment obligations in the order of around US$24,000, and the USA would have obligations of around US$600 million. In total, forty-seven of the 193 member states provide 99 per cent of the regular budget.

Peace-maintenance is also financed through obligatory dues from member states. However, each peace mission has its own financial framework so that the total expenses for peace missions change constantly according to their number and scope. The Secretary-General creates a cost-plan for each mission that must then be approved by the Fifth Committee. If the budget receives Fifth Committee approval the Secretary-General opens a unique account for the mission and sends requests for payments to member states. The level of these contributions is basically orientated on the same schedule of payments as for the regular budget, but

TABLE 1.3
The UN programme budget, 2010–11

Section	US $
I Overall policy-making, direction and co-ordination	777,439,800
II Political affairs	1,248,438,400
III International justice and law	96,855,200
IV International co-operation for development	434,311,700
V Regional co-operation for development	526,456,100
VI Human rights and humanitarian affairs	301,937,600
VII Public information	186,707,400
VIII Common support services	577,969,100
IX Internal oversight	39,438,800
X Jointly financed administrative activities and special expenses	125,248,200
XI Capital expenditures	61,265,500
XII Safety and security	239,288,500
XIII Development account	23,651,300
XIV Staff assessment	517,021,500
Total	**5,156,029,100**

Source: Data from A/RES/64/244 A-C, 24 December 2009.

TABLE 1.4

Expenditures of the UN system in US$ millions

Year	UN regular budget	UN peace-keeping	UN agencies	Total assessment spending	Total voluntary spending	Grand total
1986	725	242	1,142	2,109	4,026	6,135
1987	725	240	1,178	2,143	4,197	6,340
1988	752	266	1,349	2,367	4,997	7,356
1989	765	635	1,359	2,759	5,260	8,019
1990	838	379	1,495	2,712	5,782	8,494
1991	999	449	1,509	2,957	6,761	9,718
1992	1,008	1,697	1,731	4,436	7,159	11,595
1993	1,031	3,005	1,713	5,749	7,307	13,056
1994	1,087	3,357	1,826	6,270	7,093	13,363
1995	1,181	3,281	1,847	6,309	6,937	13,246
1996	1,112	1,522	2,057	4,691	6,054	10,745
1997	1,112	1,226	2,033	4,371	5,993	10,364
1998	1,086	995	1,792	3,873	5,411	9,284
1999	1,217	1,321	1,787	4,325	5,423	9,748
2000	1,090	2,139	1,766	4,995	4,978	9,973
2001	1,074	2,700	1,772	5,546	6,374	11,920
2002	1,149	2,284	1,739	5,172	8,245a	13,591
2003	1,409	2,501	1,761	5,671	11,076	16,747
2004	1,483	2,934	2,004	6,421	11,661	18,082
2005	1,828	4,074	2,018	7,920	13,696	21,616
2006	1,755	4,583	2,138	8,476	14,512	22,988
2007	2,054	5,148	2,198	9,400	15,570	24,970

Note: The table offers a summary of total UN expenditures. Assessed contributions expenditures are funded by payments assessed to all UN member states. Voluntary contributions are payments made to specialized UN organs and agencies not included in the assessed contributions of member states. The data presented does not include assessed contribution expenditures for international tribunals, which are a separate but relatively small item, nor do they include the Bretton Woods Institutions, which are in practice quite distinct and rarely included in UN system data, since both their governance and their source of funds are very different. The major specialized agencies include the IAEA, ILO, FAO, UNESCO, WHO, UPU, ITU, IMO and UNIDO. The major programmes, funds, and other Organs include UNCTAD, UNDP, UNEP, UNFPA, UNHCR, UNICEF, UNIFEM and UNU. In evaluating these numbers, it must be considered that the UN's scope of action has expanded significantly over time and thus the real expenditures have decreased.

Source: Data from Global Policy Forum (www.globalpolicy.org).

reductions are allowed for the poorer states. The system of dues for peace keeping, reformed on 23 December 2000 and reaffirmed in 2009, anticipates ten categories (A–J) into which member states are grouped according to their degree of financial power. Those states in categories C to J receive reductions of between 7.5 per cent and 90 per cent on the level of their dues for the regular budget, while the countries in category B must pay their normal dues. The deficits resulting from the reductions given to the C–J countries are redressed by the member states in category A, otherwise known as the five permanent members of the Security Council. Indeed, the Permanent Five carry 45.8 per cent of the costs of peacekeeping. The amounts charged to member states range from 25.9 per cent for the USA to 0.0001 per cent for countries in category J. (For the effective rates 2010–12 see UN document A/64/220/Add.1.) The budgets thus produced must pay for the running costs of the missions, including personnel (both UN personnel and locally recruited support personnel), rents, and transportation costs. Member states who 'donate' personnel receive repayments of around US$1,000 per person per month, as well as compensation for any materials used. The actual costs to a developing country member state to provide such troops or personnel is often significantly less than the provided 'reimbursement' leading to further expenditures for the wealthier states and positively attractive profits for the poorer states. Voluntary contributions to programmes and funds, however, are at the discretion of the member states. The personnel and administrative costs of these subsidiary organs are defrayed through the regular budget. The sum of the voluntary contributions significantly outstrips that of the regular budget and thus makes the operative work of the subsidiary organs possible.

Financial crises brought the UN to the brink of financial ruin in the early 1960s, and have been a steady companion of the organization ever since (Schlesinger, 2001). Through the 1990s, the financial situation of the UN ranged from precarious to catastrophic, not least because of the USA's attempt to force UN reform via unilateral reduction or withholding of dues for peace-maintenance measures. Also, other member states fell so far behind with their payments that they lost their right to vote in the General Assembly (in accordance with Article 19). In an attempt to overcome such budget problems, monies were sometimes drawn from peace-maintenance funds which in turn led to serious UN debts to troop-contributing member states. Fundamental financial reform of the UN remains to be accomplished and recommendations by the Secretary-General in his 1997 programme of reform have never been implemented. The adjustment of the scale of assessments in December 2000 was successful in settling a long-standing dispute with the USA, but the fundamental problem of the organization's complete dependence on its more powerful contributors and their willingness to pay has yet to be resolved.

Further Reading

Annan, Kofi (2000) 'We the Peoples: The Role of the United Nations in the Twenty-first Century', New York UN document (A/54/2000).

Claude, Ines L. (1970) *Swords into Plowshares. The Problems and Progress of International Organizations*, New York: Random House.

Kennedy, Paul (2006) *The Parliament of Man. The United Nations and the Quest for World Government*, London: Allen Lane.

Mingst, Karen A. and Margaret P. Karns (2000) *The United Nations in the Post-Cold War Era*, Boulder, CO: Westview Press.

New Zealand Ministry of Foreign Affairs and Trade; *United Nations Handbook*, Wellington (published annually).

Simma, Bruno (ed.) (2002) *The Charter of the United Nations: A Commentary*, Oxford: Oxford University Press.

United Nations (2008) *The United Nations Today*, Ottawa: Renouf Publishing.

United Nations Department of Public Information; *Yearbook of the United Nations*, Leiden, Boston: Martinus Nijhoff Publishers (published annually).

Volger, Helmut (ed.) (2002) *A Concise Encyclopedia of the United Nations*, The Hague: Kluwer.

Weiss, Thomas G. and Sam Daws (eds)(2007) *The Oxford Handbook on the United Nations*, Oxford: Oxford University Press.

2

Institution-Building, Regime Impact and Globalization: The Role and Function of the UN

For centuries, the history of international relations (in both the practical and academic senses) has been shaped by attempts to contain and overcome the competitive nature of the state system wherein the principal actors – states – recognize no power higher than themselves. The fundamental questions concerning how states can be brought to peacefully settle their differences is as old as the state system itself. (Griffiths, 1999) Such concerns have occupied thinkers from Niccolo Machiavelli (1469–1527) and Immanuel Kant (1724–1804) to Jürgen Habermas (b. 1929). As might be expected, their solutions have been somewhat divergent.

Since time immemorial, there have existed two primary views regarding the appropriate way to prevent war and to secure peace. These two views may best be described as the dispute between the *children of light* and the *children of darkness*. The European Enlightenment established a belief in the primacy of human goodness, human reason and human aptitude for learning. As a result, democratization –because of the demonstrable connections between the internal constitution of a state and its external behaviour – is the best way to prevent international conflict. The darker view believes the world to be anarchic and ruled by the worst of human behaviours so that only national strength and adherence to the principle of self-help can prevent conflict. Accordingly, states should not aspire to the lofty goal of 'peace', but should reach instead for the more moderate goal of 'security'.

The conflicting views propounded by the *children of light* and the *children of darkness* exemplify two different responses to the requirements of international peace and security. One side – the 'light' – believes in a multilateral world where bargaining, persuasion, consensus-seeking and diplomatic solutions predominate; the other side – the 'dark' – believes in an anarchic world where there can be no reliance on international rules, and where unilateral coercion must sometimes prevail over persuasion. To put it more dramatically: *si vis pacem para pacem* ('if you desire peace you must prepare for peace') versus *si vis pacem para bellum* ('if you desire peace you must prepare for war'). Given the far-reaching implications of this fundamental disagreement, a better understanding of the UN – which repre-sents one possible model of a multilateral world order – necessitates an examina-tion of the most important theories of states' behaviour in international relations.

Theories of International Organizations

The UN is the second practical political attempt – the first was the League of Nations – to bring order to international disorder, to minimize the oft-described 'perils of anarchy', and to entrust a global organization with the protection of world peace and international security. Since its founding over sixty-six years ago, the UN has significantly expanded its constitution and mandate but has never made any major changes to its foundational document – the Charter. During this time the UN has grown from fifty-one original member states to its current 193 member states, and it should be noted that two-thirds of the present membership were not even sovereign states at the time of the UN founding. From an organiza-tion whose primary purpose was to proscribe inter-state warfare as a political means, the UN has evolved into a multifunctional global forum where any and all the world's problems can be discussed and potentially brought closer to solution.

Independent of their judgements of the UN's work to date, there exists a consensus among observers, analysts and practitioners of international politics that the organization should be reformed. Even those who stood on different sides of the disputes over actions in Kosovo (1999) and Iraq (2003) agree that the UN's structures and procedures are no longer fully appropriate for the political reality of the twenty-first century. The goal of reform, however, requires an answer to the question of what role of a global organization the member states are willing to accept in the shaping of international politics, and in what measure they are ready to use the instruments and opportunities of such an organization for the imple-mentation of a multilateral, compromise-orientated politics. Only after this ques-tion has been answered can the debate begin over which means are the most appropriate for reaching these goals. At the same time, demand is rising for the UN to fill a gap in globalized world politics. This contradiction between the realistic possibilities for UN action and the often extremely high expectations for it creates a climate of excessive demands, and sometimes leads to an unfairly negative judgement of the UN's work. In the following theoretical discussion, the main purpose is to understand the implications of theory for various UN activities and the expected effects of international co-operation. It is not the purpose of this text to provide a detailed explanation of all the theoretical principles at stake (for comprehensive treatments, see Claude, 1970; Griffiths, 1999; Viotti and Kauppi, 2001; and Zangl and Zürn, 2003).

Adherents of the *Realist School* propose that the struggle for power and the achievement of a state's own interests constitute the most important categories for understanding international politics, because states are not subject to any higher authority with sanctioning power, and indeed *could* not be subject to such an entity. The lack of an overarching authority – one that could guarantee compliance with common decisions and basic principles – in the international system means that states seek security through the accumulation of power. Indeed, 'a feeling of insecurity born out of mutual fear and mistrust [drives] the units into a competition for power, in which for the sake of their own security they seek to pile might upon might; a struggle which remains vain, because perfect security is impossible to attain' (Herz, 1961, p. 130). States would have to relinquish sovereignty and subject themselves to a common decision-making process in order to face up to these historical exigencies, but states of the old stamp seem unwilling to do what would be required of them in this regard – especially in the realm of peace maintenance. In fact, quite the reverse is more likely insomuch as states are, and will remain, the central problem. The anarchical international system implies that war is a necessary, natural and unavoidable product of this order (Claude, 1970, p. 372). The inherent security dilemma in this anarchical international self-help system is that war and zero-sum conflicts arise almost of necessity, except when there is a fragile and continuously threatened balance of power. This is why Realists see pure inter-governmental collaboration as the only possible way of maintaining the balance of power, of avoiding war and of promoting co-operation. From this perspective, international organizations fill 'merely derivative functions, which arise out of the sovereignty and interests of their members; in their setting of goals and capacity for action, they are thus clearly determined by the readiness of their members to act' (Siedschlag, 1997, p. 227). Realists recommend traditional means of achieving security, such as national armed forces, alliances, and ad hoc collective proceedings of the rich and powerful against potential troublemakers.

The *Idealist School,* on the other hand, believes that international organizations represent an analytical construct that is not so much the designation for a particular type of institution, but rather a normative-teleological image of the development of international relations (Rittberger, 1995). Idealists make relatively little of the supposedly anarchical state of the international system where there is no central, super-state authority, but choose instead to focus on forms of co-operation that are intended to regulate that anarchy. Idealists are of the opinion that international cooperation benefits all participants, and that relations between and among individuals, various types of organizations, and states, lead gradually to a sort of universal community that by its nature tends to aid the cause of peace. Idealists also believe that variable-sum games, rather than zero-sum games, are the general characteristic of many situations in international politics and that actors consequently enjoy gains they could never have obtained through unilateral action. With the creation of a binding body of rules and regulations it is believed that a civilized world community could emerge and that community – because of its common learning process – would no longer seek to solve problems with the use of force. It is for this reason that Klaus Dicke (1994, pp. 317–33) describes international organizations as the 'catalyst, forum, and form' of inter-state cooperation. On the one hand international organizations serve states as the instruments of co-operation. On the other hand international organizations provide an ordered framework containing the rudimentary duties necessary for co-operation and normatively determining the idea of co-operation. In this idea, Dicke also indicates the normative aspect of the concept of an international organization, comprising the ideas of law or justice and peace:

> In this regard, the normative content of the concept of international organizations is that they represent the imperatives of peace and the rule of international law, while at the same time offering the possibility of realization. These possibilities for realization, meanwhile, are indeed conditioned by manifold interests and political experiences. (Ibid, p.332)

The *Institutionalist School* stands firmly in the Idealist tradition but also accepts key tenets of the Realist position. In contrast to Realists, Institutionalists believe that international co-operation is possible, and they ascribe international institutions (which provide normative regulation in specific areas of politics) a great deal more influence over the interests and behaviour of states than do the Realists. Institutionalism's relevance depends, however, on two preconditions: first, the actors must have some common interests (that is, they must see or be able to expect material advantage from co-operation); second, variations in the degree of institutionalization must be understood to have substantial effects on the behaviour of states, because if the degree of institutionalization were minimal or constant, it would make no sense to try to analyse state behaviour in terms of institutional change. The basic thesis of Institutionalism is that variations in the degree of institutionalization of international politics have significant effects on the behaviour of governments. States do not ignore the Realist power premises in their actions and as such co-operation and integration are not understood as they are by Idealists as 'rational' (and therefore relatively easily achieved processes) but rather as difficult to both initiate and maintain. State action, nevertheless, is seen as depending to a considerable extent on the existing institutional order. This institutional order influences:

- the flow of information as well as the capacity to bargain;
- governments' opportunities to observe whether other states adhere to their agreements and carry out their duties and responsibilities, which is a pre-condition for the decision to carry out one's own obligations; and
- the dominant expectations of how stable international agreements are.

According to Robert Keohane (1989, p. 150 *et seq.*), these institutions have both regulatory and constitutive aspects: they make certain actions possible for states that would otherwise have been unimaginable, they reduce costs, and they influence the role behaviour of states in relation to their concepts of self-interest. States also receive reliable information about the behaviour of other states from international organizations, which feeds back into the creation of trust and the reduction of anxiety. It is assumed that there is a tight connection between the form (i.e. the member structure and rules) and the function (i.e. the out-working activities) of institutions: changes in form lead to changes in function, and vice versa. In Table 2.1, we present the basic assumptions of the three schools more schematically.

47

TABLE 2.1
Realism, idealism and institutionalism

	Realism	Idealism	Institutionalism
The international system is primarily characterized by:	The structural feature of international anarchy	. . . also through the structural feature of interdependence	. . . also through international arrangements
The actors in international politics are:	Primarily states that orientate themselves on their self-interests	. . . also various international organizations, balancing many different interests	. . . also various international organizations, balancing many different interests
Actions are regarded as:	Rational action based on the interest of maintaining power	Rational action based on welfare interests	Rational action based on interests specific to each particular problem area
Peace on an international level can be secured by:	Balance of power and state strength	The spread and support of democracy and insight into interdependence	International institutions and balance of interests

Source: Based on discussion in Zangl and Zürm (2003, p. 140 *et seq.*).

Modern political science offers several very different answers to the question of the emergence and functioning of international organizations. Analytically, we must first distinguish between IGOs (inter-governmental organizations, whose members are state governments) and INGOs (commonly referred to as NGOs, international non-governmental organizations, whose members are non-state actors). A more precise survey would examine criteria-bundles such as geographical, sectoral or functional scope or degree of organization, as well as many other characteristics of typology or classification coming from a variety of scientific disciplines including political science, law, psychology, social psychology, and many more.

According to a minimal consensus definition, an IGO may be understood as a grouping of states created through multilateral international law contracts and having its own organs and competencies. The goal of an IGO is to facilitate co-operation among at least three states (if there were only two, it would be bilateral, not multilateral) in the political, economic, military, cultural, social arenas. Usually, the founding compact or treaty will set down not only the goals and methods of the co-operation, but also the permanent organizational structure by which these tasks are to be accomplished. These criteria differentiate international organizations from so-called international regimes, which represent a comparatively informal type of international co-operation in certain areas of politics, lying just under the threshold of true organization (Hasenclever *et al.*, 1997). Innovative research into regimes suggest that forms of co-operation that are *not* formally institutionalized are also considered regimes as long as they are identified by a certain set of principles, norms, rules and decision-making processes. This approach allows a better understanding of processes of international governance than would be possible with a purely organization-centric analysis. These regimes include inter alia the UN World Conferences that have resulted in or produced institutionalized forms of co-operation.

The degree to which states transfer sovereignty varies significantly from one IGO to another. As differentiating factors, it is useful to consider the ideal-typical concepts of *inter-governmental* versus *transnational* relations. With the former there is no relinquishment of direct sovereignty rights and ultimate authority remains with the participant states. With the latter, some aspects of sovereignty are transferred to a supra-national body, and states must reckon with the possibility of being overruled in individual cases. Supra-nationality is also manifested when an international organization can enact binding resolutions on the member states.

The UN is an international organization based on the principle of multilateral inter-governmental cooperation. This means that the states belonging to the organization work closely together, but have not transferred any direct rights of sovereignty to the organization. One exception to this is in the realm of peace maintenance, in which the Security Council may make decisions that are formally binding on all member states (and can be enforced with the application of military force). Fundamentally, however, the UN is not a supra-national organization like those present in some fields of European Union (EU) politics. It must work towards amicable solutions for every issue that is raised; its medium is that of voluntary co-operation among sovereign states. The principle of multilateralism

FIGURE 2.1
Supra-national integration and inter-governmental co-operation

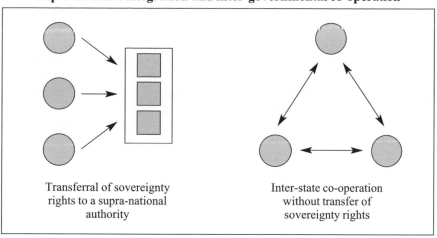

| Transferral of sovereignty rights to a supra-national authority | Inter-state co-operation without transfer of sovereignty rights |

means that multiple states must co-operate, and that this co-operation must follow established principles determining appropriate behaviour for the participating states (see Figure 2.1).

But who are the decision-makers in international organizations? If member states have the ultimate authority to make decisions according to their own national interests, then a more precise answer is needed to the question of what 'the state' actually is. First, it must be noted that the actors involved in international organizations can be divided into various categories. Governments may be the primary actors in international politics, and their representatives may have the last word, but their actions will be influenced in turn by many other actors (for example parliaments, interest groups, NGOs, advisers, the media, etc.). The theory of foreign policy decision-making processes (Haftendorn, 1990; Hill, 2003) distinguishes among three concepts for the analysis of this complex process, each of which attributes different weights to the different sources of influence:

(i)   the attempts at explanation that start from the assumption of rational, goal-orientated behaviour on the part of the actors involved (above all Realist games, rational choice models);

(ii) the contextual attempts at explanation, which incorporate the operative milieu (such as social and organizational structures) more strongly in their form of analysis (above all organizational theory); and

(iii) attempts to explain decisions with the help of the psychological context, including perceptional, adjustment and attitudinal variables (above all political psychology).

According to the Realist model of rational politics, foreign policy events are the result of conscious decisions on the parts of the governments of sovereign states, and that such decisions are made with the goal of achieving national interests. According to the organizational process model, such decisions are the product of an organizational process that is not necessarily the result of a clear understanding or idea of goals to be achieved. They result far more:

> [F]irstly, from the need such organizations have to produce acceptable results in order to achieve self-legitimatisation, and secondly from a mixture of the expectations and demands of other organizations within the government, legal authority, demands from citizens and interest groups, and not least from a bargaining process internal to the organization. (Lehmkuhl, 1996, p. 136)

The parameters of this organizational process remain largely constant, definable in each national context. In the bureaucratic politics model, more emphasis is placed on the idea that government decisions are increasingly the result of trans-governmental bargaining processes. In this model, it is neither the state nor the various organizational units that are the sole actors to be analysed, but rather the actors constitute themselves out of a multiplicity of persons and levels representing specific offices or bureaux. The result of this bargaining process is not necessarily what was sought as an optimal solution, but is rather the result of compromise, coalition-building and competition. Contrary to classical approaches, which regard the state as a rational, unitary actor capable of autonomous action, newer decision-theory approaches (for example, Neack *et al.,* 1995) start from the premise that foreign policy decisions can be defined as 'the product of a psychological selection process fully contained within the organizational complex, which purports to ascertain out of a limited and socially-defined set of problematic alternatives the one project which is supposed to bring about one of the particular end-states of things envisaged by the decision-makers' (Meyers, 1981, p. 72). The so-called 'interpretative' approaches of Political Science – which build on the assumption that 'social reality is accessible to us only as a truth-construct; realities are socially negotiated, and arise in complex interactions as the result of interpretational struggles and understandings about common knowledge' (Nullmeier, 1997, p. 101) – take this statement more seriously. An interpretative approach assumes that it is not only national power interests that influence the calculations and bargaining strategies of states, but that the institutional context is also a factor. Interests and identities 'are not the independent variable through which political processes can be explained. They are themselves far more the product and expression of international interactions and institutions. Inter-subjectively shared convictions, expectations, and collective meanings construct those structures that determine the actions of the political actors' (ibid, p. 119).

From a functional perspective, IGOs can be viewed three ways (Archer, 2001, pp. 65–111; Rittberger and Zangl, 2003, pp. 33–48):

(i)   The first view sees international organizations primarily as *instruments of state diplomacy,* meaning that states instrumentalize international organizations in order to achieve their own interests in an anarchical environment.

Agreements are not to be relied upon, because partners might at any time, according to their interests, break the agreement and take advantage of the co-operative behaviour of the other side.

(ii)   The second view interprets international organizations primarily as *arenas of international politics,* which, as lasting diplomatic structures, can address different fields of politics on different levels of co-operation. Unlike the instrumental view, here international organizations are seen more as frameworks than as means of achieving given goals.

(iii) The third view attributes to international organizations the independent quality of being *actors in international politics,* which, as causal factors, are also in a position to change the basic pattern of international politics in the sense of reducing the anarchy of its basic state.

Thus, if on one side, the analytical emphasis is placed on the co-operation-limiting structural anarchy aspect of the international system, national interests are the primary reference, and the chances of co-operation are, on balance, judged to be negative. Other perspectives tend to place the heightened possibility of co-operation, with the help of international institutions, in the central position, and start from the assumption that organizations matter. Thorsten Benner and Jan Martin Witte (2001) have suggested that a new model of international organizations ought to be developed. As theme-focused interfaces, they argue, international organizations could realize three different roles:

(i)   as negotiating platforms, they could use their scope to bring different actors together;

(ii) as managers of knowledge, they could collect information, enable learning processes, and offer advisory services; and

(iii) as implementation agents, they could implement agreements and oversee their observance.

In the future, the essential function of international organizations is likely to consist in forming 'bridges in the international system' among various actors and issue areas.

When evaluating the work of the UN it is essential to remember that it was constructed on inter-governmental principles, by which member states are the 'Masters of the Treaties', and have the last word (and expect to be consulted) on practically every decision. As we hope to show, it is also essential to differentiate by political issue area, since the UN is not a unitary actor, but rather a complex network of primary, secondary and special organs, exhibiting both various competencies and areas of responsibility, and different organizational structures. Not surprisingly, the roles of the UN (or, to put it more accurately the systems of the United Nations) in international politics are variable. Depending on the issue area, they might function primarily as an instrument, an arena, or an independent actor. Perhaps the principal characteristic of the UN, however, is its function as a forum in which the most disparate interests can be formulated and discussed in the attempt to come closer to the development of global solutions to problems. This function is regarded by every state in the world as an indispensable service. In individual issue-areas, such as (e.g.) human rights, it is possible to ascertain the beginnings of actor-orientation . . . significant UN autonomy in various issue-areas, however, remains restricted to tightly circumscribed exceptional cases, even today. (Rittberger, 1994, p. 581)

Challenges of Globalization

A crucial backdrop to the functioning and analysis of the UN is the phenomenon of globalization. The term 'globalization' (Michie, 2003; Baylis and Smith, 2008) has become a buzzword, inflated by over-use in political, publishing, and scientific debates. Furthermore, the meaning of globalization and its effects on international organizations such as the UN remain contested, (for example, what differentiates 'globalization' from 'internationalization'?) Michael Zürn (1998) has argued that the concept of 'uneven denationalization' should take precedence over globalization. Ernst-Otto Czempiel (1999) speaks of a 'self-internationalizing politics'. In the scientific/academic debate, the dividing line runs between those who see globalization as the death-knell of the sovereign statehood, and those who continue to attribute the central role in international politics to states. Globalization is, however, a dynamic historical process, which may be developing asymmetrically in various regions of the world, but nonetheless remains a viable and study-worthy worldwide phenomenon.

Globalization can generally be defined as a process in which the bonds or interactions among societies and issues are increasing in such a way that events in one area of the world have the ever increasing ability to impact societies and issues in other parts of the world. These interactions have increased first in absolute quantity, second in qualitative intensity, and third in their spatial scope. Thus there has also been an erosion of congruence of state territory, state citizens and state power, of territoriality and sovereignty, which were the markers of statehood. Action-relevant spaces are thus defined functionally, and extend beyond state boundaries. Alongside states and international organizations, new actors such as multinational corporations and a transnationally networked civil society have entered the stage of world politics.

There are different accounts as to the causes of increased globalization. In the thicket of research from many disciplines and at many levels of analysis, two paradigmatic positions may be discerned:

(i)   The first sees globalization as an exogenous process with its own logic. The driving forces are above all technological progress, the development of productive capacity, and the far-reaching changes in production relationships that come with the rise of multinational corporations, the differentiation of the international division of labour, and basic social and cultural change. Thus understood, globalization is a constituent part of a process of 'modernization' or 'westernization', in which a transition – global in tendency – from 'traditional' to 'modern' societies takes place. This process is characterized, to a certain extent, by the fact that it takes its course relatively independently of political decisions.

(ii)   The other paradigm emphasizes that it is states that have created the general framework in which the process of globalization is taking place. Globalization thus occurs not according to some law of nature, but following a political logic in the Idealistic tradition of international relations theory, which aims at a universal world-state with horizontal stratification. Even the networking of markets, for example, given all technical prerequisites, would have been impossible without politically willed deregulation.

Whatever the causes, or how such causes are evaluated, it is uncontested that the process of globalization – once it is set on its path – possesses a dynamic entirely of its own. The next task of a rational discourse on globalization is to decipher its various dimensions. For every dimension there is, of course, a whole list of the exceptions that make generalization so difficult. The degree of globalization varies with region and issue area (Scholte, 1997, p. 18):

- First, not all regions of the world are subject to globalization to the same degree. The diminishing meanings of time and space affect primarily, if not exclusively, the newly industrialized Asian countries and the rest of the OECD world. Phenomena such as multinational corporations and the use of the World Wide Web are largely confined to this region, even though other regions may be affected by these things.
- Second, globalization does not mean global unification or sameness. On the contrary, cultural diversification may even be a reaction particularly encouraged by hegemonial cultural trends in the course of globalization.
- Third, globalization has not brought on the 'end of geography'. Much more likely is the creation of new, supra-territorial spaces, which do not allow standing borders to become meaningless, but rather complement and overlay them.
- Fourth, mono-causal explanations which take, for example, technological advances, modernization, developments in productive capacity and deregulation as their point of reference, all fall short.
- Fifth, globalization is neither a comprehensive explanation for all international politics, nor is it synonymous with the victory procession of liberal-democratic government systems that has been described as the 'end of history', and is supposed to herald a stable world free of war.

The first (and the most obvious) dimension of globalization is found in economics and business. The central feature of economic globalization is that the world is divided not by territorial or geographic borders, but by economic barriers and borders. Economic globalization is manifest mainly in the integration of national political economies. (In order to understand what is entailed in economics, it is helpful to subdivide the subject into trade, capital investment, finance markets, and finance actors.) For years, world trade has grown more than world production, investments are planned globally, and a growing number of multinational corporations – the so-called 'global players' – shapes the face of economics process. Products and services are produced for a worldwide market, and capital can flow freely all over the globe and seek out the most economically efficient conditions. Between 1948 and 2000, trade increased by an average of 6.1 per cent (in real currency) every year, whereas production increased by a mere 3.9 per cent per year. Twenty-three states account for 75 per cent of world trade. The portion of world trade among industrialized countries has increased significantly since the 1980s. International capital flows have also increased enormously during recent decades. Finance markets are so tightly interwoven that the entire international finance structure can be unbalanced and forced to confront the question of necessary reforms by a single national or regional financial crisis – such as occurred in Mexico (1994), Asia (1997–8), Brazil (1999), Argentina (2002–03) or on the global level (2008 and 2011).

The increasing degree of interdependence among economies and the related broadening of world trade, along with the internationalization of production and the growing meaninglessness of time and space, have significant implications for cultures, identities and lifestyles. Growing commonalities in terms of a recognized and universal understanding of values may follow the worldwide processes of modernization, but there also exists the potential for cultural and ideological fragmentation that could threaten political structures. This threat to historically developed identities doubtless advances the cause for fundamentalist and ethno-nationalistic movements. Finally, globalization – understood as a worldwide interlinking of problem areas – has become a very important phenomenon in the realm of ecology. The ecological dimension is characterized by the understanding that harmful substances do not recognize state borders and an awareness that the global eco-system has carrying capacity. The risks of industrial development may be as old as industry itself, but in the age of globalization industrial risks take on a new quality – the place of *origin* is no longer the same as the place of *effect*. Increasingly, the risks of industrial development are abrogating the traditional categories and boundaries of state-centred politics.

Globalization cannot fail to affect international politics. The central aspect of political globalization is the erosion of state sovereignty to the extent that the traditional unit of decision-making power or *authority* – the state – and the *effects* of decision-making, which lie at the base of the all-encompassing dispositional power of the state over social conditions, is now in many areas a thing of the past. Today, the spaces relevant to action are determined primarily by function rather than by sovereign territory. The components of this process are:

- first, the growing significance of internationalized forms of political co-operation, which can in individual cases lead to the development of supranational decision-making mechanisms; and

- second, the increasing sectoralization of international politics into border-crossing issue areas with the prefix 'global', such as security, politics, environmental politics, and finance that demonstrate that the state as the sole arena for action has outlived its usefulness.

At the beginning of the twenty-first century, the international system consists of fewer than 200 states, of which (with an upward trend) 116 (approximately 60 per cent) may be described as electoral democracies (Freedom House, 2010). Using Freedom House's high standards concerning respect for human rights and the rule of law, however, only eighty-nine out of 194 states (46 per cent) are considered to be liberal democracies. Fifty-eight are considered to be partly free and forty-seven are considered to be not free (see www.freedomhouse.org). Additionally, according to the *Yearbook of International Organizations* by the Union of International Associations, there are 5,200 IGOs with international legal standing and more than 20,000 NGOs with worldwide or regional membership (UIA 2008–09, vol. 1). These numbers become somewhat less extreme if calculations are done according to the traditional method: in which case, for the year 2002, the UIA estimated that there were 251 IGOs with international legal standing, and 6,076 NGOs with worldwide or regional membership.

It has been suggested that an analysis of global political processes should be orientated on the basis of the three 'worlds' – business, society and states (Ernst-Otto Czempiel (1993; 2002)). Under this rubric, the competence of international politics to develop solutions is largely restricted to the 'world of states'. However, the increasing global interconnectedness of business, culture, environment, technology, communication, transportation, and migration have diminished states' abilities to control events and as a consequence a large number of problems remain stuck halfway on the road to a solution through international cooperation. Even with issues that remain under the direct responsibility of the state, relationships between states are adopting a pattern of reflexive interactions among members of a community of states conscious of their mutual dependence, their mutual vulnerability, and their responsibility to consider the effects on their neighbours of proposed solutions to national problems (Scharpf, 1999, p. 181).

Global Governance as a Possible Solution?

What, then, does this roughly-sketched portrait of the globalization process mean for the role and function of the UN? A significant part of the present discourse concerns whether inter-state politics should be subject to binding regulations. Such regulations would serve two aims: to further relativize state sovereignty (which is already eroding in many fields), and to assert the UN's capacity to control and influence international problems. In a world that is getting smaller, as Volker Rittberger (2000, p. 188) has maintained, the international community still relies on the duties and responsibilities that have traditionally been exercised by states, but there must be a recognition that today's states are no longer capable of fully exercising these duties and responsibilities:

There is a growing number of actors whose activities cross borders require generally binding rules in order to let them pursue both their individual and common interests, and to prevent conflicts of interest with destructive effects for either of the parties as well as for third parties.

How this transition is to be accomplished is controversial. Granting that globalization may significantly change economic, social and cultural life, representatives of the Realist School deny the need for action on the basis that the state is, and will remain, the central entity of international politics. For Idealists, globalization means a fundamental transformation of global political processes that makes the Realists' visions look increasingly obsolete. Idealists suggest that international relations are like a spider's web wherein the state is only one (important) actor of many – an actor that is no longer in a position to define what takes place on its own territory in an isolated fashion. At the same time, Idealists acknowledge the need for regulation in border-crossing issues and seek alternative steering models for the globalized world. Global governance is one attempt to meet these global challenges. Political scientists understand global governance as an alternative steering model for the international system that includes international organizations as well as informal rules and norms. The concept is not to be confused with similar-sounding ideas such as global government, but is best understood as a particular form of a politics of world order. In this process, the UN plays a central role (to which we shall return in the section discussing the various areas of UN action; on the concept of global governance, see Chapter 9).

Globalization may be understood as an indicator of the accelerating, earth-spanning interconnection of actors and fields of action. In particular, the number of issues that do not (or no longer) allow for a state-based solution is a reliable indicator of the progression that globalization has already made. Thus the central challenge for the discipline of international relations is to search for border-transcending substitutes for the dwindling steering capacities previously found at the state level, and to understand how democratic and effective governance beyond the state may be possible under these conditions. The continuing demand for 'intelligent' responses to these issues suggest that none have yet been found. We shall return to this question, and the role of the UN in this area, in more detail in Chapter 9.

The Primary Tasks of the United Nations and the Expansion of the Concept of Security

Should one ask what the concrete areas of responsibility and chief tasks of the UN are, one is likely to receive several different answers. This is partly because the UN is understood to be a global forum for international co-operation, but its more precise responsibilities are somewhat difficult to pin down. The UN was created as an all-encompassing organization in so far as it was promised far-reaching competence – its area of responsibility was the whole world – and consequently all human problems calling for international attention fall under its purview (Claude, 1970, p. 67). Actors interested in the politics of development will thus emphasize development issues, actors interested in the environment will emphasize environmental issues, and actors interested in security will emphasize security aspects.

At the foundation of the work of the UN lies a broad concept of peace that includes not only the desire to hinder the occurrence of war, but also the improvement of mankind's humanitarian and social status, the strengthening of international law, and long-term development concerns. The nearly seven-decades-old UN Charter anticipated the debate that has been occupying political scientists since (at least) the work of Johan Galtung on structural violence and the 1960s discussion of positive versus negative concepts of peace. However, this debate became much more intense in the 1990s, and has since been classified under the heading of the 'expansion of the concept of security' that concerns a horizontal broadening of the parameters of security, as well as a vertical increase in the reference points of security. It comprises three dimensions:

(i)   Economic interdependence and military-technological developments have led to the dissolution of the classical definition of security in relation to the inviolability of the nation state's territory, the retention of unlimited sovereignty, and the guarantee of national self-determination, to be replaced by a concept both spatially and substantively broader.

(ii)   Security is no longer considered to be primarily a military problem. Instead, there is an assumption that there is a total-security concept in which foreign, business, finance, environmental, development, and security politics may all be mutually optimized.

(iii)   The classical definition of security as protection from external threat is revised. The negative understanding of security is complemented by a positive understanding that allows mechanisms to be created, through the formulation of common security interests, which then work to reduce *ex ante* any non-peaceful conditions, and thereby lead to more peaceful international relations.

The concept of 'human' security (Paris, 2001) has – primarily through the *Human Development Report* of the UNDP in 1994 and the Commission on Global Governance in 1995 – established itself in UN terminology. Human security provides that state security is no longer the central issue of security; rather, it is the security of the populations living within these states that is important. The concept of human security combines traditional elements of the concept of security with the protection of human rights, the right to development, and the right to a liveable environment. The purposes articulated in the UN Charter include a broad realm of competence –from the peaceful resolution of disputes through the search for co-operative solutions to economic, social, cultural and humanitarian problems, to the encouragement of behaviour in accordance with the fundamental principles of international law – that suggests the UN is not only a means of fulfilling specific objectives, but is instead a forum for the development of a new set of basic principles for international relations. Former Secretary-General Kofi Annan, in his report 'In Larger Freedom' (Annan, 2005, p. 18) stated it thus:

> In a world of interconnected threats and challenges, it is in each country's self-interest that all of them are addressed effectively. Hence, the cause of larger freedom can only be advanced by broad, deep and sustained global cooperation among States. Such cooperation is possible if every country's policies take into account not only the needs of its own citizens but also the needs of others. This kind of cooperation not only advances everyone's interests but also recognizes our common humanity.

Despite the essentially unchanged UN Charter, the organization's areas of responsibility have dramatically expanded. This expansion is partly the result of General Assembly Resolutions (such as the Declaration on Friendly Relations of 24 October 1970, or the resolution on the definition of 'aggression' from 14 December 1974), which have provided the foundation for new UN directions. In the first forty-five years of its existence, the UN 'lived in the grip of the Cold War, prevented from fulfilling some of its core missions but discovering other critical tasks in that conflict's shadow' (Annan, 2000, p. 11).

Many authors believe that the UN has moved in a 'development aid' direction because it was thwarted in its original areas of competence (a claim regarded by others as extremely wrong-headed, see Chapter 7). But whatever the reason, it remains the case that even the core missions of the UN have undergone change. For example, at the UN's founding, the prevention of inter-state wars was considered the primary task of maintaining international peace and security, but at the start of the twenty-first century it is far more likely that internal conflicts appear on the daily agenda of work for maintaining international peace and security. The core work of the UN can be divided into three main fields, which will be analysed in more detail in Chapters 3 to 8:

- first, tasks in the area of securing world peace and international security (see Chapters 3 and 4);
- second, tasks in the area of human rights protection and the further development of international law (see Chapters 5 and 6); and
- third, tasks in the areas of economics, development and the environment (see Chapter 7).

This list of areas of competence is not exhaustive, but rather exemplifies the UN's main areas of work. Chapters 8 and 9 will offer perspectives on, and analysis of, the possible reforms that the UN must undergo, and a forecast will be attempted concerning the future role of the UN.

Further Reading

Annan, Kofi (2005) 'In Larger Freedom: Towards Development, Security and Human Rights for All', Report of the Secretary-General (UN document A/59/2005).

Archer, Clive (2001) *International Organizations*, London: Routledge.

Armstrong, David, Lorna Lloyd and John Redmond (2004) *International Organisation in World Politics*, Basingstoke and New York: Palgrave Macmillan.

Baylis, John and Steve Smith (eds) (2001) *The Globalization of World Politics*, Oxford: Oxford University Press.

Gorman, Robert F. (2001) *Great Debates at the United Nations: An Encyclopaedia of Fifty Key Issues 1945–2000*, Westport, CT: Greenwood Press.

High-Level Panel on Threats Challenges and Change (2004) 'A More Secure World: Our Shared Responsibility', New York (UN document A/59/565).

Michie, Jonathan (ed.) (2003) *The Handbook of Globalization*, Cheltenham: Edward Elgar Publishing.

Simmons, Beth A. and Lisa L. Martin (2002) 'International Organizations and Institutions', in Walter Carlsnaes, Thomas Risse and Beth A. Simmons (eds), *Handbook of International Relations,* London: Sage, pp. 192–211.

Viotti, Paul R. and Mark V. Kauppi (2001) *International Relations Theory,* Boston, MA: Allyn & Bacon.

3

The Core of the United Nations: Collective Security

If it is accepted that Article 1 of the UN Charter represents a positive concept of peace – as already discussed – an apparent incongruity soon emerges. The provisions of the operative chapters concentrate expressly on the avoidance and ending of classical inter-state conflicts and wars. Attempts aimed at the sustainable elimination of the many economic, social or humanitarian causes of violence and war – as would be expected from a broader understanding of peace – are treated with comparative brevity. The Charter's focus on inter-state conflict is understandable in light of the context, overwhelmingly influenced by the experience of the Second World War, in which the UN came into existence. The general inference drawn from the Second World War was the urgent need to eliminate war as a tool of international relations as a necessary prerequisite for the development of a comprehensive global peace. The basic principle of 'collective security' forms the basis upon which all UN efforts to ensure peace are built. Before examining the normative and organizational development of this principle through the League of Nations and the UN, it seems appropriate to lay out and discuss this idea of collective security with respect to its assumptions, its intrinsic problems and its practical potential for the maintenance of global peace.

The Principle of Collective Security: Limitations and Possibilities

The history of international relations is a history of states using force to pursue their interests. As states have moved closer together – as a result of increasing political, economic and cultural linkage and interdependence – there have been ever more frequent attempts to avoid, or at least to limit, the damage and disruption of war. The catastrophe of the First World War, however, demonstrated that non-aggression pacts, defensive alliances, reassurance treaties and carefully balanced constellations among the great powers were too fragile to create durable constraints on the will of states to pursue their interests with force. Above all, the lack of internationally accepted norms forbidding the use of force, and authoritative bodies for the maintenance of a peace built upon such norms, allowed states to appeal to their sovereignty and to fall back constantly upon the *ultima ratio regum*: war.

The League of Nations was the first attempt to address such deficits and to introduce a system of international collective security. The League of Nations was based on the assumption that all states might be capable of, and willing to, subordinate their sovereign rights and particular interests to a common interest in peaceful and stable international relations, and to take part in the creation of a global system capable of restraining its members from the threat or use of force. In contrast to a system of collective defence – whose members assure each another of assistance in the case of external threat or aggression – a collective security system is orientated towards the states organized within it, using obligations and the threat of sanctions to influence their behaviour. In its idealized form, such a system would approximate a world state with a monopoly on the use of force and executive authority with respect to the individual member states. However, the creation of such a world state remains a utopian goal. In practice, the best realization of collective security is the voluntary self-limitation of member states on the basis of an international treaty which:

- obliges the parties to settle their disputes in a peaceful manner;
- creates an organ with the authority to make judgements about the type and degree of possible violations of duties, as well as the consequences of such violations; and
- contains clear provisions for measures for the enforcement of such judgements.

The capacity for effective action under such a system, however, depends on a variety of prerequisites. First, all member states must be ready to subject their interest in a forceful alteration of the political and territorial status quo to a general prohibition on the use of force (Claude, 1970, p.250) even if they still consider themselves to be entitled to the use of force. Second, member states must be ready to act collectively against a violator of the peace, even if that means once again disregarding their own interests. Third, such a system would require an institutionalized process of peaceful dispute resolution as well as a central instance equipped with sufficient power – including military power – to implement any decisions taken. Fourth, all member states must agree upon not only the legal norms and rules, but also the procedures for the further development of them, for the purposes of dealing with violations of the peace and the measures to be taken to address them. The decisive factor for the functional efficacy of a system of collective security, however, which usurps all other prerequisites, is trust. Each member state must be able to rely upon the other members of the system to abide by the rules in a more or less permanent way. Furthermore, every peace-loving state must be able to rely on the expectation of assistance from the others in event of aggression. Such reliance requires the co-operation and assistance of all member states, but also relies upon on the effectiveness and impartiality of the central adjudicatory and enforcement body.

Criticisms of collective security arise mostly from these complex prerequisites. Adherents of the *Realist School* object to the principles of collective security insomuch as it superficially accepts a picture of international anarchy with egoistic states as the principal actors at its starting point, but fails to provide a conclusive solution to the problem of why states should overcome their mutual mistrust and the need for individual security sufficiency that arises from it. In the end, any attempt at collective security begins from the assumption that some states intend to behave aggressively; and thus strengthens the Realist precept of lingering inter-state insecurity and the permanent security dilemma (Mearsheimer, 1994, p. 30 *et seq.*). Further concerns about the efficacy of collective security accrete from the Realists fundamental objection: for example, in a state-based system where insti-tutions are controlled by states, the decisions and outcomes of institutions are always dependent on the interests of those states – i.e. the distinction between aggressor and victim is subject to states' perspective, and since the causes of war are usually very complex there is nearly always conflict between states in deter-mining which side is the aggressor and which side is the victim. Clientelism and the lack of congruence between individual state's interests would suggest that international panels might be particularly unsuited to playing the role of mediator or impartial referee. Moreover, even in unambiguous cases, states may be inter-ested in the cessation of hostilities but they might quickly part ways on how to apportion the burdens of that undertaking. The phenomenon of free-riding – a constant accompaniment to collective undertakings – undermines collective action even when there is widespread agreement concerning needs and goals. The refusal of even a relatively small number of members to support an action leads to the deceleration and sometimes even the paralysis of the collective security mech-anism – a problem made even more acute when the collective security system has to deal with several violations simultaneously. Comprehensive and obligatory norms cannot be subject to selectivity without some loss of obligation and credi-bility; on the other hand, if an attempt is made to meet every instance of aggression with the same decisiveness and unanimity, the system will very quickly find itself at the outer limits of its capacity (Roberts, 1993, p. 5).

Collective security seems to be able to promise success only against relatively small or weak states. Should a great power (with their correspondingly great mili-tary potential) appear as the aggressor the costs of engagement quickly overtake the expected benefits. This special position held by great powers can lead them to abusing collective security systems insomuch as they can usurp the decision-making body and conduct their politics under a veil of action in the collective interest (Hurrell, 1992, p. 45; Butfoy, 1993, p. 494). However, if great powers are not included in collective security systems (and their accompanying rules) the Realist perspective falls back upon a reliance on classical defensive alliances, balance of power arrangements, or concerts of the great powers. Thus, followers of the Realist school tend to conclude that:

> [B]ecause every state – and especially every great power – decides on a case-by-case basis according to its own interests whether and how a victim of aggression is to be assisted, and because democracies in particular make such decisions dependent upon the often tedious deliberation and (uncertain)

consent of parliamentary bodies, the concept of collective security proves itself to be highly unrealistic. (Link, 1998, p. 106)

Adherents of the *Institutionalist School* also criticize the concept of collective security as inappropriate for the practice of international politics. According to Ernst-Otto Czempiel (1994, p. 25 *et seq.*), the idea of collective security is a great leap forward in terms of the history of liberal/institutional theory, but has shown itself to be somewhat ineffectual in the logic of politics. Politics relies on a mechanism that does not work on a global scale.

While these criticisms might suggest that idea of collective security – with its complex and manifold prerequisites – belongs in the realm of political utopia, other critics point to the incipient problems of a *functioning* system of collective security. If violence in international relations is considered to be basically and fundamentally wrong, but a collective security system endows its central effective body with the power to legitimize the use of force, or to empower others to use force legitimately, there exists the danger that such authority could be abused. It is presupposed that collective security's underlying norms must be relatively abstract, and that an outcome decision on any issue would require significant interpretation of these underlying norms by member states. In a complex world, conflicts of value and interest are essentially programmed in, and an action considered by one group of states to be a legitimate action in pursuit of peace may represent an attempt to impose foreign ideas to another group of states, thus presenting a 'dangerous opportunity for crusaders', warns Stanley Hoffmann (1981, p. 61). External involvement increases the possibility that limited conflicts could turn into altercations with significantly larger implications and outcomes.

As it becomes more common for states' domestic concerns to be put on the agenda of collective security systems, the danger of that system then increasing the breadth and scope of the conflict is a significant concern. Interventions into smaller, chronic conflicts could in fact result in these conflicts becoming incapable of fulfilling their initiating function, which is to produce the conditions for a sustainable peace accord (see Luttwak, 1999). In place of an order created by the parties to the conflict, there will instead be an order created by an external organization and that order must be sustained against the possible opposition of one or more of the original parties to the conflict. The resulting international protectorates tie up the strength and resources of both the system and its member states in significant measure, and severely limit its ability to act in other conflicts.

The multifarious and serious objections to a system of collective security can be summed up in two queries: whether the goals of collective security might actually be impossible to achieve; and whether or not the creation of a system intended to absorb member states' individual interests and to safeguard these interests under a central organ is even feasible. Indeed, Czempiel asks if collective security is in fact a myth that has never functioned, and will never function? (Czempiel, 1994, p. 25 *et seq.*) Nye asks if states should instead concentrate on the formulation and realization of their national interests (Nye, 1999) and use their power and the application of tried and proven methods to ensure global stability – in some sense – as the sum of these counter-balancing interests?

A large part of the criticism towards collective security is in fact aimed at a straw man in the form of an overly idealized vision of what collective security is meant to achieve. The concept of collective security would shed a great deal of its ostensible utopianism if it were to be understood with respect to its normative function as a target value for international relations, and to its organizational design as a rule-based framework for the ordering of international relations. A system of collective security does not necessarily aim at setting institutions in the place of states as the central actors of international politics, and does not necessarily make classical security precautions superfluous. Instead, such a system may contribute to the creation of conditions that make the peaceful resolution of conflicts easier and more likely to enjoy success than they would under the conditions of international anarchy. From this perspective, a system of collective security complements, rather than replaces, other forms or attempts at global and regional peace maintenance (Kupchan and Kupchan, 1995, p. 54). Collective security offers an alternative way of handling conflicts; the use of institutions may not be perfectly impartial, but the initiatives and decisions of such institutions rely on compromises and the co-ordination of interests among different states that limits the effects of arbitrariness. A system lacking comparable structures must rely exclusively on ad hoc measures, thus the advantages of a collective security system are in the institutionalization of appropriate forums for consultation and the resultant reduction in arbitrary decision-making mechanisms. Collective security arrangements may also form the basis of a much more extensive system of co-operative security, in which social, economic, humanitarian or ecological problems can also be addressed through institutions.

The UN constitutes such a system of collective security. The UN has made a number of departures from its original ideal because of the constraints of reality, but has actively used opportunities to broaden the scope of its responsibilities and activities, even into the realm of cooperative security. Under Article 51, the Charter allows for individual and collective self-defence, but with the general prohibition on the use of force and the conditions laid out in Chapter VII the Charter refers every other use of force to the Security Council, and has solidly anchored these rules into international law. The elevated position of the five permanent members of the Security Council represents the concept of a concert of responsible powers, which should – in theory at least – lead to largely accepted decisions on the basis of compromise among enormously heterogeneous interests. It was in fact only on this basis that the decisive powers could be convinced to take part in the organization, although after more than fifty years of UN existence, that construction may be in dire need of reform (as will be discussed later).

The UN remains more a forum than an actor, even in its primary purpose of peace through collective measures. Furthermore, it is a forum whose is used selectively, or in many cases not at all, by its member states. This on the part of UN member states is based on the pervasive problems and ions between the Charter and the actual practice of the organization, but above all is based on a lack of trust in multilateral institutions. Before the following sections elaborate on the possibilities available for addressing this deficit, and for developing new confidence in the potential and competencies of the world organization, the normative and organizational development of the collective security system of the UN as explained in the Charter must first be described.

Still a Challenge: The General Prohibition on the Use of Force and the Exclusion of War from International Relations

In order to facilitate an effective use of agency, collective security systems require a set of general norms and rules against which its members can measure their behaviour and through which the decisions and measures of the system are legitimized. UN Charter Article 2(4) articulates a general prohibition on the use of force that stands out as fundamental among other general norms of international law: 'All Members shall refrain in their international relations from the threat or use of force against the territorial integrity or political independence of any state, or in any other manner inconsistent with the Purposes of the United Nations.' This general prohibition on the use of force – which finds its complement in Article 2(3)'s duty to resolve conflicts peacefully – represents the most extensive attempt yet to create a global order of peace on the basis of international law. This apparently unambiguous and comprehensive legal principle, however, provokes a number of questions arising from its origin, its legal scope and its practical political application.

The Development of the General Prohibition on the Use of Force

Attempts to normatively regulate inter-state relations – during times of war and during times of peace – date far back into human history. For centuries, the efforts of moral theory and then of international law were aimed at restraining the effects of war (or, as Carl Schmitt said, *'die Hegung des Krieges'*) but not at removing it altogether. As recently as 1914 and the advent of the First World War it was assumed that war and peace were naturally alternating conditions of inter-state relations. Practical, law-based efforts to banish war from international relations did not emerge until later in the Twentieth century.

The early medieval ideas of Augustine (354–430 AD) were formulated by Thomas Aquinas during the thirteenth century into the *bellum iustum* (the doctrine of just war). The *bellum iustum* allowed recourse to war only under very strict conditions: First, it required *auctoritas principis,* or the auspices of a legitimate authority. Second, the war had to be waged for a just cause (*iusta causa*) such as the punishment of injustice. Thirdly, it should be waged with the good intention (*recta intentio*) of furthering the just and fighting evil. However, the theological and scholastically influenced teachings of Aquinas do not define the standards of 'just cause' and during the conflicts of the late Middle Ages and the Early Modern period – which were marked especially by their confessional character – *iusta causa* was usually claimed by all sides. Since only one side could possibly be the true possessor of justice and truth, the appeal to *iusta causa* led not only to the demonization of the foe, but also necessitated a type of warfare intended not merely to subdue the enemy, but to bring about its near total destruction. In view of these grave difficulties, the focus on a *iusta causa* slipped increasingly into the background and attention was turned to the *auctoritas principis* to formalize conditions of just war, as follows: just war must be legitimized by the sovereign power of the ruler; just war must be formally declared, and the conduct of just war must be subject to certain rules. Furthermore, notions of justice and injustice started down a new path following the schism in Christendom and the disintegration of the medieval idea of empire that led to the demise of a generally accepted overarching authority on questions of good and evil. Following the intermediate idea of a war that might be just on both sides – *bellum iustum ex utraque parte* found primarily in the writings of Francisco de Vitoria (1486–1546) and Alberico Gentili (1552–1608) – there developed a morally indifferent concept of war, from there developed the notion of a right to war (*ius ad bellum*) deriving from state sovereignty. As predicted by Hugo Grotius (1583–1645) in 1625, in the world order created after the Thirty Years War by the Peace of Westphalia (1648) war and peace became morally neutral legal positions between sovereign states. There emerged with the 'Westphalian Order' an anarchical system of international politics, which imposed no legal or moral limitations on a state's use of power. The cabinet wars of the eighteenth century and the wars of imperial conquest of the nineteenth century could be waged under the generally accepted and poignantly formulated Clausewitzian understanding of war as the continuation of politics by other means. Even in 1918, the Netherlands refused to extradite Emperor Wilhelm II to the victorious allies on the justification that, with the unleashing of the First World War, the Emperor had merely been using the *ius ad bellum* to which a sovereign state was entitled.

As problematic as the effects of unlimited sovereignty might be seen in hindsight, it is impossible to envisage the development of contemporary international relations – wherein each state is afforded equal status and equal rights as a unit of the international system – without this principle at the foundation. The decline in thinking in categories of good and evil also had consequences for the conduct of war – there was no longer a moral requirement to comprehensively punish the loser. With war accepted as a legitimate instrument for the pursuit of interest, there emerged the need for legal regulations of its inception, conduct, and cessation. There also emerged the need for regulations as to the protection of civil populations. The law of war (*ius in bello*) became, next to the law of peace, the second pillar of international law. Although the *ius in bello* was in no way aimed at preventing war, its progressive drawing of warfare into the realm of legal norms, and its gradual dismantling of war's function of arbitration in international conflicts, created serious hurdles for any head of state who might wish to follow that route. Above all, in the efforts of the law of war to limit the damages and consequences of war for both soldiers and uninvolved civilians lay the seeds of international humanitarian law. The Hague Conventions on the Laws and

Customs of War on Land – resulting from the peace conferences of 1899 and 1907 – attempted to regulate the laws and customs of land warfare according to humanitarian considerations and are still a valid part of international humanitarian law at the time of writing.

The catastrophe of the First World War provided a dramatic demonstration of the deficiencies of an international system that merely regulated the course of warfare, and it initiated a fundamental shift in the way that major powers thought about war. It was recognized that the vast dimensions and total nature of modern warfare constituted an existential threat to the structure of the international system and to humanity in general. With the constitution of the League of Nations, based on the 'Fourteen Points' of US President Woodrow Wilson, the establishment of a partial prohibition on war was undertaken, to be guaranteed by a collective system of peace maintenance. Article 11 of the Covenant of the League of Nations disestablished the *ius ad bellum* as a subjective right of individual states: 'Any war or threat of war, whether immediately affecting any of the Members of the League or not, is hereby declared a matter of concern to the whole League, and the League shall take any action that may be deemed wise and effectual to safeguard the peace of nations.' However, in 1919, the states were still unable to push through a general prohibition on war, much less on the use of force as such. The preamble held only that:

> [T]he high contracting parties, in order to promote international co-operation and to achieve international peace and security by the acceptance of obligations not to resort to war, by the prescription of open, just and honourable relations between nations, by the firm establishment of the understandings of international law as the actual rule of conduct among Governments, and by the maintenance of justice and a scrupulous respect for all treaty obligations in the dealings of organized peoples with one another, Agree to this Covenant of the League of Nations.

Article 12 of the Covenant also required merely that disputes that are 'likely to lead to a rupture' should be submitted to arbitration, judicial settlement, or enquiry by the Council. During the phase in which the League was addressing the issue – in the case of a Council enquiry less than six months, and in cases of arbitration or judicial settlement within 'a reasonable time' – and for a period of three months after the proceedings were closed, the parties were not allowed to resort to war. In practical terms, this clause created a 'cooling-off' period of about nine months (Weber, 1995) after which, if the situation were still unresolved, recourse to war was possible. Only in the case of a unanimous recommendation by the Council, to which the parties to the conflict were willing to submit themselves, was there an actual prohibition on war (Article 15(6)). If, on the other hand, the recommendations should have been merely those of the majority, 'the Members of the League reserve[d] to themselves the right to take such action as they shall consider necessary for the maintenance of right and justice' (Article 15(7)). Even this delaying effect, however, related only to the waging of war and not to any use of force below that threshold, as long as it was declared as a measure of self-help (Guggenheim, 1932, p. 109).

In the first half of the 1920s, a number of initiatives attempted to close the loopholes and normative grey zones created by this partial prohibition on war. At the centre of these efforts stood the completion of the League's statute, especially with respect to the banning of aggressive war that was then still theoretically permissible. However, the Geneva Protocol of 2 October 1924, which described aggressive war as an 'international crime' and intended to implement obligatory arbitral jurisdiction never came into force (Wehberg, 1927). In the framework of the Western Pact, the Locarno Treaty of 16 October 1925 established a regional prohibition on aggressive war between Germany and Belgium, and between Germany and France, as well as obligatory arbitral jurisdiction between Germany and Poland and Czechoslovakia. A long list of exceptions ensured that these agreements were as full of holes as the others, but the Locarno Treaties accelerated a much more ambitious process of development that led finally to the general prohibition on war in the Briand-Kellogg Pact of 27 April 1928.

The Briand-Kellogg Pact – a Franco-American initiative named for the two Foreign Ministers Aristide Briand and Frank B. Kellogg – represented a decisive breakthrough. Whereas the Covenant of the League of Nations forbade war only under certain circumstances, and the Locarno Treaties forbade only aggressive war among specifically enumerated states, Article 1 of the Briand-Kellogg Pact finally made the unambiguous statement that:

> The High Contracting Parties solemnly declare in the names of their respective peoples that they condemn recourse to war for the solution of international controversies, and renounce it, as an instrument of national policy in their relations with one another.

The only exceptions to this prohibition remained war for self-defence and collective measures of the League of Nations. These exceptions did not represent a weakening of the general prohibition on war, but rather represented a confirmation of it. As forceful self-defence and forceful emergency aid are permissible in domestic law only against criminal actions, the rights to self-defence and collective aid at the international level worked to confirm the criminal nature of the actions against which they might be directed. In all, sixty-three countries joined the Briand-Kellogg Pact – an overwhelming majority of existing states at that time. The general prohibition on war was thus already a part of Customary International Law in the 1930s, and as such enjoyed worldwide legal validity independent of membership of the Pact.

In spite of its clear formulation and uncontested legal validity the general prohibition on war contained in the Briand-Kellogg Pact could not prevent the outbreak of the First World War – the Briand-Kellogg Pact had not included 'measures short of war' in the scope of its prohibition and the implementation of the prohibition on war had been left to the inadequate collective security system of the League of Nations. In 1945, the framers of the UN Charter hoped to overcome the structural weaknesses of the League of Nations by creating a new and more powerful system for securing peace. In the normative realm, the regulations of the Briand-Kellogg Pact with respect to the general prohibition on war were comprehensively expanded so that not only the use, but also the threat of the use of force was impermissible – a development that cannot be underestimated in terms of its effect on the shape of modern international law. It is impossible to imagine a modern international peace or security-related treaty existing without some reference to the Charter's general prohibition on the use of force. The UN's universal membership also lends the Charter's general prohibition universal legitimacy – the result of which is that the principle has entered into general international law and would continue to apply even in the event of the dissolution of the UN.

The Prohibition on the Use of Force: Concept and Extent

The regulations found in Article 2(4) of the UN Charter are more ambiguous than their language might suggest at first glance. The concept of 'force' is particularly abstruse and requires a more precise explanation in order to enable a distinction between states' legitimate use of power and states' illegitimate use of force, a necessary distinction considering that a violation of the general prohibition on the use of force can initiate both individual and collective responses – including the use of force – from the international community.

According to leading current legal opinion, the application of Article 2(4) is restricted to the use of military force between states (Randelzhofer, 2002). This interpretation does not merely replicate existing prohibitions on war (which are already established in general international law) but extends to include the use of military force not amounting to war. The General Assembly's 'Declaration on Principles of International Law Concerning Friendly Relations and Co-operation Among States in Accordance with the Charter of the United Nations' of 24 October 1970 is very telling on this point; in pursuing its goal of the further development and codification of basic norms of international law, the Declaration on Friendly Relations considers the general prohibition on the use of force to be the primary principle of state behaviour, far outweighing all others. In a thorough comment on the general prohibition on the use of force, the following rules and duties are set out:

- aggressive wars are branded as crimes against peace;
- states may not use or threaten the use of force in order to harm the existing status of international borders, and may not make use of a propaganda of aggression;
- they may not use force in measures of retaliation;
- they may not involve themselves in the formation or the support of the formation of irregular armed forces or armed bands which have as their purpose the violation of the sovereign territory of another state;
- they must refrain from the organization, incitement, or support of acts of civil war or terrorism in another state, and may not suffer the support of such actions to take place in their sovereign territory; and

- they may not obtain the sovereign territory of another state through the use of force. ('Declaration on Friendly Relations', A/RES/2625(XXV))

These comments confirm that the general prohibition on the use of force applies only to military or paramilitary force. At the same time, they also make it clear that indirect forms of the use of force that are carried out through the support of violent actions in another state also fall under this prohibition. There remain questions, however, concerning how that standard can be applied to rebel organizations or to civil wars. In its decision on the military and paramilitary activities in and against Nicaragua, the International Court of Justice (ICJ) referred expressly to the Declaration on Friendly Relations, and described the USA's arming and training of the Contra rebels – but not the USA's financial support for the Contra – as a use of force. Thus the ICJ recognized that there are permissible and impermissible forms of intervention in civil wars and uprisings, but failed to provide clear criteria for determining the difference between the two (Randelzhofer, 2002). According to the specifications of the Declaration on Friendly Relations, all forms of economic pressure are expressly excluded from the prohibitions articulated in Article 2(4) of the UN Charter (despite constant calls by socialist states (during the Cold War) and developing states (during decolonization) to include them in the prohibition on force.) The Declaration on Friendly Relations includes a prohibition on intervention – which serves to reinforce the ban on military activities – but also identifies some economic, political, and other non-military forms of pressure and/or coercion as illegitimate. Given that military and economic pressure often go hand in hand it would seem that restricting the general prohibition on the use of force to apply only to the classical military application would, at best, be problematic (Arangio-Ruiz, 1979, p. 99 *et seq.*). In practice, therefore, it is best left to the Security Council, with the broader perspective on what might constitute a threat to the peace, to decide in individual cases which forms of economic or other non-military pressure are permissible or not.

Exceptions to the General Prohibition on the Use of Force

Although the declared purpose of the United Nations lies clearly in the displacement of war and violence from the realm of international relations, the Charter does not entirely rule out the possibility of the legitimate use of force by its member states. The Charter acknowledges that states may use military or other forceful measures in pursuit of their interests, and that the use of force in defence against such states may indeed be necessary. Once again, the existence of permissible uses of force does not emasculate the prohibitory norm, but rather strengthens its basic character. The exceptions to the general prohibition which have their basis in the Charter are orientated exclusively on defence against illegal force, and thus do not constitute a covert attempt to reintroduce an *ius ad bellum*. This is made express above all in the fact that these exceptions are not unlimited, and their validity is subject to a whole list of regulations also found in the Charter. According to the UN Charter, the exceptions to the general prohibition on the use of force are:

- collective measures against a disturber of the peace on the basis of Chapter VII;
- the right of self-defence against an armed attack according to Article 51; and
- measures taken against former 'enemy states' according to Articles 53 and 107.

The general prohibition on the use of force must be understood – in theory and in practice – in conjunction with the collective security system described in Chapter VII. The prohibition of the use of force, and the duty to secure peace, are both distinct and overlapping legal duties of UN member states, the observance of which is to be overseen by the international community and the specific organs commissioned for that purpose – namely, the Security Council. In the logic of a collective security system, one member's violations of common norms must draw proportionate and appropriate measures of retaliation, up to and including the use of military force.

Article 39 of the Charter provides the normative and procedural conditions under which the use of force may be employed. First, the Security Council must determine if a threat to the peace, a breach of the peace, or an act of aggression, has occurred. Should this be the case the Security Council is authorized to issue non-binding recommendations to member states with respect to their behaviour towards the disturber of the peace (Article 40). According to Article 41 the Security Council may also issue coercive measures (sanctions) such as the interruption of economic relations or means of communication that are binding on both the target state and all other member states. If the Security Council believes that measures provided for in Article 41 'would be inadequate or have proved to be inadequate' (Article 42) in changing the peace-disturbing behaviour of the states involved, it may invoke Article 42 that allows for the use of military force under UN leadership, or by individually named member states, or by specified international organizations (Article 48). The decision to employ the use of force requires a Security Council quorum of nine votes including the concurring votes of the five permanent members. The Security Council may also choose to implement enforcement action under its authority through regional arrangements as addressed in Chapter VIII of the Charter (Article 53). These Chapter VII regulations make it clear that, except for the purposes of individual or collective self-defence as set out in Article 51 (see below), force may be used only on the basis of a Security Council determination to that effect. The Security Council may thus be said to possess a monopoly on the legitimization of the use of force.

The Security Council is not a world court, but a political decision-making committee, bound in its competences to the Charter and customary international law. Thus it is necessary to take a closer look at the situations listed in Article 39 – threats to the peace, breaches of the peace, and acts of aggression – as the bases of the Security Council's realm of responsibility. A breach of the peace occurs when at least two states undertake acts of armed combat. A breach of the peace is also determined to have occurred when an independent de facto regime (which has not been recognized as a state) uses or becomes the victim of armed force. Despite this relatively clear criterion the Security Council has determined a breach of the peace in only four cases to date: Korea, 1950; the United Kingdom/Argentina, 1982; Iraq/Iran, 1987; and Iraq/Kuwait, 1990.

An act of aggression also constitutes a breach of the peace, but in determining an act of aggression the aggressor must be named. On 14 December 1974 the General Assembly produced a definition of an 'act of aggression', which contains in Article 3 a non-exhaustive list of seven types of action, each of which constitutes an act of aggression (UN General Assembly Resolution 3314 (XXIX): Definition of Aggression). General Assembly Resolutions are non-binding on the Security Council, but can be used by the Security Council to evaluate situations and the Security Council has considered a number of actions to be acts of aggression, including Southern Rhodesia's incursion into Zambia in 1978, Israel's aerial attacks on PLO targets in Tunisia in 1985, and the South African intervention in Angola in 1985. In its formal resolutions under Chapter VII, however, the Security Council then went on to determine that each of these acts had the character of a threat to the peace. Thus far, even in relatively unambiguous cases such as Iraq's invasion of Kuwait, the Security Council has not seen fit to determine an 'act of aggression' in the sense of Article 39.

Of the three situations named in Article 39, that of 'threat to the peace' offers the Security Council the widest margin for interpretation. Despite its conceptual fuzziness and lack of straightforward legal and political intelligibility, Article 39 extends its reach to situations and actions that fall short of being an open breach of the peace or act of aggression and therefore constitutes a key instrument in the collective maintenance of peace. Article 39's 'threat to the peace' can offer non-violent solutions to brewing conflicts, rather than being constrained to wait until a conflict has already erupted into violence. The Security Council's flexibility with this concept was evident during 1990s when states' domestic events – including civil wars, mass expulsions and other large-scale human rights violations, the breakdown of state apparatus leading to the unrestrained use of force by armed bands and militias, and support of terrorist activities – were all identified as threats to international peace, justifying the implementation of collective counter-measures. In principle, any actions that might result in an armed reaction could be considered threats to the peace, including actions without immediate military force, i.e. the damming of a river. The Security Council can conceive of the notion of a threat to the peace in extraordinarily broad terms, and through consistent and expansive use of its freedom to interpret the UN Charter the Security Council has significantly extended its scope of responsibility and action. The practical effectiveness of the UN collective security system, however, has lagged somewhat behind the vistas of possibility opened up by this practice.

The UN Charter's second exception to the prohibition on the use of force consists of the natural right of a member state to defend itself – either alone or together with other states – against an armed attack (Article 51). However, the provision makes clear that the right to self-defence should not exist without restraint. Thus a gap opens up between Article 2(4) and Article 51: the right of self-defence does not exist against any and all forms of threat or use of force; only against an armed attack, and the definition of an armed attack is left open to significant interpretation. Even the General Assembly's definition of Aggression does not fully elucidate the matter, because it relates only to Article 39's phrase 'act of aggression' and is expressly not intended to regulate the right to self-defence against an armed attack ('Definition of Aggression', Article 6). However, the defi nition can at least aid in clarifying the relationship between the concepts 'act of aggression' and 'armed attack': an armed attack is a particular type of act of aggression, and not all acts of aggression can necessarily be taken to justify an invocation of the Article 51 right of self-defence. The states parties of the Rome Statute of the International Criminal Court also referred to this definition when they concretised the 'crime of aggression' (Rome Statute, Article 8) at their review conference in Kampala in June of 2010 (see Review Conference 2010: Annex III, par 1 and 2). This strict construction is in full harmony with the spirit and logic of the Charter, the central purpose of which is to reduce to a minimum the occurrence of the use of force by member states. In political practice, however, the observance of this rule is problematic.

In the classical view, an armed attack has occurred when a state employs military force to a significant extent and over a protracted period of time. Short-term border incursions and the small-scale battles that may accompany traditional military force may constitute acts of aggression in the sense of the General Assembly's 'Definition of Aggression', and are thus violations of the Article 2(4) prohibition on the use of force, but not necessarily armed attacks in the sense of Article 51. Forceful defensive measures are in fact permissible against such acts of aggression, but these measures must not become full military operations. In order to exercise the right to military self-defence, a state must be the victim of an armed attack; a generally threatening situation does not justify the use of military force. However, a state does not necessarily have to await an attack. According to customary international law, pre-emptive self-defence can be justified if an attack is imminent and all other remedies have been exhausted. This rule originates in the Caroline Case of 1837, when British forces crossed the US border into New York to fight militias supporting Canadian rebels in a riot against the Crown. During the course of this action the British burned the US ship Caroline and sent her down the Niagara Falls. In their subsequent correspondence US Secretary of State, Daniel Webster, and the British Foreign Minister, Lord Ashburton, reached an agreement that anticipatory self-defence is justified only if there is a 'necessity of self-defence, instant, overwhelming, leaving no choice of means, and no moment for deliberation', and if nothing 'unreasonable or excessive' was done (see Ackerman, 2002). Israel's actions on the eve of the Six Day War (1967) are widely perceived as an example of a legal use of pre-emptive self-defence.

The use of armed forces on the basis of abstract threats and risks, as well as military reactions against other violations of human rights and the forceful implementation of even legitimate rights upheld by arbitration proceedings or international courts, remain forbidden. The destruction of the unfinished Osirak nuclear power plant in Iraq by the Israeli Air Force in 1981 was considered non-compliant with international law and condemned by the UN Security Council (see S/RES/487 of 19 June 1981). The National Security Strategy of the USA since

September 2002, and its military operations in Iraq in 2003, however, have initiated discussion concerning the exact parameters of pre-emptive self-defence (see below and Chapter 8).

The 9/11 attacks made clear that non-state actors (such as terrorist groups) can pose a viable threat against states. In Resolution 1368 of 12 September 2001, the Security Council made clear that member states are authorized to defend themselves under Article 51 against non-state aggressors. Article 51 thus reinforces the natural right of self-defence, but limits it at the same time by tying it to the requirement that an armed attack must be either under way or imminent.

However, a state that has been attacked and intends to exercise its right to legitimate self-defence is not unrestricted in its choice of means. Such self-defence military operations are bound by the law of war principle of proportionality as much as any other military action. The further limitation in Article 51 – that a state undertaking measures in self-defence must inform the Security Council of their actions, and that those actions remain permissible only until collective security measures have been taken by the Security Council – has become somewhat meaningless. What was meant to emphasize the subsidiary character of self-defence within the framework of a collective security system has never, in practice, resulted in a state's self-defence measures being suspended as a consequence of UN involvement.

Article 51 promises the right to both individual and collective self-defence. This means that even states that are not party to an attack may hurry to the aid of a state – including the initiation of military operations – without violating the general prohibition on the use of force. The right to military support from other states is, of course, bound to the same prerequisites as the exercise of self-defence for the affected state, and above all to the existence of an armed attack and the principle of proportionality. Thus preventive use of force is still forbidden even as a measure of support. Article 51 does not, however, prevent the formation of preventive defence alliances such as NATO or the former Warsaw Pact. The right to the collective defence of a state that has fallen victim to an armed attack does not depend on whether or not that state was already part of such a defensive alliance. However, it is absolutely necessary for this kind of international emergency support that the affected state must request, or at least agree to, such aid. The right of collective self-defence may also be appealed to only by states, so that the support of parties to civil war or domestically displaced ethnic groups may not be justified through this exception to the general prohibition on the use of force.

Over the course of UN history the so-called 'enemy state clauses' of Articles 53 and 107, which were to have been the third exception to the general prohibition on the use of force, have become utterly empty of meaning. Enemy states were those that had been enemies of one of the signatories of the United Nations Charter (Article 53(2)) during the Second World War – Germany, Bulgaria, Finland, Italy, Japan, Romania and Hungary. Should it become necessary to take certain measures against these 'enemy states', regional arrangements (Article 53) and 'the governments having responsibility for such action' (Article 107), that is, the founding members of the UN, were granted special rights to exemption from the general prohibition on the use of force. These special rights related to the taking of preventive forceful measures against the 'renewal of aggressive policy on the part of any such state' (Article 53(1)), and to the implementation of such measures as normally follow a war, such as the creation and specific formulation of a peace treaty. The 'enemy state' clauses contain – as the heading of Chapter XVII shows – merely transitional security arrangements, explicable by the general uncertainty attending the effectiveness of the newly formed world organization. The 'enemy state' label was not meant to be an enduring stigma, and could be dissolved by a state's entry into the UN. Although neither Article 4 nor Article 53(2) contain such regulations in express form, it may be concluded from the principle of the sovereign equality of all member states (Article 2(1)), as well as from the Article 4 prerequisite that a state be 'peace-loving' to become a member, that once a state has entered the organization as a member, it may not suffer discrimination as an 'enemy state'. Since, in the intervening time, all the former 'enemy states' have become members of the UN and have, in some cases repeatedly, undertaken responsibility for the world's peace as non-permanent members of the Security Council, the 'enemy state' clauses have become obsolete. The high hurdles to altering the Charter, set down in Articles 108 and 109, have thus far prevented the absolute removal of these clauses. Nevertheless, the General Assembly's Resolution 50/52 (11 December 1995) has instructed that, in any future comprehensive reform of the Charter, the 'enemy state' clauses are to be deleted. At the 2005 World Summit the heads of state and government decided to remove these clauses from the Charter (World Summit, 2005, Art. 177).

Problems

As the basic constitutional norm of international law, the general prohibition on the use of force is valid worldwide and accepted formally by all states. At the same time, however, it is subject to more frequent violation than nearly any other rule of international law. Since the Charter came into force, UN member states have failed to observe the prohibition on military force in hundreds of cases. However, even in spite of the clear progress over its predecessors, the violence-reduction regime of the Charter still suffers from grey areas that make unambiguous legal and political judgements about certain forms of state use of force extraordinarily difficult to reach. Furthermore, even in cases of aggressive acts, the general prohibition imposes strict regulations and limitations on the use of force that are often difficult for the member states to accept because it is often painfully clear how ineffective the system is in providing collective security.

Logically, it follows from the definitional gaps between the general prohibition and the right to self-defence that there exist some forms of violence that states must suffer without being allowed to respond militarily. In practice, states have attempted consistently, and not without success, to interpret their right of self-defence as broadly as possible in order to justify military measures taken in or against other states. Above all, rescue operations of a state's citizens – without the agreement or consent of the state where those citizens are located – have been repeatedly undertaken in the latter decades of the Twentieth century. The most spectacular of these operations was the actions of Belgium in the Congo in 1959–60 and 1964; the Israeli storming of a captured Israeli passenger plane in Entebbe Airport in Uganda in 1976; and the failed attempt by the USA to free its citizens trapped in the US Embassy in the Iranian capital Tehran in 1980. In Grenada (1983) and Panama (1989), the USA presented the rescue of US citizens as one of several grounds for intervention. During the conflict in Rwanda in 1994, Belgian paratroopers evacuated their own and other nationals, and in March 1997, the Federal Republic of Germany carried out its very first military rescue operation to retrieve twenty Germans and forty nationals of other states from Tirana, Albania.

In no case could these countries point to a rule of international law allowing such actions. According to currently valid regulations and the leading opinion in the realm of international law, such interventions are not measures of self-defence, but are violations of the general prohibition on the use of force (Pape, 1997, p. 105 *et seq.*; see in this source also many other supporting sources). Tellingly, however, no such measures have ever been condemned by the Security Council but it cannot be concluded from the execution of such illegal actions that a Customary International Law development of a right to protect nationals abroad as part of the right of self-defence has taken place. The legal and political evaluations of most of these actions were, and remain, contested, so that neither a general state practice nor a unanimous conviction of the legal rightness of the actions (*opinio iuris*) has emerged. Customary International Law does not provide any grounds beyond those allowed by the UN Charter for legitimizing an individual state's use of force (Deiseroth 1999, p. 3087). This remains the case even in situations where a state is unwilling or unable –because of conditions where there is an acute and enduring threat to the life and limb – to secure the protection of, or to perform a rescue operation for another state's citizens. In such a case the use of appropriate and proportional means by the citizen's own state might be considered *tolerable* violations of the existing norms (Stein, 2000, p. 6).

In view of the general reluctance to use the right to self-defence as a justification for the use of military force on behalf of citizens' abroad, the legal formula of humanitarian intervention tends to be called upon more often. Thus Dieter Blumenwitz is of the view that it makes no jurisprudential sense to differentiate between the protection of one's own citizens and the support of foreign nationals in the case of massive human rights violations (Blumenwitz, 1994, p. 7). It is immediately apparent, however, that the very invocation of a right to humanitarian intervention contains within itself difficulties that strike to the very core of the general prohibition on the use of force and the UN's peace-maintenance mechanisms (see Chapter 6).

The shift in global conflict patterns from classical inter-state to intrastate disputes that occurred with the end of the Cold War placed new and grave challenges before the UN. The responsibilities of the UN and the shape of its organs had been designed to prevent or limit inter-state war, because that was the most important form of disturbance of the peace that existed at the time of its founding.

Domestic occurrences such as civil war, human rights abuses, humanitarian catastrophes, and even the genocide in Cambodia fell into the common understanding
under the scope of Article 2(7)'s prohibition on intervention, and were not
amenable to UN action. During the 1990s, in view of the quality and intensity of
violence being used in these internal disputes, the Security Council occupied itself
with a large number of them, from Iraq and Somalia through Rwanda and Haiti to
East Timor and the former Yugoslavia. The Security Council determined that
these cases constituted threats to the peace according to Article 39 of the Charter,
and thus approved forceful measures and authorized humanitarian interventions
using military means. This aggressive enlargement of the Security Council's
competence is usually seen as having happened within the bounds of the Charter
(Fink, 1999, p. 877) and sometimes even regarded as inevitable. If the Security
Council is authorized to determine that an internal conflict constitutes or results in
a threat to the peace, then its decision to take collective measures for the purposes
of eliminating that threat is in accord with both the regulations and the logic of the
Charter. The Charter does not, however, recognize any subsidiary right of self-
defence (analogous to that of states) for the affected groups of people in the case
of internal conflicts or massive human rights violations. Groups of people forced
into a threatened position may, of course, defend themselves, but they may not
appeal for help to other states in any way that might justify an exception to the
general prohibition on the use of force. Forceful humanitarian interventions may
thus take place only as collective measures under the authority of the Security
Council. When the international community accepted a responsibility to protect in
the 2005 World Summit Outcome, it highlighted the primary responsibility of the
Security Council. This means that the possibility of military protection of fundamental human rights or aid to a group of victimized people depends entirely on
the effectiveness of the UN regime (see Chapters 6 and 8). In view of the ever-
recurring inability of the Security Council to reach decisions because of the threat
or use of a veto by one of the five permanent members, there is clearly a large
discrepancy between the need for an effective regime in the protection of human
rights, and the legally permissible means available to achieve such a regime.

The North Atlantic Treaty Organization (NATO) attempted to fill in the gap in
1998 and 1999 when they first threatened and then used massive force to compel the
Serbian armed forces to leave the province of Kosovo and to cease the grave human
rights violations being conducted there. The Security Council had already imposed
an arms embargo in March 1998 (Resolution 1160, 31 March 1998) and then went
on to describe the situation as a threat to the peace in two further resolutions (Resolution 1199, 23 September 1998; Resolution 1203, 24 October 1998). Russian and
Chinese opposition, however, meant that no authorization for the use of military
force was forthcoming, so NATO acted alone and without Security Council authorization. The broad public, political, and academic discussion about the permissibility of this non-authorized use of force is not here under discussion. Regardless of the
dominant opinions concerning the moral justifications for NATO's actions, the
damage to the effectiveness of the general prohibition on the use of force and the
collective security system cannot be overlooked. With barely a respite, the general

prohibition was faced with a whole new set of challenges in the spring of 2003 by the military intervention of the USA and the Coalition of the Willing in Iraq, which also took place against the will of the Security Council (see below).

The prohibition on the use of force has been developing regressively in case-law for quite some time, not only in humanitarian cases, but also in other grey areas of international relations such as pre-emptive self-defence (as in the case of Israel against Egypt in 1967), retaliation against terrorist attacks (as in the cases of the USA against Libya in 1992 and against Afghanistan and the Sudan in 1998), or targeted killings (by UAVs in Yemen or Pakistan in the course of War on Terror after 2001). Even though the general prohibition on the use of force is legally valid independent of the effectiveness of the collective security system created to enforce it, violations of it – no matter how justified they may be as individual cases – cannot but have serious consequences for the credibility of this central constitutional norm. Every violation brings that much more harm to the prohibition and puts one more crack in the Security Council's monopoly on the legitimization of the use of force. The UN's attempt to make the system of international relations more stable and secure through legal regulation, which has prospered surprisingly well despite all the setbacks, would be doomed to ultimate failure by a further weakening or disso-lution of the general prohibition on the use of force. The possibility of developing a customary norm that would derogate from the prohibition both partly eliminate and partly complement the norms fixed by international treaty seems to hold little promise. The violent interventions of individual states or groups of states are nearly always guided by particular interests, along with the pretended or real orientation on general humanitarian goals and standards. The formation of an *opinio iuris* consistent with general state practice is thus most unlikely.

The general prohibition on the use of force has proved unable to remove war from the international scene. It has, however, become a basic norm against which both the individual and collective behaviour of states have been able to orientate themselves, and thus it is hardly possible to conceive of an international system without it. In any case, the constant divergence of state practice and rules of inter-national law leads to significant problems. Tolerating violations of the prohibition on the use of force leads only to the lowering of the threshold for violating it again, thus eroding the norm. It is imperative, then, that the collective security structure of the UN is strengthened in order that the system of international relations is not thrown back on the doctrines of *ius ad bellum,* or just war. Thus the following sections will first explain and discuss the collective security system contained in the UN Charter, and then explore the management of this system in political prac-tice (Chapter 4) and the possibilities available for its reform (Chapter 8).

From the League of Nations to the United Nations: The Organizational Evolution of Peace Maintenance

It is nearly impossible to have a full understanding of the intentions informing the founding of the UN collective security system without at least a brief look at the

League of Nations. The connection in which the two organizations are usually mentioned is that the UN was designed to address the normative and structural weaknesses and deficits of its predecessor – but such a perspective makes it too easy to overlook the far reaching developments set in motion by the League of Nations, and the organizational conditions it created, upon which the UN was able to anchor itself. This is true particularly for the basic mission of the League of Nations: to create a regime for the prevention of war based on norms of international law, and to place the responsibility for peace with an international organization.

The catastrophe of the First World War made obvious the ultimate failure of the Westphalian state system in Europe. Even during the war, a number of peace societies (for example, the Union of Democratic Control, the *Schweizer Friedensbureau,* or the League of Nations Society) as well as individuals (such as Léon Bourgeois, Henry Noel Brailford, or Matthias Erzberger) had already begun to lay plans for a post-war order on the basis of an international federation (Schücking and Wehberg, 1924, pp. 7–10). US President Woodrow Wilson relied in part on these ideas when he gave his famous 'Fourteen Points' speech before both houses of the US Congress on the occasion of the USA's entry into the First World War. In this speech, Wilson outlined the American objective for the war, and demanded that: 'A general association of nations must be formed under specific covenants for the purpose of affording mutual guarantees of political independence and territorial integrity to great and small states alike' (Wilson, 1918, p. 367/Point 14). Parallel to the Paris Peace Conference, a League of Nations Commission comprising representatives from fourteen states worked on a draft – heavily influenced by Wilson's ideas – for a League of Nations Statute. The draft work lasted from February 1919 until 28 April 1919, when the full assembly of the peace conference adopted the statute.

With only a few changes, this statute became an integral part of each of the four peace treaties signed on 28 June 1919 at Versailles, St Germain, Trianon and Neuilly. This close connection between the peace treaties and the statute of the League of the Nations was not only criticized by the defeated Central Powers, but also failed to conform to the expectations of the neutral states that had been unable to contribute their own suggestions to the statute. The Covenant of the League of Nations was thus 'introduced into a set of circumstances which removed much of its sacredness in the eyes of the world' (Schücking and Wehberg, 1924, p. 27). Connections to the peace treaties were largely external and the Covenant remained a stand-alone work with universal goals. The circumstances, however, that only the colonies and territories of the defeated powers fell under the mandate government system of Article 22, and that a number of the areas given up as part of war liquidation were transferred to the League (Eupen-Malmedy, Saargebiet, Danzig, Memel) had the effect of eviscerating the Covenant's chances of acceptance.

Membership of the League was in principle open to all states but there was a clear differentiation made between founding members and those who joined later. The original members were the signatory powers of the First World War peace treaties (with the obvious exception of the defeated powers – Austria, Bulgaria, Germany and Hungary) and the thirteen neutral countries. Of the thirty-two signatory states to the peace treaties, Ecuador, Hedjas (a part of which was later to be Saudi Arabia) and the USA decided not to ratify the peace treaties, and thus did not enter into membership of the League of Nations (a two-thirds majority in the federal assembly was required for the admission of new members). Furthermore, permission for membership was contingent upon the applicant state's acceptance of an armed forces and armaments arrangement determined by the League of Nations. Since such arrangements could be decided upon only by unanimity, the differentiation of member status became a matter of significant political relevance – the original members were able to place requirements on new members that they themselves did not have to observe. Nevertheless, twenty-one states – including all the defeated powers of the First World War – became members of the League of Nations. The right to withdraw from the League of Nations (with a two-year term of notice) was contained within the statute and nearly one-third of the membership (nineteen in total) eventually made use of this provision, including the German Reich (1933), Japan (1933), and Italy (1937). Also, according to the Covenant, 'any Member of the League which has violated any covenant of the League may be declared to be no longer a Member of the League by a vote of the Council concurred in by the Representatives of all the other Members of the League represented thereon' (Article 16). The only state to be so treated was the Soviet Union, on 14 December 1939, as a result of its attack on Finland. By that time, however, the League was already essentially defunct.

According to its Covenant, the League's primary bodies were the Assembly, the Council, and the Permanent Secretariat (Article 2). The official seat of the entire League was in Geneva, Switzerland, as was the Permanent Secretariat. The sessions of both the Assembly and the Council also generally took place in Geneva. All members were represented in the Assembly by a delegation, and each delegation had one vote. Non-members who were parties to a dispute that the League of Nations wished to address could be invested with a vote and involved in the Assembly's sessions. The Assembly possessed comprehensive competence with respect to all the League of Nation's areas of activity and to all questions touching on world peace; it was effectively able to deal with and make recommendation on any issue. The Council consisted of both permanent and non-permanent members, the total number of which changed several times in the course of the League's history. In 1920, when the Covenant came into force, there were intended to be five permanent members (the 'representatives of the allied and associated powers' of the peace treaties: France, Great Britain, Italy, Japan and the USA) and four non-permanent members that were to be chosen by the Assembly. However, as a result of the USA declining to enter the League of Nations, its permanent seat remained free. A permanent seat was created for Germany on its entry in 1926, and for the Soviet Union when it joined in 1934, and the number of non-permanent members was increased over the course of two phases to eleven.

The Council usually reached its decisions and recommendations through consensus, unless the Covenant specified that some lesser quorum was sufficient for particular issues. In the event that members of the Council became involved in a dispute, their votes were suspended so they were unable to exercise a veto over any decision reached in their own cases. The Council, which usually met in five (later four) regular sessions each year (and also met as necessary for ad hoc sessions) was allowed the same comprehensive competencies as the Assembly, the result of which was that the two bodies were in a relationship of competitive responsibility. This problem was alleviated to some extent through a practical division of labour: the Council, as the smaller body and the one that met more frequently, dealt with the more urgent matters (Weber, 1995), while the Assembly was left with *everything else*. The Permanent Secretariat, under its two Secretaries-General, Sir James Eric Drummond (until 1933) and Joseph Louis Avenol (until 1940), constituted the administrative body of the League of Nations. The Secretary-General enjoyed the services of two Deputy Secretaries-General, three Under-Secretaries-General, and an international bureaucracy divided into departments and staffed primarily by personnel recruited from the civil service of the member states.

The Covenant created a dual system of collective security for the purpose of sustaining world peace and security: first, the prevention of war through an institutionalization of peaceful processes for dispute resolution; second, the provision of a sanctions mechanism for the purposes of ending ongoing wars. The Covenant's partial prohibition on war obligated all its member states to take part in a 'cooling-off process' (see above) in any situation of dispute that might conceivably lead to war. The point of this process was to submit the matter of dispute either to an arbitration process, to the Permanent International Court, or to the Council itself. The Council had six months to investigate the situation and to complete a report, and the court or arbitration process was to have a specific time frame within which it could operate. During this phase, and including a further period of three months after all these processes should have been carried out in full, no party was allowed to resort to war. In the case that one of the parties to the dispute should accept the judgement, arbitration, or unanimous recommendation of the Council, an absolute prohibition on resort to war came into force. Should a Council recommendation be given by mere majority it was left to the parties to the dispute to decide (after the cooling-off period) whether or not to pursue their objectives through war.

One of the gravest weaknesses of this set of regulations was that no use of force falling below the threshold of actual war came under the scope of its prescriptions. Thus the question of when permissible use of force becomes impermissible remained open. Such ambiguities were of great significance for the effectiveness of the collective security measures. Such collective measures, on a spectrum ranging from economic and political boycott to military force, were to be implemented by all the members of the League and taken against non-members of the League, but because of the lack of a clear definition of aggression there existed a great deal of uncertainty about the conditions necessary for the implementation of forceful measures in general, and the scope of the member state's duty to contribute military resources in particular. At the beginning of the 1930s, the League of Nations did nothing about Japan's invasion of northern China. When Japan withdrew from the League of Nations in 1933, the organization became even more powerless to prevent the outbreak of the Sino-Japanese war in 1935. In practice, the League of Nations exercised its ability to sanction only once – in the Abyssinia War of 1937 – when the Council laid an (ultimately ineffective) embargo on Italy. The Soviet aggression against Finland in December 1939 did lead to the ejection of the Soviet Union from the League, but in view of the outbreak of the Second World War in September of that same year, it was already clear that the League of Nations had failed as a collective security system.

The usual culprits blamed for the failure of the League of Nations are the deficits and ambiguities in the normative underpinnings of the Covenant – particularly that the Covenant contained only a partial, not a full, prohibition on war. Structural weaknesses in the organization itself, however, must also share some of the blame. The institutional connections between the League of Nations and the execution of certain provisions of the Paris Peace Treaties drew the organization – fairly or unfairly – into the cross-hairs of the defeated powers' unrestrained revisionist mania (Weber, 1995) an thus accelerated its demise. Above all, the League of Nations did not succeed in including all the great powers of the day. The USA preferred a separate peace to the Paris treaties. In 1933, after the German National Socialists' seizure of power, the German Reich withdrew from the League of Nations, as did Japan. The Soviet Union did not join until 1934. Thus the League was never able to become a universal organization. On 18 April 1946, at the twenty-first Session of the Assembly, the League was dissolved.

All the same, it would be a mistake to dismiss the League of Nations as a total failure. Even if states were not yet ready to embrace this revolutionary new idea of how to prevent war and secure peace, and were unwilling to use the global system as a clearing-house for questions of global security, the League of Nations stands as a watershed in the history of ideas in international relations (Guggenheim, 1932, p. 272 *et seq.*). Its ultimate failure in the face of the catastrophe of the Second World War did not lead to a general conviction that the ideas and norms at the foundation of the League of Nations were utopian or superfluous. Instead, the need for an effective system of collective security was dramatically emphasized. With the UN Charter, the world made a second attempt to establish such a system.

The Collective Security System of the UN Charter

Just as the League of Nations had done before it, the UN mounted its collective security system on two pillars: the prevention of war, and common enforcement action against disturbers of the peace. In contrast to the League of Nations, however, the UN Charter introduced a comprehensive prohibition on both the threat and use of force into international law (Article 2(4)) and in doing so alleviated a significant portion of the regulatory ambiguities and normative grey zones. Beyond this, the UN succeeded in inducing all the great powers of the time to participate in the new organization, and in creating the Security Council as a potentially powerful and capable organ for taking on primary responsibility for the maintenance of international peace and security (Article 24).

However, the growing evidence of the East–West conflict of the Cold War made it clear that the consensus of great powers necessary for an effective security system would be all but impossible to achieve in practice. The Security Council – the most important main body of the organization – was to all intents and purposes hamstrung for decades. As a result, the collective security system of the UN was not implemented as the Charter's framers had intended. Instead, the Charter was used to create new instruments of peace maintenance (such as observation and 'blue helmet' missions). Following the demise of the bipolar world order of the Cold War, the Security Council continued to extend its area of competence and to reach decisions on enforcement measures, and this was always done in harmony with the relevant norms and rules of the Charter. It is, however, important to briefly explain the collective security system as originally imagined by those who drafted the Charter, and how all of the deficits and weaknesses that attend it are an essential part of the explanation concerning why UN practice deviates so much from the ideal. Above all, the Charter's weakness lies in its intentions and claims, which far outstrip the practical political possibilities offered by a world of states. The practice of both the organization and its member states will be examined in the following chapters.

Article 2(3)'s duty to resolve disputes peacefully, as well as the general prohibition on the use of force that follows logically from it (Article 2(4)) constitute the normative core of the UN collective security system. Their relationship to the two other central constitutional principles of Article 2 – the principle of sovereignty (Article 2(1)) and the prohibition on intervention (Article 2(7)) – can thus be interpreted to mean that a state's pursuit of political goals, however that pursuit may be conducted, must be subject to the collective interest of world peace and international security. Member states accept this hierarchy of principles as a condition of organization membership, and thus it has become a part of Customary International Law and is effective beyond the scope of the Charter. Because such normative principles can offer no guarantee of their own observation, however, the UN Charter Chapter VI further specifies the principles and processes of pacific settlement of disputes. Chapter VII measures are described as measures that can be taken collectively by the organization against a renegade member states in the case of threats to the peace, breaches of the peace or acts of aggression.

The Charter situates the Security Council at the very centre of the UN's collective security system and accords it the primary responsibility for international peace and security. The Security Council is an executive organ with extensive authority to evaluate international and domestic events with respect to their potential to endanger the peace. It is also the only main body with the authority to make decisions that are binding upon all member states (Article 25).

Chapter VI: The Pacific Settlement of Disputes

Chapter VI sets out a number of legal duties for member states arising from Article 2(3) and regarding the forms and processes of the peaceful resolution of disputes. Article 33(1) requires that:

[t]he parties to any dispute, the continuance of which is likely to endanger the maintenance of international peace and security, shall, first of all, seek a solution by negotiation, enquiry, mediation, conciliation, arbitration, judicial settlement, resort to regional agencies or arrangements, or other peaceful means of their own choice.

This introductory Article of Chapter VI places the primary responsibility for such efforts on member states; the role of the Security Council in this Chapter remains largely restricted to that of moderator or of catalyst to the various suggested processes. Any member state may bring a matter of dispute to the attention of the Security Council. The Security Council may also, on its own authority and according to Article 34, undertake to examine any situation with respect to its potential to threaten the peace and issue recommendations on its resolution (Article 36). All the same, the Security Council may not issue binding measures in any processes of peaceful dispute resolution – a suggestion for mediation may only be offered when all parties to the dispute have asked the Security Council for advice (Article 38).

Regarding the tension between sovereign statehood and collective action, Chapter VI accords primacy to the former. The essential limitation on state sovereignty – aside from the prohibition on the use of force – lies in a state's obligation to actively seek a peaceful resolution. There is no obligation to produce a certain result or to abide by any third-party declaration. Later statements of the General Assembly designed to clarify the processes of dispute settlement merely confirm the dominance of the principle of sovereignty, rather than indicating possible paths to new forms of conflict resolution through collective efforts. In particular, the 'Manila Declaration on the Peaceful Settlement of International Disputes' of 15 November 1982 (UN General Assembly Resolution A/RES/37/10) declares itself 'devoted to the fetish of sovereignty' (Tomuschat, 1983, p. 734) when it states that processes of peaceful dispute resolution should not be seen as incompatible with the principle of sovereign equality. Emphasis on sovereignty is surely not inappropriate for an international organization formed upon the membership of states – indeed, intervention and external pressure are unlikely to create a sustainable solution, especially in the early phases of a dispute.

In contrast, co-operation and institutionalized conflict settlement before an arbiter or the ICJ, or upon appeal to the Secretary-General, are tried and tested methods of preventing war and maintaining peace (see Mani 2007, pp. 304 *et seq.*). The credibility of such methods, however, depends upon the assumption that all parties to the dispute are equal. This principle of the equal rights and equal worth of states, and with it the anticipation of a lasting consensus or compromise, would be contradicted by an early third-party intervention that had not been agreed to by all parties to the dispute. At the same time, Czempiel (1994, p. 141) is to be sympathized with when he complains that the obligation to take part in the Chapter VI processes is not particularly emphasized, and that the functions of the Security Council and the barely-alluded-to General Assembly remain similarly modest. Greater obligations and more specific processes would further limit the scope of judgement and thus the sovereignty of states, but it is precisely in such actions that the nature and intent of a collective system of peace maintenance lie. Furthermore, staggered regulations could be created in such a way as to make mediation or arbitration through the Security Council obligatory only if the parties to the dispute are to come to a peaceful solution through their own efforts, and the threat to peace continues to exist.

The objection that a higher degree of obligation in regard to processes of peaceful dispute resolution would constitute an unendurable limitation of sovereignty is less convincing in light of the fact that – in the case of a failure of consensus processes – the Charter anticipates the imposition of much greater limitations on sovereignty through force. Furthermore, the permissible measures against a state – such as trade embargoes – may themselves cause considerable damage and disadvantage to states that are not even party to a dispute (when they must, for example, limit their political or economic relations with a state under sanction). The introduction of binding processes of peaceful dispute resolution would thus represent no unacceptable check on state sovereignty, but rather a moderating intermediate step. On this vital point Chapter VI of the Charter is stuck far short of where it needs to be to maintain international peace. The principle weakness in peaceful dispute resolution remains the often insufficient political will of states to make use of the framework at all, and their unwillingness to subject themselves to decisions in particular cases. If the preventive treatment of conflict is ever to be firmly anchored in the system of international relations, a thorough revision of Chapter VI will be imperative.

Chapter VII: Action with Respect to Threats to the Peace, Breaches of the Peace and Acts of Aggression

While Chapter VI builds as much as possible on the idea of consensus and compromise among equal and sovereign states, Chapter VII offers the Security Council the opportunity to implement coercive measures against the will of the state or states involved. Formal requirements must be met before coercive measures can be implemented; peaceful attempts at dispute resolution must have failed and a threat to or breach of the peace must remain. The spectrum of available measures ranges from non-violent sanctions to the application of military force, including limitations on sovereignty up to and including the practical suspension of sovereign rights. Transitional administrations possessing state-like authority and capabilities were thus set up by the Security Council in Cambodia, the former Yugoslavia and East Timor, and the sovereign authority of the territorial state was, at least temporarily, revoked.

In order for the Security Council to become active under Chapter VII, the legal and procedural prerequisites of Article 39 (the first article in Chapter VII) must be met. First, the Security Council must determine, whether one of the three situations on which its authority is based exists – is there a threat to the peace, a breach of the peace or an act of aggression? (Security Council resolutions, however, do not usually refer to single articles but instead indicate a more general term such as 'acting under Chapter VII' or it determines that a situation 'constitutes a threat to the peace'.) Should such a determination be reached, the Security Council may either issue recommendations or may decide to implement coercive measures under Articles 41 and 42. The difference between recommendations and such measures is that recommendations are not binding on either of the states to which they are addressed or on the other member states of the organization. Other than that, the Charter does not differentiate them clearly from coercion. Thus it remains unclear whether the Security Council may recommend forms of behaviour which, if undertaken by member states, might take on the form of coercive measures with respect to the target state – for example, the breaking off of commercial relations. The existence of clear regulations for coercive measures in Articles 41 and 42 rather mediates against this possibility so that the Security Council is restricted to recommendations that would not, if followed, have an adverse effect on the target-state's rights guaranteed by the Charter and in general international law. One example of this might be the Security Council's recommendation that member states cease to deliver arms and weapons to a particular state, or that they assist a victim of attack in the exercise of its right to self-defence. Another option short of coercive measures is for the Security Council to advocate the observance of preliminary measures according to Article 40. This happens quite often in practice, mainly in the form of demands that combat activities, or other activities threatening the peace, be discontinued.

The coercive measures in Articles 41 and 42 are the core of Chapter VII. They are by their very nature conducted against the will of the target state, and furthermore do not require the agreement of any state not belonging to the Security Council. Thus they constitute the narrow area in which the UN can in fact exercise supra-national functions. These measures are not forms of punishment, but are rather forms of collective pressure that can be exercised by the UN when it wishes to influence a member state to change its peace-disturbing behaviour. They are thus permissible only so long as the disturbance to the peace lasts, and must be lifted once the disturbance no longer exists. Consistent with the nature of the UN as a consensus-orientated international organization, these measures are being used rather infrequently. Over the course of UN history, non-violent sanctions (see Chapter 4) have been imposed in only twenty-three cases (twenty-one times since 1992). In only three cases (Korea 1950, Iraq 1990 and Libya 2011) has the UN imposed military force.

Article 41 contains a broad palette of measures ranging from the full or partial interruption of economic relations, transportation, and communication to the breaking of diplomatic relations. This non-exhaustive list may be extended as per the judgement of the Security Council to include other appropriate measures. In the exercise of its authority under Article 41, the Security Council created an international criminal tribunal for the former Yugoslavia through Resolution 827 (25 May 1993) for the purposes of prosecuting various grave violations of international humanitarian law. A year later, the same step was taken for Rwanda (Resolution 955, 8 November 1994). The Security Council has made efforts to tailor Article 41 sanctions more effectively to specific institutions or persons rather than imposing them on entire countries and societies (for example in Resolution 1718 of 14 October 2006, the Security Council prohibited the export of luxury goods to North Korea).

Should the Security Council conclude that peaceful sanctions would be inadequate or have proved to be inadequate it may have recourse to land, air, and sea military forces which are necessary to maintain or restore the peace (Article 42). In other words, the Charter does not delineate any hierarchical order of escalation in which the effects of softer measures must be evaluated before the Security Council can employ military force. There are also no express regulations laid on the Security Council with respect to the intensity of military force it may employ. However, since the Security Council is bound both to the Charter and to Customary International Law – and despite the large space left to it for political judgement – it must remain bound to a set of principles. Above all, the Security Council must ensure that the measures employed must be appropriate to the intended purpose, and that the measures must be consistent with proportionality.

Responsibility for the implementation of the measures determined by the Security Council lies either with the Security Council itself or with member state(s) or state(s) so authorized by the Council (the latter option is articulated in Article 42 wherein the use of 'air, sea or land forces of Members of the United Nations' is mentioned). In the logic of Chapter VII member states should make their armed forces, assistance and facilities available to the Security Council in order to contribute to the maintenance of international peace and security. According to Article 43 this should happen on the basis of special agreements or arrangements between the Security Council and member states. In practice, however, no such arrangement has ever been met. The regulations in Article 43(3) require member states to enter into such special agreements only if the Security Council should so request; otherwise, there is no obligation to conclude or ratify such documents. To date, the Security Council has taken no such initiative, so that no member state is currently obliged to make troops available to the Security Council. Any Article 42 measures may thus be taken under the authority of the Security Council only on the basis of voluntary *ad hoc* arrangements.

In that regard, Article 48(1) must be understood in the context of its being subject to member states volunteering the necessary actions and mechanisms for carrying out Security Council's decisions, and that volunteerism may be undertaken by all, or only by some, or even by just one Member State – such decisions shall be carried out by member states themselves or by their 'appropriate international agencies of which they are members'. (Article 48(2)) This opens the door to mandated missions that are requested by the Security Council, but not conducted under its direct guidance or supervision. The most prominent example of such a mission has been the Gulf War of 1990–91. Since the mid 1990s the mechanism of Chapter VII mandated peace missions has been undertaken extensively by western states in NATO and the EU in Bosnia-Herzegovina, Kosovo, and Afghanistan (see Chapter 4). The Council may also utilize 'regional arrangements or agencies' (Article 53(1)) in the Chapter VIII sense, for the implementation of coercive measures. This was the case in the former Yugoslavia, where missions were conducted through the OSCE and the EU.

Similar to Article 43 – which has remained essentially a dead letter – Article 47's provisions for the creation of a Military Staff Committee have effectively been ignored. A Military Staff Committee, which was intended to be composed of members (or their representatives) of the General Staffs of the Security Council permanent members (Article 47(2)), holds a significant position as the only subsidiary organ to be written into the Charter. The remit of the Military Staff Committee is to advise and support the Security Council in all military questions regarding the maintenance of world peace (Article 47(1)), and to be responsible for the strategic leadership of the armed forces placed at the Security Council's disposal (Article 47(3)). In practice, however, it has remained one of the most curious of all the UN bodies (see Grove 1993). For nearly forty years, at two-week intervals, military representatives of the armed forces of the Security Council permanent members held informal meetings without ever discussing matters of substance. Since the beginning of the 1990s, these meetings have taken place among the military advisers of the respective UN delegations of each of the Security Council permanent members. Occasional suggestions to the effect that the Military Staff Committee ought to be integrated into the leadership of UN peacekeeping operations have never been pursued and the Military Staff Committee has never been able to develop any substantive military or political functions. Any attempts, however, to abolish this dormant subsidiary organ have been rejected by the permanent members of the Security Council. At the 2005 World Summit an agreement was reached, but only to request the Security Council 'to consider the composition, mandate and working methods of the Military Staff Committee' (World Summit, 2005, Art. 178).

In complete contrast to Chapter VI (the pacific settlement of disputes), Chapter VII (action with respect to threats to the peace, breaches of the peace and acts of aggression) places great demands on the collective engagement of member states, far outstripping the practical political realities. A certain amount of solidarity among the organization's members is necessary for the completion of special agreements on the provision of troops for collective security measures – a solidarity that member states do not wish for, and indeed probably cannot achieve. The extent of the abstract collective interest in peace is usually too small in specific cases for states to endanger their soldiers' lives for the sake of general obligations and the UN therefore lacks a key element of a quick and effective collective security system. The use of military force is not an impossible task for the UN – as the practice of the 1990s since the Iraq/Kuwait Gulf War of 1990–91 has shown – but the processes necessary for its implementation have demonstrated themselves to be significantly more complicated and protracted than possibly imagined. The example of the Gulf War of 1990–91, however, demonstrates that when the political constellations are favourable and there exists a high degree of convergence of interest among the acting member states, even very large-scale and rapid operations fall within the realms of possibility.

The UN's dependency upon such 'coalitions of the willing', however, pierces to the heart of the principle of collective security. The fact that states must be *willing* to take part in common action, with such willingness resulting primarily from a particular interest in the matter at hand, is almost guaranteed to lead to selectiveness as to which missions are undertaken. The decision for or against collective measures thus orientates itself not upon the requirements of the current conflict, but upon the degree of interest other states have in that conflict's solution. The complex peace missions of the 1990s have shown that collective measures are dependent not only upon the availability of *willing* states to implement them, but also upon the availability of states with the technological, financial and other *capabilities* to do so. The selectivity born of interest that emerged among industrialized countries after the failed action in Somalia is impossible to ignore. It also raises suspicions that certain states may attempt to instrumentalize the collective security system for the pursuit of their own interests. Such developments have caused the effectiveness and legitimacy of the system to fall into crisis. However, the composition, voting processes, and modes of activity of the Security Council are not designed to alleviate this suspicion in any way. The power distribution within this most powerful of the main bodies closely mirrors political positions at the end of the Second World War, as though they could remain unchanged over half a century, and as though the Security Council's claim on the observation of its determinations could continue to be accepted by all sides. A more balanced representation of all regions of the world in the permanent membership of the Security Council is thus just as necessary a change as the modification of its voting procedures and the abolition of the veto.

Chapter VIII: Regional Arrangements

It has already been discussed that the UN accords considerable meaning to regional arrangements. Article 52 articulates that regional organizations – insofar as they are in accord with the purposes and principles of the UN – should attempt to resolve local disputes peacefully on their own before involving the Security Council. The founders of the UN believed that proximity mattered in terms of regional organizations having a better understanding of situations. The founders were similarly aware that it would lighten the UN's own burden if regional organizations assumed some of the workload. Proximity to a situation can, however, be a disadvantage as well as an advantage. It is sometimes more acceptable for conflicting parties to suffer external intervention from neutrals instead of from neighbours. Article 52 refers to the role of regional organizations only in the peaceful resolution of disputes – it remains the case that any coercive measures would have to be authorized specifically by the Security Council under Article 53. Experts in international law are not in agreement, however, on what constitutes a regional arrangement in the sense of Chapter VIII (for example, strict constructionists decline to include military alliances such as NATO in the category of regional arrangements). The definition that has emerged in practice requires merely some regional association and a membership roster smaller than that of the UN. The list thus comprises such institutions as the Arab League, the Organization of American States (OAS), the African Union (AU), and the Organization for Security and Co-operation in Europe (OSCE), as well as NATO and EU, and the UN has often authorized or empowered such regional arrangements to implement peace missions. Prominent examples include the implementation of the Dayton Accords from December 1995 in Bosnia-Herzegovina (IFOR/SFOR), as well as the placement of peacekeepers in Kosovo (KFOR) since June 1999, both of which are under the leadership of NATO, support missions by the EU in Africa (DR Congo, 2003; 2006) and Chad/Central African Republic (2008–09), or EU stabilizaton missions as in Bosnia-Herzegovina (since 2004).

The greater involvement of regional arrangements presents risks as well as opportunities. Advocates emphasize the amount of work taken off the shoulders of the UN, as well as an improved international division of labour. Such advocates seek greater involvement by regional arrangements and furthermore seek the possibility of delegating to them the decision to use forceful measures. Critics suggest that such actions would lead to a hollowing-out of UN responsibilities in its very core areas that would more likely to lead to a two-tier system of peace maintenance (with the high-tech missions of the industrialized countries on one side and the ill-equipped UN deployments on the other). (See Chapters 4 and 8.)

The Limits of Collective Security: The UN and the 2003 Iraq War

The Iraq Question (Berdal, 2003; Cordesman, 2003; Kubbig, 2003) put the mechanisms of collective security to a serious and multifaceted test. The Iraq Question was about more than finding the proper strategy for the containment of dictators allegedly armed with weapons of mass destruction, and the future face of the crisis-prone Near East – it also concerned who has the right to make decisions about appropriateness of preventive military measures; on which international legal the grounds these might be undertaken; and what relationship they might bear to the general prohibition on the use of force.

Efforts to find a solution to the Iraq crisis within the framework of the UN have occupied the international community for more than a decade. After Iraq invaded Kuwait in August 1990, and then ignored Security Council resolutions and non-violent sanctions to withdraw, a broad coalition of twenty-eight states – authorized under Security Council Resolution 678 of 29 November 1990 and under the leadership of the USA – intervened militarily and liberated Kuwait (Operation Desert Storm) in January 1991. After Iraq's defeat and their withdrawal from Kuwait, a number of conditions were imposed with the intent of maintaining Iraqi compliance. Resolution 687 (April 1991) created a ceasefire agreement that was intended to hold only as long as Iraq co-operated with the UN; the newly created United Nations Special Commission on Iraq (UNSCOM) and the International Atomic Energy Agency (IAEA) were given the task of the control and demolition of Iraqi weapons of mass destruction. All atomic, biological, and chemical weapons, weapon parts, and establishments for their production were to be destroyed, and Iraq was to remain under constant supervision so that it could not resume development, production, or acquisition of such weapons.

A re-evaluation of the existing policy of international containment against Iraq was of decisive importance in the assessment of the legitimacy of any war against that state. It was here that the advocates and opponents of military action in Iraq differed in their judgements, and here that the fault line between the USA and its Coalition of the Willing and their opponents ran, in the Security Council and else-where. When the UNSCOM and IAEA inspectors started their work in 1991, all members of the Security Council had been in relative agreement and supported their work unanimously. The inspections proved to be very difficult to carry out because of Iraqi non-co-operation – Iraq was required to disclose any questionable programmes voluntarily; but it did not do this. Although the original time-plan for inspections (set for one year) were totally confounded, there were nonetheless an impressive number of ballistic delivery systems and combat agents destroyed, and a significant network of surveillance cameras and measuring points installed for early warning of renewed attempts at armament in the period between 1991 and 1998. However, the unanimity of, and therefore the pressure coming from the Security Council increasingly gave way over this period, and ultimately Iraq refused all co-operation. Resolution 1134 (October 1997) drew attention to Iraq's unco-operative behaviour, but it was not supported unanimously. It was suggested that because US inspectors also worked for the US Central Intelligence Agency (CIA) their work for UNSCOM was being compromised and this gave Iraqi leader Saddam Hussein a welcome a pretext for refusing compliance with Security Council resolutions (see Ritter 2005, part III).

The Iraq situation began to escalate in spring 1998, after many incidents, including a last-minute agreement between Iraq and the UN to prevent a military intervention by the USA and the UK. But the 'cat and mouse game' of Saddam Hussein's regime went on: Iraq acknowledged openly that it no longer intended to co-operate, and the conflict over inspections in the presidential palaces finally led to the total withdrawal of UNSCOM inspectors on 16 December 1998. Following this, the USA and the UK decided – without the approval of the Security Council – to carry out Operation Desert Fox, the largest military action undertaken since the end of the 1991 Gulf War. In a four-day air operation, Iraq's military potential was hugely weakened. Security Council authorization was neither requested nor received; Russia, China, and France protested the attacks, and the international public discussion was also nearly unanimously negative. Another inspection attempt was made in December 1999. The corresponding Resolution 1284 of 17 December 1999 was supported by only two of the Security Council permanent members, the USA and the UK. The other three permanent members abstained. For nearly three years, UNMOVIC inspectors were unable to work on location, at least in part because of the lack of backing from the Security Council, and because Iraq refused to co-operate. It was only under decisive military pressure that the weapons inspectors were allowed to return on 27 November 2002 (under Resolution 1441, passed unanimously on 8 November 2002 after weeks of diplomatic tug-of-war). In it, Iraq was given a 'final chance' to fulfil the requirements of the 1991 ceasefire resolution, to make its weapons programmes available for inspection, or to provide reliable proof that such programmes no longer existed. Should co-operation not be forthcoming, Iraq was threatened with 'serious consequences'.

The Split between Interventionists and Inspectionists

The head of UNMOVIC, Hans Blix, and his counterpart from the IAEA, Mohamed El Baradei, presented the Security Council with regular reports on the status of Iraqi co-operation. Progress was made, but deficits still existed. The two 'camps' within the Security Council were unable to come to a common understanding of the political meaning of the reports. The USA, the UK, Spain, and Bulgaria argued that Iraq was *not* co-operating fully and was thus far in violation of Resolution 1441. France, Russia, China and Germany saw progress being made and argued that there were insufficient grounds to break off the inspections and to take military action; they supported an expansion of the inspections, a clear time-plan with which Iraq's willingness to co-operate could be reliably evaluated, and above all the avoidance of any action that might lead to war. German foreign minister Joseph Fischer warned urgently against war with Iraq in his address to the Security Council on 7 March 2003, suggesting that it would be better to exhaust the peaceful means available and to support weapons inspections. It was not apparent, he said, that a radical solution needed to be sought when less extreme instruments still existed. Germany, France and Russia claimed in their common declaration of 15 March 2003, that Iraq was, in fact, 'in the process' of disarmament.

The Security Council remained deeply split between Interventionists and Inspectionists. French, German, Russian and Chinese suggestions were directly opposed to Anglo-American plans, and demonstrated moreover that there was no hope of a unanimous understanding of the situation in Iraq. It was in the context of this deadlock that the USA made clear that, if necessary, it would act without Security Council authorisation. The inspections needed neither more time nor more personnel, but rather the full co-operation of Iraq. Iraqi co-operation, however, was not forthcoming. This position was re-emphasized at a tripartite American–British–Spanish summit in the Azores on 16 March 2003, and Iraq was given a final deadline. The USA and its partners suggested that the authority of the Security Council, and indeed the whole UN, was under threat if its Resolutions could be ignored without any adverse consequences. US President Bush insisted that in matters of its own security, the USA did not need permission from the UN to act; and that if the UN could not reach a decision to act it was merely proving its irrelevance and displaying its true nature as a 'talking shop'. On 20 March 2003, the military intervention was begun without Security Council authorization.

According to the USA's 2002 National Security Strategy – since classical security precautions such as deterrence or arms control offer no support against terrorist organizations and despots – the USA must be in a position to strike its enemy before the enemy can attack. The 'pre-emptive measures' or 'pre-emptive strikes' mentioned in the strategy do not, however, relate only to recognized dangers or immediate threats. Even abstract risks could justify recourse to such measures (see Chapter 8). The USA is also ready, if necessary, to carry out these so-called pre-emptive (in fact preventive) measures alone. In particular, it is willing to act without UN involvement, whose functions and responsibilities are not mentioned at all in the entire security strategy. The US administration has long insisted on the right to sovereign decision-making, independent of international norms or bodies, for the purposes of ensuring the security of the USA – and this includes the decision to use military force. In the US administration there was a camp that considered international norm and decision-making systems for the limitation or prevention of violent unilateral action to be completely unrealistic and unwanted (Glennon, 2003). Such thought is supported by a school of international legal thinkers who insist that the norms of international law are valid only for those states that have consented to them or accepted them. This 'state consent' argumentation strikes at the core of the UN. The organization was created specifically – in the aftermath of the catastrophic failure of the Westphalian system with its *liberum ius ad bellum* in the disaster of two World Wars – to remove states' sovereign rights to war and violence as political means, and to place these instead under the control of an international body. The US position, however, was not shared by the majority of the international law community (Tomuschat, 2003).

What did this particular marginalization mean for the UN? Would the US precedent result in worldwide instability as other states arrogate to themselves the right to act unilaterally without Security Council authority? Is the entire international order of capable international organizations and international law – that has the UN at its centre – at stake?

With their decision to end the months-long political tug-of-war in the Security Council, and to prepare a violent end for the Iraqi regime without the mandate of the community of nations, the USA and its coalition partners did more than set the UN and its system of collective security to another serious test. This situation, far more than previous cases of the UN's and the Security Council's marginalization, carried with it the potential for a real existential crisis for the world organization. When NATO intervened in the Kosovo in 1999 without a Security Council mandate, the states of the 'western camp' were at least able to maintain a unified position, which then found wider acceptance when it ended largely successfully. Furthermore, NATO made sure that the Kosovo question came back to the UN and that the subsequently necessary civil and military peacekeeping was legitimized through the Security Council. The overt split in Security Council permanent members on the Iraq crisis – two for intervention, and three against – merely accelerated and brought into the open a dramatic development that has been under way for some time. In the conduct of its most important core task – the maintenance of international peace and security – the UN is facing a fork in the road: can the organization maintain its concept of institutionalized and norm-based multilateralism, or will a world hegemony that meets its needs for international co-operation with loose and changing *ad hoc* coalitions dominate?

It is obvious that international legal norms do not disintegrate when they are broken once or twice by a single state or power, and that the competencies and procedural norms of the Security Council remain valid even when force is used without its authorisation. However, the USA, as by far the strongest and most capable power, has the potential to cause significant harm to the international legal order and its major organ. It is certainly not being insinuated that the USA is deliberately trying to return the world to previous epochs of international law, but rather that some of its leading thinkers assume that the USA will continue for a long time to be in a position to maintain the global balance of a *pax americana* (Kagan, 2003, p. 115 *et seq.*), perhaps supported by a 'league of democracies'. On the other hand, there exists significant doubt as to whether this unipolar order really would function better than the existing one. The emerging over-extension of American forces in a large number of crises, and the difficulties the USA has encountered in coping with the post-war situation in Iraq, suggest however that the US may very well be a little too self-confident to gamble away a global order accepted by the over-whelming majority of states.

European states carried their own responsibility for the splintering of the unanimous position of the Security Council in February/March 2003 and the subsequent marginalization of the Security Council that followed. France had originally suggested a two-step process in Iraq: that after a final ultimatum (such as that in Resolution 1441), if Iraq continued to violate UN requirements, then possible military steps should be discussed. France thus signalled its willingness, at least in principle, to consider a military solution. However, in January 2003, France began to call for indefinite extensions for the inspections – even before the weapons inspectors' reports were received, and then escalated its opposition to any possible military measures with the threat of a veto. France's actions were understandably interpreted by the USA as a breach of the previously agreed-upon plan. At the same time, the USA and UK saw their position coming under ever greater pressure because of questionable evidence, rapidly alternating justifications for war, and an apparently more-compliant Iraq (albeit in a very feeble sense). The Cheney–Rumsfeld camp (in the USA) had been against the Security Council route from the beginning and now regained its influence over US President Bush. The basis for a common solution to the Iraq problem crumbled visibly when Germany blocked itself by assuming – for domestic political reasons – a strict anti-war position even if the Security Council succeeded in passing a resolution. Furthermore, when agitating loudly against Washington's policy on the Iraq situation, Germany denied itself its traditional role as an honest broker between the USA, and France and Russia.

The failure to pass the required Security Council resolution – at the hands of its most important members – produced the worst results for everyone. The Iraq War could not be prevented, and attempts at prevention did not encourage Washington's willingness to bring the issue back before the Security Council in the foreseeable future. There was also little reason for celebration in the unilateralist camp: its victory over the 'irrelevant' Security Council showed itself to be somewhat superficial as soon as it became clear that the stabilization of the region, as well as the control of WMD proliferation, required capable international organizations and multilateral arrangements. The damage to the UN and to the principle of multilateral peacekeeping was and is considerable – and attempts to restore the damage will require a great deal of effort from all sides.

The course of the Iraq War 2003 demonstrated that the Security Council cannot exercise a policy of containment over the USA – and this will likely remain the case for any other emerging great power. The UN may be of use and significance to the USA, but in light of the existing power gradient, this dependency might not appear as immediate or as obvious to the USA. Instead of further endangering the Security Council and the UN with continued attempts to contain the USA, it would seem to promise more success to reintegrate the USA back into the Security Council as *primus inter pares* – such would include the acceptance of its status and the readiness of the members to co-operate more in the fields that carry particular importance for the USA. This would not be a capitulation to the right of the strongest, but a precept of political wisdom. The history of the transatlantic relationship shows that the USA is more amenable to influence from co-operative partners than from objectors. On the other hand, it lies in the nature of the 'paradox of American power' (Nye, 2002) that the USA needs friends and partners. Both sides would do well to keep this decades-long experience in mind.

Further Reading

Claude, Inis L. (1965) *Swords into Plowshares. The Problem and Progress of International Organization*, London: University of London Press.

Hurrell, Andrew (1992) 'Collective Security and International Order Revisited', *International Relations* (1), pp. 37–55.

Kupchan, Charles A. and Clifford A. Kupchan (1995) 'The Promise of Collective Security', *International Security* (1), pp. 52–61.

Opitz, Peter J. (2010) 'Collective Security', in Helmut Volger (ed.), *A Concise Encyclopedia of the United Nations*, 2nd revised edition, Leiden/Boston: Martinus Nijhoff Publishers, pp. 33–41.

Orakhelashvili, Alexander (2011) *Collective Security*, Oxford: Oxford University Press.

Randelzhofer, Albrecht (2002) 'Art. 2 (4)', in Simma, Bruno (ed.), *The Charter of the United Nations: A Commentary*, Oxford: Oxford University Press, pp. S.112–35.

Weber, Hermann (1995) 'League of Nations', in Rüdiger Wolfrum, with Christiane Philipp (eds), *United Nations: Law, Policies and Practice*, 2 vols, Dordrecht, Boston, Leiden: Martinus Nijhoff Publishers, pp. 848–53.

4

The Changing Practice of Peace Maintenance

The UN Charter provides a very clear general prohibition on the use of force in international relations but as discussed in previous chapters, the use of force has not been eliminated from the international system. Instead, violence and conflict have continued to appear in various guises on the world stage. The UN has responded to these changes, and the legal ambiguities concerning the collective use of force, by developing various mechanisms of peace maintenance. But before the UN's practice of peace maintenance is analysed it will be useful to consider a brief empirical note on the development of violence and war, as well as the UN's instruments for tackling these altering challenges.

Since the UN's founding in 1945 there have been more than 230 wars that have claimed more dead than the casualties suffered in the Second World War (the exact number of wars varies slightly according to definition and research method, see Figure 4.1). Since the early 1960s, the number of wars occurring worldwide increased almost continuously for three decades, with a peak occurring at the beginning of the 1990s. Despite the drastic reduction in the frequency of war between 1992 and 1997 there was no confirmation of the optimistic assumption that the number of wars could be permanently reduced. War in the so-called 'OECD world' (i.e. war between the thirty-four member states of the Organisation for Economic Co-operation and Development) has become rare, and it is also the case that democracies generally do not fight wars against each other because of similar modes of conflict resolution in their internal and external behaviour (i.e. the Democratic Peace Theory). External to these observations, and seen from a global point of view, however, war remains 'a companion to the process of social development' (AKUF, 2000, p. 11) and a 'central part of political effectiveness even in the 21st century' (Hoch, 2001, p. 17). On the edges of the 'zones of peace' there is a certain grey area to be found, characterized primarily by instability. Some analysts have even argued that the world is now finding itself on the way from a Cold War to a 'hot' war (Parsons, 1995) or a 'deadly peace' (Carnegie Commission, 1998).

Following the work of Hungarian peace researcher István Kende, the *Arbeitsgemeinschaft Konfliktursachenforschung* (AKUF, Working Group for Research into the Causes of War), defines war as a 'violent mass conflict exhibiting all of the following characteristics':

96

FIGURE 4.1
Number of wars conducted world-wide every year

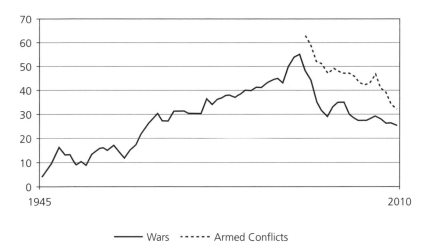

Source: Data from Working Group for Research into the Causes of War (AKUF 2000; Schreiber 2010, p. 1)

- two or more armed forces take part in the combat, of which at least one is the regular armed force (military, paramilitary groups, police units) of a government;
- there must be a minimum level on both sides of centrally-directed organization of the parties to the conflict and of the combat, even when this means nothing more than organized armed defence or planned assaults (guerrilla operations, partisan warfare and so on); and
- the armed operations take place with a certain continuity, and not merely as opportunistic, spontaneous collisions; that is, both sides operate with a planned strategy of some kind, whether the combat takes place in the territory of one or more communities, and whether the engagements are long or short. (Schreiber, 2010, p. 9)

By this definition, thirty-two wars/armed conflicts were waged in 2010, of which:

- ten were in Africa (e.g. Central African Republic, Chad, the Democratic Republic of Congo, Somalia, Sudan);
- ten were in Asia (e.g. India, Pakistan, Southern Thailand);
- ten were in the Near East and Middle East (e.g. Afghanistan, Iraq, Palestine);
- two were in Latin America (Colombia and Peru).

The AKUF differentiates among five types of war, although intermediate forms may also occur in practice:

(i)   anti-regime wars, where the struggle is for the overthrow/defence of a government or for a change in the political system or social order;
(ii)   wars of autonomy/secession, where the struggle is for greater regional autonomy within a state or federation, or for secession from a state or federation;
(iii)   wars of decolonization, where the struggle is for liberation from a colonial ruler;
(iv)   inter-state wars; and
(v)   other wars. (Ibid, p. 8)

Furthermore AKUF discriminates between wars/armed conflicts with and without the involvement of external parties. Classical inter-state war (the prevention of which was the driving force behind the creation of the UN) has become an increasingly peripheral phenomenon. According to the AKUF criteria, all wars in 2010 were internal conflicts (many of them with external parties involved, however). Of these, the largest portion (thirteen) were wars of autonomy or secession, in which a violent regime change was being attempted. The second largest portion (twelve) were anti-regime wars.

A new type of warfare has begun to emerge in place of traditional inter-state war (see Creveld, 1991; Kaldor, 2007; Münkler, 2004). Such new wars can manifest themselves in many different ways – public and private, intra- and inter-societal, international and national – as well as with regional and local parties to conflict. These types of wars can combine elements of classical war, civil war, organized crime, and planned large-scale violations of human rights; they can also be characterized by the privatization of the application of force. Over the course of, and as a result of, such changes, the state's monopoly of war is being eroded, and as a consequence it has become difficult, and will continue to become more difficult, to determine the precise locus from which a military danger arises. A state's claim to being the sole authority with the right to the use of military force may have led to a number of wars, but it also served to stabilize international relations insomuch as it limited the number and types of actors able to cause wars. The decline in inter-state war is at least partly a result of states' observation of the general prohibition on the use of force. Also, the decline in inter-state war must be correlated with the decline in military power as an effective tool against the perils of contemporary threats (i.e. nuclear threats and terrorism), and with the notion that it no longer seems palatable to legitimize the use of military power for the pursuit of a state's individual national interest. However, the privatization and economisation of violence and war and the 'return of security politics to the Middle Ages' is eroding any newly-won stability, and the borders between traditional inter-state war and internal conflict are becoming more and more blurred (see Münkler, 2004, p. 74 *et seq.*).

The conduct of conflicts is not the only element to have diversified; the causes of conflict have also become more diverse. The struggles of ethnic groups for independence, the violent exercise of the right to self-determination, fundamentalism and other religious or ideological extremism, terrorism, classical power struggles and regional conflicts, and destruction of the environment and the scarcity of vital resources are all potential future sources of conflict that might lead to violence. Global inequality – sometimes described as 'global apartheid' – is also an increasing source of conflict. It is now weak states, rather than strong states, that present the most potential for creating instability in the international system. Weak states offer fertile ground for the development of sub-state or private violent actors that may become active within failed states as warlords, or that may export violence to other states and societies.

Furthermore, traditional armed forces also seem to be undergoing their own process of significant change that is often encapsulated by buzzwords such as 'post-modern warfare', the revolution in military affairs (RMA), and information warfare (Morgan, 2000; Arquilla and Borer, 2007). These terms, however, seem to point in two different directions. On the one hand, they outline the development of ever more expensive weapons systems that are far more precise and designed also to minimize one's own losses (i.e. unmanned aircraft, satellite-guided steering systems, and the possibilities for attacking an opponent's infrastructure through cyber-warfare). On the other hand, such developments can also be characterized under the heading of asymmetric warfare since the technologies are not aimed at combating similarly-equipped opponents, and problem states and aggressive non-state actors now have almost unrestricted access to the means of unconventional warfare. The dangers of unconventional warfare have been raised to previously unheard-of levels as a result of the proliferation of biological and chemical or nuclear weapons and their respective carrying systems. The basic truism of security politics – that no scenario, no matter how vile, is unthinkable – holds true here; and it is practically guaranteed that what is thinkable will at some point be attempted.

Public discourse concerning the new face of war was brought to the fore following the asymmetric and unconventional nature of the 9/11 terrorist attacks. At the heart of this debate was two questions: (1) whether or not the 9/11 attacks, which were led by private non-state actors, should be categorized as a 'war' or if the attacks should instead be categorized as a 'crime', and (2) whether or not the measures of defence subsequently undertaken by the US and its allies were an appropriate response? The deep qualitative changes taking place in the conduct of war in the international system has been ongoing for decades but has accelerated significantly in the last twenty years. Even though it remains difficult to draw a clear picture of the current situation – because it is still so much in flux – some overarching trends and essential developments may be identified:

(i) globalization, with its increasing interdependence amongst open societies creates new vulnerabilities that can be targeted by state and non-state actors;
(ii) progressing erosion of state sovereignty and the simultaneous decrease in the state's capability of keeping the promises of overall security to its citizens;
(iii) a soaring privatization in the use of force and violence by an increasing number of sub-state and/or non-state actors as well as states;

(iv) growing significance of asymmetric forms of warfare using insurgencies and (international) terrorism as dominant strategies;
(v)   the mix of war actions with crimes;
(vi) blurring borders between the classical spheres of internal and external security.

These trends increasingly characterize the nature of modern wars and conflicts, and as a consequence now form an essential part of the framework in which strategists and planners in international politics and in the military must consider their options.

The changing forms of war require a modified understanding of the instruments of peace maintenance. The first distinction to be made in the context of the UN is the above-mentioned distinction between securing the peace, in Chapter VI, and peace enforcement, in Chapter VII (see Table 4.1). When it became clear that the Charter-based system of collective security was unable to respond to contemporary conditions in a way that the writers of the Charter intended, it became necessary to develop alternative forms of peace maintenance.

TABLE 4.1
UN approaches to preventing and managing conflicts

Collective security	Theory and practice whereby all states thwart an aggressor state by joining together against him. Attempts to prevent the outbreak of conflict, but if a breach of peace or an aggression attack occurs, it is met with collective measures, including military force.
Arms control and disarmament	Efforts to persuade states to limit, reduce, or eliminate specific types of weapons.
Preventive diplomacy	Practice of engaging in diplomatic interventions before the outbreak of conflict. Includes confidence-building measures, fact-finding missions, demilitarised zones or monitoring hot spots through the use of peacekeeping forces or surveillance technology.
Peacemaking	Various techniques by which disputes and hostilities are settled, such as consultation, arbitration, mediation by the SG, conciliation and good offices, investigations and recommendations by the SC.
Peacekeeping	The use of multilateral forces to achieve several different objectives: observation of truce and ceasefire lines; separation of forces, promotion of law and order; provision of humanitarian aid and intervention.
Peace Enforcement	Efforts to bring an end to hostilities by coercive measures authorized by the SC such as sanctions or the use of military force.
Peacebuilding	Post conflict activities to prevent the return of violence, strengthen and preserve peace, such as development aid, civilian administration, and human rights and election monitoring.

These new approaches allowed the UN to continue to support its Charter-based purposes and principles without going against the interests of the Security Council permanent members, nor infringing upon the sovereign equality of the other member states.

The emergence of UN observer missions or peacekeeping troops – the so-called 'blue helmets', so-named for their conspicuous blue headgear – has been the most visible and prominent peace-maintenance measure. However, looking for a Charter-based textual reference to the blue helmets is a vain enterprise and no such reference will be found. Additionally, and because of their many-sided character, it is also very complicated to provide a precise definition of blue-helmet missions – they encompass the dispatching of everything from civilian observer missions to military units. In the sixty-plus years of peacekeeping history numerous different types of peacekeeping operations have been developed, all belonging officially to the genus of peace missions, but their concrete manifestations could hardly be more different from each other.

The classic version of peacekeeping is not based on force – its central element is that 'there is no peacekeeping if there is no peace to keep' – and thus constitutes an important modification of the principle of collective security. The contradiction between acting 'in concert' and exercising compulsion was resolved in peace-keeping practice to the advantage of the 'in concert' side, and the peacekeeping concept was further developed under an informal 'Chapter 6½' definition (i.e. situated somewhere between Chapters VI and VII, the classic consensus-orientated processes of peaceful dispute resolution (such as mediation efforts) and information-gathering missions and the implementation of forceful measures of compulsion). As already discussed, the Chapter VII option existed largely only on paper during the Cold War – although the Security Council discussed the possible use of coercion in countless cases of a threat to or breach of the peace, it had in fact adopted them only in a few exceptional cases (the empowerment of specific states to undertake military operations under the leadership of the USA in North Korea in the summer of 1950, an economic boycott against then-Southern Rhodesia in the winter of 1966, and an arms embargo against South Africa in autumn of 1977). The Security Council was weakened significantly by the permanent members' ability to veto decisions; although results differ depending on the counting method, the veto was used approximately 240 times until 1990 (118 times by the USSR, 69 times by the USA, 32 times by the UK, 18 times by France, and 3 times by China) (Mingst and Karns, 2000, p. 28). Occasional attempts by the General Assembly – in cases of a self-blockade by the Security Council – to win more authority remained largely without noticeable effect. The most prominent attempt by the General Assembly to break a Security Council gridlock was the aforementioned Uniting for Peace Resolution of November 1950, in which the General Assembly successfully attempted to recommend the use of forceful measures. However, in the 1960s the Security Council reasserted its primary responsibility for the maintenance of international security as enshrined in Article 24.

In more than forty years of classical UN peacekeeping (1948 to the end of 1988), the UN initiated a total of sixteen peace missions, some of which continue to the present day (see Table 4.2). UN peace missions were awarded the Nobel Peace Prize in 1988, and since its 1988 renaissance – made possible by the Cold War détente and the subsequent end of the bipolar world order – the number of missions to be initiated and completed has grown markedly. From 1948 to October 2011, there were a total of sixty-six such missions, some of which have been Chapter VII operations (see Tables 4.3 and 4.4).

The UN has adopted the typology of 'generations' of peace maintenance in categorizing its peace missions, as follows (for other categorizations see Jett, 2000, pp. 21, 34; and Debiel, 2003, pp. 221–4):

(i)   The 'first generation' is characterized by classical peacekeeping, comprising traditional military observer missions and 'blue helmet' operations in buffer zones for the supervision and safeguarding of already-concluded peace treaties or ceasefires (e.g. truce observation in Israel/Palestine since 1948 or the Observation of Disengagement on the Golan Heights since 1974).

(ii)   Missions of the 'second generation', after 1988–9, are distinguished by a far more complex set of tasks such as securing and assisting processes of political transformation, reconciliation, election processes, or institution-building. In these increasingly complex missions more and more civilian personnel like police officers or administrative experts served alongside with the soldiers (e.g. Namibia's transition to independence from 1988–90 or the Transitory Authority in Cambodia from 1992–4).

(iii)   Those missions of the 'third' generation mixed elements of peace maintenance and peace enforcement by deploying peacekeepers in ongoing conflicts, thus bringing them between the warring parties where they suffered considerable losses (e.g. Somalia 1992–4 or Bosnia and Herzegovina 1992–5).

(iv)   Missions of the 'fourth' generation are multi-dimensional and largely involve comprehensive responsibilities up to and including the exercise of civil administrative functions. Deployed in post-conflict scenarios, these peacekeeping missions more and more form a non-dissolvable entity with (civilian) peace-building capacities in their effort for the reconstruction of war-torn states (e.g. East Timor 1999–2001).

The Development of Classical Peacekeeping (First Generation)

The first large UN mission was UNTSO (see Table 4.2) initiated in June 1948 and still ongoing. (Prior to this mission, in October 1947, the General Assembly had resolved to set up a special committee for the support of peaceful development in the Balkans – UNSCOB – but it was not subject to UN jurisdiction.) Although the term 'peacekeeping' had not yet been used explicitly, the original purpose of this mission was that of the contemporary understanding of the word – the safeguarding of a ceasefire, in this first case following the first Arab–Israeli war of 1948. In November 1947, the General Assembly had approved a plan for the partition of

TABLE 4.2
UN peace missions, 1948–88

Mission name	Time period	Location
UNSCOB	1947–51	Special Committee for the Balkans
UNTSO	Since June 1948	Mission for the supervision of the cease-fire in Palestine
UNMOGIP	Since January 1949	Military observation group in India/Pakistan
UNEF I	November 1956–June 1967	First emergency force in the Sinai
UNOGIL	June 1958–December 1958	Observer group in Lebanon
ONUC	July 1960–June 1964	Operation in the Congo
UNSF	October 1962–April 1963	Security force in Western New Guinea
UNYOM	July 1963–September 1964	Observer mission in Yemen
UNFICYP	Since March 1964	Peacekeeping troops in Cyprus
DOMREP	May 1965–October 1966	Mission in the Dominican Republic
UNIPOM	September 1965–March 1966	Observer mission in India/Pakistan
UNEF II	October 1973–July 1979	Second emergency force in the Sinai
UNDOF	Since June 1974	Observer force for the breaking up of troop contact between Syria and Israel
UNIFIL	Since March 1978	Interim force in Lebanon
UNGOMAP	Aprril 1988–March 1990	Good offices mission in Afghanistan
UNIIMOG	August 1988–February 1991	Observer group in Iraq/Iran

Source: Data from UN Department of Peacekeeping Operations.

Palestine that was intended to create two states: one Arab and one Jewish. The plan was rejected by the Arab states. In May 1948, the UK ended its mandate in Palestine, the Jewish population in Palestine declared the state of Israel despite the Arab rejection of partition, and rioting and violence followed between the Arab and Jewish populations of the territory. At the end of May 1948, the Security Council demanded (in Resolution 50) an end to the hostilities in Palestine, and determined that the ceasefire should be safeguarded by a UN mediator and a group of military observers. The first group arrived in the region in June 1948 and has continued to undertake various tasks since then. The maximum size of the force has hovered around 200 but by the end of the 1990s was costing around US$30 million per year.

The second large mission also took place in the context of an inter-state conflict. This time, it involved the maintenance of the ceasefire between India and Pakistan (UNMOGIP). By January 1948 the Security Council had determined (in Resolution 39) to create a commission for India and Pakistan to mediate between the parties. After a ceasefire was reached in June 1949 under the Karachi Accord, the Security Council passed Resolution 91 in March 1951 to establish UNMOGIP to oversee the ceasefire. Since then, approximately fifty military observers have continued to monitor the border with the task of investigating complaints of cease-fire violations and communicating the results of their investigations to both parties to the conflict as well as to the UN Secretary-General. Despite constant disagreements over the creation of the mandate, the mission has continued to exist to the present day with expenses in the region of US$8 million (1998) paid from the UN's regular budget.

Over the course of a single decade, from 1956–7, eight new missions were established, ranging from observer troops (UNOGIL in Lebanon, UNYOM in Yemen, DOMREP in the Dominican Republic, and UNIPOM in India and Pakistan) to comprehensive missions that have been given complex and novel sets of tasks (UNEF I in Egypt, ONUC in the Congo, UNSF in New Guinea, and UNFICYP in Cyprus).

Of particular importance is the first use of the UN's emergency troops, known as the United Nations Emergency Force (UNEF I) in Egypt. UNEF I existed from November 1956 to June 1967 and is usually regarded as the birth of classic peace-keeping. The peacekeeping troops – numbering around 6,000 at the height of the mission in February 1957 – were tasked with the cessation of hostilities between Egyptian and Israeli forces; specifically to ensure the withdrawal of French, Israeli and British troops from Egyptian territory and to act as a buffer after that with-drawal. As the Israeli–Egyptian conflict intensified, the Security Council –inca-pacitated by the French and British vetoes – was unable to condemn either the Egyptian annexation of the Suez Canal or the Israeli aggression. In the absence of any Security Council action, the General Assembly attempted to enter the fray with the Uniting for Peace Resolution. First, the General Assembly condemned both the Israeli occupation of Egyptian sovereign territory in the Sinai and the Egyptian blockade of the Suez Canal under Resolution 997 of 2 November 1956. Second, the General Assembly recommended the introduction of peacekeeping troops. The entire General Assembly procedure was legally contested, but because of the agreement of the parties to the conflict, it did not count as compulsion in the sense of Chapter VII (in which case the Security Council would have had to be responsible). Furthermore, the lack of opposition may have stemmed from the fact that neither of the superpowers, nor any other major power, had an interest in opposing this arrangement and insisting on the sole right of the Security Council to act. The result was that the Security Council did not oppose the procedure, and the General Assembly was able to request Secretary-General Dag Hammarskjöld to oversee the implementation of the Resolution and report to the Security Coun-cil and the General Assembly should further measures appear to be necessary.

Conflicts over the legal basis of peace-maintenance measures did, however, continue to arise. The USSR and France, along with others, refused to provide financial support to UNEF, and also later refused financial support to ONUC in the Congo (with the argument that they were in conflict with the UN Charter because, according to Article 24(1), it is the Security Council alone that carries primary responsibility for the maintenance of peace). The issue was put to the ICJ that then defined the functional responsibilities of both the Security Council and the General Assembly (Sucharipa-Behrmann, 2001). In practice, there has developed an acceptable form of cohabitation for these two bodies, although since the 1960 Congo crisis the Security Council has been more assertive in reserving initiative and decisional authority for itself.

The Secretary-General played an increasingly prominent role in the lead-up to UNEF, and exerted a great deal of influence how the mission took shape. General Assembly Resolution 998 (4 November 1956) requested that the Secretary-General produce a plan within 18 hours for how to post an international emergency force with the consent of the affected parties. General Assembly Resolution 1000 (5 November 1956) created the international peacekeeping force under the command of a UN-designated military general. According to Ernst-Otto Czempiel (1994, p. 114 *et seq.*):

> The UN force could not possibly and was not intended to resolve the Near East conflict. It could not force the conflicting parties to desist from the use of force. But as long as the parties to the conflict were willing [to desist from the use of force], the UN troop could wedge itself between them, and preserve the situation for the longer term . . . The consent of the parties involved is decisive. It is not of a fixed, but rather of a flexible extent, and it can be influenced and stretched. Should it erode or break, the instrument of peacekeeping becomes unfit.

Secretary-General U Thant – who succeeded Dag Hammarskjöld – recalled UNEF in May 1967, citing the lack of consent by the conflicting parties and the fact that Egypt was demanding UNEF withdrawal. It is important to note that although the conflict had not been resolved, UNEF I had held the region in a state of peace for ten years.

UNEF entered the history of international peacekeeping on the strength of one particular circumstance. In the run-up to the first large-scale peacekeeping mission, Secretary-General Dag Hammarskjöld formulated important fundamental principles for an emergency force and communicated them in various reports to the General Assembly and the Security Council. This force was to become the model for further missions of classical peacekeeping:

- *Consent of the parties to the conflict.* Classical 'blue helmet' missions cannot take place against the will of the affected states. Rather, all parties involved in a process of conflict resolution must come to a consensus, through a ceasefire or a peace treaty, regarding a 'blue helmet' peacekeeping mission. The agreement of the affected parties is the *conditio sine qua non* of this type of peace mission. A consensus decision not only eases the problem of the soldiers' acceptance in their mission area, but is also an important prerequisite for the willingness of member states to provide troops, because it minimizes the danger that the 'blue helmets' will be drawn into combat situations.
- *Direct responsibility of the UN.* In contrast to military operations conducted in Korea, during the first Gulf War, and more recently in the Balkans, UN peacekeeping missions are as a rule not only authorized by the Security Council, but also conducted under the operational leadership of the Secretary-General. In the UN Secretariat, a special main department was created specifically for the planning and implementation of peacekeeping missions: the Department of Peacekeeping Operations (DPKO). The military leadership of the mission falls

upon a Force Commander named by the Secretary-General, and the political leadership is usually carried out by a Special Representative of the Secretary-General (SRSG). As a rule, UN peacekeeping missions are financed through a unique budget, raised for each separate mission through a cost-sharing process among member states. Soldiers and civil servants for the mission are provided by member states, but any other assistance necessary is usually acquired locally. Although the 'sending states' retain responsibility for their troops and civil servants in a general sense and for the purposes of labour law, observer missions and peacekeeping troops in the field function effectively as subsidiary organs of the Security Council. This status is of decisive importance for the acceptance of peacekeeping missions by states that might otherwise not allow the presence of troops in their sovereign territory.

- *Neutrality.* Inextricably tied to the principle of party consent is the principle of the neutrality of the peacekeepers. The 'blue helmets' constitute a buffer zone between the armed forces of the conflicting parties, and are intended to prevent the resumption of combat activities. The provision of 'good offices' – such as facilitating a meeting of negotiating delegations in buildings belonging to the peacekeeping mission – is one of many other acceptable 'blue helmet' tasks. Any involvement in the conflict – even if one side has flagrantly violated the conditions of the ceasefire – is expressly forbidden. The neutrality issue also requires that due diligence is given to ensuring a balanced regional representation is the composition of the force.
- *Use of weapons only in self-defence.* While observer missions are usually conducted by unarmed military experts, members of a peacekeeping force have the use of light, hand-held weapons. Such weapons are intended for self-defence only, but this can take place in relation to the implementation of the mandate. The conditions under which 'blue helmets' might use their weapons were – until the 1990s – understood very narrowly in order to give parties no pretence for drawing UN troops into the conflict.

The initial successes of UNEF meant that, by the beginning of the 1960s, there was a great deal of optimistic expectation bound up with UN peacekeeping missions. This optimism was expressed inter alia through the ambitious UN deployment into the Republic of Congo (ONUC) from July 1960 to June 1964. ONUC was originally conceived in order to oversee the withdrawal of Belgian troops from the Congo but the mission did not hold very closely to Secretary-General Hammarskjöld's principles. Starting with Resolution 143 (July 1960) and including a total of four further Security Council resolutions, ONUC's mandate was expanded continuously and at its height consisted of approximately 20,000 troops. From its original mandate of overseeing Belgian troop withdrawal, ONUC eventually grew to involve the protection of the territorial integrity of the Congo, the prevention of the outbreak of civil war, and the support of the government in its attempts to create a civil service. Security Council Resolution 161 (February 1961) allowed ONUC peacekeepers to use their weapons in the service of their mission, and not just for self-defence. The result of this was that – contrary to the original concept – peacekeepers became one of the parties to the conflict. After initial success, ONUC became the first 'major peacekeeping failure' (Jett, 2000, p. 24). The UN was drawn increasingly into the unresolved internal conflicts of the Republic of Congo, member states were pursuing very different interests, and disagreements over the mission's mandate and financing were rife. In the summer of 1964, following the Congolese refusal to extend the mandate, the operation was brought to a close. The lessons of the Congo mission, described somewhat exaggeratedly by William Durch as 'the UN's Vietnam' (1993, p. 12), made a lasting impact on the UN and its conception of peacekeeping. In the decades that followed, no other peacekeeping mission came close to size and complexity of ONUC. Indeed, the goals of peacekeeping have become significantly more modest. The UN recalled Hammarskjöld's original principles and sought in particular the consent of the parties involved before any mission was undertaken. The Security Council also managed to reassert its position as the only body that could mandate and oversee peace missions.

The UN mission in Cyprus (UNFICYP; still ongoing at the time of writing) is another prominent example of classic peacekeeping. UNFICYP was created by Security Council Resolution 186 (March 1964) in an attempt to prevent further conflict between Greek and Turkish Cypriots. In the years that followed, however, UNFICYP was unable to halt the violence and eventually undertook the forceful partition of the island state. A ceasefire was accomplished in 1974 and UNFICYP's mandate has been extended every six months since to oversee the agreement and to secure the partition buffer zone. More than 1,200 UNFICYP soldiers have been deployed since 1964 and various secretaries-general have made attempts at mediation to resolve the conflict. UNFICYP has suffered a great deal of criticism, most particularly the charge that the decades-long UN presence is in fact removing any pressure for the two sides to reach a lasting agreement. Despite these and other accusations (and the fact that UNFICYP itself has suffered 180 fatalities) the mission has ensured that there has been no escalation of the conflict since 1974.

A large number of potential peacekeeping missions were prevented from taking place by the antagonism between the Eastern and Western blocs – and their blockade of the Security Council – during the Cold War. During the 1970s, those missions that did succeed in winning approval were focused on the conflict in the Near East. Three missions in one decade were undertaken in the region: (1) in October 1973 the second Emergency Force (UNEF II) entered the Sinai; (2) in June 1974 an observer mission (UNDOF) was deployed to the Golan Heights; and (3) in March 1978 the interim force in Lebanon (UNFIL) was begun. All three missions (the latter two of which continue to exist at the time of writing) are classic 'first generation' missions. It should be noted, however, that the consent of the parties was temporarily not forthcoming in Lebanon, and so the UNFIL was for a time restricted to humanitarian aid activities. After the 2006 Lebanon war, UNIFIL's mandate was expanded to inter alia monitoring the cessation of hostilities between Lebanon and Israel as well as accompanying and supporting the Lebanese Armed Forces (LAF) in the south as Israel withdraws its armed forces.

Furthermore UNIFIL has been tasked with assisting the LAF in establishing zones free of armed personnel, and other assets and weapons, (other than those of the Government of Lebanon and of UNIFIL) between the Blue Line and the Litani. UNIFIL also gives assistance to the Government of Lebanon in securing its borders and other entry points (see S/RES/1701, 11 August 2006). Since 2006, force numbers have increased considerably from approximately 2,000 to more than 12,000 soldiers in order to fulfil these complex mandates.

Following UNEF II, UNDOF and UNFIL, no new missions were undertaken until the end of the 1980s. It was not until 1988 and the establishment of UNIIMOG and UNGOMAP (the first of which was an observer force overseeing the ceasefire between Iraq and Iran, the second a supervision of the withdrawal of Soviet troops from Afghanistan) that there was a peacekeeping renaissance. UNIIMOG conformed to the classical peacekeeping profile as an unarmed observer group, but UNGOMAP was a new type of 'good offices mission' not mandated directly by the Security Council; but merely given its approval.

If one were to add up the experiences of the first four decades of UN peace-keeping, it would certainly produce a mixed result. Every mission, however, is a special case that cannot run according to a pre-set plan of precise detail. The ideal set out in the Charter (and in particular the extensive regulations in Chapter VII) has proven to be less than practical and has resulted in the innovation of 'blue helmet missions'. Such missions were aimed primarily at assisting the parties to a conflict towards a resolution, or in 'lay[ing] the violent portion of the conflict to rest' (Kühne, 1993, p. 19) insofar as the parties were willing and able to do so. 'Blue helmet' missions were a means of damping conflict, not solving it. This apparently unambitious goal was not the result of modesty or a lack of confidence in the UN's competence to solve conflicts, but developed as a result of conceptual restraint, strategic ingenuity, and in response to what is practicable. In most cases, this modest goal has been achieved, although often at the cost (as in Cyprus) of a long-term presence, significant financial obligations, and UN casualties. Should these limitations be abandoned, however, as they were in the Congo, the outcome of many more missions would likely be negative.

Peacekeeping after the Cold War (Second and Third Generation)

The thawing of Cold War relations between the USA and the USSR in the late 1980s practically catapulted the UN – after decades of relative impotence – back into the centre of international politics. The Security Council – whose permanent members had essentially halted the work of the Council with the practically habit-ual use of their vetoes during the Cold War – achieved a previously unknown capacity to reach decisions and take action. The number of vetoes dropped to almost nil and there was an explosion of resolutions and measures taken by consensus. Suddenly, blue helmets were no longer an 'exotic peripheral phenom-enon of international peace and security politics', but rather 'one of its most important pillars' (Kühne, 1993, p. 18).

The 'expansion period' of peacekeeping occurred at a time of fundamental political upheaval on a global scale, during which the lingering consequences of the Cold War had to be dealt with in Asia (Afghanistan, Cambodia), Africa (Namibia, Angola, Mozambique), and Latin America (El Salvador, Nicaragua). Iraq's invasion of Kuwait destroyed any hope of a world free of inter-state war, and the collapse of states in Africa (Somalia) and Europe (Yugoslavia) created an all-new set of challenges for the UN. Increasingly, the organization was confronted with states' internal conflicts rather than conflicts between states. The competencies of the Security Council thus expanded to include actions that would previously have been considered impossible because of the Charter's prohibition on intervention. This expansion of competencies was both the result of, and a necessary condition for, the creation of a new generation of peacekeeping missions.

Fourteen new missions were begun between 1988 and 1992 – nearly as many as in the previous forty years combined. According to DPKO, in January 1988 there were 11,121 soldiers, police, and civilians operating in a total of five missions worldwide at the cost of approximately US$230 million. By the end of 1992, there were nearly 100,000 peacekeepers in fourteen missions, costing around US$4 billion. Six new peace missions were begun in 1993 alone, and despite a temporary de facto moratorium in the mid-1990s the number of missions increased to fifty-six by the end of the century.

If classic peace missions were distinguished primarily by their function as a buffer between the armed forces of the (usually state) parties to the conflict, mandates of the 'second generation' were characterized by an ever-widening spectrum of tasks that a peace missions were expected to fulfil, such as: aid for states in transitional periods or undergoing processes of national reconciliation, support for processes of democratic consolidation, disarmament and reintegration of the parties to civil wars, repatriation of refugees, and the temporary undertaking of quasi-sovereign competences for an entire country. The novelty of this phase is appropriately described by Dennis Jett (2000, p. 23 *et seq.*): '[F]or the first time, the UN assumed temporary authority over a territory in transition to interdependence, added civilian police to a PKO, became involved in a civil war, established a large-scale operation, and allowed the peacekeepers to carry arms.'

The composition of these peace missions (and their personnel) required serious changes commensurate with this new 'to-do' list. While classical operations relied primarily on soldiers, the 'second generation' missions increasingly required the integration of civilian experts, for example, in the areas of civil policing, the administration of justice, humanitarian aid, public administration, and the organization and supervision of elections.

Security Council Resolution 632 (16 February 1989) gave the UN Transitional Assistance Group in Namibia (UNTAG) an extensive mandate in support of the state's transition to independence from South Africa. Between April 1989 and March 1990, more than 8,000 soldiers and civilian experts escorted the country through the cessation of hostilities, the withdrawal of the South African troops, the creation of opportunities for the repatriation of refugees, the preparations for elections, and the construction of a new legal and political order. An independent Namibia was admitted to the UN in April 1990. A decisive measure preceding the Namibia mission was the creation of the first Angola Verification Mission (UNAVEM I) in January of 1989 to oversee the withdrawal of Cuban troops who had been intervening in Namibia from bases in Angola.

In November 1989, the UN began a mission in Central America that was to last for around two years. Resolution 644 (7 November 1989) created the Observer Mission in Central America (ONUCA) to support Costa Rica, El Salvador, Guatemala, Honduras and Nicaragua in the maintenance of the obligations they had undertaken with respect to a peaceful coexistence with one another. The critical job of the 260 military observers – strengthened by an 800-strong infantry battalion and countless civilian workers – was the demobilization of around 20,000 Nicaraguan Contras as a pre-condition for free elections in Nicaragua (the implementation of those elections was overseen by another UN mission). A separate mission was begun in El Salvador in April 1991 (ONUSAL) to initially supervise the observation of human rights and then to support the ceasefire that was later negotiated between the parties to the civil war. The Iraq–Kuwait observer mission (UNIKOM) was also begun in April 1991 as a more traditional peacekeeping operation – it was created to guard the demilitarized border zone in the aftermath of the large-scale international military operation that had been mandated by Security Council for the liberation of Kuwait from Iraq.

Security Council Resolution 745 (28 February 1992) created the UN transitional authority in Cambodia (UNTAC) for the purposes of overseeing the implementation of the peace agreement that had been signed in October 1991 between the warring sides in the Cambodian civil war. It was clear from the beginning that such a mission could not limit itself to a passive readiness to provide aid, but must behave, instead, like a transitional administration. Based on the success of the multi-faceted operation in Namibia the UN was encouraged to take on its largest ever peacekeeping mission. More than 22,000 soldiers and civilian experts organized free elections under UN auspices, supported the drafting and promulgation of a constitution, helped in the creation of a state administration and infrastructure, and enabled refugees and displaced persons to return to their homes. UNTAC – the most expensive peacekeeping mission in the history of the UN – was brought to a close in September 1993.

The development of 'second generation' peacekeeping doctrine was gradual insofar as the missions were still largely post-conflict; i.e. missions were conducted in a relatively peaceful context and under the protection of an existing peace agreement or consent of the parties. A number of post-1992 missions, however, did begin to experience difficulties with the hallowed principles of 'blue helmet' operations, thus heralding the slide into the 'third generation' of peacekeeping missions.

UNOSOM in Somalia was the first time since ONUC that a peacekeeping mandate was given under Chapter VII and included the use of military force. Despite early signs of success, the mission – the UN's first humanitarian mission – failed to disarm the warring clan militias and was unable to provide consistent humanitarian aid to the Somali population. Following the deaths of twenty-four UN peacekeepers from Pakistan, the blue helmets abandoned their neutrality and once again became a party to a conflict where they were supposed to be impartial. UNOSOM was closed in November 1994 and complete troop withdrawal was scheduled for no later than 31 March 1995. In total 132 'blue helmets' – and an unknown number of Somalis – died during the course of the mission. The second Somali mission (UNOSOM II, March 1993 –March 1995) suffered primarily from the fundamental problem that the 'blue helmets' were regarded as not going in to support an existing peace, but to compel one. Suffering heavy losses UNOSOM II joined the conflict instead of stopping it.

The UN Protection Force in the Former Yugoslavia (UNPROFOR) on the other hand tried for a long time to stick to the classic peacekeeping formula. It soon became apparent, however, that a proven instrument becomes useless when it is applied in a context for which it was not designed, i.e. 'Blue helmets' were deployed despite the lack of a reliable peace agreement. UNPROFOR was begun in Croatia in 1992 to keep the conflicting parties away from one another, but is slowly broadened to include Bosnia-Herzegovina. Eventually, UNPROFOR's mandate evolved into an intervention to protect the civilian population from massive human rights abuses. Secretary-General Boutros Boutros-Ghali warned several times that peacekeepers should not be given tasks for which their training and rules of engagement (ROE) were not suitable. The new mandate, however, was not accompanied by appropriate changes either in the military outfit or in the legal and political definition of the ROE. There were numerous cases of 'blue helmets' being taken hostage or used as human shields. Frequently unable to tell where the 'fronts' were (because they might consist of anything from regular forces to warlord bands) peacekeepers were caught between them rather than keeping them apart, and leadership and command eventually splintered among the UN, the troop contributing states, and other co-operating organizations. UNPRO-FOR remains a less than sparkling chapter in the history of the UN. Responsibility for military peacekeeping in Bosnia-Herzegovina was transferred to NATO in the winter of 1995–6.

'Third generation' peacekeeping mandates – which were expanded to include compulsion and military force – fall into two very different categories.

First, the failed missions in Somalia and the former Yugoslavia symbolize the beginning of the crisis of UN peacekeeping. Pictures of dead US Rangers in Somalia (though not being part of the UN mission) or UN troops being held hostage in Bosnia caused a dramatic drop in the readiness of many member states to send their soldiers into danger in difficult missions. The overrunning of a UN safe zone in Srebrenica by Bosnian Serbs in July 1995 (resulting in the deaths of over 8,000 Bosnian Muslims who had been in the protection of the UN forces) became a symbol of the UN's failure in concrete situations of conflict. Robust intervention was left to the NATO-led Implementation Force (IFOR, later the Stabilization Force (SFOR)) carried out in the winter of 1995. In Rwanda in 1994, UNAMIR troop commanders were facing the possibility of genocide on a massive and horrific scale. UNAMIR Force Command requested to be allowed to take action to prevent the genocide, but instead the UN reduced the mission after the massacres began (Carlsson *et al.,* 1999). Operation Turquoise (summer 1994) was subsequently empowered to use military force to prevent the continuation of genocide in Rwanda, but it was too little, too late and occurred only *after* more than 800,000 people had been murdered. These failures caused the UN to be regarded by large sections of the public in a somewhat unfavourable light; the UN looked like an incompetent paper tiger. It became clear that fundamental analysis of the political and social conditions in the target-country needed to be undertaken in order to produce a clear peacekeeping mandate, and that the appropriate means to the achievement of these mandates must be made available before the missions could make any sense of the situation. At the time of the first Chapter VII peacekeeping mission, the UN had possessed nothing like such capabilities. Furthermore, the sobering experiences in Somalia, Bosnia and Rwanda, coupled with UN peace missions taking place in the context of conflicts that had already broken out into violence and hostilities, have demonstrated that the UN and its special organizations must work towards the *preventive* regulation of conflicts.

Second, the UN Transitional Authority in East Slavonia (UNTAES) mission from 1996 to 1998 with its 'robust mandate' to realize the peaceful transfer of contested territory – the Region of Eastern Slavonia, Baranja and Western Sirmium – to Croatia was effectively completed. The UN Support Mission in Haiti (UNSMIH) was also considered as a success: between 1993 and 1994, it removed a military dictatorship and reinstated the democratically elected president (UNSMIH was only possible, however, in conjunction the actions of US forces). The International Force for East Timor (INTERFET) – empowered by Security Council Resolution 1264 (15 September 1999) to restore peace and security in East Timor – however, received a more equivocal evaluation. The Security Council came to a speedy and unanimous decision to intervene in the conflict only two weeks after the beginning of the massive expulsions and killings that followed the Independence Referendum of 30 August 1999. Furthermore, INTERFET was able to rapidly control the situation under Australian military leadership. However, despite widespread observation that violence was likely to follow the referendum in East Timor, the UN did not outfit the subsequent UNAMET mission – tasked with executing and overseeing the referendum – with its own security component. Instead, the UN relied upon the security assurances of the Indonesian government and had to bear a good deal of the responsibility for the subsequently necessary military intervention. Missions in both Haiti and in East Timor failed to create a lasting peace in those places. After initial improvements and stability, there was in both cases a return to large-scale violence – that required new and intensive efforts by the international community – following the withdrawal of UN support. Along with other cases in Africa and the Western Balkans, the UN experience in Haiti and East Timor served to highlight that the emerging new task of post-conflict peacebuilding was for long-lasting deploymentsand complex missions tailored to the specific need of the situation in the countries concerned.

Peacekeeping and peacemaking have becoming ever more closely tied together, and require mutual success. Cases such as Bosnia-Herzegovina, Kosovo, and East Timor demonstrate that the challenge is not only to prevent the resumption of hostilities through a deterrent military presence (a robust mandate), but to create new structures in all relevant political, social, and economic areas, and to recreate a stable community after the breakdown of order. Complex peace missions in an often fragile post-conflict environment have become the 'fourth generation' of UN peacekeeping challenges.

Complex Missions and Peacebuilding (Fourth Generation)

Since the end of the 1990s growing efforts have been required from the international community to cope with an ever-increasing number of crises and conflicts worldwide, and it is in this environment that the UN has returned to the stage as a major player in the maintenance of international peace and security. In 2011 the total number of UN peace missions reached sixty-six, by October 2011 approximately 121,800 peacekeepers were active in fifteen peace operations and one political mission lead by the DPKO – among them approximately 85,000 soldiers (troops and military observers) and 13,000 civilian police from 114 contributing member states. The presence of some 20,000 international and local civilians and some 2,200 UN Volunteers provides further proof that UN peace operations are more and more based on a civilian pillar. For the fiscal year 2011–12 the UN's peacekeeping budget totals an all-time high of approximately US$7,06 billion (see Table 4.4). As of 2011, a total of 2,918 UN personnel had died in the course of their duty with more than 1,200 of those fatalities occurring since 2000 (all data from the DPKO).

Following a long period of crisis, the recent increase in peacekeeping mandates indicates member states' growing confidence in the UN's capabilities to conduct large-scale peace missions. However, this renaissance of the UN peacekeeping is in danger of overcharging the existing structures of the organization: the DPKO and relevant Field Support (DFS) comprises approximately only 650 personnel but it is required to meet increasingly complex demands for the continued success of missions. The ever-increasing demand for UN peacekeeping, and the serious challenges that confront the UN as a result, is not merely the result of the outbreak of new conflicts. Often, it is the increasingly complex requirements of existing missions that are over-extending the UN: the mission in Somalia has been required to deal with 'spillover' effects of the conflict such as piracy and regional destabilisation; the mission in Lebanon has been criticized for not eradicating the underlying causes of the conflict and now has to deal with the potential return of violence; the missions in Haiti and in East Timor again were withdrawn before a sustainable order was created and required the redeployment of troops to prevent the states' backslide into anarchy; the mission in the Congo proved to be entirely unrealistic so that amendments and reinforcements became necessary. Demands on peacebuilding missions like in Sierra Leone or in Burundi have required complex qualitative re-evaluation as the mission has become more challenging, especially with the regard to the recruitment of vetted experts and the sustainable flow of resources for long-term engagements.

TABLE 4.3

Completed UN peace missions, 1989–July 2011

Mission name	Time period	Location
UNAVEM I	January 1989–May 1991	Angola verification mission
UNTAG	April 1989–March 1990	Transitional assistance group in Namibia
ONUCA	November 1989 –January 1992	Observer group in Central America
UNIKOM	April 1991–October 2003	United Nations Iraq–Kuwait observation mission
UNAVEM II	June 1991–February 1995	Angola verification mission
ONUSAL	July 1991–April 1995	Observer mission in El Salvador
UNAMIC	October 1991–March 1992	Advance mission in Cambodia
UNPROFOR	February 1992–March 1995	Protection force in the former Yugoslavia
UNTAC	March 1992–September 1993	Transitional authority in Cambodia
UNOSOM I	April 1992–March 1993	Operation in Somalia
ONUMOZ	December 1992–December 1994	Operation in Mozambique
UNOSOM II	March 1993–March 1995	Operation in Somalia
UNOMUR	June 1993–September 1994	Observer mission in Uganda/Rwanda
UNOMIG	August 1993–June2009	Observer Mission in Georgia
UNMIH	September 1993–June 1996	Observer mission in Haiti
UNOMIL	September 1993–September 1997	Observer mission in Liberia
UNAMIR	October 1993–March 1996	Assistance mission for Rwanda
UNASOG	May 1994–June 1994	Aouzou Strip observation group (Chad)
UNMOT	December 1994–May 2000	Mission of observers in Tajikistan
UNAVEM III	February 1995–June 1997	Angola verification mission
UNCRO	March 1995–January 1996	Confidence restoration operation in Croatia
UNPREDEP	March 1995–February 1999	Preventive deployment force in the FYR Macedonia
UNMIBH	December 1995–December 2002	Mission in Bosnia-Herzegovina
UNTAES	January 1996–January 1998	Transitional authority in East Slavonia (Croatia)
UNMOP	January 1996–December 2002	Mission in the Croatian peninsula of Prevlaka
UNSMIH	July 1996–July 1997	Support mission in Haiti
MINUGUA	January 1997–May 1997	Guatemala verification mission
MONUA	June 1997–February 1999	Observer mission in Angola
UNTMIH	August 1997–November 1997	Transitional mission in Haiti
MIPONUH	December 1997–March 2000	Civilian police mission in Haiti
UNPSG	January 1998–October 1998	Civilian police mission in Croatia
UNOMSIL	July 1998–October 1999	Observer mission in Sierra Leone
MINURCA	April 1998–February 2000	Mission in the Central African Republic
UNTAET	September 1999–May 2002	Transitional authority in East Timor
UNAMSIL	October 1999–December 2005	Mission in Sierra Leone
MONUC	November 1999–June 2010	Stabilization Mission in the Democratic Republic of the Congo
UNMEE	July 2000–July 2008	Mission in Ethiopia and Eritrea
UNMISET	May 2002–May 2005	Mission of Support in East Timor
ONUB	June 2004–December 2006	Operation in Burundi
UNMIS	January 2005–July 2011	Mission in Sudan
MINURCAT	September 2007–December 2010	Security Mission in the Central African Republic of Chad

Source: Data from UN Department of Peacekeeping Operations.

Throughout the 1990s and early 2000s, missions were prone to failure as a result of unrealistic mandates that could not be effectively implemented by peace-keepers. Mandates were often tailored to best-case scenarios, whilst the conditions in the theatre were those of the worst case (see Brahimi 2000, paras 48–64). In an attempt to address this issue the Brahimi Report recommended that missions receive more regular and robust mandates and respective rules of engagement. The problem still existed, however, that mandates often lacked the appropriate equipment to meet these more regular and robust mandates. Furthermore, the new mandates were increasingly directed to post-conflict situations that looked as far forward as the reconstruction of state institutions, and even entire states, from the ruins of war (see Call and Wyeth, 2008). Since the 1992 publication of Secretary-General Boutros-Ghali's 'An Agenda for Peace', post-conflict efforts have fallen under the auspices of 'peacebuilding' that has become more and more linked to peacekeeping. Thus new kinds of so-called complex or integrated missions – the instance of which has become the rule rather than the exception – have emerged (see Eide *et al.*, 2005). Complex or integrated missions are built less and less on standard concepts and instead demand individualized designs and capabilities. Integrated missions encompass a broad spectrum of tasks, requiring an increasing number of civilian experts in fields such as policing, law enforcement, justice, administration, economic recovery, reintegration of refugees and former combatants, and infrastructure or health services (see Table 4.5). As a consequence, the recruitment of experts and force generation is a demanding task, as is the required command and control to support and sustain the troops and civilian capacities deployed.

Mission experts are tasked with executive functions (if foreseen by the mandate), but above all they are tasked with overseeing the creation of local or national authorities' institutions. For example, in Kosovo, UNMIK (alongside NATO, the EU, and the OSCE) executed full sovereignty over the former Serbian province for approximately ten years to facilitate the province's path to statehood (the statehood of Kosovo, however, remains contested by a large number of UN member states including China and Russia). In other cases such as in Afghanistan (UNAMA) or in the Democratic Republic of Congo (MONUSCO) the UN assists national governments in the construction of relevant institutions. Such missions have become challenging tasks for the UN as the institution attempts to balance classical military security functions with civilian assistance – more so because most member states do not have sufficient reserves of qualified civilian personnel at their disposal (see Chesterman, 2004; Bellamy *et al.*, 2010, p. 153 *et seq.*). The lack of appropriate personnel has resulted in delayed achievements in the Balkans, in Haiti, and in central Africa. (For details on international peace missions see Bah, 2009.)

Post-conflict peacebuilding is time-consuming and demands considerable perseverance from both the target state and from the international community (see Paris, 2007, p. 416 *et seq.*). The longer a state or society suffers from civil war and persistent violence, the longer it usually takes to create trust between the different ethnic or religious groups, and the longer it takes to then foster societal

TABLE 4.4
Ongoing UN peace missions (as of October 2011)

UNTSO	**UN Truce Supervision Organization**
Mandate:	Supervision of the ceasefire in Palestine
Begun:	1948
Strength:	148 military observers supported by 94 international civilian personnel and 120 local civilian staff
Fatalities:	50

Costs (Appropriations for 2010–11): US$60,704,800

UNMOGIP	**UN Military Observer Group in India and Pakistan**
Mandate:	Supervision of the ceasefire in the Kashmir Valley
Begun:	1949
Strength:	38 military observers supported by 25 international civilian personnel and 51 local civilian staff
Fatalities:	11

Costs (Appropriations for 2010–11): US$16,146,000 million

UNFICYP	**UN Peacekeeping Force in Cyprus**
Mandate:	Supervision of the ceasefire in Cyprus
Begun:	1964
Strength:	857 troops and 63 police supported by 40 international civilian personnel and 112 local civilian staff
Fatalities:	181

Costs (Approved budget July 2011–June 2012): US$58,204,247

UNDOF	**UN Disengagement Observer Force**
Mandate:	Supervision of the ceasefire on the Golan Heights
Begun:	1974
Strength:	1,036 troops, 43 international staff, and 102 local civilian staff
Fatalities:	43

Costs (Approved budget July 2011–June 2012): US$50,506,100

UNIFIL	**UN Interim Force in Lebanon**
Mandate:	Supervision of the ceasefire in Lebanon and the monitoring cessation of hostilities, assistance to Lebanese Government and armed forces (since 2006)
Begun:	1978
Strength:	12,349 total uniformed personnel, 351 international civilian, and 656 local civilian staff
Fatalities:	293

Costs (Approved budget July 2011–June 2012): US$545,470,600

MINURSO	**UN Mission for the Referendum in Western Sahara**
Mandate:	Supervision of the ceasefire in the Western Sahara
Begun:	1991
Strength:	224 total uniformed personnel including 27 troops and 197 military observers, 4 civilian police, 98 international civilian personnel, 162 local civilian staff, and 18 UN Volunteers
Fatalities:	15

Costs (Approved budget July 2011–June 2012): US$63,219,300

UNMIK	**UN Interim Administration Mission in Kosovo**
Mandate:	Creation of a civilian transitional administration
Begun:	1999
Strength:	8 military observers, 8 civilian police, 144 international civilian, 234 local civilian personnel, and 25 UN volunteers
Fatalities:	54

Costs (Approved budget July 2011–June 2012): US$$47,874,400

UNMIL **UN mission in Liberia**
Mandate: Support for the implementation of the ceasefire agreement
Begun: 2003
Strength: 7,782 troops and 130 military observers, 1,288 civilian police, 471 international
civilian personnel, 997 local staff, and 233 UN Volunteers
Fatalities: 160
Costs (Approved budget July 2011–June 2012): US$525,612,730

UNOCI **UN Operation in Côte d'Ivoire**
Mandate: Supervision of the situation in Côte d'Ivoire
Begun: 2004
Strength: 8,974 troops, 193 military observers, 1,276 police, 397 international civilian
personnel, 736 local staff, and 267 UN Volunteers
Fatalities: 78
Costs (Approved budget July 2011–June 2012): US$486,726,400

MINUSTAH **UN Stabilization mission in Haiti**
Mandate: Supervision of the situation in Haiti
Begun: 2004
Strength: 8,728 troops and 3,524 civilian police, 564 international civilian personnel, 1,338
local civilian staff, and 221 UN Volunteers
Fatalities: 164
Costs (July 2011–June 2012): US$ 793,517,100

UNMIT **UN Integrated Mission in Timor-Leste**
Mandate: Support of the government in consolidating stability in the face of a major politi-
cal, humanitarian and security crisis
Begun: August 2006
Strength: 1,194 police and 33 military observers, 396 international civilian staff, 890 local
civilian personnel, and 193 UN Volunteers
Fatalities: 10
Costs (Approved budget July 2011–June 2012): US$196,077,500

UNAMID **African Union/UN Hybrid Operation in Darfur**
Mandate: Protection of civilians and humanitarian staff, monitoring and verifying imple-
mentations of agreements
Begun: July 2007
Strength: 17,759 troops, 311 military observers and 4,526 civilian police, 1,136 interna-
tional civilian personnel, 2,834 local civilian staff, and 480 UN Volunteers
Fatalities: 75
Costs (Approved budget July 2011–June 2012): US$1,689,305,500

MONUSCO **UN Organization Stabilization Mission in the Democratic Republic of the**
Congo
Mandate: Supervision of the arms embargo, ensuring the effective protection of civilians
and humanitarian personnel, helping the government in strengthening its military
capacity and consolidating state authority
Begun: July 2010
Strength: 17,010 troops, 746 military observers and 1,241 civilian police, 983 international
civilian personnel, 2,828 local civilian staff, and 580 UN Volunteers
Fatalities: 29
Costs (July 2011–June 2012): US$1,419,890,400

UNISFA **UN Interim Security force for Abyei, Sudan**
Mandate: Demilitarizing and monitoring peace in the disputed Abyei Area
Begun: June 2011
Strength: 4,200 troops, 50 police (authorized)
Costs: (Approved budget July 2011–June 2012): not available

UNMISS **UN Mission in the Republic of South Sudan**
Mandate: Consolidating peace and security and to help establish conditions for development
Begun: July 2011
Strength: 7,000 troops, 900 police (authorized)
Costs: (Approved budget July 2011–June 2012): not available

Source: Data from UN Department of Peacekeeping Operations.

confidence in new state institutions and structures. Peacebuilding efforts face a large number of dilemmas and hurdles including but not limited to: reconciliation processes after years of atrocities, legal prosecution of those responsible for large-scale crimes against humanity, and socio-economic measures for ensuring future prosperity. Another problem arises when external peacebuilding intervention starts to weaken local ownership and leads to the establishment of long-term protectorates administered by the international community (see Paris, 2004; Paris and Sisk, 2009). However, the tragic examples of Angola, Rwanda, and Sierra Leone in the 1990s and more recently the examples in East Timor and Haiti prove that a hasty termination of international assistance and support of newly created institutions might lead to a society's relapse into violence (see Annan, 2005, para. 114). It remains a major task for the UN to develop appropriate patterns of securing the transition from war to lasting peace (see below, on peacebuilding commission).

Peacekeeping Reform Attempts since the 1990s

The large number of new – and increasingly complex – peacekeeping/peacebuilding functions were tasked to an organization that was not ready for them in terms of experience, doctrine, equipment, headquarters, capacities, or skilled

TABLE 4.5
Elements of complex peace missions

Security, show of force	Creation of a secure environment, which facilitates political solutions; control of the observation of ceasefires, borders, troop withdrawals and peace agreements; possibly the creation of a buffer zone between the conflicting parties; enforcement actions against objectors or insurgents
Humanitarian aid, Disarmament, Demobilization and Reintegration (DDR)	Relief for refugees, displaced persons, victims, Reducing the amount of weapons and opening alternative perspectives for a civilian life beyond violence
Institution building/ state building	(Re-) building legitimate governmental institutions, esp. in the security sector (military, police, law enforcement), justice, administrative structures, schools, health services, infrastructure
Economic and social development	Enhancement of economic recovery and self-sustainability social justice
Transitory authority	Mandatory execution of sovereign functions by UN authorities
Interagency co-operation	For example, with NATO, EU, OSCE, AU or sub regional organizations such as ECOWAS

personnel. Meeting the requirements of new types of mission turned out to be a difficult learning process for the UN. Over the course of only a few years, and in an increasingly complex political environment, the organization had to develop a new task profile and operational form of peacekeeping that had little in common with the missions of the 'first generation'. It was imperative that peacekeeping structures and procedures be markedly improved. A daunting task, but as noted by Winrich Kühne (1993, p. 93), traditional peacekeeping did not develop overnight, but was rather 'a permanent learning process on the basis of trial and error'.

An Agenda for Peace

On 31 January 1992 – at its first session at the head-of-government level – the Security Council charged the Secretary-General with the analysis of peacekeeping, and recommendations for how to comprehensively strengthen and make more efficient the UN's capabilities in this area. Secretary-General Boutros Boutros-Ghali presented his 'Agenda for Peace' in June 1992. In addition to clarifying and classifying key terms and ideas, the Agenda for Peace created a new concept of peacekeeping. The Secretary-General identified five distinct but closely related task-areas:

(i)   *Preventive diplomacy*: The goal of this is to minimize tensions and to eliminate the causes of those tensions *before* a conflict erupts. The essential elements are confidence-building measures, the creation of structures for fact-finding missions, early warning in all relevant areas of tension, demilitarized zones, and preventive missions.

(ii) *Peacemaking with civilian and military means*: Chapter VI should be taken more seriously and improved systematically. Furthermore, sufficient means for third parties in conflict mediation must be made available. Chapter VII measures (peace enforcement) should be implemented consistently; according to the Secretary-General, this means that there must be armed forces made available to the Security Council in the sense of Article 43.

(iii) *'Blue helmet' peacekeeping*: the preconditions for the use of this instrument should be adjusted conceptually to fit the changed types of conflicts; beyond that, it is necessary to conclude agreements with the member states regarding their readiness to provide troops, and to solidify through written agreements a much better level of financial and logistical support.

(iv) *Post-conflict peacebuilding*: a ceasefire does not constitute a lasting peace. The post-conflict period must be given a great deal more attention, including the disarmament of warring parties, mine-clearing, the resettlement of refugees, political reordering, and the reconciliation of the parties.

(v)   *A conflict-specific division of labour between the Security Council and regional organizations*: better use should be made of the co-operation with regional arrangements mentioned in Chapter VIII. That Chapter states that localized conflicts should be resolved peacefully through the active efforts of such regional organizations, before the Security Council is activated. In the case that coercive measures need to be used, however, the empowerment of the Security Council would still need to be sought.

The Agenda for Peace was never implemented in its entirety, but the basic structure and conceptual framework for reform remains valid. Over the course of the 1990s, the DPKO was completely restructured and its personnel increased in order to improve and streamline the work of around 100,000 personnel in seventeen different missions around the world. The DPKO planning process was streamlined in co-operation with other departments of the Secretariat (see below).

The Brahimi Report

With all this in mind, in spring 2000, Secretary-General Kofi Annan charged an independent panel of experts – under the chairmanship of the former Algerian foreign minister Lakhdar Brahimi – with a comprehensive analysis of the abilities and capacities of the UN in the field of peacekeeping. The experts were also requested to formulate recommendations on how to address the existing shortcomings in UN peacekeeping and improve its operational capabilities. The report, presented in summer 2000 and passed on to both the General Assembly and the Security Council (Brahimi, 2000) is characterized by a frankness that is unusual in such documents. The first paragraph states that:

> The United Nations was founded, in the words of its Charter, in order to 'save succeeding generations from the scourge of war.' Meeting this challenge is the most important function of the Organization, and, to a very significant degree, the yardstick by which it is judged by the peoples it exists to serve. Over the last decade, the United Nations has repeatedly failed to meet the challenge; and it can do no better today.

Implementation of internal recommendations occurred comparatively quickly, but member states somewhat dragged their feet on the measures left for their implementation. In October 2000, and then again in June 2001, the Secretary-General presented reports on the status of his own efforts, the decisions already taken, and the remaining obstacles (Annan, 2000a; 2001). Included in the June 2001 report were proposals from the Special Committee on Peacekeeping Operations and the recommendations of an external group of professional management consultants. (This latter group also conducted the first tests of effectiveness and economic viability to be undertaken on a UN department, in this case the DPKO.) The fifty-seven recommendations of the Brahimi Report can be grouped into three categories:

- first, reminders that a fundamental re-orientation in the creation of the political and strategic framing conditions for peacekeeping missions is necessary;

- second, demands that the DPKO create the necessary personnel and structural preconditions for the execution of complex peace missions;
- third, demands for tangible results from the member states.

Complex peacekeeping missions have often failed as a result of their mandates being unrealistic and impossible for troops to fulfil. It was also often hard to differentiate the precept of neutrality – eminently important for the success of peacekeeping missions – from mere indifference. The Brahimi Report emphasized that no failure had shaken the credibility of UN peacekeeping missions more seriously than their constant hesitation to differentiate between victim and aggressor.

What is striking is that nearly all Security Council resolutions concerning international peace and security have cited 'threats' to the peace, i.e. they have utilised the weakest category in Article 39. The term 'breach of the peace' has been used in only four cases, and acts of aggression are mentioned only where they are regarded as constituting a threat to the peace. The panel members thus stressed to the Secretary-General the imperative need to avoid telling the Security Council only what it wants to hear, and being forthright about what it must know when determining the scope of a mission. Co-ordination between the Security Council (where decisions are made) and the Secretariat (where planning and implementation is organized) must be improved and intensified. Similarly, troop-contributing member states must be included during the phase of creating the mandate in the Security Council. More than just having a clear mandate, the peacekeeping troops must also be in a position where they can execute that mandate with robust measures if necessary. The experience of a number of UN-led and NATO-led peacekeeping missions has demonstrated that a peacekeeping force that is armed with a clear mandate and suitable deterrent armaments is involved in far fewer combat situations (and is more successful in fulfilling its mandate) than a poorly armed force with convoluted rules of engagement.

Standby Capabilities

The period immediately following a ceasefire is of decisive importance to a peace mission's success. Accordingly, the Brahimi Report recommends that classical peacekeeping operations should be deployed within thirty days (or for more complex operations, within ninety days) of a Security Council Resolution to that end. The report also recommends that the Secretary-General should be authorized to begin recruiting personnel and to begin using financial resources as soon as a Security Council mandate is in sight. The report also suggests that leadership training for missions should be improved, and that mission leadership should be brought together earlier in the planning process for the purposes of better co-ordinating of their respective tasks. The rapid availability and readiness of peacekeeping personnel is, however, also tied to the readiness of member states to volunteer such forces, and speedy and effective participation by member states is presupposed on the notion that they possess the necessary capacities to have such personnel available. The UN Standby Arrangement System (UNSAS) has been under active construction since the mid-1990s in an effort to abate the challenge of sourcing available peacekeeping personnel. UNSAS is a data bank of member states' capacities that they wish to make available to the UN. The resources registered by member states can be differentiated into operational units, including but not limited to: infantry, air-defence and artillery units, support units such as command and signal troops, logistics units, and specially-qualified individuals such as military observers, refugee aides, infrastructure experts, medical specialists, administrative experts, and judges. In total, member states have registered approximately 150,000 personnel with UNSAS. In spite of this impressive number, there still exist serious deficiencies with respect to particular specialties and equipment. An overwhelming number of the available forces consist of operational units, and of these, most are light infantry. Most of these forces come from developing countries and have only the most skeletal equipment of their own, and an extremely limited or non-existent capacity to supply their own logistical needs. These support units are very expensive – because of the qualifications and specialized technical capabilities they need – and can usually be supplied only by the wealthier industrialized countries, but it remains the case that they are not being provided in the necessary numbers. As a result, UNSAS has turned out to be less efficient than expected in practice. Member states' commitments were not that reliable and capabilities reported to UNSAS have often been used in other frameworks. This is especially true for the expensive force enablers and multipliers owned by the industrialized countries. They tend to deploy these capacities in mandated missions under the control of EU or NATO rather than providing them for UN missions. Force generation for UN peace missions continues to be difficult work for the Secretariat and often causes delays to the deployment of peace missions.

The multinational Standby High Readiness Brigade (SHIRBRIG) is one such symptomatic example of the lacking preparedness of wealthier industrialized member states to provide for UN peace missions. SHIRBRIG's sixteen member states (Argentina, Austria, Canada, Denmark, Finland, Italy, Ireland, Lithuania, the Netherlands, Norway, Poland, Portugal, Romania, Slovenia, Spain and Sweden) had pledged for six earmarked infantry battalions or regiments plus all the necessary support elements for a possible deployment. SHIRBRIG had a permanent base in Hovelte, just north of Copenhagen, in Denmark, with a 15-person multinational Planning Element. The other fifty or so members of the brigade staff (as well as the actual troop units) remained stationed in their home states. SHIRBRIG was registered ready with UNSAS in January 2000. SHIRBRIG was first deployed with the UN Mission in Ethiopia and Eritrea (UNMEE) in early 2001; in the subsequent years SHIRBRIG supported UNMIL in Liberia as well as UNAMIS and UNMIS in Sudan (primarily with HQ and planning capacities, since member states refused to make troops available for deployment). In 2008, however, SHIRBRIG member states surprisingly decided to terminate all activities with the UN and the African Union. By the end of June 2009 SHIRBRIG was closed, not least due a priority shift among some of its member states to assign their shrinking capacities to other arrangements like EU Battlegroups or the NATO Response Force (NRF). SHIRBRIG should serve as a valuable example when, in the future, regional organizations such as the EU are considered for UN peace missions (see Koops, 2007).

Some better experience has been had with member states providing 'on-call' lists to the Secretariat. These lists name military and civilian experts who can be made available within the space of seven days for mission preparation. The introduction of new logistical standards and the creation of the UN Logistics Base (UNLB) in Brindisi, Italy, also improved more rapid deployment and better supply of missions in the field.

In the end, adequate and reliable financing is one of the decisive factors in the success of a peace mission. In the past, the refusal to deliver funds – especially by large industrialized countries – contributed significantly to financial crises in the UN's peacekeeping activities. The UN has been in debt to a number of personnel-contributing states for considerable sums for many years. Peace missions are all financed through their own individual budgets, which must be co-operatively established by member states. In December 2000, after years of difficult negotiations, member states succeeded in reforming the financing regulations for peacekeeping missions (which dated from 1973) to reduce dependency on a few main contributors, and to distribute the burden according to a ten-part scale. This new regulation was possible only after the USA was able to reduce its peace mission financing to 25 per cent of the overall costs (as a consequence of which the USA became relatively reliable in its payments of the regular contribution) and because a number of other member states declared themselves willing to pay more into the UN's coffers. This constituted a serious improvement in the future operational capacity of the UN in the area of peacekeeping.

Changes within the Secretariat

The UN has had to undergo hard learning processes in terms of successfully adjusting its peacekeeping concept to the requirements of new and increasingly complex types of deployments. The surge in peacekeeping at the end of the Cold War rapidly overcharged a Secretariat that was not prepared to cope with these new kinds of challenges. The DPKO was desperately undermanned with regard to the operational guidance and supervision of tens of thousands of soldiers and civilians in a growing number of missions that no longer worked according to the principles of classical peacekeeping, and it also lacked experience and the necessary doctrine for large-scale deployments to ongoing conflicts as well as to fragile post-conflict situations. After initial success in Namibia and Cambodia, the setbacks suffered in Somalia, Rwanda, and the Balkans highlighted the need for new structures, new procedures, and new capabilities to meet the new requirements.

The creation of the Executive Committee on Peace and Security (ECPS) – launched by Secretary-General Kofi Annan in 1997 – was one of the first major peacekeeping reform efforts. Convened under the auspices of the Department of Political Affairs (DPA), ECPS has since been working as a kind of system-wide framework of co-ordination for all stakeholders in UN peace efforts. The changing compositions of UN peace missions has since been reflected in the DPKO with measures such as the implementations of a police division, a mine action service, field logistics and other relevant branches. The former lessons learned unit has been upgraded into a Policy, Evaluation and Training Division (led by an Assistant Secretary General) and, in 2007, Secretary-General Ban Ki-Moon conferred responsibility for peace mission planning and conduct on two separate departments: the DPKO that continues to administer the deployments politically and executively and the Department of Field Support (DFS) that provides finance, logistics, technology and human resources to the missions (see Ban, 2007).

In 2008 the two departments jointly published a new concept paper reflecting the recommendations of the Brahimi Report and other key findings of DPKO best practice (see DPKO/DFS 2008). This so-called Capstone Doctrine intends to create a common understanding of terminology and concepts in the area of peacekeeping and to give some general orientation to Secretariat staff as well to external partners by sketching the basic principles and guidelines for the planning and the conduct of UN peacekeeping operations. It provides a clear view on how the DPKO and the DFS imagine a proper Integrated Mission Planning Process (ibid., p. 54 *et seq.*) or the 'Art of Successful Mandate Implementation' (ibid., part III). In practice, however, the concept has to be very flexible and has to be especially open to national prescriptions and caveats by the personnel contributing member states and/or co-operating institutions. Without doubt, successive Secretaries-General have made decisive steps forward in terms of reforming the Secretariat to manage the growing demands posed by international peacekeeping. However, any success in the Secretariat must be metered against member states' continuing refusal to provide the ECPS with sufficient strategic analysis and information (as was proposed by the Brahimi Report in order to improve DPKO's overall capabilities of preparing, deploying and commanding missions). The continuing problems with member states' unwillingness to sustain UN peace efforts suggest that further reforms steps are still required. Two ongoing reform projects, the 'New Horizon Initiative' of the DPKO and the 'Global Field Support Strategy' of the DFS will be considered in Chapter 8.

The Peacebuilding Commission

'Fourth generation' peacekeeping missions require precise mandates based on thorough assessments of situations and tailored to the specific needs of the target state. Over the course of more than ten years of 'fourth generation' peace missions, however, the UN did not sufficiently develop the appropriate administrative and operational capacities to completely master these challenges. The 2004

Report of the High-Level Panel on Threats, Challenges and Change (HLP) stated: 'Our analysis has identified a key institutional gap: there is no place in the United Nations system explicitly designed to avoid State collapse and the slide to war or to assist countries in their transition from war to peace' (High-Level Panel, 2004, para. 261).

The Security Council is responsible for managing acute crises of international peace and security, but after the initial crisis – once a consolidated peace or at least persistent security is achieved – recovery assistance generally falls under the mandate of ECOSOC. States that have been able to overcome violence but have not yet achieved lasting stability often find themselves trapped between UN bodies, in a vicious gap between institutional competencies and without co-ordination of relief. Approximately half of such states relapse into violence within five years (see Annan, 2005, para. 114). In response to this institutional gap – and to effect sustainable implementation of strategies for peace and recovery and to reduce the risks a return to war – the HLP recommended the creation of a peace-building commission (PBC) whose core functions should be:

[T]o identify countries which are under stress and risk sliding towards State collapse; to organize, in partnership with the national Government, proactive assistance in preventing that process from developing further; to assist in the planning for transitions between conflict and post-conflict peacebuilding; and in particular to marshal and sustain the efforts of the international community in post-conflict peacebuilding over whatever period may be necessary. (Ibid, para. 264)

Secretary-General Kofi Annan furthered upon this proposal in his 2005 report 'In Larger Freedom', which specified his own ideas of structure, functions, and working procedures of such a commission in an explanatory note (see Annan, 2005b). At the 2005 World Summit, heads of states and government decided to establish a peacebuilding commission (see World Summit, 2005, para. 97 *et seq.*). The General Assembly (A/RES/60/180, 20 December 2005) and the Security Council (S/RES/1645, 20 December 2005) subsequently adopted parallel resolutions on the creation of the PBC, thus bringing into being the UN's first subsidiary organ that reports to two main bodies. Both PBC resolutions requested the Secretary-General to establish a standing Peacebuilding Fund (PBF) funded by voluntary contributions as well as a small Peacebuilding Support Office (PBSO) with the Secretariat.

The PBC was established as an intergovernmental advisory body mandated to carry out the following primary tasks:

(a) to bring together all relevant actors to marshal resources and to advise on and propose integrated strategies for post-conflict peacebuilding and recovery;
(b) to focus attention on the reconstruction and institution-building efforts necessary for recovery from conflict and to support the development of integrated strategies in order to lay the foundation for sustainable development;

(c)   to provide recommendations and information to improve the coordination of all relevant actors within and outside the United Nations, to develop best practices, to help to ensure predictable financing for early recovery activities and to extend the period of attention given by the international community to post-conflict recovery. (A/RES/1645, para.2)

The PBC is required to fulfil two functions: (1) to develop overall concepts and general guidelines and (2) to tailor specific missions for specific states. In order to fulfil both functions the PBC meets in two basic configurations: the organizational committee and the country-specific meetings.

The organizational committee is the PBC's nucleus, comprised of thirty-one UN member states, including seven members of the Security Council, seven members of ECOSOC, five of the ten top providers of assessed contributions to UN budgets, and five of the ten top providers of military personnel and police to UN missions. To ensure adequate regional representation and the inclusion of states with post-conflict recovery experience, a further seven members are elected from the General Assembly. Each PBC member is eligible only for one of these five categories, which they serve for a renewable term of two years. (Regarding the seven PBC members elected from the Security Council, it was decided in a separate resolution (S/RES/1646, 20 December 2005) that five of the seven should be the Permanent Five, and that the remaining two should be elected annually from non-permanent members of the Security Council.)

Country-specific meetings are not composed of a fixed membership but are comprised of members invited by the organizational committee, including but not limited to: the country under consideration, neighbouring countries, members of relevant regional organizations, top UN envoys, troop, and police contributors, donors and financial organizations. As of October 2011 six countries are on the agenda of the PBC: Burundi, Guinea, Guinea-Bissau, the Central African Republic, Sierra Leone and Liberia.

The PSBO – comprised of only fifteen staff – gives assistance to the work of the PBC and mainly serves as a knowledge centre for best practices on peacebuilding. The PBSO also assists the Secretary-General in the co-ordination of UN actors in the field of peacebuilding. Furthermore the PBSO is in charge of administering the PBF, which is supported by voluntary contributions from member states, organizations, and individual donors. In 2010 the PBF was allocated US\$1,96,000,000 to support more than 100 projects in fifteen countries

The HLP's original idea that the PBC should be an early warning mechanism for the prevention of state failure and/or civil war was not realized in the PBC's eventual mandate (during the World Summit debate, representatives from many developing countries refused to give approval for the creation of a commission with the autonomy to act independently). According to its founding resolution the PBC is only allowed to address specific country situations on request from the Security Council, or if the Security Council is not seized with the matter, from ECOSOC, the General Assembly, the Secretary-General, or from a country on the verge of violence. All PBC activities and expressions must be based on consensus and PBC proposals are non-binding. The PBC is by no means empowered to proactively pursue peacebuilding efforts. On the contrary, it is dominated by the Security Council and its permanent members, and as an intergovernmental body it is subject to the national interests and opportunistic calculations of its members. On the other hand, the PBC is a unique body bringing together all relevant actors and involving them in developing state-specific strategies for economic and social recovery as well as for state building processes.

To date, the PBC has achieved progress in Sierra Leone and Burundi, the first two states under its consideration. The situations in Guinea-Bissau and the Central African Republic, however, have deteriorated considerably under the watch of the PBC – mostly due to the dramatic demise of their internal situations. At the time of writing talks with Liberia just had begun. The three authors of the 2010 review report on UN peacebuilding architecture draw a sobering balance, when they state that 'despite committed and dedicated efforts, the hopes that accompanied the founding resolutions have yet to be realized' (Anderson *et al.*, 2010, p. 3). The report criticizes the PBC's limited interaction with the Security Council and other key players in the UN system, and noted the lack of synergies and inadequate weight of the PBSO within the Secretariat. Peacebuilding in the UN is at a cross-roads and enhanced efforts are required from member states to address post-conflict situations in a comprehensive and determined manner. Some approaches to this end will be discussed in Chapter 8.

Remaining Challenges

Although there have been some significant and positive developments, peacekeeping has experienced some sizable crises and tests with respect to its original areas of responsibility. The industrialized states in particular – who have their own functional security organizations such as NATO and EU and are able to form effective ad hoc coalitions – have lost confidence in the UN's ability to handle the political and military leadership of complex peace missions. Hesitation or refusal to provide human, material, and financial support to UN peace missions has consequently shifted competences from the Security Council to regional alliances, as has been the case in the Balkans and in Afghanistan where Security Council authority has been limited to granting mandates (which essentially amounts to the adoption and endorsement of agreements reached outside the Security Council's procedures).

During the first decade of the new century, industrialized countries have increasingly focused on mandated missions in their own areas of interest. For instance, NATO has deployed more troops to Afghanistan than the UN has deployed to sixteen missions worldwide. At the same time, general support for the UN has more and more been limited to small-scale participation in UN peace-keeping missions, and such support has often been manifest in the form of merely symbolic support to UN operations in Africa. Thus a kind of two-tier system of peacekeeping has been created, visible in the basic types of missions that have emerged and distinguishable by the institutional responsibility for their establishment and command:

- UN-led missions still form the largest number of international peace operations. Such missions are based a Security Council mandate to which member states contribute personnel and capabilities on the request of the Secretary-General. The Secretary-General carries the political responsibility for the conduct of the mission, and usually appoints a Special Representative (SRSG) as the civilian Head of Mission, a Force Commander, and a Police Commissioner (if required). Operational planning, formulation of the rules of engagement (RoE), and the clarification of all political, legal, organizational and administrative questions is conducted by the relevant Departments of the Secretariat, particularly the DPKO and the DFS. The financing of all UN-led missions is contributed by member states according to the scale of assessments adopted by the General Assembly (see A/64/220/Add.1, December 2009).
- During the course of the 1990s many industrialized countries started to resist assigning their troops/civilian personnel to the UN, preferring instead to conduct missions in the frameworks of regional organizations (i.e. NATO or EU). Such missions are mandated by the Security Council under Chapter VII, but are conducted independently in terms of political responsibility and the modes of conduct. At a first glance, 'stand-alone missions' – such as the EU-led EUFOR Althea in Bosnia-Herzegovina, or NATO-led KFOR in Kosovo or ISAF in Afghanistan – are advantageous for the UN because it removes primary responsibility for the risks and costs of the missions outside the organization. Closer consideration, however, demonstrates that the industrialized countries are utilizing their expensive capabilities in their own areas of interest while refusing to provide the same high-value assets to the UN. High-tech missions belong to NATO and the EU, ill-equipped missions belong to the UN forces – thus the problems of a two-tier peacekeeping becomes blatantly clear.
- A third basic type of international peace operations is formed by hybrid missions, in which the UN collaborates with other organizations such as the AU or the EU. In the case of the African Union/United Nations Hybrid operation in Darfur (UNAMID) – which even carries the 'hybrid' in its name – the UN and the AU jointly run the operation on the basis of a single common Security Council resolution (S/RES 1769, 31 July 2007). Another hybrid example occurs when a UN operation is supported by another actor under a separate mandate, for example, the 2003 EU mission 'Artemis' deployed under a secondary mandate to provide a 'bridging force' in the east of the DRC until the arrival of UN troops. In another support operation in the DRC (EUFOR) the EU provided support to the UN Organization Mission in the Democratic Republic of the Congo (MONUC) during the potentially problematic presidential elections in the Fall of 2006. The EU also deployed to Chad/Central African Republic in 2008 to prepare the region for the UN Mission in the Central African Republic and Chad (MINURCAT). Hybrid missions allow the UN to co-operate with relevant regional actors in order to generate capabilities that would otherwise be unavailable to the organization. EU deployments, however, demonstrate the UN's dependency on the goodwill of the supporting

institution, which remains in full command of its assets. In the DRC and in Chad/Central African Republic the EU provided its support to the UN only on the basis of fixed end dates and without consideration of the potentially changing situational requirements in the country. The problem of two tier peacekeeping also occurs in those combined deployments, when two distinct missions are taking place parallel to one another without common objectives and structures.

The UN's claim to be a global system for peace maintenance with comprehensive responsibility, and its legitimate claim to the international observation of the norms and rules set down in its Charter, has thus been brought under increasing scrutiny. The accusation that wealthier industrialized states are using the UN selectively for the pursuit of their own interests has gained significant support, particularly from the developing countries' corner. The danger has grown such that the UN will become increasingly marginalized in the core areas for which it was founded. Such apprehensions go far deeper than the survival of the UN – they concern a fundamental question of principle, i.e. whether issues of world peace and international security will remain within the compass of a collective security system, or whether they will return to states and regional alliance systems. This question becomes even more urgent as internal conflicts with countless direct and indirect effects on the international system draw ever more military interventions on humanitarian grounds in their wake. Were such an option to reside de facto with states on an ad hoc basis to exist, it would sooner or later erode the international legal order that has survived so many other obstacles. Despite all the fragility of the UN system, there still exists a wide consensus among states that it is an indispensable one. The experiences with different generations of peacekeeping operations make it evident that the UN as an inter-state organization cannot replace states in the exercise of their responsibilities for the peace of the world. But it also became clear that states are in need of collective instruments to address the problems of inter-state wars, internal conflicts, humanitarian disasters, or state failures. Despite a number of severe setbacks, international peace missions under the umbrella of the UN continue to be necessary tools in a turbulent world in which new crises and conflicts tend to increase the demand for collective action (see Bah, 2009, i).

From the very beginning, UN peacekeeping has been a project that has had to undergo perpetual change and reform, and this will be true for the future as well. Peacekeeping and peacebuilding will be constituted less on the basis of a settled and accepted set of principles and rules, and more on the specific necessities of the target country. This will necessitate the establishment of new forms interaction between the UN and other stakeholders in the maintenance of peace and global stability, a challenge addressed by the Secretariat in its 'New Horizon Initiative' launched in 2009 (see DPKO/DFS 2009). Before this vision for a comprehensive reform of UN peacekeeping is discussed in Chapter 8, the next sections will examine the achievements and remaining challenges of the recent and ongoing reforms.

Sanctions as an Instrument of Peace Maintenance

At the same time – after the end of the Cold War – that the Security Council was beginning to be able to reassert its competencies with regard to using coercive measures against threats to international peace and security, it was also beginning the renaissance of its use of non-military sanctions. (Stremlau, 1998). Non-military sanctions can be used in connection with many different issue areas, and can include activities such as the cessation of all political or cultural contact, embargoes of every kind, and the criminal prosecution of individuals in war crimes tribunals (such as the International Criminal Tribunal for Rwanda (UNICTR) and those for the International Criminal Tribunal for the former Yugoslavia (ICTY)). The list of possible sanctions articulated in Article 41 of the UN Charter is not meant to be exhaustive; within the framework of the Charter the Security Council may use any measures it deems appropriate for the prevention or ending of disturbances of the peace. Sanctions are not international criminal punishments, but a means of exercising political pressure to move states to change their policies in certain directions. There are two basic models of how sanctions should work, based on two different basic assumptions:

- The first follows from the belief that the government of the affected country is a rational actor. Thus, if the costs of the sanctions outweigh the benefits of the sanctioned behaviour then the government (or the potentate or dictator, or whoever the sanctions are targeted against) will change its or his/her behaviour to comply with the Security Council's directions.
- The second model aims at the creation of political pressure within the target state itself. Economic sanctions, in particular, tend to affect the general population adversely; their suffering is then expected to lead to the strengthening of an opposition group or party and a weakening of the regime, thus leading to a change in policy.

Sanctions are only effective against states that have an interest in co-operative international relationships; they must have at least a limited investment in being part of a pluralistic political order. Isolationist regimes are comparatively immune to sanctions of this kind.

All UN member states have a legal obligation to implement Security Council resolutions pertaining to sanctions (Article 25). Member states may maintain relationships with the target state only in areas that are not specifically limited by sanctions. The Security Council can create sanctions committees (as subsidiary bodies of the Security Council) to supervise sanctions implementation. These committees (comprised of all fifteen members of the Security Council) oversee the states' implementation sanction measures primarily by receiving and evaluating reports requested from member states. Additionally, the committee considers submissions by member states requesting exemptions from the measures, and can also make judgements in ambiguous cases. Sanctions are now largely tailored to specific actors within a state, rather than being applied to the entire state. To this end, sanctions committees maintain lists of individuals and entities with respect to the sanction's purposes and member states can request committees to add or to delete names from the respective list. In the absence of the Security Council's own supervisory forces, committees can appoint independent expert panels or investigative panels to commission reports on sanctions violations, i.e. smuggling, trafficking of illicit goods, etc. (see Cortright *et al.*, 2007, p. 361 *et seq.*). Committees also may work with other organizations or with member states on a case-by-case basis.

The 1990s were often called the 'decade of sanctions' (Cortright and Lopez, 2000): the Security Council had rediscovered coercive measures below the threshold of the use of force, and wasn't afraid to use them. Before 1990, the Security Council made use of its right to impose non-military mandatory sanctions only twice (in then Southern Rhodesia in 1968–79 and in South Africa 1977–94). By comparison, the Security Council made use of its right to impose non-military mandatory sanctions thirteen times since the beginning of the new century. This surge in the use of sanction has been attributed to the increasingly complex demands of international peacekeeping. Sanctions were used in the classic way against Iraq, the former Yugoslavia, and Ethiopia/Eritrea, all of which were involved in inter-state wars of some kind. Sanctions were also used in Angola, Liberia, and Sierra Leone, where the goal was to force an end to civil war. In Somalia and Haiti, the purpose was to improve humanitarian conditions; in Libya, Afghanistan, and Sudan, sanctions were used in response to states' involvement in international terrorism.

Again, however, the balance sheet shows mixed results. The initial enchantment with this 'new' instrument of peacekeeping – more a manifestation of euphoria that the Security Council was able to make decisions at all than of a rational expectation based on examples of practical success – soon gave way to disillusionment. The very first set of sanctions, levied against Iraq for its aggression against Kuwait, failed to lead to a change in Iraq's politics. In Haiti, Somalia, and the former Yugoslavia (amongst other cases) sanctions proved ineffective even as a less-costly alternative to military intervention. Sanctions came under increasing criticism because of the grave humanitarian problems that often accompanied their (usually non-effective) use. A reasonable expectation of effectiveness is an essential pre-requisite to the legitimacy of international sanctions – ineffective compulsion quickly loses its legitimacy when the side effects are worse than the problem that the measures were intended to address.

Many of the sanctions applied by the UN during the 1990s lacked clarity of purpose and did not adequately consider the careful targeting of the measures (Kulessa and Starck, 1997, p. 4 *et seq.*). The less specific the sanction – above all embargoes, prohibitions on the landing of planes, and isolation – the more serious their side effects relative to success in the achievement of their goal. For example, the arms embargo on the former Yugoslavia had no detrimental effect, for a long time, on the Serbs' capacities for hostilities – it did, however, make it difficult for the Bosnian Muslims to defend themselves. The lack of a supervisory body led to countless violations of embargo provisions, partly caused by the lack of sufficient surveillance resources, but also the result of the intrinsic impracticality of a comprehensive embargo with many exceptions. The history of sanctions against Saddam Hussein's Iraq demonstrates that even when sanctions are applied in accordance with the two basic precepts suggested for their success – rationality of government lead and suitable conditions for the creation of internal political pressure – it is often the case that they can create more problems that they solve. (Cortright and Lopez, 1995). In Iraq, the increasing misery of the civilian population did not lead to pressure on the Hussein regime for political change, rather they increased his ability to repress his subjects. Saddam Hussein was able to use the dramatic humanitarian situation to brush aside the problem of his weapons of mass destruction (WMD) – the ostensible reason for the sanctions – and split the Security Council on the question of the sanctions policy.

Non-specific sanctions can have negative effects on the economy, the vulnerable populace, and/or the political opposition (Kulessa, 1998, p. 32). In 2000, the Security Council established an informal Working Group on General Issues of Sanctions in order to evaluate recent experience with sanctions and to 'develop general recommendations on how to improve the effectiveness of United Nations sanctions' (Vassilakis 2006, p. 4). In 2006, the Working Group published a short but concise report highlighting that in order to make targeted sanctions effective, 'appropriate action must be taken at all decision-making levels: the Security Council, the sanctions committee, member states and their administrative agencies' (ibid.). The Working Group's deliberations and recommendations on the design, implementation, and monitoring of sanctions – thereafter known as 'smart sanctions' – have been reflected in more recent sanctions measures, such as those applied against Iran (2006, 2010), on the Democratic People's Republic of Korea (2006, 2009) and on Libya in 2011. Regarding Iran, an embargo was applied on all proliferation-sensitive nuclear and ballistic missile programmes-related devices, a ban was applied on the export/procurement of any arms and related materiel from Iran and on the supply of certain conventional weapons, and a travel ban was applied against certain assets and on designated persons and entities (see Resolution 737, 23 December 2006 and Resolution 1929, 9 June 2010). Regarding the Democratic People's Republic of Korea, a ban was applied against the export of luxury goods to the state (see Resolution 1718 (2006) and Resolution 1874 (2009)). In the case of Libya a broad spectrum of sanctions was established including a referral of the situation to the prosecutor of the International Criminal Court, an arms embargo, a ban on flights, asset freezes and travel bans for the Qadhafi clan (see Resolution 1970 (2011) and Resolution 1973 (2011)).

Complaints by humanitarian agencies and member states concerning the negative side effects of sanctions led to the establishment of a Focal Point for Delisting. Created by the Secretary-General (pursuant to Security Council Resolution 1730 (2006)) the Focal Point attempts to improve transparency and fairness for individuals and entities on sanction lists by enabling petitioners to submit requests to have their names deleted from the relevant sanctions lists. The Focal Point assumed work in July 2007 and has since processed fifty-three requests, resulting in twelve individuals and seventeen entities being delisted (as of September 2011). For requests concerning the so-called 'Consolidated List' of Al-Qaida and Taliban sanction subjects, the Security Council established the office of an independent ombudsperson in 2009 (see Security Council Resolutions 1267 (1999), and 1904, 17 December 2009).

The notion behind such measures is for sanctions to hit harder at the parties directly responsible for the offensive policies, and to keep adverse consequences for the rest of the populace and any third parties to a minimum. The implementation of sanctions as a 'surgical strike' applied against specific targets in the framework of a consistent policy of avoiding escalation, however, requires clear legal and political rules. There must be a transparent decision-making process and a consistency of application, but there must also be an effort to anticipate and moderate potential negative side effects. It is also necessary to consider and address the potential limitations incurred against the rights of third-party states. Article 50 allows states affected indirectly by sanctions to present their problems to the Security Council, but there exist neither rules of procedure nor mechanisms for compensation to address these complaints. The creation of a compensation fund could contribute to a fairer distribution of burdens – and solidarity – within the member states community. The experience of the 'decade of sanctions' has created new perspectives on the use of this sensitive instrument that will remain on the UN agenda for the foreseeable future.

Disarmament and Arms Control in the Framework of the United Nations

The UN is also concerned with the control, limitation and reduction of member states' military power potential. There is a conceptual distinction to be made between 'arms control' and 'disarmament'. Arms control is aimed at the political control of arms processes through bilateral, multilateral, or global treaties; disarmament means the quantitative and qualitative reduction of weapon stocks and military personnel.

The Charter requests member states to protect international security 'with the least [possible] diversion for armaments of the world's human and economic resources' (Article 26). It is implied that certain levels of armaments are necessary, both for the implementation of forceful measures determined upon by the UN and for maintaining the right to self-defence as foreseen by Article 51. However, in political science literature, the function and effect of armaments measures are a matter of debate. On the one hand, there is the view that armaments lead to diminished security and exacerbate the security dilemma described in Chapter 2. But on the other, it is argued that a certain level of armament is absolutely necessary for the stabilization of the international system. Depending on which view is held, the value of disarmament and arms control will be estimated differently. Deputy director of the UN Institute for Disarmament Research (UNIDIR) Christophe Carle (1999, p. 17) describes this tension thus:

[d]isarmament can come to fruition only if the international environment is perceived as increasingly benign. But it is also true that disarmament itself is

part of the international strategic scenery. Its onset and progress can contribute to creating and reinforcing the very conditions that engender perceptions of security instead of insecurity. Unfortunately that virtuous cycle is as difficult to initiate as the opposite vicious circle is easy to fall into.

After the end of the Cold War, there were many successes in disarmament. Between 1990 and 1998, military spending in nearly every region of the world (with the exception of east Asia) went down, conventional and nuclear arsenals were drastically reduced, and countless disarmament and arms control treaties were signed or re-activated. The total share of the global product spent on military purposes, however, continues to hover at around 2 per cent – significantly more than is spent on development aid. Since 9/11, a number of countries have begun to increase their military spending. For example, the US defence budget was US$296 billion in 2001, but this number climbed to US$329 billion in 2002 and was up to US$663,7 billion by 2010 (see also Figure 4.2).

Along with disarmament successes following the Cold War, there also came a number of new risks to international peace and security. Proliferation of nuclear and biological weapons of mass destruction, along with carrier systems for these warheads, has increased. So too has the proliferation of small arms. Fifteen years after the end of the Cold War, the debate concerning the best methods for creating armaments stability has intensified. The methods available to the UN in the realm of disarmament and arms control are both manifold and limited at the same time (for an overview, see Brauch, 2010 BICC, 2000; SIPRI, 2000; Lang and Kumin, 2001). The UN's activities exist primarily in the realm of creating global agreements with the participation of as many states as possible (these are not meant to be in competition with, or take the place of, existing bilateral or multilateral efforts of individual states or groups of states). The Charter twice addresses the issue of disarmament. In Article 11, it is written that the General Assembly may 'consider... the principles governing disarmament and the regulation of armaments, and may make recommendations with regard to such principles to the Members, or to the Security Council, or to both'. In Article 26, the Security Council is tasked with the creation of plans 'to be submitted to the members of the United Nations for the establishment of a system for the regulation of armaments'.

Within the UN itself, there are a large number of offices and committees involved with these issues. In the Secretariat, the UN Office for Disarmament Affairs (UNODA) led by the High Representative for Disarmament promotes global norms for disarmament. UNODA organizes conferences, supervises individual disarmament regimes, and co-operates with related agencies like the IAEA or the CTBTO preparatory commission. Additionally the Office publishes the UN Disarmament Yearbook as well as occasional papers explaining the current status of disarmament every year. The General Assembly – namely in its First Committee 'Disarmament and International Security' – deals with questions of disarmament at every yearly session and has successfully passed several important resolutions on the subject, including 'Nuclear Disarmament' (A/RES/65/56, 8

FIGURE 4.2
World-wide military spending, 1987–2009 (US$ bn)

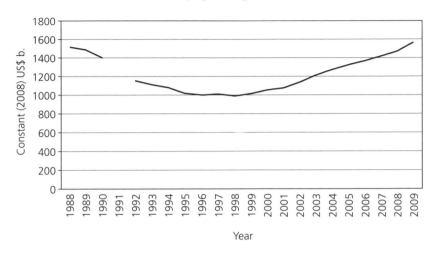

Note. The gap in the data probably reflects the unreliability of the data in this period.

Source: Data from Stockholm International Peace Research Institute (SIPRI).

December 2010) that urges all 'nuclear-weapon States to take effective disarmament measures to achieve the total elimination of these weapons at the earliest possible time'. In 1978 the General Assembly installed the UN Disarmament Commission (UNDC) as a subsidiary organ comprising all UN member states, but because of the need for consensus on all issues, it is often not even possible to agree on the agenda for the meeting, so that the conclusion of binding agreements on substantive issues is practically inconceivable, and over the course of more than a decade the UNDC has failed to produce any substantive results. The Security Council has been active only occasionally on disarmament issues. Its most prominent was the demand placed upon Iraq in 1991 to destroy all chemical and biological weapons and to submit to an inspections regime; the outcome of these efforts is well known. The Security Council has been trying to prohibit an alleged nuclear weapons programme in Iran since 2006. Of greater significance is the Geneva Conference on Disarmament (CD). The Conference encompasses sixty-five states (as of October 2011) as a single standing multilateral forum to discuss issues of disarmament, arms control, weapons of mass destruction (WMD) and non-proliferation. Formally, the CD is an independent body but it has very close ties to the UN – the UN services the CD through its Geneva Office and secures CD finances as part of its regular budget. Global disarmament agreements negotiated under the auspices of the UN include, but are not limited to:

- the Biological and Toxin Weapons Convention (BTWC, in effect since 1975);
- the Nuclear Non-Proliferation Treaty (NPT, 1968; extended indefinitely in 1995);

- the Chemical Weapons Convention (CWC, 1997);
- the Comprehensive Nuclear Test-Ban Treaty (CTBT, ready for ratification since 1996);
- the Anti-Personnel Landmines Convention (APLC, 1999);
- the Convention on Cluster Munitions (CCM, 2010).

Countless UN special organizations supervise specific disarmament agreements (for example, the CTBTO preparatory commission for the implementation of supervision mechanisms of the Test-Ban Treaty). In December 1991, the General Assembly established the UN Register of Conventional Arms, an initiative launched as a global confidence-building measure. All UN member states are invited to report their weapon trades to the Register on a voluntary basis. Since the Register was installed within UNODA in 1991, 173 states have reported at least once; bit reporting rates have declined continuously in the 2000s. In 2010, UNODA received only sixty-nine reports, the lowest number since the Register's inception.

The work of the United Nations in disarmament can be summarized in the following list of functions:

- the development of new efforts through non-binding exchanges of information and ideas;
- the presentation of different national positions before the broad forum of the global public;
- the articulation of concrete tasks for processes that might also take place outside the UN framework;
- the exercise of moral pressure on rule-breakers with the goal of influencing them to co-operate;
- the provision of organizational aid to interested states which will not or cannot maintain their own apparatus for disarmament or arms control;
- the introduction of a larger number of states to the obligations previously decided upon by a smaller circle; and
- the oversight of agreements already reached, through special organizations or regimes.

The disarmament environment at UN thus 'makes it possible for the initiators to float test-balloons, for the interested to develop an idea in discourse, and for the critics to articulate their objections and perhaps have a substantive influence on the initiators' (Barker, 1990, p. 183). It is also true, however, that many important steps taken in this realm have been at the periphery of, or even outside, the UN. This was particularly visible at the 2005 World Summit where issues of proliferation or WMD were largely left alone. The will of member states to use the UN as a multilateral forum and communication platform for disarmament arrangements varies greatly from one issue to the next, preventing fundamental progress in this area.

Prevention as a Task of the United Nations

Another important field of action is the prevention of crises and conflicts. In July 2000, the Security Council requested the Secretary-General to create a report on the prevention of armed conflict. This subsequent 2001 report by Secretary-General Kofi Annan contained twenty-nine recommendations for strengthening preventive thinking and the creation of long-term strategies, including, an increased reliance on the International Court of Justice and the Secretary-General, better co-ordination of the UN system with respect to the goal of prevention, the rapid implementation of peacekeeping reforms, and increased contributions to development aid. The report's recommendations were reaffirmed in the 2005 World Summit Outcome Document (Chapter III, Art. 74). In July 2006, the Secretary General delivered his 'Progress Report on the Prevention of Armed Conflict', stating that although there has been important normative, political, and institutional progress concerning the prevention of conflict, an unacceptable gap remains between rhetoric and reality. The report suggests that reliance on external actors can be crucial in helping to prevent conflict, but that success in this area is facing a lack of co-operation on the part of sovereign governments (see Annan, 2006a).

The term 'conflict prevention' tends to be sprinkled liberally in the strategy papers of international organizations and national governments, but it is a thankless task. When conflict prevention is successful, its contribution is often ignored because it is not often possible to prove which measures had a direct causal relationship to the cessation of a crisis or conflict. When conflict prevention is unsuccessful, there is rarely a serious analysis of the causes of failure. Instead, the issue is rife with general – and ultimately meaningless – conclusions such as 'too late' or 'not handled decisively enough'. The unique dynamic of each crisis is also usually noted – often with some justice – as being only partially amenable to external control. This, along with the rather spongy and indistinct character of what is understood under the heading of 'conflict prevention' leads to the issue being relegated to mere political rhetoric. In reality, conflict prevention is less an independent field of action than a new perspective on politics:

- First, conflict prevention is a cross-cutting task, in which foreign, development, financial, trade, environment, and security policies all play an essentially equal role, and can (and must) complement one another. Trouble spots such as Kosovo, Macedonia, or Afghanistan prove that a strong military component for the compulsion of peace is necessary, but that any success at stabilization may very easily be lost through inadequate civil capacities and a lack of sustained post-conflict attention.
- Second, conflict prevention requires the co-operation of the most diverse actors, including international organizations (IGOs), non-governmental organizations (NGOs) and states. Purely national strategies not bound into a multilateral concept can thus contribute very little. On the contrary, as the crisis management in the Balkans demonstrated, differing national strategies practically guarantee ineffectiveness.

- Third, conflict prevention in the potential conflict region must exist on several levels and be aimed not only at the political and military decision-makers, but also at various social groups. Such a structure, with multiple themes and actors, obviously requires an enormous amount of co-ordination at both national and international level in order to avoid repetition or competition and to achieve a meaningful division of labour.

In order to better understand conflict prevention, it is necessary to first ask some important questions: What are the chances of early checks on crises having any success? Has the current understanding of prevention been a failure, or is it no longer appropriate for the new security conditions? On which levels should preventive politics be active, and is it necessary in extreme cases to understand 'prevention' in a military sense in order to be able to react to novel forms of conflict? In response, it is helpful to first differentiate among some of the different forms of preventive politics (Varwick, 2003):

- Crisis prevention can be understood generally as a systematic and forward-looking effort of the international community or individual states to prevent potentially violent crises, or as a contribution to the transformation of violent conflicts into peaceful modes of resolution. Prevention politics are aimed not at avoiding conflict altogether, but rather at influencing those processes which lead to the use or escalation of *force*. Whether this should be called violence- or conflict-prevention, conflict transformation, or war prevention, is a matter of secondary importance.
- Chronologically, it is possible to distinguish between early or primary prevention of the emergence of a violent conflict and the prevention of the escalation or spread of an already existing, but limited, violent conflict. The prevention of flare-ups from concluded conflicts lies more in the realm of peace consolidation. For every point on the time axis, there are appropriate and inappropriate mechanisms to be applied, and these can also differ from crisis to crisis.

A further categorization follows from the concepts of operative and structural prevention:

- Operative prevention relates to measures taken at short notice in the hope of preventing or regressing an escalation. Instruments can include civil measures, offers of mediation, sanctions, incentives and so on, as well as military measures on various levels.
- Structural prevention, on the other hand, relates to mid- to long-term measures aimed at the deeper causes of conflicts and crises. Here, also, the list of available methods is very diverse: fighting poverty, sustainable development policy, environmental policy, arms control and, the encouragement of regional integration, but also security principles such as deterrence, balance-of-power politics, collective or co-operative security arrangements, and the strengthening of the Security Council's monopoly on the legitimization of the use of force that goes along with such arrangements.

The success of crisis prevention depends primarily on the capacity to negotiate, which involves knowledge of the relationships among various effects as well as the accurate ascertainment of concrete link-points in crises and conflicts. Above all, success requires the readiness and the willingness to negotiate, which in turn depends on many factors – at the political decision-making level, there are the questions of 'national' interest, cost–benefit calculations and internal support. At the international systemic level, the sovereignty principle and the prohibition on interference in 'domestic affairs' set strict limits on effective prevention.

A structural problem for preventive politics is the oft-lamented gap between early recognition of a crisis (early warning) and the practicability of early action to avert that crisis, a point made clear by the Secretary General in his 'Progress Report on the Prevention of Armed Conflict' (Annan, 2006a). Knowledge about the causes of conflicts, and the factors that allow conflicts to spiral into a crisis and then into a violent confrontation, is multifaceted. This is true for both the structural and operative dimensions. Diverse offices in ministries, bureaux, services, international organizations, and non-state actors prepare information, conduct analyses, and present recommendations for action – often making all this information available to the public. An unexpected crisis outbreak is generally the exception rather than the rule; crises usually have lead-times, amenable (and usually subject) to analysis. The connections between conflict and global inequality, poverty, lack of perspective, and the disintegration of state structures are well known, but despite this knowledge and resultant efforts at global development, the linkage has yet to be effectively addressed. In 2009, the worldwide figure for military spending was around US$1,5 trillion, but the figure for official development aid provided by the OECD states was only around US$133 billion. The goal for industrialized countries to reserve 0.7 per cent of their national product for development aid has been achieved in only a few cases since the 1970s (see Chapter 7). Regional conflicts have been analysed from countless different perspectives, and their threat to international security extensively described, yet it remains the case that there is still no sustainable solution in sight.

The gap between early warning and early action is dramatically evident in two crisis situations, the backgrounds of which have since been well-documented and will not be discussed here:

(i)   In the case of genocide in Rwanda, there was plenty of early warning. As previously mentioned, Operation Turquoise took place only *after* 800,000 people had already been slaughtered (a slaughter that happened despite the presence of UN 'blue helmets' (UNAMIR)). The UN chose not to authorize the strengthening of the 'blue helmet' force or the Force Commander's request to take preventive measures, and instead *reduced* the force when the violence began. At the time of writing, it is estimated at the UN that a deployment of around 5,000 soldiers in April 1994 would have been sufficient to check the genocide.

(ii)   In the case of Kosovo, there was no lack of suggestions for solutions to the conflict, but rather a lack of a common strategy. Thus it took nearly a decade after the suspension of Kosovo's autonomy for the international community to decide to proceed with military intervention. In the Balkan peace efforts, Kosovo was generally bracketed out of the discussion because it was clear that the parties would never agree over it. Too many attempts at mediation and civil mandates had already foundered on the refusal of the conflicting parties to accept any plan for peace, or on the Serbian government's refusal to accept mediation. NATO's military action in the early summer of 1999 was not a preventive effort, but a reaction to a humanitarian catastrophe that had been giving off warning signals for some time. The early recognition of the conflict at the expert level was unfortunately never implemented on the political side.

The international community has learned from its failures in Rwanda and Kosovo and now recognizes that there can be no 'black holes' (states or regions that sink into chaos without external interference) in world politics. Sooner or later all black holes become a threat to international peace and security. It has also been recognized that there ought to exist some established mechanism to intervene quickly in specific crises. Whether such an instrument would actually be used – if available – is another question.

The ways in which war can be prevented and peace secured are manifold. Our understanding of the causes of conflict is greater than it ever has been; the resources and instruments to deal with such conflict are – at least in principle – readily available. This does not mean that all conflicts are solvable, nor that the escalation of a conflict into a crisis is dependent solely on whether there is external engagement or not. Rather, it means simply that the prevention of crises depends to a large extent on the presence of actors ready and willing to take preventive action. For this to be the case, prevention-politics must be placed at the top of states' lists of foreign policy and security policy priorities. The main obstacle to the prevention of conflicts and their escalation into violence lies less in a lack of knowledge about potential conflicts and crises, and in the lack of political will to act when such crises are identified. The creation and mobilization of political will – how to transform a 'culture of reaction' to a 'culture of prevention' (Annan, 2002a) – will be the ongoing task of the UN.

The UN and International Terrorism

The UN reacted immediately to the 9/11 terrorist attacks. With a speed and unanimity that even UN optimists had barely believed possible, the UN made decisions and determined on measures with far-reaching legal and political implications. It seemed as if the unprecedented challenges presented by 9/11 were heralding a renaissance of the UN as the central actor in global crisis- and conflict-management.

The 9/11 attacks affirmed the comprehensive character of international terrorism. All of the global powers – and certainly all of the Security Council permanent members – felt existentially threatened by the events of 9/11, the challenges of which became an important test for the UN. Member states' confidence in the organization's ability to address terrorism proved to be a new starting-point in terms of reaffirming the organization's indisponsibility on the global stage (see Chapter 9). The results of this renewed confidence, however, will depend on the organization's ability to fulfil the two basic functions fighting global terrorism:

- First, and in the short-term, the creation of a political and legal framework for the immediate military engagement of terrorists, their networks, and their state and quasi-state supporters. Military actions, however, constitutes only one small part of a broad spectrum of measures in the proceedings against terrorism. The UN will also be judged on its success in developing and applying comprehensive legal and political instruments for the defeat of terrorism.
- More important in the mid- and long-term, however, will be the production of sustainable strategies aimed at combating the causes of terrorism, not least the support and popularity that terrorist organizations often find in poor and oppressed societies. Support of economic and social development, as well as of a more equitable distribution of the fruits of globalization, belongs to the sworn central tasks of the UN.

In the weeks and months following 9/11, the concrete initiatives and activities of the UN were concentrated on political and legal measures to fight terrorism, as well as on the stabilization of the new regime in Afghanistan. In these, and in the years to come, the UN faces a large duty in terms of addressing the multifaceted phenomenon of international terrorism.

Legitimization of the Military Action

The Security Council passed Resolution 1368 on 12 September 2001, one day after 9/11. Resolution 1368 called on all member states to strengthen their efforts in the prevention and combating of terrorist activities, and to develop intensive inter-state co-operation for this purpose. Resolution 1368 made clear that member states would be required to counter the terrorist threat by *all* available means. Furthermore, it reaffirmed member states' Charter-based right to individual and collective self-defence. On this, and on the basis of the much more extensive Resolution 1373 (28 September 2001), the USA and its allies deployed military troops against Osama bin Laden, the Al Qaeda network and the Taliban regime in Afghanistan. Resolution 1368 did not specifically articulate a right of self-defence against terrorism, but the whole context of the Resolution made it clear that this was the idea being expressed: a general reference to a right already explicitly articulated in the Charter, without any connection to the object of the Resolution, would have been utterly superfluous. The Security Council made it clear that a member state attacked by terrorists could use the same means against them as a member states would use against a state aggressor. The right to self-defence was dependent on establishing that an armed attack – as understood in the sense of

Article 5 – had taken place. Of utmost importance was discovering who carried original responsibility for the attack (in order to know where to direct the response). Establishing the source of an attack is usually relatively simple – in the case of an inter-state war the agressor is usually quite apparent – but the suspected aggressor in the case of 9/11 was an amorphous, decentralized, transnational network with no openly recognized structure or form. Nevertheless, the evidence brought forth by the USA and its allies, coupled with the public announcements made by Osama bin Laden and other spokesmen of Al Qaeda, constituted sufficient grounds for the defensive measures eventually decided upon.

More difficult was the question of how to involve Afghanistan, or rather the Taliban regime, in the military action. Afghanistan had not carried out an armed attack on the USA, but it had played host to bin Laden and had refused to extradite him even at the binding request of the Security Council. The state of affairs in Afghanistan – particularly the presence of the Al Qaeda supporting Taliban government – had long been considered a threat to international peace and security and had been the source of a long line of Security Council Resolutions (the last being Resolution 1333 on 19 December 2000). Taliban support for bin Laden constituted an aggressive action according to both the Declaration on Friendly Relations (24 October 1970) and the General Assembly's definition of Aggression (14 December 1974), and even though General Assembly outcomes are not binding on member states, the same criteria was used to support the ICJ decision that the USA's support of terrorists and armed bands in Nicaragua was illegal. The ICJ described the USA's arming and military training of Nicaraguan Contras as an act of aggression that might activate Nicaragua's right to self-defence; an analogous use of this understanding in the case of Afghanistan makes it very clear that the USA's self-defence against Afghanistan was legitimate. That the USA and its allies believed their actions in Afghanistan to be within the scope of their rights under the UN Charter is evident in the fact that all military measures undertaken by the USA in Afghanistan have been reported to the Security Council as per Article 51, and have been recognized and approved by the Security Council.

It has already been discussed that actions in self-defence do not require Security Council authorization. That the USA sought integration with, and approval from the UN, with regard to its defensive measures against Afghanistan carries essential political meaning. Resolution 1373 states unambiguously that terrorist acts pose a threat to international peace and security, thus the American military action in Afghanistan must also be considered in the context of addressing international terrorism. The support of the Security Council – as the possessor of the monopoly on the legitimization of force – is even more important in light of the fact that international law contains no regulations comparable to those in domestic law, according to which aggressors may be called to answer for their deeds. This means that military means, in particular, tend to be contested not only politically, but also legally. The support of the Security Council thus constitutes a further basis of legitimization. The activation of the Security Council, its ongoing occupation with the problem of fighting terrorism, and not least the fact that the states involved are acting on its Resolutions and observing the Charter's provisions, have all heightened the reputation of the somewhat long-suffering central organ of the UN.

A fight against an enemy who is difficult to identify is particularly suited to demonstrating the importance of a multilateral organization for decision-making and legitimization. The determination of whether a state lies under sufficient suspicion of co-operation with terrorists in order to justify military action should not be left to the sole judgement of the state desiring to take such action. If such sole judgements were have the final say, the global fight against terror would certainly slide into the mill of individual state interests and be ground to nothing. This decisive lesson, however, did not impede American action in Iraq 2003 – conducted by President George W. Bush against an allegedly imminent WMD terrorist attack – and conducted without Security Council authorisation. It later became clear that there had been no threat of WMD attack (indeed, there were no WMDs found in Iraq) and it also became clear that the US decision to 'go it alone' without Security authorisation had severely harmed the Security Council as global decision-making body and had also compromised international measures taken to address terrorism. In the wake of the 2003 Iraq War, violence against the International Assistance Force (ISAF) and even against UNAMA personnel increased in post-Taliban Afghanistan (and elsewhere) with aggressors blaming the 'War on terror' as a pretext for the exertion of military dominance over Muslim countries.

The Security Council's ability to achieve the authority intended for it by the Charter – that of being the highest custodian of international war and peace – is dependent on the will of member states, and particularly the will of the Permanent Five. Questions concerning the legitimacy of Security Council decisions in the 'War on Terror' have also reignited discussion about Security Council reform (see Chapter 8).

Other Legal and Political Measures

Transnational terror networks constitute a global threat to international peace and security. The defeat of such a threat lies with individual states that must take preventive and other measures (through legislation and criminal procedure) to hinder the formation of terrorist groups and the conduct of terrorist attacks, as well as bringing to justice those responsible. An effective collective procedure requires the existence of internationally accepted norms and standards, upon which state-based regulations can be based. Since the Convention on Offences and Certain Other Acts Committed on Board Aircrafts (14 September 1963) e efforts to create such internationally-accepted standards have led to thirteen UN conventions, countless resolutions and declarations of the General Assembly and Security Council, and a large number of regional agreements dealing with forms of terror and ways of fighting it (see Table 4.6 for a synopsis of the major international instruments).

Despite these advancements, there has been no success in producing a binding definition of 'terrorism'. The definition of terrorism is a particularly fraught debate: a number of states that support liberation movements in 'illegally-occu-

TABLE 4.6
International conventions on terrorism

1963	Convention on Offences and Certain Other Acts Committed On Board Aircraft (*Aircraft Convention*)
1970	Convention for the Suppression of Unlawful Seizure of Aircraft (*Unlawful Seizure Convention*)
1971	Convention for the Suppression of Unlawful Acts against the Safety of Civil Aviation (*Civil Aviation Convention*)
1973	Convention on the Prevention and Punishment of Crimes Against Internationally Protected Persons (Diplomatic Agents Convention)
1979	International Convention against the Taking of Hostages (*Hostages Convention*)
1980	Convention on the Physical Protection of Nuclear Material (*Nuclear Materials Convention*)
1988	1988 Protocol for the Suppression of Unlawful Acts of Violence at Airports Serving International Civil Aviation, supplementary to the Convention for the Suppression of Unlawful Acts against the Safety of Civil Aviation (Extends and supplements the 971 *Montreal Civil Aviation Convention*) (*Airport Protocol*)
1988	Convention for the Suppression of Unlawful Acts against the Safety of Maritime Navigation (*Maritime Convention*)
1988	Protocol for the Suppression of Unlawful Acts Against the Safety of Fixed Platforms Located on the Continental Shelf (*Fixed Platform Protocol*)
1991	Convention on the Marking of Plastic Explosives for the Purpose of Detection (*Plastic Explosives Convention*)
1997	International Convention for the Suppression of Terrorist Bombings (*Terrorist Bombing Convention*)
1999	International Convention for the Suppression of the Financing of Terrorism (*Terrorist Financing Convention*)
2005	International Convention for the Suppression of Acts of Nuclear Terrorism (*Nuclear Terrorism Convention*)

pied territories' want to prevent any definition that includes such 'legitimate struggles for self-determination'. It was this position – held by a small group of states headed by Pakistan and Egypt – that led to the breakdown of efforts to produce a comprehensive convention on terrorism in November 2001. The 2004 HLP described terrorism as 'any action that is intended to cause death or serious bodily harm to civilians or non-combatants, when the purpose of such an act, by its nature or context, is to intimidate a population, or to compel a Government or an international organization to door to abstain from doing any act' (HLP, 2004, para. 164). The formula for this definition was reiterated by Secretary-General Kofi Annan in his 'In Larger Freedom' report, but it was not endorsed at the 2005 World Summit. In October 2010, the Sixth Committee of the General Assembly established a working group with a view to finalizing the work on the terrorism convention. In its first report, presented only four weeks after its inception (UN document A/C.6/65/L.10), the Working Group proposed a draft text prepared by a small 'Group of Friends of the Chair' on the preamble and central articles of a comprehensive convention that included a concise definition of what has to be considered as an offence under the convention (Article 2). The draft sections as well as outstanding issues will require longer consideration and discussion by member states, a process that eventually might eventually result – as intended by the Chair of the Working Group – in a UN high-level conference that could eventually pass the comprehensive Convention. Although a Convention would surely have served the international community well in its past decisions, it must not be forgotten that existing conventions provide a comprehensive legal and political instrument under which nearly all forms of terror can already be legitimately pursued. States have, however, proved themselves exceptionally hesitant to ratify these conventions (passed by overwhelming majorities in the General Assembly) and incorporate them into their domestic law.

Under Resolution 1373 (28 September 2001), the Security Council made use of its authority to accelerate the implementation of a few basic regulations into state domestic law. Once it was determined (in accordance with Article 39) that the terrorist attacks constituted a threat to the peace, the Security Council then placed the decisions and requirements in the operative section of the Resolution under the auspices of Chapter VII, i.e. it made the catalogue of measures to be taken binding on all member states. Thus it is now every member states' obligation to prosecute every form of financial support of terrorism as a criminal activity, to freeze any related assets, and to forbid any and every form of direct or indirect financial support for terrorist attacks. The Security Council thereby set the International Convention for the Suppression of the Financing of Terrorism (passed in 1999, but ratified by only five states) into effect. As far as the active support of terror is concerned, it is required of all member states that they deny terrorists any haven or base of operations, and to ensure that acts of terrorism count as felonies under their national law. Furthermore, the Security Council appealed to member states to strengthen the exchange of operational information for purposes of prevention and prosecution of terrorist acts, and to pay more attention to the close connection between terrorism and international organized crime. The Security Council formed a Counter-Terrorism Committee (CTC) for the oversight of these obligations – all member states were required to report (within ninety days) any measures undertaken or decisions made with respect to Resolution 1373. Between 2001 and 2006, only 113 member states provided such reports to the CTC. Pursuant to Resolution 1624 (2005) – which followed the 2001–06 tenure of its predecessor Resolution) – only seventy-nine states have provided their reports to the CTC since 2006 (as of August 2010).

The Security Council has advanced considerably in the direction of a substantial progressive development of international law. A broad palette of legal and political measures, supported by verbal acclaim but in fact implemented only by a minority of states, should now be implemented in national law by way of compulsion. In the years following the onset of the War on Terror, the Security Council repeatedly resorted to Article 39 in order to impose new legal obligations on member states. In Resolution 1540 (28 April 2004) the Security Council obliged member states to take legal action to prohibit any non-state actors acquiring WMD capabilities, to prevent WMD proliferation, and to control the means of WMD delivery. Again, the Security Council established a committee to supervise member states' compliance. In subsequent resolutions (1673 of 27 April 2006, and 1810 of 25 April 2008) the Security Council extended the mandate of the 1540 committee until 2011 and demanded intensified efforts to promote the full implementation of Resolution 1540. Resolution 1566 (8 October 2004) again calls upon member states to bring to justice any person that commits or supports terrorist acts.

Concerning the formal legal pre-requisites, there is nothing about this rather unusual behaviour of the Security Council that could give cause for complaint. For the purpose of restoring international peace and security, the Security Council enjoys an extraordinarily wide scope of judgement, and according to Article 25, member states have all obligated themselves to accept and support any decision of the Security Council. Under Resolutions 1373, 1540, 1566, etc., the Security Council has executed a number of meaningful measures out of the endless loop of the ratification procedure and thus warned member states that they need to be conscious not only of their sovereign rights, but also of their obligations in the process of developing a workable international law. The immediate ratification of the Convention for the Suppression of the Financing of Terrorism by a large number of states can certainly be considered as a Security Council success story. Considering even the apparent limitations thus imposed on states' sovereign rights to self-legislate, many states have welcomed this type of compulsory development of international law as it provides politicians a method of by-passing domestic political objections to the implementation of such policies.

However, the Council's extensive use of Article 39 is not without risk. The Security Council is the watchdog of international peace and security but it is not the world's supreme legislator. Despite the large scope of interpretation applied to Article 25, the Security Council lacks any means of ruling over the national legislatures of member states. A threat to the peace entitles the Security Council to take coercive action against Member states, but these competences are exemptions from the fundamental principle of sovereign equality of all UN member states (Article 2(1)) and cannot continue to be exerted once the threat has been averted. Behaviours that were justified in the immediate aftermath of 9/11 can become problematic once the immediacy of the threat has diminished. Indeed, the ongoing involvement of the Security Council in elementary sovereign rights of member states has increased widespread distrust in the Security Council in general and its Permanent Five members in particular, thus leading to an accelerated loss of authority and credibility of the Organisation's centre of power.

The United Nations' Anti-terrorism Architecture

In addition to Security Council and General Assembly initiatives to allow for member states' legal use of instruments against international terrorism, the UN has also implemented an institutional framework of its own to counter terrorism. The Security Council has set up three committees: the Al Qaeda and Taliban Sanction Committee (Resolution 1267), the Counter Terrorism Committee (CTC) (Resolution 1373) that afterwards received an Executive Directorate (2004), and the 1540 Committee on the prevention of WMD proliferation. Together with the

Working Group based on Resolution 1566, these subsidiary bodies help to enable the Security Council to refine its own anti-terrorism activities. Providing strategic information and preparing decisions, they are the most powerful and effective bodies in the Organisation's anti-terrorism architecture.

Following the 2005 World Summit's unequivocal condemnation of all forms of terrorism, Secretary-General Kofi Annan published his landmark report 'Uniting Against Terrorism' (Annan, 2006b). The report recommended a number of counter-terrorism strategies: dissuading groups from resorting to terrorism or supporting it; by denying terrorists the means to carry out an attack; by deterring States from supporting terrorist groups; and by developing State capacities to prevent terrorism. The report catalysed further debate in the General Assembly and lead eventually to the adoption of the ever first Global Counter-terrorist Strategy (see A/RES/60/288, 8 September 2005). The plan features four major packages of measures:

- measures to address the conditions conducive to the spread of terrorism e.g. the eradication of poverty or the implementation of the Millennium Development Goals;
- measures to prevent and combat terrorism, e.g. by encouraging the CTC to co-operate with member states on the implementation all kinds of anti-terror activities;
- measures to build States' capacity to prevent and combat terrorism and to strengthen the role of the United Nations system in this regard, e.g. by taking action against money-laundering or by developing best practices to prevent terrorist attacks; and
- measures to ensure respect for human rights for all and the rule of law as the fundamental basis of the fight against terrorism, e.g. by the support of strengthening the function of the UN High Commissioner for Human Rights with regard to counter-terrorist activities.

In order to assist UN member states in fulfilling their responsibilities for the implementation of the Global Strategy, and to enhance co-operation and co-ordination between all anti-terrorism stakeholders within the UN system, the Secretary-General brought into being a Counter-terrorism Implementation Task Force (CTITF). At the time of writing the Task Force comprised thirty-one UN entities ranging from DPKO and DPA, to Security Council committees, the IAEA, WHO and UNDP. To fulfil its tasks CTITF has built six working groups on issues like conflict prevention, the prevention of terrorist WMD attacks, or the protection of human rights while countering terrorism.

As in any other field, UN counter-terrorist actions largely depend on member states' will and preparedness to comply with the legal framework established by the organization. Indeed, member states' officials and member states' reports are only too quick to agree that international terrorism constitutes a global challenge that requires a determined collective and comprehensive response. In practice, however, member states that take most benefit from a stable world order prefer national strategies or actions within the framework of their own alliances like NATO or EU. But as the records in Afghanistan, in Iraq, or elsewhere show, even the most powerful nations face constraints. The 'division of labour' favoured by Washington in recent years – in which the USA and its allies accomplish the military victory and then the UN takes on the dangerous, expensive, and obstacle-strewn work of repatriating refugees and rebuilding the state – is not likely to to work for the long-term future. For the purposes of the fight against terrorism in particular, and for a stable world in general, states need organizations that are capable of action, and the organizations need the active and long-term support of their member states.

Whether or not the role of the UN will find find broader recognition in the wake of international terrorist atrocities such as 9/11 – and the emergent recognition of this mutual dependency – remains to be seen.

Further Reading

Annan, Kofi (2002) Prevention of Armed Conflicts, UN document (A/55/985), New York.
Boutros-Ghali, Boutros (1992) 'An Agenda for Peace', UN document (A/47/277), New York.
Brahimi Report (2000) *Report of the Panel on United Nations Peace Operations,* UN document (A/55/305-S/2000/809).
Bellamy, Alex J., Paul Williams and Stuart Griffin (eds) (2010) *Understanding Peacekeeping,* 2nd edition, Cambridge: Polity.
Call, Charles T. and Vanessa Wyeth (eds) (2008) *Building States to Build Peace,* Boulder, CO: Lynne Rienner.
Paris, Roland (2004) *At War's End. Building Peace after Civil Conflict,* Cambridge: Cambridge University Press.
Paris, Roland and Timothy D. Sisk (eds) (2009) *The Dilemmas of Statebuilding: Confronting the Contradictions of Postwar Peace Operations*, London and New York: Routledge.

5

The United Nations and Human Rights: Normative Development, Codification and Definition

The protection of human rights is the second original area of responsibility for the UN. As with the first area of responsibility – the maintenance of international peace and security between states – the development of UN-based universal human rights was born of the experience of the World Wars. Just as the horror of the First World War gave force to the idea that states should no longer enjoy the right to resort to war, the Second World War and the genocide against European Jews (among other grave and large-scale violations) made clear the need for an effective protection for basic human rights. The notion that every human being has a dignity of his own – from which inborn and inalienable rights can be derived regardless of age, sex, religion, ethnicity, nationality or regional or social background – constitutes one of the founding principles of the UN. The effective protection of these rights was believed to be achievable through binding international norms and collective mechanisms for the implementation of such norms. However, the content of the term 'human rights' is so unclear as to make a commonly accepted definition barely possible and in turn UN protection of these human rights remains largely unworkable.

The consciousness of a close relationship between world peace and respect for human worth has had a long tradition in intellectual history, and was elevated further in the public consciousness during the Second World War thanks largely to the efforts of American president Franklin D. Roosevelt to include a comprehensive catalogue of human rights in the Charter of the world organization he hoped to see created. The idea of universal human rights was embraced by a large number of intellectual and civil organizations and was highlighted at the San Francisco Conference as a possible element of the charter. However, in keeping with the objections presented by the Soviet Union and the UK, it quickly became clear that the protection of human rights would find only a limited mention in the Charter. Compared to the chapters on the prevention of war and the maintenance of peace, which were written in an operational style, the protection of human rights remained programmatic and was not subject to a legal or institutional formulation. Indeed, states specifically created strong defensive instruments for themselves under Article 2(7) dealing with the prohibition of intervention. The notion that states – and their fiercely protected sovereignty – should be subject to external scrutiny and enforcement was a non-starter at the UN and states were hesitant to outfit their newly created world organization with constitution-like competencies in the realm of the protection of human rights. This becomes understandable when one considers that hardly any other form of state behaviour belongs more immediately to the realm of 'domestic affairs' than the way that a state or society deals with individuals, and it is precisely the goal of an international human rights regime to institute the legal regulation of this internal relationship, and to oversee its implementation. It is therefore hardly surprising that the protection of human rights has taken place precisely along the fault line between collective regulatory competence and the sovereignty principle and that the discussion has primarily concentrated on the problem of the exact parameters of core human rights – those human rights that are subject to universally valid norms and standards that cannot be derogated by states. The discussion also concerns the question of how these standards can be created and maintained, and in what form and by what means the community of states is authorized to act against individual members of the community in the case of a breach. It would seem to be appropriate first to regard these general problems of the protection of human rights before the specific way the UN has handled the situation is addressed.

During the course of the second half of the twentieth century the notion of universal human rights went 'global' in a completely unprecedented fashion. Countless declarations, treaties and conventions created a global normative framework to the extent that the Universal Declaration of Human Rights is now the most-translated and most widely promulgated international document in existence. The globalization phenomenon, not least in the realm of communication, has given human rights a prominent place on the global media agenda. However, in spite of both the general and specific acknowledgements of human rights (Kühnhardt, 1991, p. 29) violation remains widespread and the standards enshrined in the various treaties have generally failed to find their way into positive state law. Furthermore, the international struggle against terrorism has generally resulted in human rights being confined in favour of public security requirements, even in a number of democratic states (see Mertus and Sajjad, 2007; Robinson, 2002). Basic legal standards in the field of privacy, secrecy of the post, personal data, etc., are being more and more reduced, and new hurdles and obstacles are being built against those who might traditionally seek and be delivered protection under a human rights-based agenda. Indeed, some states use the fight against international terrorism as a pretext for intensified repression against ethnic or religious minorities, dissidents or political opposition, whilst continuing to find willing partners in their democratic neighbours (many of whom have themselves transgressed from being principal promoters and defenders to being similarly subject to scrutiny). A brief examination of the torture (and torture-like procedures) conducted in Abu Ghraib, along with the practice of targeted killings without trial and enforced disappearance and rendition of alleged terrorists reveals how muddy the waters have become.

The weakness of human rights lies in the still-inconclusive nature of the conceptual framework. The idea of human rights suggests a material and legal clarity, which, on closer inspection, simply does not exist. Borrowing from the historical development of the idea, it has become customary to speak of three 'generations' of human rights:

(i)   the first generation comprises the classical liberal rights protecting individuals against the arbitrary judgement or violence of state or society: the rights to life, liberty of conscience, speech, religion and the rule of law;
(ii) the second generation extends to rights of individual claims on and participation in social, economic and cultural realms, such as the right to work, to humane working conditions, to a materially-secure existence, or to health; and
(iii) the rights of the third generation aim more at collective goals: the right to development, to a clean environment and to peace. These are rights of solidarity, which none the less take the individual into consideration indirectly as the original bearer of rights.

The various understandings supporting each of these 'generations' reveal categorical differences in the perceptions of human rights that grow out of the world's cultural plurality and in turn seriously undermine the idea of an indivisible and globally-accepted standard of human rights norms. The western democracies tend to promote the civil liberty rights of the first generation. During the Cold War, however, the socialist states tried constantly to redefine participation rights in connection with an ideologically based concept of peace into socialistic human rights (Kühnhardt, 1991, p. 251 *et seq.*), and in the years since the states of the southern hemisphere have claimed that the realization of collective rights – especially the right to development – is a pre-requisite to the implementation of other civil rights (Howard, 1997/8, p. 99 *et seq.*). Many developing countries putting forward this third generation argument are motivated by one (or both) of two goals:

(i)   they wish to decouple their material claims on industrialized states from western conditions regarding western conceptions of human rights; and
(ii) the argument is to a great extent about defending against demands for participation and democratization coming from within: collective human rights of the third generation often present – for example, in the case of 'Asian values' – legitimizations for (neo-)authoritarianism and the stabilization of the authority of the indigenous elites.

As accurate as these objections may be, democracies' own practice regarding human rights has hardly convinced of their superiority. This applies first to the recognition that human rights may be violated even in mature democracies, as –

besides the difficulties shown above in the context of the struggle against terrorism – the annual reports of Amnesty International or Human Rights Watch make
clear. Even more, however, it applies to the problem of double standards, when
industrialized countries on the one hand condition development aid on the fulfilment of human rights requirements, and on the other overlook serious human
rights abuses when these take place in countries of great political or economic
importance.

Despite these ongoing and problematic issues, the UN might feasibly be the
best-suited global forum for the task of human rights/civilizational standard-
setting to finally be accomplished. It is suited to this task as is no other international organization. As in the case of most other matters of international concern,
however, the UN is dependent on the personal, financial, material and above all
political, support of its member states. In Chapter 6, the means and opportunities
available to the UN in the realm of human rights protection will be analysed in the
context of the discussion that has just been sketched out above.

Human Rights in the UN Charter

A universally valid list of codified norms and rules is essential for the effective
protection of human rights on a global scale. However, as has already been shown,
the founding member states of the UN acted with the utmost restraint and care
when framing the UN Charter's provisions on human rights and their protection,
so that no inclusion of a comprehensive catalogue of human rights in the Charter
was possible. Human rights did not even rate an article of their own, let alone a
whole chapter. The limited number of provisions on human rights goals or
obligations that did find their way into the Charter is spread out over a number of
Chapters and Articles dealing ostensibly with other matters. However, a few
epochal changes were in fact introduced:

- first, a programmatic framework for the development of international protection of human rights was created in the Charter;
- second, binding norms and mechanisms were integrated into the Charter,
  through which the organization was also given competence to engage with
  concrete human rights situations inside the member states; and
- third, in this way it was made clear that human rights, as a collective legal good,
  were to be removed from the exclusive disposal of states.

Thus the Charter of the United Nations became the first international law treaty to
be built – among other things – on universal respect for human rights (Boutros-
Ghali, 1995, p. 5) . Even in the Preamble, 'faith in fundamental human rights, in
the dignity and worth of the human person, [and] in the equal rights of men and
women' is emphasized. In Article 1(3), it is named as one of the binding purposes
of the organization to 'promot[e] and encourag[e] respect for human rights and for
fundamental freedoms for all without distinction as to race, sex, language, or reli-

gion'. Although human rights are articulated without concrete definition or description, the prohibition on discrimination contains a rule that can be applied with no need of further modification. The validity of a basic idea of rights for all individuals independent of their origins or convictions is a constitutive element of the Charter's framework for the protection of human rights (Tomuschat, 2000, p. 432). The prohibition on discrimination, which is re-emphasized in the operative provisions of Article 1(3), constitutes an independent normative element that creates an immediate legal obligation for the member states (Riedel, 2002).

The programmatic formulation of this purpose can be found in Chapters IX and X. First, in Article 55(c), the close connections among economic, social and humanitarian welfare and world peace are underlined. Then, in binding terminology, the United Nations promotes 'universal respect for and observance of human rights and fundamental freedoms' with special attention to the prohibition on discrimination. In practical terms, this meant that the organization's first order of business was to develop a definitional basis explaining which human rights and fundamental freedoms should be included under the umbrella of international protection. The United Nations fulfilled this requirement with the creation of the International Bill of Human Rights and other treaties following from it, such as the International Convention on the Elimination of All Forms of Racial Discrimination; the Convention against Torture; and the Convention on the Rights of the Child. A general obligation for standard-setting in the area of human rights can also be drawn from the language in Article 55(c) (Riedel, 1998, p. 25), which the United Nations has attempted to meet over the decades of its existence with an almost unimaginable number of resolutions and declarations.

The programmatic framework also answers the question of which organs and committees are responsible for the realization of this task. Article 60 places responsibility on the General Assembly and ECOSOC, which operates under the authority of the General Assembly. Article 68 requires ECOSOC to form functional commissions to support it in the realization of its multifaceted duties. The only commission of this kind actually specified by name is that for the promotion of human rights. In immediate fulfilment of this provision, ECOSOC formed the Human Rights Commission of the UN in 1946. Originally occupied with the development of a normative foundation in the form of the International Bill of Human Rights, the commission had evolved since the 1960s, and in particular in the 1990s, into an effective organ for overseeing the protection of human rights worldwide. It was supported in this work by the Commission on the Promotion and Protection of Human Rights, which was created in 1947 by ECOSOC as the Sub-Commission on Prevention of Discrimination and Protection of Minorities, and renamed in 1999. A second sub-commission for the protection of the freedom of information began its work in 1952. In 1946, ECOSOC also created what started out as a sub-commission, but what then became the independent Commission on the Status of Women. The newest functional commission of ECOSOC to concern itself with human rights issues is the 1995 Commission on Social Development. At the 2005 World Summit, however, after intensive discussions on the credibility and seriousness of the Commission on Human Rights, the heads of state and government decided to dismantle this body and replace it with a newly created Human Rights Council (see below, Chapter 6).

The Charter does not stop at the programmatic framework, but also makes clear that the fulfilment of human rights obligations depends also in large part on member states' readiness to take substantial steps to implement protection of human rights in their domestic realms. The General Assembly and ECOSOC are also given competency for concrete action. According to Article 13, the General Assembly can instigate investigations and issue recommendations as a contribution to the realization of human rights and fundamental freedoms. Article 62 gives ECOSOC the right to issue recommendations regarding the observance and realization of human rights. These competencies, which are neither supported by an ability to sanction nor backed up by the authority to check the human rights situation of any particular Member State against its will, seem modest at first glance. However, the decisive breakthrough is that an international organization had been given the right to involve itself in the human rights problems of its membership Thus the United Nations was given a potential for action that both complements and goes beyond the treaty obligations of international law contained in the International Bill of Human Rights, which the organization was able to build upon slowly over the following decades (Boutros-Ghali, 1995 , p. 9).

This is true in particular of the gradual overcoming of Article 2(7)'s limitations on intervention. The codification of the sovereignty principle and of the resulting prohibition on involvement in states' domestic affairs helped the states to balance against the organization's claims to collective regulation, especially in the area of human rights. Furthermore, in this area the Charter placed only very weak legal requirements on the states. Article 56 requires member states, in pursuit of the goals listed in Article 55, 'to take joint and separate action in cooperation with the organization'. This expression, however, amounts to little more than a stressing of the Article 2(2) duties of states to abide by the provisions of the Charter. Only the continued politics of obstruction in the case of discrimination was recognized specifically by the General Assembly as a violation of the duties in Article 56. In view of the weak legal obligations in the Charter, it is hardly surprising that repressive regimes could use Article 2(7) successfully as a means of defence against external criticism for decades (Weiss, 1996, p. 57), and that the operative work of the UN bodies dedicated to human rights remained relatively weak.

With the passing and ratification of each human rights document, the self-confidence of the General Assembly and the Human Rights Commission in dealing with human rights violations within states also grew. Involvement has become the rule, and the burden of proof has shifted so that a state accused of serious human rights violations must now provide public proof of its progress (Baum, 1999, p. 247) instead of being able to point to the prohibition on intervention. Not least, the Security Council's practice of intervention during the 1990s contributed significantly to the spreading of the belief that human rights and world peace stand in an indissoluble relationship to one another. Beginning with Resolution 688 of 5 April 1991 concerning the protection of the Kurdish population in northern Iraq, the Security Council has repeatedly described large-scale human rights violations as threats to the peace, against which it could intervene to the limits of its power of sanction. In December 2001 the International Commission on Intervention and State Sovereignty (ICISS) – implemented by the Government of Canada – submitted a report on the 'Responsibility to Protect' in which the commission underscored that it is the primary responsibility of states to protect their citizens' human rights. The commission also claimed that the principle of non-intervention would yield to the international responsibility to protect, in the event that a population suffers serious harm and the government is unwilling or unable to prevent such harm (see ICISS, 2001, XI). The 'Responsibility to Protect' was subsequently adopted by attending heads of state and government at the 2005 World Summit, as a reminder to states of their obligations to safeguard the fundamental rights of their citizens and to offer international assistance to governments to exercise this responsibility. Leaders also declared the determination of the international community to take coercive action against severe human rights violations like genocide, ethnic cleansing or crimes against humanity if diplomatic measures should fail (World Summit, 2005: paras 138 and 139; see below Chapter 6) The notion and substance of human rights as a collective legal good capable of transcending the state has thus been declared emphatically not only in the Charter, but also in UN practice. Indeed, the UN has succeeded in significantly expanding its options for human rights action over and against states via dynamic interpretation and an ever more decisive use of the rather modest tasks and authorities assigned to it by the Charter. The prohibition on intervention continues to be described in restrictive terms, but human rights have been defined to be no longer a part of those 'matters which are essentially within the domestic jurisdiction of any state' (Art. 2(7); Riedel, 2004, p. 18). The UN has thus become not only a forum for, but also one of the central actors in, the international protection of human rights.

The International Bill of Human Rights

Although the attempt to insert a comprehensive catalogue of human rights in the UN Charter failed, the newly founded world organization immediately began to work on the protection of human rights. During its first session in June 1946, ECOSOC created the Human Rights Commission whose first, and for a long time *only* task was the creation of an International Bill of Human Rights. Under the leadership of Eleanor Roosevelt, the eighteen experts of the Commission created a multi-step process in an attempt to resolve the basic contradiction between state sovereignty and increasingly binding international human rights, First, a Declaration should be written to express a universal understanding of 'human rights'. Second, international treaties should be established between states to protect these universal rights. Third, institutions and instruments should be established for the implementation and protection of these universal human rights. A first draft of a Human Rights Statute was created within just one year. After intensive discussion in the General Assembly's Third Committee and at the General Assembly plenary meeting in Paris, on 10 December 1948, the Universal Declaration of Human Rights was passed in the form of Resolution 217A (III). The Declaration was passed without opposition by forty-eight of the fifty-six members of the UN; the USSR and five allied socialist states, as well as Saudi Arabia and South Africa, abstained (on the making of the Universal Declaration see in detail Morsink, 1999).

The first two articles of the Universal Declaration codify the principle of equality and the resulting prohibition on discrimination. Article 3 contains the first specific enumeration of the human rights to be protected: 'Everyone has the right to Life, Liberty, and Security of Person.' The Universal Declaration continues with a number of other civil and political rights including prohibitions on slavery and torture, the claim to be dealt with according to the rule of law and to a process of fair trial, the protection of privacy and property, the freedoms of conscience and assembly, and the right to form a family. The Universal Declaration also established the right to a nationality and to claim asylum – neither of which was a self-evident proposition in 1948. Article 21 articulates the right to political participation, which has subsequently developed into the right to democracy. Article 22 constitutes the second main pillar of the Universal Declaration, in which it is stated that:

> [everyone], as a member of society, has the right to social security, and is entitled to realization, through national effort and international cooperation and in accordance with the organization and resources of each state, of the economic, social, and cultural rights indispensable for his dignity and the free development of his personality.

These basic claims are further elaborated upon in articles dealing with the rights to paid work worthy of human dignity, an adequate standard of living, education, and participation in cultural activities are all laid down. Article 28 promises all human beings the entitlement to live in a social and international order in which the rights enumerated in the Universal Declaration can be realized. One can already hear in this provision a premonition of the so-called 'third generation' of human rights. Article 29 in particular shows the influence of the Asian-Confucian culture by laying duties to society upon the individual, and making it possible to limit individual rights through laws that are in harmony with the purposes and principles of the UN. In Article 30, on the other hand, the extent to which human rights may be limited is articulated in the provision that they may not be abolished by any state, group or individual.

As a General Assembly resolution the Universal Declaration carries no legally binding effects for member states – but it was for precisely this reason that its approval was possible by member states. Implementation was the sole responsibility of individual member states, and the fulfilment of the Declaration's claims was subject to no external control. The Declaration's real triumph was the success of the Human Rights Commission in putting together a universally acceptable inventory of human rights in the space of thirty articles.

The creation of a legally binding treaty for the protection of human rights proved to be a long and difficult process, made even more difficult by the onset of the Cold War and the impossibility of consensus between the two camps, and it soon became very clear that such differences – not only in the material–legal realm, but also in the matter of mechanisms for implementation – would make the passing of a uniform treaty impossible (Boutros-Ghali, 1995a, p. 43 *et seq.*). The Human Rights Commission 1949 18-article draft for a Human Rights Pact contained no provisions on economic, social or cultural rights but the inclusion of such rights was specifically required by the then-socialist states (Strohal, 2001). At the request of ECOSOC, the General Assembly decided in 1950 (in Resolution 421 (v), Section E) that civil and political freedoms as well as the economic, social and cultural rights were interconnected and interdependent, and demanded the inclusion of appropriate regulations in the draft. The Commission then produced fourteen further suggested articles, as well as a further ten directives for the implementation and supervision of the legal duties in the signatory states. Legal problems, however, arose very quickly. Negative civil rights on the one hand, and positive economic, social and cultural rights on the other cannot be implemented and monitored by the same mechanism. Under pressure from western states, the General Assembly thus revised its original position and asked the Human Rights Commission to make two separate pacts. In order to protect the unity of the International Bill of Human Rights, it required that both pacts contain as many common regulations as possible and be passed in a common acceptance process. The final drafts produced by the Human Rights Commission were not accepted by the General Assembly, but instead subjected to an article-by-article discussion in the General Assembly's Third Committee. This discussion – which included all UN member states – consumed a period of twelve years during which time the various sides sought to win the votes available from the newest member states as they emerged from the process of decolonization. This long period was necessary in order to form a consensus in a heterogeneous community of nearly 120 states. Eventually, on 16 December 1966, these efforts produced the International Covenant on Civil and Political Rights (ICCPR), including an optional protocol for individual complaints, and the International Covenant on Economic, Social, and Cultural Rights (ICESCR), accepted unanimously through Resolution 2200 A (XXI). These treaties are also sometimes known as the Civil Covenant and the Social Covenant, for short.

The two covenants contain very different sets of rights. In the ICCPR, the classical negative civil–liberal rights dominate, which build in general from the prohibition on discrimination and the equal rights of men and women. The individual guarantees can be grouped into four different categories according to the scope of their application and the extent to which they may be derogated:

- *Protection of the individual sphere*: the rights to life, to freedom from slavery and servitude, to recognition as a legal person, to protection of the private sphere and of personal honour, to free profession of religions and world-views, to protection of the family, and to protection of children.
- *Protection of the social position of the individual*: the right to personal freedom and security, the liberty of movement and free choice of residence, to protec-

tion for aliens from arbitrary deportation, to the free practice of religion, and to freedom of expression. The freedom of expression is already specifically limited in the covenants so that war propaganda and the incitement to national- ist, racist or religious hate must be forbidden by law.

- *Protection of position in the polity*: political rights, such as the right to take part in governance and public affairs, the right to vote, and the right to equal access to public office. These general claims are complemented through the right to freedom of assembly and the freedom to form political and labour parties and unions.
- *Judicial rights*: the principle that no one may be condemned for an activity that was not a crime at the time it took place, and the entitlement to a legal and fair trial, as well as a right to the enforcement of punishments in a humane manner. Some efforts were made to limit the use of the death penalty: it may be used only on the basis of a law and in cases of especially grave crimes. It may not be used against persons who had not reached eighteen years of age at the time of the crime. On 15 December 1989, the second optional protocol to the Interna- tional Covenant on Civil and Political Rights for the Abolition of the Death Penalty was adopted. As of January 2011, it had been ratified by seventy-three states.

While the rights contained in the ICCPR can be transformed into state duties with- out further action, Article 2(1) of the ICESCR requires the state signatories

> to take steps, individually and through international assistance and co-opera- tion, especially economic and technical, to the maximum of its available resources, with a view to achieving progressively the full realization of the rights recognized in the present Covenant by all appropriate means, including particularly the adoption of legislative measures.

For a long time it was assumed on the basis of this formulation that states were obliged only to *promote* such rights, and that a large degree of freedom was allowed to them in this undertaking. This perspective, however, overlooks the fact that the ICESCR also includes a number of immediate positive rights, such as the protection of children, the right to unionize, and the right to equal pay for equal work. In spite of these utterly differentiated implementation obligations, the ICESCR's guarantees have been considered to be far looser than those of the ICCPR. This finds expression also in the notion that the framework of the ICESCR permits no individual or group complaints process. The ICESCR protects three kinds of rights:

- *Economic rights*: the right to work, the right to just and reasonable working conditions, the right to form unions, and the right to social security.
- *Social rights*: protection of the family and in particular protection of mothers and children. These regulations are enhanced by obligations placed on the state to create an appropriate standard of living for all people. Finally, the claim to a

very high degree of physical and psychological health, implying concrete duties for the state.
- *Cultural rights*: entitlement to education, which obliges states to provide free elementary level education. The right to take part in cultural life and in scientific progress is included, along with the right to scientific and artistic freedom.

As in the ICCPR, the general negative rights of the prohibition on discrimination and the obligation to the equal treatment of men and women are included in the ICESCR. Both covenants contain nearly identical Preambles, and both also articulate the right to self-determination of peoples in deference to the states newly emerged from decolonization.

The Covenants differ, however, in two essential points: the extent to which rights may be limited, and the process for their implementation. With respect to the limitation of rights, the ICESCR contains an all-encompassing general clause articulating that rights may be limited only on the basis of a law, and only for the purpose of promoting 'the general good in a democratic society'. In contrast, the ICCPR contains individual regulations referring to the way in which, and the degree to which, each right may be restricted. States are, however, also allowed the option of suspending rights in a state of emergency. Any state making use of this provision must inform the other parties to the treaty, but need not provide specific reasons for doing so, or the specific measures it has taken or intends to take. This particular limitation clause is among the most enduring weaknesses of the ICCPR. With respect to the implementation of rights, the ICESCR requires only periodic reporting wherein states must give an account of the status of the fulfilment of their duties to the Committee for Economic, Social, and Cultural Rights. The ICCPR requires a three-step process that includes periodic obligatory reports and also encompasses the optional state or individual complaints processes.

The covenants came into force on 3 January 1976 (ICESCR) and 23 March 1976 (ICCPR with first optional protocol) after each had undergone a ten-year adoption phase and after thirty-five states had deposited instruments of ratification for each covenant with the Secretary-General. As of October 2011, 160 states had entered the ICESCR and 167 the ICCPR. The optional protocol to the ICCPR on the individual complaints process has been ratified by 114 states. However, these two covenants serve as an example that the decades-long discussion regarding precisely which human rights are to be protected has yet to come to a definitive conclusion. Many states, (including most Asian member states) prefer a phased model, in which social standards must first be secured before civil rights can be considered (Thomsen, 1998, p. 25). Other states have ratified the covenants only with restrictions, such as, for example, the People's Republic of China, which ratified the ICESCR on 27 March 2001 with a reservation relating to the right to form unions. The USA has ratified the ICCPR, but not the ICESCR, which it signed in 1977.

Notwithstanding the long period of its development and the remaining deficits in its implementation, the International Bill of Human Rights constitutes a breakthrough in global efforts for effective human rights protections. On the basis of this document, human rights have been established in the global public conscious-

ness as a collective good, the protection of which falls on the same level of importance as the maintenance of global peace. The 'relativization from below of state
sovereignty' (Kälin, 1998, p. 12) that has accompanied the internationalization of
human rights has opened up manifold opportunities for states, international
regimes and the organizations of the global community to become involved in a
state's human rights situations without that state being able to appeal to a prohibition on intervention in their domestic affairs. A number of other international
special protection agreements have also arisen from the Universal Declaration of
Human Rights, and with these, a comprehensive codification of the human rights
deserving of protection has been achieved; see Table 5.1.

TABLE 5.1
Central human rights agreements of the UN

Instruments	States-party*	Signed but not ratified
International Convention on the Elimination of All Forms of Racial Discrimination	175	5
International Covenant on Civil and Political Rights	167	5
1st Optional Protocol to the ICCPR on Individual Complaints	114	5
2nd Optional Protocol to the ICCPR on the Abolition of the Death Penalty	73	3
International Covenant on Economic, Social and Cultural Rights	160	7
International Convention on the Elimination of All Forms of Discrimination Against Women	187	2
Optional Protocol to the Convention on the Elimination of Discrimination against Women	102	14
Convention Against Torture and Other Cruel, Inhuman or Degrading Treatment or Punishment	149	11
Convention on the Rights of the Child	193	2
Optional Protocol to the Convention on the Rights of the Child on the involvement of children in armed conflict	143	18
Optional Protocol to the Convention on the Rights of the Child on the sale of children, child prostitution and child pornography	150	17
International Convention on the Protection of the Rights of All Migrant Workers and Members of Their Families	45	15
Convention on the Rights of Persons with Disabilities	105	57
International Convention for the Protection of All Persons from Enforced Disappearance	30	63

* States, which became members of the treaties by ratification or accession; current status of ratifications available under www.ohchr.org.

Source: Data from Office of the UN High Commissioner for Human Rights (October 2011).

Comprehensive Protection of Human Rights

The early value placed on the development of a comprehensive protection of human rights is evident in the varied nature of the activities of the Human Rights Commission and its Sub-commission on the Promotion and Protection of Human Rights, the Commission on the Legal Status of Women (also founded in 1946–7), ECOSOC, and the General Assembly itself. Initial efforts predominantly sought to provide adequate help to groups of people who had been victims of frequent and/or serious human rights violations. By 1952, the General Assembly passed the Convention on the Political Rights of Women (drafted by the Commission on the Legal Status of Women) which was followed by a number of other resolutions and conventions that eventually lead to the legally binding 1979 Convention on the Elimination of All Forms of Discrimination against Women (CEDAW). The General Assembly and ECOSOC then turned their attention to the issues of human trafficking and the exploitation of sex workers; the protection of the rights of refugees and stateless persons; and humane conditions for prisoners (for an overview, see Boutros-Ghali, 1995, chapter III).

The UN's activities in the field of human rights have produced a dense web of standards and norms which might initially appear confusing, but these combined efforts have contributed significantly to the creation of human rights standards as an important measure of the legitimacy of state actions (Tomuschat, 2000, p. 435). Here only international instruments that are both legally binding and include mechanisms for implementation will be discussed.

Elimination of Racial Discrimination

The raw memory of the Holocaust, the racial discrimination of South Africa's apartheid system, and the emergence of newly independent former colonies, ensured that the International Convention on the Elimination of All Forms of Racial Discrimination (CERD) was given high priority at the UN; the drafting of which was considered even more urgent by the fact that the Human Rights Covenants (which would also prohibit racial discrimination) remained far from concluded. The Convention was adopted on 21 December 1965, and came into force on 4 January 1969 following the deposition of the required twenty-seven instruments of ratification. As of October 2011, 175 states had joined this, the first of all the UN legal instruments to include an international supervision mechanism and provisions for individual complaints processes. Racial discrimination is understood broadly to mean every differentiation, exclusion, limitation or privileging based on race, skin-colour, descent or national origin that has as its purpose or effect the prevention or restriction of an equal recognition, enjoyment or exercise of human rights and basic freedoms in economic, social, cultural or any other area of public life. A specification of the concept of 'race' has still not been presented, for very good reasons: such a specification might restrict the spectrum of marking characteristics which may not be used to justify unequal treatment to those that are merely biological or external.

The Committee for the Elimination of Racial Discrimination, formed on the basis of Article 8 of the Convention, starts from the assumption that membership in a particular group follows from an individual feeling of belonging to that group. The Convention requires its signatory states to pursue an active policy for the elimination of racial discrimination through the abandonment of discriminatory activities on the part of the state, the legislative prohibition of discriminatory activities on the part of non-state actors, and the promotion of organizations and programmes with integrative functions. As the high number of ratifications shows, the Convention has been accepted by the overwhelming majority of the global community, and is firmly anchored in state civil and criminal law. At the same time, even in the states parties (states which became members of a treaty by ratification or accession), racial discrimination has by no means been fully eliminated. In everyday life and speech, a number of deep-rooted stereotypes and prejudices exist – consciously or not – with the constructed concept of 'race', and are constantly reinforced. It thus requires particularly vigorous efforts to introduce a change in consciousness on the many social levels that cannot be regulated by legal directive. The UN therefore tried, with the World Conference against Racism (August 2001 in Durban, South Africa) to give a further impulse in this direction, and to keep the problem of racism firmly on the agenda of the state community and the global civil society.

Protection of Women's Rights

The equal rights of men and women are anchored in the Preamble as well as Article 1(3) of the UN Charter. Subsequently, and for the first time, the principle of equal rights was included in a binding international legal document – and this at a time when such a belief was hardly to be taken for granted even in the western democracies. Despite this progress there remained concerns right through the 1980s that the discussion of women's rights was not a legitimate part of the discussion of human rights in general and it has only been since the 1990s that the human rights dimension of women's rights – particularly in the case of violence against women (Gottstein, 1998, p. 82) – have routinely appeared in UN documents. Deriving from the Charter's provisions, the Commission on the Legal Status of Women has developed many activities, which have eventually led to various conventions, declarations, and resolutions of the General Assembly. The efforts of the Commission were aimed at the achievement of equal rights with respect to marriage, citizenship, equal position in education and employment, and political rights. A further area of activity was the creation of specific negative rights for women, for example in their role as mothers, or with respect to the fight against trafficking in women and girls, or to the exploitation of sex workers (see for many examples and further sources, Wolfrum, 1995).

Along with the progressive development of standard setting, the UN initiated a number of measures to advocate for the recognition of the human rights of women into the global public consciousness. For example, the 1975 'International Year of the Woman' included the first World Conference on Women in

Mexico City where a World Action Plan for the equalizing of the position of women was passed. Also at this conference the International Research and Training Institute for the Advancement of Women (INSTRAW) was founded as an autonomous research institute of the UN. A 'Decade of the Woman' began in 1976 and in 1980 another World Conference on Women took place in Copenhagen. The UN Development Fund for Women (UNIFEM) was founded and integrated into the UN's existing development programme at the conclusive conference of the 'Decade of the Woman' in Nairobi in 1985. However, the most important result of the 'Decade of the Woman' – at least in the legal codification process – was the Convention on the Elimination of All Forms of Discrimination Against Women (CEDAW), which came into force in 1981. Born of proposals put forward at the 1975 World Conference in Mexico City, this Convention brought together all the provisions that had until then been regulated in separate instruments, including the prohibition on discrimination, the requirement of equal treatment, and the requirement for special protection. The Convention has since been ratified by 187 states, and has been heralded as the central human rights instrument for women at both the Vienna Human Rights Conference in 1993 and the Fourth World Conference on Women in Beijing in 1995. As a strategy for the further development of the protection of women's rights and the gradual realization of equal treatment, it was suggested in the Beijing Declaration and Platform for Action – the conference's concluding document – that there should be a systematic integration of the gender perspective into all areas of life, a system entitled 'gender mainstreaming' in UN terminology. Gender mainstreaming essentially means that all state and social measures and actions worldwide should be examined with respect to their gender-specific effects. Despite this progress CEDAW remains one of the most disputed and contested human rights treaties and continues to elicit tremendous reservations from some (especially Islamic) member states. In October 1999 the General Assembly adopted an Optional Protocol the CEDAW that allowed individual complaints to the Women's Rights Committee. It entered into force on 22 December 2000 and counts at the time of writing 102 states parties.

There is hardly any field of international protection of human rights that is subject to the number of culture-related objections as the rights of women. In fact, at the twenty-third special session of the General Assembly ('Beijing+5') in June 2000 found rather sobering results concerning the progress of women's rights: moderate successes were identified alongside renewed attempts to weaken the norms and standards developed in Beijing. Further efforts on behalf of women's rights – possibly a fifth world conference – will undoubtedly be necessary. The long-term success of the Action Platform and its strategies will require more than goodwill, it will require a fundamental rethinking of the traditional understanding of the role of gender in nearly all societies. The example of the gradual progressive development of the idea of human rights, however, shows that such ambitious projects are, at least theoretically, realizable (for a provisional balance of the efforts taken in favour of women's rights, see Schoepp-Schilling and Flinterman, 2007).

The Convention Against Torture

The act of torture, and associated acts of cruelty and humiliating treatment and punishments, constitutes some of the most obvious violations of human worth and human rights. The abolition of such practices – which are unfortunately still widely used in a large number of states – is the goal of the Convention Against Torture and Other Cruel, Inhuman or Degrading Treatment or Punishment (CAT) which came into force in June 1987. As of October 2011, 149 states had ratified the Convention. Article 1 defines torture as:

> any act by which severe pain or suffering, whether physical or mental, is intentionally inflicted on a person for such purposes as obtaining from him or a third person information or a confession, punishing him for an act he or a third person has committed or is suspected of having committed, or intimidating or coercing him or a third person, or for any reason based on discrimination of any kind, when such pain or suffering is inflicted by or at the instigation of or with the consent or acquiescence of a public official or other person acting in an official capacity.

In the detailed provisions of its first section the convention obliges all states parties to take effective legal measures for the elimination of torture, and excludes all 'extraordinary circumstances' such as war, internal instability, or the declaration of a state of emergency, as grounds for derogation. The advent of the age of global terrorism, and the associated questions of whether and under which conditions torture might be acceptable as a means for the prevention of large-scale damage – such as in time bomb scenarios and/or the use of weapons of mass destruction (see Massimino, 2007, p. 282 *et seq.*) – raises significant and important questions. Any attempts, however, to justify torture or pre-forms of torture like painful interrogation and waterboarding are decisively rejected by the vast majority of states, governments and societies even under the auspices of anti-terror efforts. All instances of torture constitute a crime that must be met with appropriate punishments. The criminal prosecution of suspected persons can be undertaken by any state in whose sovereign territory a suspect happens to be located. As with the other instruments mentioned thus far, a special committee was set up for the CAT, which enjoys extensive authority to investigate cases.

The Convention on the Rights of the Child

The protection of the rights of children has been pursued by the UN since it's founding. In such work the UN was able to build on the work of the League of Nations (and the League's 1924 Declaration of the Rights of the Child) and also drew upon the rights of children expressly emphasized in both the Universal Declaration of Human Rights and the two Human Rights Covenants. Subsequently, the UN's Children's Fund (UNICEF) was created in December 1946 and has become one of the most effective subsidiary organs of the UN. The Declaration of the Rights of the Child was passed by the General Assembly on 20 November 1959 and was the first document of the UN to concern itself exclusively with the rights of children. The Declaration, in turn, served to initiate various activities for the mobilization of worldwide interest that culminated in the Convention on the Rights of the Child adopted by the General Assembly on 20 November 1989. The Convention quickly became one of the most ratified international agreements with sixty-one governments signing on during the first day on 26 January 1990 (Boutros-Ghali, 1995, p. 81). At the time of writing, 193 states (with notable exceptions being the USA and Somalia) have ratified the Convention.

Any person who has not yet reached the end of his or her eighteenth year of life is counted as a child, unless national law stipulates the age of majority as being younger than that. The signatory states are obligated to guarantee, or to protect through legislative precautions, the rights laid down in the Convention for all children within their sovereign territory. In total, the Convention contains fifty-four individual provisions, in which the classical negative civil rights, but also the economic, social and cultural participation rights of the child are articulated. The states parties have agreed to take all legislative, administrative and other measures including international co-operation in order to realize these rights. States must also submit regular reports to the Committee on the Rights of the Child to enable that body to exercise supervisory control over their progress.

However, the absence of any other review processes makes the Convention rather weak in reality. Once again, though, it cannot be overlooked that it was the same lack of hard enforcement mechanisms that made it easier for states to accept the norms laid down in the Convention. It was in this way that worldwide standards could at least be introduced, then later successively expanded and realized. On 25 May 200, after six years of preparation, the General Assembly passed two additional protocols to the Convention on the Rights of the Child intended to improve the protection against trafficking in and sexual abuse of children, and the protection of children involved in armed conflicts, respectively. Both protocols were signed by a large number of states during their first appearance at the UN Millennium Summit on 5 September 2000, and came into effect after a relatively short ratification processes in January and February of 2002. The additional protocols currently have 143 and 150 states parties, respectively.

Despite these efforts and progress, children remain the victims of grave human rights violations, particularly in the realms of sexual exploitation and child labour (Schellinski, 1998, p. 142 *et seq.*), and in military conflicts where children are forced to become child soldiers (Kreuzer, 2001, p. 308). The UN Conferences from the 1990 World Summit for Children (New York) through the 1996 World Congress against Sexual Exploitation of Children (Stockholm, with a follow-up conference in Yokohama 2001) to the 2000 International Conference on War-affected Children (Winnipeg) have made clear just how massive the dimensions of the problem are.

The Convention on the Protection of the Rights of Migrant Workers

Globalisation has resulted in more and more people migrating in order to find work outside their home regions or countries. According to the Office of the

High Commissioner for Human Rights, more than 150 million migrants live outside their home countries, often being confronted with working conditions far beneath ILO or WHO standards, and with the high risk of being victimized as a result of illicit recruitment and trafficking. In the absence of labour unions or lobbies, and often working without papers and permissions in shade-economies, these people often lack the materials or support to defend themselves against exploitation and abuse. The General Assembly adopted the International Convention on the Protection of the Rights of all Migrant Workers and Members of their Families (MWC) on 18 December 1990 in order to provide migrant workers and their families with a basic set of legal protection. The MWC is an attempt to formalize the status and treatment of migrant workers during the entire migration process from departure to return home (Article 1(2)), and also provides a category system for the different types of migrant worker. Part III (Articles 8–35) establishes an elaborate set of human rights for the workers and their families without distinction between documented (legal) and undocumented (illegal) workers. Additional rights for migrants with a regular status are anchored in Part IV (Articles 36–56); Part VI obliges states parties to promote sound, equitable, humane and lawful conditions for workers and their families. The Convention is monitored by a committee of fourteen independent experts (up from ten experts since the 41st state party) who are elected by secret ballot by the states parties. Thus the Convention imposes international standards binding on both host states and the states of origin. However, it took until 1 July 2003 (nearly thirteen years until the twenty-first document of ratification was deposited) for the Convention to enter into force and as of October 2011 the Convention's state party numbers only forty-five. The long process of ratification and the fact that no single industrialized country has acceded to the Convention suggests that migrant workers will continue to face significant difficulties. Also, despite the definition articulated in Part I of the convention, a common understanding and use of the term 'migrant worker' has yet to emerge, and the Convention's provisions concerning the rights of 'illegal workers' continue to often be in conflict with, and therefore secondary to, the legal systems of the majority of the industrialized countries. Subsequent conferences and consultations – on the initiative of the Secretary-General (2003), in the ILO (2004), at the World Summit (2005) and in the General Assembly (2006) (see OHCHR, 2005, p. 15 *et seq.*) – have also failed to achieve more than non-binding declarations of intent. Without improved support – and particularly without the improved support of countries receiving migrant workers – the Convention will remain the weakest of the major human rights treaties.

The Convention on the Rights of Persons with Disabilities

The records of human history show that persons with disabilities have often been invisible in social and professional life. Indeed, persons with disabilities have often been considered as objects of treatment, care and shelter instead of holders of individual human rights. At present there are 600 million disabled people in the world, most of who are limited from, or barred completely from equal participation in society.

There has been a step-by-step paradigm shift in some countries that has served to refocus disability awareness away from medical prevention and rehabilitation towards social equalization of the persons concerned. However, even at the UN questions of disability have been discussed more as a matter of social or health policy than as a human rights issue (see Degener, 1995). The 1981 UN 'International Year of the Disabled' lead to the 1982 World Programme of Action concerning Disabled Persons and the subsequent proclamation of the UN Decade of Disabled Persons (1982–92). It was during this decade that NGOs began disclosing and publicly naming member state violations and violators of disabled persons human rights and initiated calls for the equalization of disabled persons. The resultant twenty-two 'Standard Rules on Equalization of Opportunities of Disabled Persons' (A/RES/48/96 of 20 December 1993) laid the groundwork for the General Assembly to 'establish an Ad-hoc Committee, open to the participation of all member states and observers of the United Nations, to consider proposals for a comprehensive and integral international convention to promote and protect the rights and dignity of persons with disabilities' (A/RES/56/168 of 19 December 2001; see Quinn and Degener, 2002). Following the work (and draft resolution) of a forty-person working group on the issue, the Convention on the Rights of Persons with Disabilities (CRPD) entered into force on 3 May 2008. To date, 105 countries are states parties to the Convention. In its fifty articles the CRPD comprehensively defines the specific rights of disabled persons including equality and non-discrimination (Article 5), accessibility to all areas of social life (Article 9), the right to life (Article 10), equal recognition before the law (Article 12), access to justice (Article 13) and the right to live independently and to be included in a community (Article 19). The CRPD also obliges all states parties to ensure and promote these rights (Article 4), to implement them into their national law (Article 33) and to strengthen international co-operation in favour of these rights. Similar to other major human rights treaties the CRPD also established a monitoring committee (Article 34), consisting of twelve independent experts. Without doubt the CRPD is a major step forward for the equal recognition of disabled persons – the provisions in the Convention are tailored to the specific needs of disabled persons; they give clear orientation to the states parties' governments and societies to meet those legal, administrative and organizational arrangements necessary for a life in dignity and the Convention articulates binding standards that can be verified by civil society, the public and the media, and not least can be sued for by the right-holders themselves. However, it is too soon to tell if the CRPD will be successful, and the extent to which this new human rights instrument will work.

International Convention for the Protection of All Persons from Enforced Disappearance

The most recent international human rights instrument to come into effect was the International Convention for the Protection of All Persons from Enforced Disappearance. The Convention became active on 23 December 2010; thirty days after the twentieth state party (Iraq) had deposited its ratification document with the UN Secretary General.

The phenomenon of 'disappearance' of persons is long known and its reasons various, ranging from voluntary departure or escape from prosecution, to kidnapping, and as a consequence of conflict or natural disasters The issue of enforced disappearance as an matter of human rights concern, however, exists recently as a specifically narrow concept. As observed by Manfred Nowak (2002, p. 7) enforced disappearance in its contemporary context can be traced back to Adolf Hitler's 1941 'Night and Fog Decree', wherein there exists accounts of the arbitrary seizing of persons who disappear without a trace as a tactic of intimidation. Enforced disappearance remained in the global consciousness throughout the 1960s and 1970s as a tool of military dictatorships in Latin America but has since become a 'truly universal phenomenon, with tens of thousands of disappearances in all regions of the world' (ibid., p. 8).

Since the late 1970s the international community has become increasingly concerned with the issue of enforced disappearance. In 1980, the UN Commission on Human Rights created the Working Group on Enforced or Involuntary Disappearances (Resolution 20 (XXXVI) of 29 February 1980) comprising five independent experts. The Commission's original mandate – to examine relevant questions concerning disappearance – has since been extended to include assistance to families in determining the fate and whereabouts of disappeared relatives (see CHR resolution 2004/40 of 19 April 2004). In its non-binding 'Declaration on the Protection of all Persons from Enforced Disappearance' the General Assembly (A/RES/47/133 of 18 December 1992) condemned any act of enforced disappearance as an offence to human dignity (Article 1) and stated that, 'No circumstances whatsoever, whether a threat of war, a state of war, internal political instability or any other public emergency, may be invoked to justify enforced disappearances' (Article 7). Nine years later, under Resolution 2001/46 of 23 April 2001, the CHR established an 'Inter-sessional open-ended working group to elaborate a draft legally binding normative instrument for the protection of all persons from enforced disappearance'. In 2003, the representatives of forty CHR-members – plus a large number of observers – drafted a convention text that was later adopted by consensus in the Working Group. Subsequently the convention text was adopted by the newly created Human Rights Council on its first session in June 2006 and also approved by the General Assembly (by unanimous vote) on 20 December 2006.

The Convention confirms the prohibition of enforced disappearance and excludes any circumstances that might be invoked for its justification (Article 1). The Convention defines enforced disappearance as

> the arrest, detention, abduction or any other form of deprivation of liberty by agents of the State or by persons or groups of persons acting with the authorization, support or acquiescence of the State, followed by a refusal to acknowledge the deprivation of liberty or by concealment of the fate or whereabouts of

the disappeared person, which place such a person outside the protection of the law. (Article 2)

The states parties are obliged to ensure that enforced disappearance constitutes an offence under national criminal laws (Article 4), and also that widespread or systematic practice of enforced disappearance is considered a crime against humanity (Article 5). The Convention also contains provisions concerning measures to be taken by states parties for prevention of enforced disappearance and measures to ensure its criminal prosecution (Articles 6–12). The Convention also emphasizes international co-operation and mutual legal assistance between the states parties (Article 14), and the protection of victims. Article 17 excludes any kind of secret detention and Article 18 demands all states parties to 'guarantee to any person with a legitimate interest in this information' access to basic information such as information concerning the supervising authority and the whereabouts of the detained person. Article 24 defines 'victim' as 'the disappeared person and any individual who has suffered harm as the direct result of an enforced disappearance' and requires the states parties to ensure in their national laws, that victims 'have the right to obtain reparation and prompt, fair and adequate compensation' (para. 5 *et seq.*).

The Convention also establishes a Committee on Enforced Disappearance, consisting of ten independent experts who work according to self-established rules of procedures. As will be discussed in Chapter 6 this Committee has a set of relatively strong competences at hand that *inter alia* allow it to take urgent action at the request of persons with a legitimate interest (Article 30), or bring a case of widespread or systematic practice of enforced disappearance to the attention of the General Assembly (Article 34). The Committee is limited, however, in that it can only exert its competences with respect to cases of enforced disappearance occurring after the entry into force of the Convention (Article 35).

The entry into force of the International Convention for the Protection of All Persons from Enforced Disappearance marks a decisive step in providing a legally binding instrument to prevent this evil and to prosecute those responsible. Its eventual effectiveness, however, will depend on a quick ratification by the large number of its signatories (30 by October 2011), the entry of new states parties, and on the willingness of states to enforce the Convention in their own national laws and politics.

The Interdependence of Human Rights

The concept of 'third generation human rights' refers to international solidarity rights and collective positive rights such as the right to peace, to a healthy environment, and to development, which are all far more abstract and in many ways more vague than the individual liberty rights of the ICCPR or the participation rights of the ICESCR. The terminology of 'third generation human rights' first began to appear in the late 1970s and 1980s, but the underlying ideas are certainly much older (Esquivel, 1989). Political efforts relating to these third generation rights have their roots in the process of decolonization which took place in the 1950s and 1960s, during the course of which the number of developing countries increased dramatically. Commensurate with their growing weight in the General Assembly, new states used the forum of the UN to lay their demands for substantial support in overcoming their social and economic challenges on the doorsteps of the industrialized countries.

The December 1960 Declaration on the Granting of Independence to Colonial Countries and Peoples was aimed at establishing international standards of justice, in which the peoples' right to self-determination and to participation in economic and social development were brought into line with the UN's efforts for world peace and international security. Nine years later, the General Assembly reiterated this approach in the Declaration on Social Progress and Development (Resolution 2542 (XXIV) of 11 December 1969). The Declaration provided a catalogue of the means and methods for the formation of a global development process. So-called 'third generation human rights' were first addressed under that name by then-UNESCO Human Rights Division leader Karel Vasak in 1974, but it took almost a decade – at the time the issue was largely overshadowed by the East–West ideological battles of the Cold War – for the General Assembly to pass the Declaration on the Right to Development (A/RES/41/128) on 4 December 1986. In this declaration, the right to development is considered to be an inalienable human right, on the strength of which all people, and peoples, have a claim to participate in, to contribute to, and to draw use from a process of economic, social, cultural and political development in which all human rights and basic freedoms can be fully realized. In view of the polarized debate over the existence of a human right to development, the results of the vote were surprisingly unanimous: 143 votes supporting the decision and eight abstentions against one non-supporting vote (the USA).

Third generation human rights achieved their breakthrough at the Vienna Human Rights Conference in the summer of 1993. In the conference's unanimously adopted concluding document of 25 June 1993 – entitled the Vienna Declaration and Programme of Action – 171 participating states professed their belief in the universality, indivisibility and interdependence of human rights, and underlined such rights as significant to and necessary for world peace. Democracy, development and the observation of human rights were seen as mutually strengthening goals. The right to development was given a broad interpretation and precise content. A healthy environment, a general right to participate in the fruits of scientific progress (especially in medical and information technology), forgiveness of developing countries' debts, and the fight against extreme poverty were all named as goals or prerequisites for the international protection of human rights. Despite these aspirations, the results of the Vienna conference have been the subject of serious criticism from several sides. Franz Nuscheler (1996, p. 11) asks, for example, what 'development' in fact means and suggests that the vagueness of its description will be inflated into a 'right to everything'. Nuscheler further criticizes the 'lazy compromise' by which the western states have essentially won the agreement of the developing countries to the universality of civil and political rights with tactical concessions regarding the right to development. There exist also technical legal objections; for example, that third generation human rights are so extremely imprecise that they lose their legal character. The question is also proffered concerning whether states, which have a duty to guarantee certain rights to their citizens, can simultaneously enjoy the right to make claims of their own. This criticism, however, overlooks the fact that state-structural principles such as the welfare state or the rule-of-law state are clothed in abstract formulations and made concrete only through specific guarantees (Riedel, 2004, p. 28). In this process of concretization, the right to development functions as a representative for all third generation human rights, even though progress on individual and/or specific human rights has remained sharply limited. The Millennium Declaration of September 2000 and the Millennium Development Goals (MDG) oblige states to take concrete steps in the fight against poverty and illness as well as in the promotion of education, again underscoring the interdependence of the three generations of human rights (see Ramcharan 2007, pp. 456–8). Although it is still not possible to bring suits for damages arising from these rights, as soft law they have the effect of creating standards for the further construction and implementation of the international protection of human rights.

An overview of the most important activities and instruments the UN has undertaken or produced in the course of its efforts for a comprehensive protection of human rights shows that the phase of standard-setting and codification is nearing its close. After the entry into force of the International Convention for the Protection of All Persons from Enforced Disappearance on 23 December 2010 there is hardly any area of human rights for which international norms have not been developed and accepted by the overwhelming majority of states. What is just as important, however, is that in nearly all areas, the actual realization of human rights protection lags far behind the almost universal profession and recognition of these rights (see Gareis 2009, p. 37 *et seq.*) Aside from the difficulties already mentioned regarding universal acceptance of a codex of human rights and the resistance of many states and societies towards following such norms, in many parts of the world the simple lack of opportunities for ensuring of such rights – especially participatory rights – is also responsible for this state of affairs. Hence, the focus of international politics has to be on the improved observation of human rights and on the mechanisms for their safeguard and protection.

Further Reading

Alston, Philip (ed.) (2004) *The United Nations and Human Rights: A Critical Appraisal,* Oxford: Oxford University Press.

Amnesty International, *Annual Reports.*

Chesterman, Simon (2001) *Just War or Just Peace. Humanitarian Intervention and International Law,* Oxford: Oxford University Press.

Fields, A. Belden (2003) *Rethinking Human Rights for the New Millennium,* Basingstoke: Palgrave Macmillan.

Oberleitner, Gerd (2007) *Global Human Rights Institutions*, Cambridge: Cambridge Polity Press.

Smith, Rhona K.M. (2007) *Textbook on International Human Rights*, 3rd edition, Oxford: Oxford University Press.

Steiner, Henry J. and Philip Alston (2000) *International Human Rights in Context,* 2nd edition, Oxford: Oxford University Press.

Tomuschat, Christian (2008) *Human Rights. Between Idealism and Realism,* 2nd revised edition, Oxford: Oxford University Press.

Weijers, Hanna (ed.) (2009) *The Office of the High Commissioner for Human Rights. Selected Basic Documents and Background Materials*, Nijmegen: Wolf Legal Publishers.

6

Human Rights Protection: Institutional Framework and Code of Practice

The effective protection of human rights requires more than the general codification of norms and general appeals for their observation – human rights must be integrated into states' own legal systems, and there must be reliable mechanisms for the supervision and enforcement of these human rights. However, the same problem confronts the international protection of human rights as confronts any form of external intervention into the sovereign principle. As a result, states have avoided the creation of any overarching international human rights law and have instead turned to treaty-based options for human rights inspections and implementation. The competencies of the UN human rights committees have therefore essentially been limited to normative work. This chapter will first examine the core international human rights treaties and explore their different practices and applications.

The basic controversy concerning how to monitor states' conduct with regard to their various human rights treaty obligations was addressed with the adoption of 'state reports'. Such state reports obliged states to report regularly on the status of their implementation and observation of the agreed-upon norms to one of the committees formed by the provisions of the treaty. The state reporting process – a modality that works in concert with and protects the principle of state sovereignty (Tomuschat, 1995c) – was first developed during negotiations on the civil and social covenants, i.e. the International Covenant on Civil and Political Rights (ICCPR) and the Rights, but was first given effect as an obligatory instrument under the International Convention on the Elimination of Racial Discrimination (ICERD, which ended up pre-dating the civil and social covenants). There are now nine core international human rights treaties (see Table 6.1) and each of the eight treaties that followed ICERD have automatically subjected state-parties to the duty to report – a control procedure conducted under the responsible committee, but not expressly regulated. In practice, however, the procedural regulations of the various committees have all developed provisions that reporting states may be represented by their own deputies in any investigations processes, and may provide additional information or statements. The state reporting process is concluded with 'general remarks', and each committee handles the writing of its own reports and recommendations differently. The state reporting process allows states a large degree of control over the information that is self-reported, i.e. it relies on states' own sense of obligation to conduct the report seriously and honestly. It must also be kept in mind, however, that the public treatment of the reports and the opportunity for actors such as NGOs to collect follow-up information (see Otto, 1996; Liese, 1998) means that states even remotely concerned with international reputation will have an interest in candid and transparent reporting.

Unlike the widely accepted mechanism of state reporting, the process for state complaints (i.e. complaints against other states) is obligatory only in ICERD. In other treaties – including the ICCPR and in the International Convention against Torture and Other Cruel, Inhuman or Degrading Treatment or Punishment (CAT) – the mechanism for state complaints is tied to a voluntary subjection clause and it is not present at all in any other of the core international human rights treaties. The state complaints process is rooted in the notion that states should function as a watchdog for the observance of an objective order (Partsch, 1995) and that states should not – at least according to the intention of the process – use the process to serve their own interests. Complaints procedures are conducted confidentially, but records reveal that the process has never been utilised by any state party to any of the nine core international human rights treaties. The procedure, however, has found its way into various regional human rights agreements, such as the European Convention on Human Rights or the most important African human rights document: the African [Banjul] Charter on Human and Peoples' Rights (27 June 1981).

Efforts to protect human rights by making individuals the subjects of international law find expression in an individual complaints process known as the 'communication process' (the UN has introduced the term 'communication' in order to avoid using the term 'complaint'). The communication process is intended to provide every individual the opportunity to present themselves before an international committee, to provide that committee with information about violations to their personal rights, and to seek help. Four of the most important human rights treaties now include the individual communication process, although it is not obligatory and is subject to voluntary self-subjection by states. In the case of the ICCPR, this self-subjection takes place by way of the ratification of an optional protocol; in CAT and ICERD, it takes place through a simple declaration of agreement. The UN Charter has little to say on the subject of personal petitions – they are mentioned only in Article 87(b) in relation to the now-defunct Trusteeship Council wherein the inhabitants of trustee territories can ask the Trusteeship Council to investigate violations of their individual rights. Since the 2005 World Summit, the entirety of Chapter XIII, including Article 87, has been deleted from the Charter. The UN Human Rights Commission initially declined to give itself a communication procedure (see ECOSOC Resolution 75 (V), 5 August 1947). The subsequent de facto powerlessness of the UN to monitor and implement human rights standards lasted for more than twenty years, until ECOSOC – under pressure from the Human Rights Commission – revised its position in Resolutions 1235 (XLII) of 6 June 1967 and Resolution 1503 (XLVIII) of 27 May 1970. These resolutions allowed the Human Rights Commission to accept and investigate, under specific conditions, individual communications and public statements on these communications (Tomuschat, 1995a), a procedure that has been carries over to the new Human Rights Council that replaced the Commission in 2006 (see below).

Treaty-Based Bodies

The task of overseeing the implementation and maintenance of treaties' agreed-upon norms generally went to committees specifically established for that purpose. The procedures, decisions, and reports of these committees are detailed exhaustively in the Treaty Body Database at the office of the UN High Commissioner for Human Rights in Geneva (see Table 6.1).

Despite numerous commonalities, the various monitoring committees exhibit a number of differences in their practices.

TABLE 6.1
Treaty-based monitoring bodies

		Date	Monitoring body
ICERD	International Convention on the Elimination of all Forms of Racism	21 December 1965	CERD
ICCPR	International Covenant on Civil and Political Rights	16 December 1966	CCPR
ICESCR	International Covenant on Economic, Social and Cultural Rights	16 December 1966	CESCR
CEDAW	Convention on the Elimination of all formsof Discrimination Against Women	18 December 1979	CEDAW
CAT	Convention against Torture and Other Cruel, Inhuman or Degrading Treatment or Punishment	10 December 1984	CAT
CRC	Convention on the Rights of the Child	20 November 1989	CRC
ICRMW	International Convention on the Protectionof the Rights of all Migrant Workers and Members of their Families	18 December 1990	CMW
CRPD	Convention on the Rights of Persons with Disabilities	13 December 2006	CRPD
CPED	International Convention For the Protection of all Persons from Enforced Disappearance	20 December 2006	CED

The Human Rights Committee of the ICCPR

The Human Rights Committee of the ICCPR was established in 1976. The eighteen members of the Committee serve a four-year term and are elected by secret ballot from a list of suggestions submitted by the states parties in a special assembly called by the Secretary-General. Each states-party may nominate two of its own nationals, but elected members are required to work impartially and do not serve the Committee as representatives of their states. As a rule, the Committee meets three times a year in New York or Geneva, and is supported in its work by a secretariat located with the High Commissioner for Human Rights in Geneva. The overwhelming majority of the Committee's work is concentrated on the examination of state reports. Each new signatory state must present a report within six months of the time the treaty came into effect for that state, detailing the measures it has undertaken for the realization of the rights contained in the treaty. After the initial state report, the state is subject to the Committee's requests for further reports at five-year intervals and the Committee may require additional reports if it becomes aware of possible human rights violations. NGO participation is given a great deal of weight in the process of examining the reports for the purposes of providing additional information and encouraging greater openness and honesty in the reports. Discussion of the reports is public and closes with the publication of the Concluding Observations, in which both the achieved progress and the outstanding deficiencies and points of criticism are frankly stated.

Individual communications against a state are subject to the state having ratified the first optional protocol to the ICCPR, and the communication procedure exists only under very strict conditions. The right to complain ('communicate') is available only to persons who have experienced a violation of their human rights, and they must have fully exhausted the domestic processes available to them for complaint. Even then, communication will only be accepted if the matter is not under current consideration by any other international body (such the European Court of Human Rights). The examination of the communication takes place in confidence. The decision of the Committee – known as 'views' – are not binding judgements, but are modelled as such and include both a legal appraisal of the complaint and recommendations for restitution. The Human Rights Committee of the ICCPR publishes its 'views' as an annex to its yearly report to the General Assembly, thus contributing to the mobilization of public pressure on the states involved to observe the legal evaluation and recommendations of the Committee. In comparison with regional human rights regimes such as the European Convention on Human Rights, and the binding judgements of the European Court of Human Rights, the competencies of the Human Rights Committee appear to be limited. They are, however, of decisive importance for the overwhelming majority of people, and peoples, who have no access to more effective regional regimes.

The Committee for ICESCR

Unlike the ICCPR, the International Covenant on Economic, Social and Cultural Rights (ICESCR) did not initially contain provisions for the creation of a special committee for the supervision of its activities. Instead, states were required to submit their reports to ECOSOC via the Secretary-General. ECOSOC then reviewed the reports with the assistance of the Human Rights Commission and in co-ordination with other specialized agencies. In 1985, however, ECOSOC created a Committee on Economic, Social and Cultural Rights (CESCR) to deal with this task (see Resolution 1985/17, 28 May 1985). Members of CESCR are nominated by ICESCR state-parties, but elected by ECOSOC (regardless of ECOSOC members' affiliation to ICESCR), so that the CESCR is in reality a subsidiary body of a UN principle organ. CESCR meets twice a year for three weeks, plus an additional one-week pre-sessional working group meeting, and is supported by the Office of the High Commissioner for Human Rights (OHCHR). CESCR's only control instrument is the state reports. After the initial state report, which must be presented by the state within a year of the treaty's coming into effect, state reports must be presented at five-year intervals. Initial examination of the state reports is carried out first by the pre-sessional working group (comprising five experts), who draft a number of questions relating to the report and any additional information provided by external parties such as NGOs. The state that submitted the report has six months to respond to these questions, and must present themselves for an oral presentation before the Committee presents its Concluding Observations. In its General Comments, the Committee attempts a more concrete interpretation of the treaty provisions that constitute standards for the relevant norms, but are not legally binding (Riedel, 2004, p. 40). In 2008, in an attempt to invigorate the observation of the rights anchored in the Social Covenant, an optional protocol to the ICESCR was adopted by the General Assembly that allowed for individual complaints to the CESCR (see A/RES/63/117, 10 December 2008). To date (as of October 2011), the Optional Protocol has only thirty-eight signatories and only four states parties and requires another six ratifications before its entry into force.

Two circumstances make the CESCR a rather weak instrument of control. First, the participatory aspect of the covenant is difficult to adjudicate because the boundaries of participation are defined by the state rather than any external objective criterion – many states ratified the covenant with reservations. Second, the Committee's only tool in its task as a monitoring instrument is the state reporting process – it does receive additional information from independent sources but the overall usefulness of the process depends in large upon states' willingness to co-operate. Furthermore, the labour-intensive procedure of examining state reports threatens to overwhelm the Committee. It remains to be seen if the Optional Protocol – if it becomes legally binding in the future – would significantly improve the monitoring and protection of rights articulated in ICESCR.

The Committee for ICERD

The Committee on the Elimination of Racial Discrimination (CERD) – the body of independent experts that monitors implementation of ICERD – was established on 10 January 1970. Members of CERD are elected from the states parties for a four-year term, and OHCHR in Geneva is responsible for supporting the Committee's work. For the exercise of its monitoring functions, it has the use of state reports, as also has procedures for both state and individual complaints ('communications').

The reporting system requires parties to submit comprehensive reports every four years, as well as additional reports on any particularly important developments. A member of CERD is named as the *rapporteur* for each report; the *rapporteur* must present his/her evaluation of the status of the Convention's goals in the state involved, and may make use of the aid of independent experts and organizations. During the public discussion of the reports, the relevant governments may also present their perspectives. The Committee's Concluding Observations is forwarded to the General Assembly's Third Committee for further advice. One of the newer developments with CERD is that it now attempts public proceedings against states that fail to submit their reports, or whose reports evince a drastic need for action.

To date, the state complaints procedure has never been utilised and approximately only a quarter of the 175 states parties have made a declaration submitting them to the individual communications procedure.

Committee on the Elimination of Discrimination against Women

The Committee on the Elimination of Discrimination Against Women (CEDAW) – the body of independent experts that monitors the implementation of the Convention on the Elimination of all forms of Discrimination Against Women – was established in 1981 and consists of twenty-three independent experts elected by the states parties. Like other treaties, CEDAW's primary instrument is state reports, which are examined in a process similar to the ones described above for the other bodies. CEDAW submits yearly reports to ECOSOC (and the General Assembly's Third Committee) and to the Secretary-General (and the Commission on the Status of Women). Since 22 December 2000, the long-overdue optional protocol for the enabling of an individual communications procedure has been in effect, but it has only been ratified at the time of writing by 102 of the 187 states parties, and thus plays only a secondary role in the work of the Committee.

CEDAW is hemmed in to a far greater extent than any of the other treaty bodies as a result of the numerous reservations made by states made at the time of ratification. Even in states that have no official regulations debarring women from certain rights, many of CEDAW's recommendations have not been implemented on the grounds of cultural peculiarities or customary law. Article 20 reveals states' apparent lack of will to create an effective monitoring and implementation organ for women's rights: it states that the Committee 'shall normally meet for a period of not more than two weeks annually' in New York for the purposes of reviewing the state reports. In 1995 the General Assembly adopted an amendment of Article 20 allowing states parties to fix the term of the annual meeting (see A/RES/50/202, 22 December 1995). The amendment, however, needs the acceptance of two-thirds of CEDAW's state-parties for its entry into force, but by October 2011 only sixty-four out of 187 state-parties had notified their support to the Secretary-General. As a temporary measure the General Assembly authorized CEDAW to convene three annual sessions, each of three weeks and preceded by a pre-sessional working group. (A/RES/60/230, 23 December 2005, para. 14). This extended working time usually allows the Committee to invite eight state-parties (fourteen, if the Committee meets in parallel chambers) to present their state reports for consideration. The relevant country *rapporteurs* – based on remarks made by the pre-sessional working group – then provides lists of issues with regard to the reports to be considered in the upcoming session. Having examined the state reports, the Committee can formulate (under Article 21) general Recommendations for states' fulfilment of their obligations under the Convention. To date, the Committee has issued twenty-eight General Recommendations, covering a wide range women's rights, including but not limited to: violence against women (1989, 1992); female circumcision (1990); equality in marriage and family relations (1994); and the protection of human rights for older women (2010). At each session the Committee also considers individual complaints under the Optional Protocol, a process that is being prepared by a five-member Working Group on Communications. So far, the Committee has received eighteen complaints and taken fourteen decisions ('views'), eight of which were on the inadmissibility of the complaint, five were in favour of the victims, and in one admissible case the Committee saw no violation of the Convention by the state-party.

On the basis of the reports and subsequent recommendations, a number of substantial – and even some temporary – improvements have taken place in a number of countries regarding the legal protection of women's rights. Nevertheless CEDAW and the work of its monitoring body continues to be the source of bitter contention among different religious and cultural groups, and continues to be a catalyst for ongoing debate on the universal understanding of human rights.

Committee on the Convention against Torture and Other Cruel, Inhuman or Degrading Treatment or Punishment

The Committee on the Convention against Torture and Other Cruel, Inhuman or Degrading Treatment or Punishment (CAT) – the body of independent experts that monitors the implementation of the Convention of the same name – consists of ten experts chosen *ad personam* by the states parties. In addition to the obligatory state reporting procedure, CAT can utilize both the state complaints and individual communication procedures (although the former is, in practice, completely meaningless). Both state complaints and individual communications can occur only with appropriate declarations on the part of the signatory states. CAT is similar to the other previously described monitoring bodies in its *modus operandi* and procedural rules. However, the mechanisms by which CAT can initiate an investigation extend beyond those available to other monitoring bodies – CAT may examine any 'reliable information' that indicates the existence of systematic torture in a state party. This clause enables NGOs to communicate directly with CAT and to provide the Committee with information to instigate investigations. There is also a Working Group on the Optional Protocol to CAT which would enable sub-commissions to make investigative visits to correctional facilities or other facilities of signatory states in which people may be held under arrest. The competencies foreseen in the draft protocol for the sub-commission are broadly constructed and would represent a significant step forward in the protection against torture if states were to ratify it. Experience with other such voluntary mechanisms of submission to specific procedures, however, would suggest that the ratifications will be forthcoming from states where torture is a marginal human rights concern – states that might be subject to such investigation are unlikely to voluntarily enter into such obligations.

Committee on the Convention of the Rights of the Child

The ten experts who form the Committee for the Convention of the Rights of the Child (CRC) are responsible for monitoring the most widely accepted human rights treaty. Commensurate with the co-operative and holistic approach of the Convention, its monitoring committee works with the other human rights committees – mostly UNICEF – from its seat in Geneva. The only monitoring tool that the CRC has at its disposal, however, is the state reporting process. The two optional protocols, passed on 25 May 2000 and coming into force at the beginning of 2002, on the rights of children involved in armed conflicts and protection against child-trafficking and prostitution, both also contain their own requirements for state reporting. The CRC may also request additional reports as it sees fit, and thus has what approaches a right to investigation.

Committee on the Convention for the Protection of the Rights of All Migrant Workers and their Families

The Committee on the Convention for the Protection of the Rights of All Migrant Workers and their Families (CMW) – the monitoring Committee for the implementation of the Convention of the same name – came into force on 1 July 2003. Ten independent experts were initially elected by the assembly of the states parties, to be increased to fourteen members once the 41st state ratifies the CMW (see Article 72). The CMW meets twice a year at UN headquarters in New York. States parties are obliged to submit state reports to the UN Secretary-General on the legislative, judicial, administrative, and other measures they have taken to put into effect the provisions of the Convention and the Secretary-General then forwards the reports to the CMW for consideration. An initial state report is required from each state-party within one year of joining, and follow-up reports must be presented every five years thereafter, or upon the Committee's request. Individual communications may also be submitted to the Committee. As of October 2011, the Committee had convened fifteen sessions, to consider states' initial and follow-up state reports. However, a number of state reports have been submitted reluctantly and only upon the Committee's specific request (see CMW Report 2009, Annex III, UN document A/64/48). During its 13th session, the CMW issued a General Comment on the situation of domestic migrant workers, which identified them as migrant workers in the understanding of Article 2, paragraph 2 of the Convention and thus extending its protective provisions to this group (aee CMW/C/12/CRP.2/ Rev.2).

Committee on the Rights of Persons with Disabilities

The Committee on the Convention on the Rights of Persons with Disabilities (CRPD) – the monitoring Committee for the implementation of the Convention of the same name – elected twelve independent experts at their first conference in October 2008 (membership will increase to eighteen after the 80th ratification or accession to the Convention). The Committee convened its first meeting in February 2009. Members of CRPD serve a four-year term and are eligible for re-election only once. The CRPD's main source of information are states reports – initially submitted by states within two years of their entry into force of CRPD and at least every four years thereafter. States reports may also be requested of states at any time by CRPD. The Secretary-General can make the state reports available to all UN member states, and CRPD may make suggestions and general recommendations on each state report. An Optional Protocol – ratified by twenty-nine states – allows individual complaints ('communications') to CRPD.

Committee for the International Convention for the Protection of all Persons from Enforced Disappearance

The states parties of the International Convention for the Protection of all Persons from Enforced Disappearance (CED) met for the first time on 31 May 2011 at UN headquarters in New York to elect the first ten members of the monitoring Committee for the implementation of the Convention. As with other treaty monitoring bodies, the general work of the CED, whose first meeting was scheduled 8–11 November 2011, consists of considering states' reports. In cases of urgency, however, the CED can receive requests from a disappeared person's relative, legal representative, counsel, or otherwise authorized persons, and can demand relevant information from the state party concerned. The CED can then produce recommendations, including interim measures, for locating and protecting the disappeared person. Furthermore, the Committee can have its members undertake visits to states of concern if it receives reliable information indicating that a state- party is in violation of the Convention. Of course, such visits are only possible in consultation with and approval by the state-party concerned. The CED also has the authority to bring a matter of urgent concern to the attention of the General Assembly, i.e. if it receives credible information that enforced disappearance is being practised on a widespread or systematic basis in the territory under the jurisdiction of a state-party (see Article 34). Such provisions make the CED fairly strong in comparison to other treaty monitoring bodies, however, as the youngest such monitoring body, the CED has yet to give proof of its effectiveness.

Summary

Human rights treaties – unlike the Declarations and Resolutions of the General Assembly – constitute binding international law. The treaties' relatively weak monitoring mechanisms, however, mean that the implementation and monitoring of human rights standards often fails to achieve the desired outcomes. Some of the treaties' procedures, such as the bodies preparing state reports or field missions to various states, have become accepted practice, while other efforts, such as the attempt to have local investigations or to grant a right of initiative to the treaty bodies, remain stuck in their embryonic phases. Committees often struggle to adequately address the large amounts of issues that are submitted to them during their relatively short sessions, and there is a distinct effort underway to speed up the examination process by bundling and harmonizing issues. As a result, some human rights problems are being lost in the fray. In order to address these deficits, it might be helpful for committees to establish common guidelines for the writing of reports. Such efforts should seek to eliminate standardized reporting (that often blurs the characteristics of specific human rights issues) and should concentrate on integrating country-specific human rights into regional arrangements and national law. In view of the now-comprehensive inventory of human rights norms, it seems that, in the future, emphasis should be placed on the improvement of the monitoring mechanisms rather than on the suggestion of ever more refined rules with very questionable prospects of realization (Riedel, 2004, p. 54).

Human Rights Protection by UN Organs

The decisive advantage of human rights treaties – that they are legally binding – applies only to states that have submitted themselves to the respective treaty. In order to close the gap between the universal claims of basic human rights standards and the more limited treaty memberships, and to augment the none-too-effective treaty mechanisms, the UN has gradually expanded its human rights monitoring competencies with respect to its member states. The UN's capacities as a human rights monitoring body are based in various General Assembly and ECOSOC Resolutions that have sought to reinterpret existing Charter provisions. However, this process of re-interpretation of the Charter's jurisdictional scope means that the resultant mechanisms are considered 'political' rather than 'juristic' (Alston, 1994, pp. 1–21). The political character of UN human rights protection is underscored by the fact that their work is carried out by representatives of the various state governments, who are bound to follow their governments' instructions, as opposed to independent experts, as in the treaty bodies. UN committees are thus rather more flexible than those of the treaty bodies, but they are also more susceptible to the temptation to orientate their work along considerations of political opportunity, and thus to the problem of double standards.

The Charter gives original jurisdiction over questions of human rights to its main bodies, but it is mostly subsidiary bodies – the UN Human Rights Commission (now the UN Human Rights Council) and the UN High Commissioner for Human Rights – that are concerned with the specific protection of human rights. First among these was the Human Rights Commission – a functional commission of ECOSOC that also worked closely with the General Assembly's Third Committee on the drafting of Declarations and Resolutions. In 2006, the Human Rights Commission was replaced by the UN Human Rights Council (a subsidiary organ of the General Assembly). The UN High Commissioner for Human Rights (UNHCHR) – attached to the Secretariat – plays a somewhat different role. The office was created as a result of a political decision, specifically a General Assembly Resolution, but the High Commissioner and his/her colleagues are members of the UN International Civil Service and are thus not bound by any member state instructions or directions. The High Commissioner acts on behalf of the Secretary-General, and in the name of the UN.

The UN Human Rights Council

The creation of the UN Human Rights Council (the 'Council') was decided at the 2005 World Summit. The HRC was created as a replacement for the Human Rights Commission that had functioned for decades as the UN's central inter-state agency in the field of human rights – first promoting standard setting and later increasing its mandate considerably to consider all relevant human rights issues, from the further development of standards, through the investigation of human rights violations, to the issuing of recommendations for the better implementation of human rights norms in domestic law (Baum, 1999, p. 242). This commission's expansion of competencies was made possible by ECOSOC Resolution 1235 (1967) and ECOSOC Resolution 1503 (1970): Resolution 1235 permitted the Commission to deal with the human rights situations in a few specified countries; Resolution 1503 permitted individual petitions. The Commission vested special *rapporteurs* or working groups with country-specific mandates for the observation of specific human rights issues such as disappearances, torture, child trafficking, or the right to development. During its annual spring sessions the Commission made (legally non-binding) remarks or recommendations on the implementation and observation of human rights in member states. The Commission was always a political body, however, and controversies between different sections and members of the Commission became more and more polarizing, especially when the US was voted off the Commission in 2001, or when Libya chaired the Commission in 2003. In his 2005 report to the General Assembly, Secretary-General Kofi Annan deplored that:

> [The] Commission's capacity to perform its tasks has been increasingly undermined by its declining credibility and professionalism. In particular, States have sought membership of the Commission not to strengthen human rights but to protect themselves against criticism or to criticize others. As a result, a credibility deficit has developed, which casts a shadow on the reputation of the United Nations system as a whole. (Annan, 2005, para. 182)

Annan proposed to the heads of state and government the creation of a smaller standing Human Rights Council to abide by the highest human rights standards (ibid., para. 183). Although Annan articulated a clear outline of the new Council (which found its way into the draft of a final document presented by General Assembly President Jean Ping) it took another six months of intense negotiation among member states to establish the Council. The Human Rights Council was born on 15 March 2006 (see A/RES/61/251) at which time the Commission terminated its work.

It quickly became clear that states and governments would claim a dominant role in the Council's working procedures. As a result, the Council shares many similarities with its predecessor in a number of crucial areas. The Council has a broad mandate, including the responsibility 'for promoting universal respect for the protection of all human rights and fundamental freedoms for all', the right to 'address situations of violations of human rights, including gross and systematic violations', and to 'promote the effective coordination and the mainstreaming of human rights within the United Nations system' (ibid., paras 4 and 5). The Council has its seat in Geneva, where an office consisting of the president and four vice-presidents directs the work of the Council (the Council's administrative work is also supported by the Office of the High Commissioner for Human Rights). The Council consists of forty-seven member states. As in the Commission, Council membership is based on the principle of equitable geographical distribution, as follows:

- Africa (13 seats);
- Asia (13 seats);
- Latin-America and the Caribbean (8 seats);
- Western European and other states (7 seats);
- Eastern Europe (6 seats).

Council members are elected by secret ballot majority in the General Assembly, and serve for a term of three years with the opportunity of one immediate re-election. Council membership can be suspended by a two-thirds vote in the General Assembly if a Council member commits gross and systematic violations of human rights. Unlike the Commission, the Council works throughout the year; it has to convene at least three regular sessions of a total duration of not less than ten weeks and may hold special sessions as needed, and upon the request of a Council member with the support of one-third of the membership.

On its fifth regular session – and after one year of preparation – the Council finalized its institution-building (A/HRC/RES/5/1) and instituted the guidelines and mechanisms of its work, as follows:

- **Universal Periodic Review (UPR):** An entirely new instrument created by the Council to periodically review of the human rights situation in all member states. The UPR started in April 2008 and will complete its first cycle during its twelfth session in late 2011 – at which point it will restart the entire review

process. Each member states is discussed on the basis of a state-report, a coun-
try-specific file provided by the OHCHR, and a dossier compiled by the
OHCHR comprising reports by stakeholders, civil society, the media, and
NGOs.

- **Special procedures:** Special *rapporteurs* or working groups on the examination of the human rights situation in certain member states, known as 'country
  mandates' (such as Sudan, Haiti, the Democratic People's Republic of Korea,
  Myanmar, or the occupied territories of Palestine) or on specific human rights
  issues, known as 'thematic mandates' (such as arbitrary detention, the right to
  food, torture, or freedom of opinion). At the time of writing there exist eight
  country mandates and thirty-three thematic mandates with fifty-five mandate-
  holders (see OHCHR 2011, p. 2 *et seq.*).
- **Advisory Committee:** A body of eighteen international human rights experts
  that functions like a think-tank and provides expertise to the Council on its
  request.
- **Complaint procedures (also known as the 1503 procedure):** Named for
  ECOSOC Resolution 1503 of 27 May 1970, the complaints procedure allows
  individuals (and groups of individuals) to submit complaints or communication
  in cases of well-founded suspicion of massive and systematic human rights
  violations in a particular country. The 1503 procedure is only available when
  the complainant has exhausted all other measures available them. The Council
  has established two working groups on the consideration of individual communications. All such procedures are conducted in closed sessions, and the
  complaints procedure is entirely confidential.

Despite fears that the Council would merely replicate the work of the Commission
in a new guise, the Council inherited some well-proven procedures and mechanisms from the Commission. The work of independent mandate-holders remains
crucial for neutral fact-finding and balanced, non-partisan assessments (although
the code of conduct passed by the Council in July 2007 (A/HRC/RES/5/2) might
look like a disciplinary instrument). The UPR is designed as a co-operative mechanism that does not practise public accusation and condemnation of political
adversaries (as it was practiced in many of the debates in the Commission) but
serves as a symmetric discourse between countries and cultures on human rights
and their observation worldwide. The Council's instruments, combined with the
direct election of its members from the General Assembly, means that it is able to
exert much more political weight that was possible by the Commission under the
ECOSOC (see Rathgeber, 2010).

Back in 2006, the US and Israel were vocal opponents to the creation of the
Council. Since then, these and a number of additional member states have
remained sceptical of the Council. The regional membership criteria in the Council, along with its generally low (and very generalized) membership threshold
means that Council seats are often filled by states with questionable human rights
records. Countries like China, Cuba, Pakistan, or Russia – in the eyes of many
western democracies – do not belong to the camp of intrinsic human rights defend-

ers. Indeed, there are no serious hurdles to human rights violators wishing to sit on the Council and it appears almost impossible to dismiss a systematic wrongdoer from the Council after they are elected. Work on institution-building, and in the UPR, has largely been conducted in a positive and constructive manner, but the results of the special sessions raises serious questions about the impartiality of the Council. In six of seventeen special sessions (as of October 2011) the Council occupied itself with Israel and concluded these sessions with resolutions that strongly condemn Israel (largely for its use of military violence with respect to Palestine (see A/HRC/S-1/ of 18 July 2006; A/HRC/S-2/2 of 17 August 2006; A/HRC/S-3/2 of 20 November 2006; A/HRC/S-9/L.1 of 12 January 2009, A/HRC/S-9/2 of 27 February 2009; A/HRC/S-12/1 of 21 October 2009 – resolutions largely sponsored and carried by majorities of authoritarian states, and usually against the negative votes or abstentions of western democracies). In the case of Darfur conflict in Sudan, the Council has only expressed its 'concern regarding the seriousness of the human rights and humanitarian situation in Darfur' (Decision S-4/101, 13 December 2007). A similarly weak resolution was passed by the Council concerning the Democratic Republic of the Congo (A/HRC/RES/S-8/1, 1 December 2008). Though criticism of Israel's strategies in Lebanon and Palestine are certainly justified, the Council's asymmetric assessment of human rights violations raised doubts about the seriousness of the Councils efforts to maintain a neutral and objective handling of the cases considered.

On the other hand, the Human Rights Council quickly reacted on the crackdowns of anti-government demonstrations in North Africa in early 2011, held special sessions on Libya (February 2011) and Syria (April and August 2011) and strongly condemned the regimes' violence against civilians. On 1 March 2011 the General Assembly referred to HRC resolution S-15/1 of 25 February 2011 when it suspended Libya's membership in the Council (A/RES/65/265). In other cases, the Council has found clear words and has promoted a consistent course of actions, as was the case concerning the refusal of Burma/Myanmar's military junta to admit international relief after the flood disaster of 2007. Similarly, in special sessions in 2009 and 2010, the Council considered the impact of the world financial crisis on elementary human rights, as well as the situations in Sri Lanka, Haiti, and Côte d'Ivoire.

Like its predecessor, the Human Rights Council is a political committee in which the widely differing understandings of the type and scope of international protection of human rights find lively expression. Delegates generally conform to interpretations of human rights that are not derived from a universal understanding or universal norm, but rather conform to interpretations based on the political system, the religious belief, and the cultural heritage of their state. A large number of states – especially from Asia and Africa – argue that national and cultural peculiarities should be given more consideration in the way that the agreed-upon norms are guaranteed. Western democracies in particular tend to accuse these states of practising human rights relativism under the cover of cultural differences. The general response to this accusation is that the West also practises an inconsistent politics of double standards, and that it ignores human rights violations in its own spheres of interest. The intrinsic tension between the principle of sovereignty and collective implementation of human rights remains a major theme of discussion, and area of contention, in the Council – just as it was in the Commission. The Council's composition of member states means that it cannot but reflect the political, economic, social, and cultural heterogeneity of its members. This reality cannot be overcome by the tailoring of an international body or by confrontation, sanctions, or boycotts. The international protection of human rights depends on the willingness of the states to negotiate and bring forward basic norms and mechanisms. Even if it is not yet capable of achieving everything that it set out to do, the world needs institutions like the new Human Rights Council in order to keep the process moving forward. In this regard, it was a positive signal set by the US to re-join the HRC in 2009; the Council itself substantially gained international confidence in its impartiality by its determined occupation with the situation in Libya and Syria. The key to the Council's success lies in the hands of the states, governments and societies: if they fail to use the opportunities offered by the Council, it might experience the fate of the former Commission.

The UN High Commissioner for Human Rights

Shortly after the founding of the UN the Secretariat formed its own human rights department. Known since 1982 as the UN Human Rights Centre, the original seat of this department was originally in New York but was moved to Geneva in 1974. Through all it's progressions, however, the Human Rights Centre has never developed a mandate to allow it to develop into an operative organ with its own competencies for action.

Following the end of the Cold War, there was an international push for human rights that culminated in the 1993 Vienna World Conference on Human Rights. The Vienna Conference paved the way for General Assembly to Resolution 48/141 (20 December 1993) and the office of UNHCHR. Recognizing that primary responsibility for the implementation, observation, and protection of human rights lies in the hands of governments, one of the major tasks of the High Commissioner is to provide assistance to governments and other international organizations and bodies. Today OHCHR describes its major tasks and activities as split into four main categories:

(i)   *Mainstreaming human rights*: among the core purposes of the OHCHR is the promotion of fundamental rights as set down in the Universal Declaration of Human Rights, but also as contained in the human rights covenants and other treaties. As the primary UN body for the promotion and protection of human rights, OHCHR is tasked with the implementation of human rights perspectives in all UN actions, programmes and missions.

(ii) *Partnerships*: the OHCHR co-operates with all actors in the field of human rights protection, governments, civil society, national human rights institutions, and international institutions including but not limited to the International Labour Organization, UNICEF, and the International Criminal Court.

(iii) *Standard-setting and monitoring*: this includes the contribution of knowledge and expertise on human rights issues to all UN bodies occupied with human rights. So OHCHR functions as the secretariat of the Human Rights Council (see above) whose work it supports by giving assistance to the special *rapporteurs* and independent experts as well as by providing country-specific information for the Universal Periodic Review.

(iv) *Implementation on the ground*: in recent years OHCHR has extended its field activities and its country-specific work. Regional and country offices – as well as human rights components within UN peace missions – help to identify and name human rights problems and provide assistance to and co-operation with governments, international bodies, or NGOs in the development of solutions. This can be assistance in law making, human rights education or in other implementation procedures; it also can be the monitoring of human rights situations within countries or societies (see www.ohchr.org).

One major area of work for OHCHR is in field missions, the number of which has increased considerably over the past two decades. By 2011, OHCHR was running ten regional offices or centres that each address specific human rights issues, co-ordinate human rights actors in countries, or provide assistance to the UN country teams within the region. The regional offices/centres are based in Addis Ababa (East Africa), Yaounde/Cameroon (Central Africa), Pretoria (South Africa), Bangkok (South East Asia), Suva/Fiji (Pacific), Beirut (Middle East), Bishkek (Central Asia), Panama City (Central America), Santiago de Chile (South America), and Qatar (South-west Asia and the Arab Region). There are country offices in Bolivia, Cambodia, Colombia, Guatemala, Mexico, Nepal, Togo, and Uganda, as well as two stand-alone offices in Kosovo and Palestine. Each of the offices are based on special arrangements with the respective governments. These offices analyse the human rights situations in the country, report publicly and offer assistance to the government in implementing human rights protection measures. An increasing field of activity for OHCHR is in UN peace missions – such activities do not only help to prevent human rights violations in the mission country (through analysis or public reports) but also serve to monitor the compliance of UN peacekeepers' conduct with human rights standards. Furthermore, OHCHR has made arrangements with the Resident Coordinators of UN activities in an increasing number of countries (up to twenty-one by the end of 2010) to help ensure the integration of human rights issues in the respective country.

To a certain extent, the OHCHR is the supervision centre of all the UN's human rights activities, and its duties are to provide a framework and a coherent strategy over a cross-cutting set of tasks. This particular role of the OHCHR is underscored by the High Commissioner's membership in the Secretary-General's Senior Management Group. The High Commissioner also occupies the rank of an Under-Secretary-General, and is nominated by the Secretary-General and approved by the General Assembly for a four-year term of office with the option of extension. The first High Commissioner – José Ayala Lasso of Ecuador – left the office in early March 1997. Former Irish President Mary Robinson served as the second High

Commissioner from 1997 to 2002. The former leader of the Office for the Coordination of Humanitarian Affairs in the UN Secretariat, Sergio Viera de Mello of Brazil, held the office from 2002 until his tragic death in a bomb attack in Iraq on 19 August 2003. Following de Mello's death, the office was led by an acting High Commissioner, Bertrand Ramcharan of Guyana. Between 2004 and 2008, the office was held by Louise Arbour of Canada, and has been served by Navanethem Pillay, a lawyer from South Africa, since 1 September 2008. The UNHCHR acts under the authority of the Secretary-General and the General Assembly, but the High Commissioner enjoys a large measure of autonomy that finds frequent expression in extensive rights of initiative. The High Commissioner may – under his/her own competence – enter into dialogue with governments, offer them help, offer recommendations to UN organs, and call public attention to existing problems and deficiencies. An important step in the improvement of the OHCHR's capabilities was accomplished in 1997 when it integrated with the UN Human Rights Centre. At the same time, the office of a Deputy High Commissioner was created, intended to free the High Commissioner from administrative tasks to enable them to concentrate on operational activities. The current Deputy High Commissioner – Kyung-wha Kang of South Korea – has held this position since January 2007.

The primary activities of the High Commissioner involve quiet diplomacy and co-operation with various governments. The High Commissioner must respect state sovereignty and national authority and thus walks a very thin line between co-operation and the exercise of public pressure. In particular, the exercise of this task by first High Commissioner Ayala Lasso subjected him to multiple accusations concerning lack of transparency and too much consideration of states. Many NGOs also complained that there was a lack of co-ordination between the UNHCHR and their own information and perspectives. Subsequently, High Commissioner Mary Robinson placed greater emphasis on country reports and worked to integrate fact-finding trips with a larger country strategy, and showed a much greater willingness to engage with the public. High Commissioner Louise Arbour concentrated very much on the evolution of instruments for early warning and early reaction to human rights violations.

The creation of OHCHR constituted a massive qualitative leap for the UN in the strategic bundling of its human rights activities – acting as a central promoter, bringing global publicity and attention to human rights, and functioning as a peer contact for governments and NGOs. However, OHCHR is not immune to the financial difficulties that are present across the rest of the UN. As of the end of 2011, OHCHR comprised about 900 staff, including some 240 human rights officers working in UN peace missions worldwide. Although funding to OHCHR was increased from US$54 million to US$141,4 million between 2005 and the biennium of 2010–11, OHCHR funds represent less than 3 per cent of the UN's regular budget and OHCHR continuously relies on voluntary contributions, which rose from US$15 million in 1994 to a peak of US$119,9 in 2008 but then slipped to US$109,4 million in 2010 (see OHCHR 2011a, p. 78). Though considerable progress has been made in enhancing the work of OHCHR the question of lasting and sustainable support by the Organisation remains on the agenda (more data from www.ohchr.org.).

Human Rights Protection: New Fundamentals and Perspectives

The discussion of human rights and their effective protection took one of the top places on the 1990s global agenda. The end of the Cold War indicated that the ideological blockade that had obstructed the creation of a worldwide concentrated strategy for improving the protection of human rights might now be overcome. Above all, many persons who had fought for democracy and human rights – and had been subject to imprisonment and persecution as a result – were then able to reach high political office and leading social positions. Europe in particular coalesced around a common understanding of human rights. Similarly in Africa and Asia, more and more movements began to demand multi-party systems, rights of political participation, and human rights standards. In Latin America, most of the military dictatorships were toppled .

Two important developments followed the end of the Cold War. On the one hand, catalogues of human rights were established in numerous new constitutions, and the ratification of existing human rights treaties became a new priority. On the other hand, waves of violence flared up all over the world in countless civil wars and wars of secession as well as in the activities of majority populations toward national minorities. This included everything from large-scale human rights violations to ethnic cleansing and genocide. Through the rapidly-developing global network of information media, the pictures from countries in crisis found their way ever more quickly into the households and consciousness of the world public (Debiel and Nuscheler, 1996, p. 19). Above all, in western states the so-called 'CNN effect' – the usually selective pressure on decision-makers created by mass media news portrayals of crisis – created considerable political pressure to act to avert massive human rights violations.

Such developments also found expression in the UN Security Council where détente between the USA and the Soviet Union had already led to an increased capacity for action. Following the collective action against Saddam Hussein's Iraq in the first Gulf War, optimism grew regarding a multilateral 'new world order', the central axis of which was to be the UN, and in the framework of which the global protection of human rights was to be pushed forward. The UN engaged itself in new ways for the protection of human rights, going well beyond the mechanisms to be found in its Charter and associated treaties. Two of the most important such instruments – UN humanitarian intervention and UN International Criminal Tribunals – were established during this time and will be discussed below.

From Humanitarian Interventions to Responsibility to Protect

Beginning with Resolution 688 (5 April 1991) on the situation of the Kurds in northern Iraq, the Security Council continued throughout the 1990s to involve itself with human rights and humanitarian situations in various countries, demanding steps for their improvement and undertaking measures up to and including the use of military force. Despite its largely human rights-based mandate, the situation in northern Iraq could also be viewed plausibly as a potential threat to international peace and security (because of the potential involvement of Turkey in an inter-state war), but only a year later the Security Council declared with respect to the situation in Somalia (an entirely internal situation) that the scale of human rights violations constituted a threat to international peace and security (Resolution 794, 3 December 1992). This resolution – passed unanimously and without even passing mention of the possible international consequences such as mass migration of refugees – marked the first time an entirely internal affair was qualified as a threat to international peace and security. The mandated military action UNITAF (Restore Hope) was thus the first UN military intervention on purely humanitarian grounds and represents a significant development in the Security Council's gradual expansion of functional responsibilities.

This process opened the UN to extensive opportunities for intervention on humanitarian and human rights grounds. As already discussed, Article 2(7)'s prohibition applies only to intervention in matters that are essentially within the domestic jurisdiction of a state. Furthermore, it does not apply when the Security Council decides to take enforcement measures under Chapter VII. Of course, the prerequisite for the use of such measures is an Article 39 determination that international peace has been threatened or broken, or that an act of aggression has taken place. But the concept of a threat to the peace is not clearly defined and allows the Security Council a great deal of freedom to use its own judgement (for several sources, see Pape, 1997, p. 128). Events that constitute threats to international peace and security (as agreed upon by the Security Council) are automatically withdrawn from the *domaine reservé* of states. An expansive interpretation of Article 39 thus allows the Security Council broad powers of action, described by Dieter Blumenwitz as the 'key element for an effective protection of human rights within the framework of the UN' (Blumenwitz, 1994, p. 7). Bartl remarks correctly that the language in Resolution 794 is of international humanitarian law, not violations of human rights (Bartl, 1999, p. 133). However, as shown by Pape (1997, p. 44 *et seq.*), human rights law and international humanitarian law build off the same basic norms and have the same purpose: to protect the individual. Ebock claims that six Security Council Resolutions of the 1990s on humanitarian intervention show that the Council's decisions were premised in large part on human rights considerations (2000, p. 263 *et seq.*).

The Security Council has mandated a number of humanitarian interventions (conducted either by 'blue helmets' or by the armed forces of an authorized state or states) on the basis of this broadened notion of international peace and security. The record of these operations, however, is somewhat mixed. The hope of the early 1990s to be able to contribute to the worldwide implementation of human rights through military intervention very quickly gave way to the recognition that such a task went well beyond the UN's competencies and capabilities. Along with the already-discussed conceptual and technical problems attending collective military action, new questions arose concerning the endangerment of civilians for the purpose of delivering them aid (Smith, 1998). Furthermore, high casualty numbers suffered by intervening states – above all in Somalia and the former Yugoslavia – significantly reduced states' readiness engage on the basis of human rights protection. Democratic regimes in particular must be able to justify to their constituencies the grounds on which they are risking the lives and welfare of their soldiers and civilian mission workers. A Security Council decision to intervene comes from Security Council members. In short, Security Council action is usually dependent on member states' national interests and considerations. This leads to mission selectivity that appears quite incompatible with the inalienable and indivisible nature of human rights and has grave consequences for both the 'forgotten regions' and for the moral integrity of the intervening powers.

The core legal, ethical, and political problems of human rights-based military intervention came to the fore in spring 1999 with NATO operation in Kosovo. Although the Security Council had described the humanitarian situation in Kosovo as a threat to the peace on numerous occasions (in Resolution 1199 of 23 September 1998 as well as several other statements), any authorization of the use of military force was made impossible by the veto threats of Russia and China. In weighing the protection of human rights to the Kosovar Albanians and observing the Charter's general prohibition on the use of force, NATO made the decision to undertake an action *praeter legem*: that is, outside the formal prescriptions of international law. The worldwide discussion of the legal permissibility, the ethical responsibility, and the political opportunism of this step is too complex to be reviewed here (see Chesterman, 2001). However, the incident demonstrated the instability of both the normative and legal frameworks for decision-making.

The ever deteriorating situation in the Darfur region of Sudan highlights another aspect of selectivity in this regard: although the UN Security Council has been seized of the matter since 2004, it has strongly condemned the grave human rights violations (S/RES/1591, 29 March 2005), has repeatedly declared the situation to be a threat to international peace and security, and has deplored the deteriorating situation (see most recently S/RES/1841, 15 October 2008) no decision has been made regarding an effective intervention to end the genocide-like crimes being tolerated – if not encouraged – by the Sudanese government. With two permanent members of the Security Council – China and Russia – having major economic interests with and ties to the Sudanese government the Security Council has been unable to enact measures beyond the establishment of a 'Panel of Experts' (S/RES/1591/2005) or the creation of a weak UN-AU hybrid mission (UNAMID, S/RES/1769/2007), none of which have helped to improve the situation. The western democracies in the Security Council occasionally articulate their concerns about human rights violations in Darfur in strong words, but do not appear at all inclined to commit themselves to putting diplomatic pressure on China or Russia. The most significant decision by the Security Council on the issue of Darfur has been transferring the inquiry of crimes committed to the Prosecutor of the International Criminal Court, whose substantial findings convinced the Court to issue arrest warrants against top Sudanese leaders (see below).

How should states, and international organizations, handle large-scale human rights violations? In an attempt to answer this question Canadian Prime Minister Jean Chrétien established the International Commission on Intervention and State Sovereignty (ICISS) – often referred to as the 'responsibility to protect' (R2P) – in

September 2000. The 2001 report underlines the primary responsibility by states and governments for the prohibition of human rights crimes, and proposes that the international community should give assistance to national authorities in their efforts to this end. R2P also claims, however, that the responsibility to protect should yield to the international community if governments are either unable or unwilling to meet their obligations. In such cases, the UN Security Council should be the central institution for the legitimization of international action. Crucially, however, R2P does not suggest the Security Council is the *only* legitimizing institution. In cases where the Security Council is unable to come to a decision or unable to produce a mandate, interventions by the international community should still be possible as long as a number of other criteria are met. The 2005 World Summit Outcome Document accepted R2P in principle but imposed considerable limitations on its enactment. For instance:

> Each individual State has the responsibility to protect its populations from genocide, war crimes, ethnic cleansing and crimes against humanity. This responsibility entails the prevention of such crimes, including their incitement, through appropriate and necessary means. (Paragraph 138, World Summit Outcome Document)

As such (and also in paragraph 139 of the 2005 World Summit Outcome Document) R2P is not accepted as a mechanism for the protection of human rights in general, but only in cases of genocide, war crimes, crimes against humanity and ethnic cleansing. Any coercive action against a state or a government is admitted exclusively under the auspices of Chapter VII of with the Security Council as the sole legitimizing body, which referred to R2P in its Resolutions 1970 of 26 February 2011 and 1973 of 1 March 2011 authorizing the use of force against Libya in order to protect civilians against Al Qadhafi's troops. Although R2P has found its way into international (customary) law, it remains an emerging norm that will have to be elaborated upon and made operational in the future (see Ban, 2009). R2P has, by no means, become an alternative norm that would allow states to bypass the Security Council and the existing system of legitimization of the use of force (R2P and the problems of intervening into domestic jurisdiction will be discussed more detailed in Chapter 8). Security Council reform, and the development of clear criteria for the permissibility of human rights-based military action, are indispensable prerequisites for the consistent use of R2P, and until progress is made in this area, it is likely that the UN, member states, and regional arrangements will undertake humanitarian intervention only in exceptional cases, otherwise they will continue to rely on political and economic measures.

International Criminal Jurisdiction

Treaties and procedures for the international protection of human rights are generally characterized as efforts to bring the individual to the forefront of international law. Human rights violations do not simply 'occur'; they are initiated and conducted by people. Thus it is clear that in complement to human rights-based international law there must also be international criminal norms to which perpetrators can be called to account for their individual guilt.

It was not by chance that the first efforts to codify international criminal norms emerged at the same time as the prohibition and ostracism of war in the 1920s. The civilian victims were too numerous and it became evident that modern war constituted the most horrifying violation of humanitarian norms that could be imagined. However, attempts to bring German Emperor Wilhelm II to justice for unleashing the First World War, and for the violations of the Hague Conventions and other laws and customs of warfare that had been committed in the course of that conflict, ultimately failed. Thus, it was not until the international military tribunals at Nuremberg and Tokyo following the Second World War that war criminals were tried on the basis of international criminal law. The introduction of the offence of 'crimes against humanity' made it possible to prosecute crimes that had been carried out by a state against its own civilian population, for example, the murder of German Jews by the Nazi regime. The traditional conceptualization of sovereignty – already weakened by the partial prohibition on war introduced by the Charter of the League of Nations, and the total prohibition of the Briand-Kellogg Pact – was further eroded by the Nuremberg and Tokyo trials insomuch as these processes denied sovereign immunity to its subjects.

The UN's efforts to further formulate and codify the Nuremberg Principles, however, remained unsuccessful for a long time against the backdrop of the Cold War. Furthermore, states were (and are) reluctant to subject their political activities to international judgement and possible condemnation. The creation of the Convention on the Prevention and Punishment of the Crime of Genocide (9 December 1948) was followed by various unsuccessful attempts by the UN International Law Commission (ILC, founded by the General Assembly in 1947) to create a statute for an international criminal court. In 1954, the ILC presented a code of crimes against the peace and security of humanity, but its discussion was postponed indefinitely by the General Assembly and its development was not resumed until well after the establishment of the 1974 Definition of Aggression. It was not until the mid-1990s that the ILC was able to present another statute for the creation of an international criminal court (1994) and a code for international crimes (1996) (on this development, see Ferencz, 2001) that eventually found expression in the Rome Statute of the International Criminal Court, passed in 1998 and coming into force on 1 July 2002.

During ILC consultations, the development of international criminal law was accelerated from another direction – the decision of the Security Council to create an International Criminal Tribunal for the Former Yugoslavia (ICTY, Resolution 827, 25 May 1993) to be based in the Hague, Netherlands. Preceding this decision, in October 1992, an independent expert commission had been sent to investigate the humanitarian situation in the former Yugoslavia, on whose report the Security Council had relied heavily in its determination that the situation represented a threat to the peace (Resolution 808, 23 February 1993). With Resolution 808, the Security Council gave the Secretary-General the task of examining the possibility of creating a criminal court. On 3 May 1993, Secretary-General Boutros Boutros-Ghali presented a report composed partly from ILC drafts, statements from thirty member states, and statements from the OSCE, the International Committee of the Red Cross, and a number of other NGOs. In this report, Boutros-Ghali recommended that the Security Council create an international criminal tribunal on the basis of Chapter VII as a non-military sanction for the restoration of peace. The draft statute appended to the report was put into effect under Resolution 827 (ICTY Statute). The following year, one of the ways in which the Security Council reacted to the genocide in Rwanda was the institution of a second international criminal tribunal, the International Criminal Tribunal for Rwanda (ICTR, Resolution 955, 11 November 1994) based in Arusha, Tanzania.

As *ad hoc* courts, the jurisdictions of both tribunals are restricted in many senses. This is especially true in terms of which crimes they are able to prosecute: the ICTY may prosecute grave violations of the 1949 Geneva Conventions, violations of the laws and customs of war, genocide, and crimes against humanity. The jurisdiction of the ICTR includes genocide, crimes against humanity, and violations of the general Article 3 of the Geneva Conventions as well as the second Protocol Additional to the Geneva Conventions. Since the Security Council has no competence to legislate, the crimes over which these tribunals were to have jurisdiction had to be carefully worded so that they were firmly rooted in existing international law. In order to avoid violating the principle of *nullum crimen sine lege* (no *ex post facto* crimes), only Customary International Law crimes could be included (see number 33 *et seq.*, of the Secretary-General's report of 3 May 1993). According to Article 24 of the ICTY Statute and Article 23 of the ICTR Statute, only prison sentences either of limited duration or for life – not the death sentence – may be handed down for the punishment of the indicated crimes (this is in contrast to the International Military Tribunals of Nuremberg and Tokyo where the death penalty was allowed). For the safekeeping of the accused during the pre-trial detention period, tribunals' host states provide the use of prison space to the UN. Sentences are served in prisons volunteered for this purpose by UN member states. Those already sentenced by the ICTY are serving sentences in Finland, Germany and Norway. For the ICTR the United Nations established an UN Detention Facility (UNDF) in Arusha, both for the detention of suspects and for the imprisonment of convicted persons.

Both tribunals have the same structure. They consist of a jurisdictional organ with three Trial Chambers and one Appeals Chamber, an Office of the Prosecution, and a Registry. The Rwanda Tribunal does not have the use of its own Appeals Chamber; it has been sharing with the ICTY. The judges are nominated by the Security Council and confirmed by the General Assembly for a four-year term with the option of reappointment. The fourteen full-time justices of the ICTY have the assistance of up to nine *ad litem* justices, should the caseload increase significantly. The prosecutor is named by the Security Council on the nomination of the Secretary-General. Following the appointments of Richard Goldstone (South Africa), Louise Arbour (Canada) and Carla del Ponte (Switzerland), this most prominent post in the ICTY has been held since 1 January 2008 by Belgian law professor and prosecutor Serge Brammertz (for details on the structure and functioning of the ICTY, see Morris and Scharf, 1995). Both Tribunals initially shared one Office of the Prosecutor, but these Offices were separated on 15 September 2003, at which time Hassan Bubacar Jallow of Gambia was appointed Prosecutor for the Rwanda tribunal and his Office was moved to Arusha.

Following an initial phase of only the most hesitant progress – for which the blame fell mainly on the reluctance of states to deliver accused citizens – both tribunals have evolved into effective courts. On 28 June 2001, the 39th indicted suspected war criminal was brought into pre-trial detention in the Netherlands. That suspect was Slobodan Milosevic, the first ever head of state to be held answerable before an international court. In 2006 Milosevic died in detention in Scheveningen before his trial could be completed.

As of October 2011, 161 persons have been indicted under the ICTY. There are thirty-five ongoing cases, of which fourteen cases are currently at trial (amongst them former president of the Serbian Republic in Bosnia and Herzegovina Radovan Karadzic), five cases are currently at pre-trial, and sixteen cases are in appeals. One suspect – former Serbian politician Goran Hadzic – remains at large. Of the 126 concluded cases, sixty-four accused have been sentenced, thirteen accused have been acquitted, and thirteen accused have been transferred to national jurisdiction. Twenty cases have been withdrawn and sixteen accused have died before or after their transfer to the Tribunal.

There are currently fifty cases in progress at the ICTR (as of October 2011), of which ten cases are currently at trial, one case is currently in pre-trial, and nineteen cases are in appeals. Ten suspects remain at large. Of the forty-eight concluded cases, thirty-two accused have been sentenced (among them that of the former Rwandan Prime Minister Jean Kambanda), eight accused have been acquitted, and three accused have been transferred to national jurisdiction. Two cases have been withdrawn and three accused have died before or after their transfer to the Tribunal.

The 'legal intervention' of the Security Council in founding criminal tribunals as a non-military sanction for peace maintenance led to fundamental debates in political science and international law, as well as in the public sphere. A few authors have questioned the authority of the Security Council to create courts on the basis that no state has given the Security Council sovereignty over criminal affairs, and that the Security Council arrogated to itself a legislative competence that is not contained in the Charter. In response, it may be maintained that the Security Council did not create any new law with the statutes of the tribunals but simply made use of existing Customary International Law. However, the group of crimes known as 'crimes against humanity' – referred to in Article 5 of the ICTY Statute – remained highly contested. The scarcity of state practice with respect to this type of crime allows serious doubts as to its status under Customary International Law (see Hasse, 2000). The Secretary-General's report (see no. 48), however, starts from the assumption that the relevant norms had been part of Customary International Law since the Nuremberg and Tokyo tribunals. Both the Trial and Appeals Chambers of the ICTY shared this opinion in their judgement of the Dusko Tadic case, as follows:

A prohibited act committed as a crime against humanity, that is with an awareness that the act formed part of a widespread and systematic attack on a civilian
population, is, all else being equal, a more serious offence than an ordinary war
crime... Dusko Tadic was aware that his acts were part of, and contributed to,
the crime against humanity committed by Bosnian Serb forces against the non-
Serb population of opstina Prijedor. (ICTY Trial Chamber Proceedings,
www.icty.org/sid/7492)

There has also been scepticism regarding the ability of an international criminal
tribunal to contribute to international peace. However, it must be presumed that
the threat of punishment will have at least a general deterrent effect on potential
perpetrators who might earlier have counted on the protection of their sovereign
immunity. Objections raised against the ICTY are answered by the growing recognition extended to it through the submission and extradition of persons for whom
an arrest warrant has been issued. A number of high-ranking functionaries – such
as the chair of the Croatian Defence Committee General Tihomir Blaskic, and the
former president of the Republika Srpska, Biljana Plavsic – have submitted to and
been sentenced by the ICTY. The former Federal Republic of Yugoslavia recognized the ICTY's legitimacy with the delivery of their former head of state Slobodan Milosevic. The Republic of Serbia similarly recognized the ICTY's
legitimacy when its authorities arrested the former Head of State of the Republika
Srpska Radovan Karadzic (arrested in Bosnia-Herzegovina on 21 July 2008,
transferred to the ICTY on 30 July 2008) and the long-wanted Serbian General
Radko Mladic (arrested 26 May, transferred to the ICTY on 3 June 2011).

The International Criminal Court

The significance of the ICTY and the ICTR cannot be underestimated in the
creation of the International Criminal Court (ICC). The Statute for a Permanent
International Criminal Court was voted into existence at the conclusion of the
Rome Conference on 17 July 1998 – of the 148 participating states, 120 voted for
acceptance, twenty-one abstained, and only seven voted against. Among the 'no'
votes were the USA, Israel, China, Iraq, Yemen, Qatar and Libya. (In the case of
the USA, the Bush government turned the USA's passive resistance into an open
struggle against the ICC with President George W. Bush taking the unprecedented
step of withdrawing the signature of his predecessor President William J. Clinton.)
In 2002, the USA achieved the practical suspension of ICC jurisdiction for citizens
of non-states parties engaged in peacekeeping missions (see Security Council
Resolution 1422, 12 July 2002), but this practice ceased in 2004 after it was
disclosed that US service-members in Iraq had been responsible for severe human
rights violations. Although it is extremely unlikely that citizens of the USA would
ever be prosecuted in the ICC – because of the complementary nature of its jurisdiction – the Court has suffered serious harm as a result the USA's behaviour.

After unexpectedly swift ratification by more than sixty states, the ICC Statute
came into effect on 1 July 2002. As of October 2011, 118 states were full members

of the Rome Statute, and a further thirty-three had signed, but not ratified the statue. From the perspective of the international protection of human rights, the importance of this development cannot be overestimated. The creation of the ICC is the culmination of a decades-long process of bringing individuals to the centre of international law – with respect to both an individual's need for protection under international law, and their individual responsibility for their actions under international law – an action tantamount to a weakening of state sovereignty. Article 1 of the ICC Statute gives the Court complementary jurisdiction – i.e. when the legal apparatus of the relevant state is either unwilling or unable to uphold their obligation to investigate and prosecute those accused of serious crimes under international law, the ICC will assume responsibility for fulfilling that duty on behalf of the international community (see ICC Statute, Article 17). The authority of the ICC is therefore not quite as far-reaching as that of the ICTY or the ICTR – both of which may take over processes in progress in respective states if they should consider it necessary. The meaningfulness of the ICC, compared to the international tribunals, is evident in the fact that the ad hoc tribunals were the result of Security Council enforcement measures under Chapter VII, while the ICC is a treaty in which the parties agreed voluntarily to transfer some of their sovereign rights to the Court.

Article 5 of the ICC Statute lays down four core universal crimes: genocide; crimes against humanity; war crimes; and the crime of aggression. Genocide, crimes against humanity, and war crimes are articulated in detail in Articles 6 to 8 of the ICC Statue – the provisions of Article 6 correspond largely with those of the 1948 Genocide Convention; Article 7, on crimes against humanity, is based on the provisions in the ICTY and ICTR statutes (with the major difference being that these crimes are no longer bound to the coexistence of a conflict for their objective criminality, see Kaul, 1998, p. 127); and Article 8, on war crimes, extends the pre-existing definition of war crimes under International Customary Law to apply also to states' internal conflicts. The definition of the crime of aggression, however, was initially postponed due to differences among the states parties. On 11 June 2010, the Review Conference accepted an Article 8 bis as an amendment to the Rome Statute on the crime of aggression, which is therein defined as

> the planning, preparation, initiation or execution, by a person in a position effectively to exercise control over or to direct the political or military action of a State, of an act of aggression which, by its character, gravity and scale, constitutes a manifest violation of the Charter of the United Nations. (Review Conference 2010: Annex III, para. 1)

With regard to acts of aggression, the amendment refers to General Assembly Resolution 3314 (XXIX) of 14 December 1974. For the crime of aggression, there has still been no success in creating a commonly accepted definition and translating it into concrete criminal activities. The practical introduction of this criminal norm thus remains contingent on a decision of the assembled states parties. Article 25 states that the jurisdiction of the Court is over natural persons who can be called to answer for their individual criminal responsibilities. With exceptional clarity, Article 27 denies immunity to sovereign actors, including heads of state, and Article 28 regulates the criminal responsibility of military superiors. According to Article 77, the punishments available are prison sentences up to and including life terms. In addition to prison sentences, fines may be levied, and criminally acquired properties may be confiscated. Article 11 states that the Court is responsible only for crimes that take place after the Statute's entry into effect. For this, it was necessary (Article 126) for sixty states to ratify the Statute.

In contrast to the ad hoc tribunals, the ICC constitutes a permanent international court with obligatory jurisdiction. At the same time, the ICC's jurisdiction is also subject to certain regulations. Automatic jurisdiction for the crimes mentioned in the Statute can occur only when, according to Article 12(2), either the state in whose territory the crime took place or the state to whom the suspected perpetrator belongs is a party to the ICC. Thus, crimes that take place in an internal conflict in a state that is not a party to the ICC are not subject to the ICC's jurisdiction, even if the victims of the crimes were citizens of a state party. With respect to war crimes, Article 124 provides that the states parties

> may declare that, for a period of seven years after the entry into force of this Statute for the State concerned, it does not accept the jurisdiction of the Court with respect to the category of crimes referred to in article 8 when a crime is alleged to have been committed by its nationals or on its territory.

These limitations are somewhat mitigated by the fact that non-parties to the Statute may accept the jurisdiction of the ICC for a particular case, and that the Security Council may refer a situation to the ICC under Chapter VII, when it suspects that a large number of crimes have been committed (Article 13(b)). If such a step is undertaken by the Security Council it must be considered a coercive measure according to Article 41 of the Charter binding on all member states – therefore the issue of whether or not a state has ratified the Statute and is a member of the ICC becomes irrelevant. Security Council Resolution 1593 of 31 March 2005 referred the situation in the Darfur region of the Sudan to the ICC so that the prosecutor could start investigations and indict the relevant persons for committing genocide, war crimes, and crimes against humanity. Most prominently, the Court issued arrest warrants for sitting Sudanese President Hassan Omar al-Bashir, and Sudanese Humanitarian Affairs Minister Ahmed Haroun. That the ICC prosecutor was acting under Chapter VII of the Charter is very important provision for the effectiveness of the Court – should the system be effective in bringing Sudanese politicians to the Court when Sudan has not ratified the Statute, it will represent a huge step forward in preventing states or their leaders from avoiding responsibility for their crimes by simply refusing to sign or ratify the Statute.

It was also significant in the case of the al-Bashir and Haroun warrants that China and USA – vocal opponents of the ICC – supported the involvement of the Court through constructive abstention, thus showing acceptance of the principle relevance of this institution. On 26 February 2011 the Security Council referred the situation in Libya to the prosecutor of the ICC by a unanimous vote (S/RES/1970). Under the same conditions, however, the permanent members of the Security Council remain in a privileged, practically untouchable position.

The structure of the ICC comprises four organs: the Presidency, the Chambers, the Office of the Prosecutor and the Registry (see Schabas 2007, Chapter 11). The Presidency consists of the President of the Court and two Vice-presidents, who are elected for a three years term by their fellow judges. Song Sang-hyun of South Korea has been President of the ICC since 11 March 2009, following Philippe Kirsch of Canada. Vice-presidents are Fatoumata Dembele Diarra of Mali and Hans-Peter Kaul of Germany. There are eighteen independent judges (including the Presidency), appointed by the Assembly of States Parties for a nine-years term without re-election, who build the three divisions of the Chambers.

- **The Pre-trial Division** is composed of six judges in two pre-trial chambers. The Pre-trial chamber is also entitled to issue arrest warrants or summonses to appear if it is convinced that the respective person has committed crimes under the jurisdiction of the Court.
- **The Trial Division** is composed of seven judges with criminal trial experience. Three judges of the Division carry out the judicial functions of the Trial Chamber.
- **The Appeals Division** is composed of five judges (one of them is the President of the Court).

The Office of the Prosecutor is lead by a world-class lawyer – currently Luis Moreno-Ocampo of Argentina – who is responsible for the conduct of investigations, which he can assume on referral by a state-party (Art. 14), *proprio motu* on communications from individuals and organizations (Art. 15), and at the request of the Security Council (Art. 13b). The Registry is the main administration and support organ of the Court.

Since the Court assumed work in 2003, three situations have been referred to it by states parties: the Central African Republic, the Democratic Republic of the Congo, and Uganda. In the situation in Uganda the Pre-trial Chamber issued five arrest warrants against leading members of the Congolese militia called the 'Lord's Resistance Army' (one of which, for alleged LRA Deputy Army Commander Raska Lukwiya, has been withdrawn following his death on 12 August 2006.) In the situation of the Democratic Republic of Congo there have been five arrest warrants issued, of which three cases are in pre-trial, one case is at trial and one suspect is still at large. In the situation of the Central African Republic, one arrest warrant has been issued for Jean-Pierre Bemba Gombo whose case is currently in pre-trial. As mentioned above, the Security Council mandated the ICC to investigate the Darfur situation in Sudan, a non-state-party of the Rome Statute. Of the six warrants issued across four Sudanese cases, two accused are currently at trial, one case was withdrawn at pre-trial stage, and three other accused – including President Hassan Omar al-Bashir – remain at large. In March 2010, Pre-trial Chamber II authorized the prosecutor to open an investigation *proprio motu* in the situation of Kenya in relation to crimes against humanity committed between 1 June 2005 and

26 November 2009. To date, six warrants have been issues across two cases, of which all six are at trial. In October 2011 the ICC opened a trial against Laurent Gbagbo, the former President of Côte d'Ivoire. At the time of writing, fourteen cases in seven countries had been brought to the ICC.

It is still too early to assess whether or not the ICC might become an effective actor in the field of human rights protection. The achievements of the ad hoc Tribunals for Rwanda and Yugoslavia give space for optimism, as does the establishment of so-called hybrid courts in Cambodia and Sierra Leone where the UN and national legal authorities co-operate in the prosecution and trials of alleged criminals. As a result of these developments, impunity for top political or military leaders no longer exists, and severe human rights violations are no longer an acceptable norm in the international legal system. But without the compliance and co-operation of the states, norms and judicial procedures matter for very little. The referral of the Sudan situation to the ICC under a constructive abstention by the US and China and their support of the referral of the Libya case can be considered as encouraging signals – the US opposition to the ICC, in particular, has become less consistent and less credible than ever before. The road from the Nuremberg and Tokyo Tribunals to a standing International Criminal Court was long, but it still remains that case that more time and more effort will be required to fully convince state actors that justice should prevail over interests.

Summary and Further Challenges

Despite progress, the global discourse on human rights still faces the task of producing a universally accepted understanding on a comprehensive and consistent code of the human rights that can be guaranteed and protected under international law. Concretely, such an accomplishment would involve the integration of the standards and norms established in international covenants and treaties into national law, the breathing of real life into them, and the decisive and effective use of the available instruments for their implementation. There are good chances that this might all, in fact, be brought to fruition. In the 1990s, the fall of socialism showed the unbroken attractive power of a western understanding of human rights in combination with democratic forms of government. The course of the economic crisis in Asia following 1997 also showed that democratic states in Asia, such as South Korea and Thailand, are able to bring their problems under control more quickly and in a more sustainable way than can authoritarian systems such as Indonesia. Even in industrialized states there is growing awareness that humankind cannot live on liberty alone. What might emerge from such is the global acceptance of a non-hierarchical inter-dependence of all three generations of human rights. This requires inter-cultural dialogue and a willingness to learn from all states and cultures involved in the human rights discourse. At the political level, it also means the progressive re-evaluation of the classical notion of state sovereignty. Elementary human rights, as a global legal good, are removed from the realm of control of individual states. The nexus between human rights and international stability in the globalized world imposes duties on states on the same level as the obligations to peaceful resolution of disputes and the prevention of war. This excludes isolation with reference to sovereignty rights just as much as it excludes the instrumentalization of human rights in the pursuit of national interest.

Following 9/11 and the Global War on Terror, however, new problems have emerged – the protection of human rights has lost its high position in the public's attention, at least temporarily and it is not only in the USA that questions of security have dominated the political discussion since the terrorist attacks in New York and Washington DC (Robinson, 2002). Across most democratic states, the need to guarantee citizens' and non-citizens' basic individual human rights has taken a back seat to the exigencies of public safety and security. Standards for basic rights are lowered, and new hurdles for refugees or asylum-seekers are constructed. In states where the human rights situation was already precarious – such as in China, Russia, or Pakistan – the fight against international terrorism serves as a pretext for the further aggravation of their handling of minorities and political opposition. Many western democracies are not only overlooking this fact, but are also positively accepting as partners states and regimes which – only a few years before – were pariahs of the international community because of their human rights practices. Questions must be asked concerning the seriousness of western democracies in their commitment to the standards they supposedly advocate. Human rights, it would seem, are not sacrosanct; they are still deeply rooted in the political culture of states and societies. Human rights have a stable normative foundation, but it remains to be seen if normative goals can be matched with effective operational progress. Human rights regained some footing at the 2005 World Summit, not as a central player, but it was at least given a more prominent place on the international agenda. The development of an integrative universal understanding of human rights is immensely important. Although monitoring mechanisms have been created, the sovereignty principle means that such mechanisms have remained 'rudimentary attempts at real and effective implementation mechanisms' (Riedel, 2004, p. 52). More work has to be done to convince states of the usefulness of a universal understanding of human rights.

The slow process of gradually bringing states into various human rights treaties demonstrates states' willingness to move in this direction. Compared to compulsory duties, obligations entered into freely have a far greater chance of becoming embedded in the political consciousness of a state or a society. Interventionism of whatever kind for the protection of human rights will remain subject to the suspicion of unilateral pursuit of national interests as long as the causes for intervention are determined selectively by the active and powerful states. This does not mean that military intervention for the protection of human rights could ever be necessary or justified, but it does mean that, as in the area of peacekeeping, they should be exceptional instances and carried out by the community of states as a whole.

Further Reading

Broomhall, Bruce (2003) *International Justice and the International Criminal Court. Between Sovereignty and The Rule of Law*, Oxford: Oxford University Press.

Evans, Gareth (2008) *The Responsibility to Protect: Ending Mass Atrocity Crimes Once and For All*, Washington, DC: Brookings Institution Press.

Nowak, Manfred (2003) *Introduction to the International Human Rights Regimes*, Leiden, Boston: Martinus Nijhoff Publishers.

O'Flaherty, Michael (2002) *Human Rights and the UN: Practice before the Treaty Bodies*, Leiden, Boston: Martinus Nijhoff Publishers.

Ramcharan, Bertrand G. (2002) *The Security Council and the Protection of Human Rights*, Leiden, Boston: Martinus Nijhoff Publishers.

Robertson, Geoffrey (2003) *Crimes Against Humanity. The Struggle for Global Justice*, New York: New Press.

Schabas, William A. (2007) *An Introduction to the International Criminal Court*, 3rd edition, Cambridge: Cambridge University Press.

Steiner, Henry J. and Philip Alston (2007) *International Human Rights in Context*, 3rd edition, Oxford: Oxford University Press.

Weijers, Hanna (ed.) (2009) *The Office of the High Commissioner for Human Rights. Selected Basic Documents and Background Materials*, Nijmegen: Wolf Legal Publishers.

7

Economic, Development and Environmental Questions in the United Nations: Problem Areas and Institutional Design

In his Millennium Report to the General Assembly, Secretary-General Kofi Annan used the metaphor of the 'world as global village' to emphasize the extent of global interdependence. (Annan, 2000, p. 9 *et seq.*) Imagine a village of 1,000 people where the current world demographics are reflected on the population: around 150 people would live in the 'nice part of town', 780 would live in the poorer quarters (some of them with insufficient nutrition) and 70 people would live in a neighbourhood in transition. Two hundred people would possess more than 86 per cent of the total wealth, while nearly 500 people would have to survive on barely US$2 dollars a day. Two hundred and twenty of the villagers would be illiterate, fewer than sixty people would own a computer, only twenty-four would have internet access, and more than 500 would never have used a telephone. Some areas of the village would be relatively safe, but others would be plagued by organized violence. In the last few years, there would have been an increasing number of natural disasters that hit the poorer quarters comparatively hard. The average temperature is climbing, and the threat of further environmental catastrophes looms large. Addressing the problems in this 'global village' is a major aspect of the UN's work. Next to peacekeeping and the protection of human rights, activities in the socioeconomic and development areas constitute a third major area of duties for the UN.

There have been progressive improvements in the areas of socio-economics and development since the beginning of the new century. Despite rapidly rising populations across most of the developing world – a growth from 4 to 5 billion between 1995 and 2005 – poverty levels have fallen. The proportion of people living in extreme poverty – defined as less than US$1 per day – fell from 28 per cent to 21 per cent. The rates of undernourishment and infant-mortality also dropped and life expectancy rose to an average of sixty-five years (see UN Millennium Project, 2005, p. 13 *et seq.*). Such positive trends, however, do not tell but half the truth. Newly industrialized states like China, Brazil, or India developed significantly above the average whilst the progress of development has deteriorated in many regions of Sub-Saharan Africa. In fact, disparities in global socio-economic indicators – such as life expectancy, infant mortality, literacy rates, and nutrition – demonstrate degrees of inequality tantamount to what has been termed 'global apartheid'. The North–South 'conflict' – the relationship between the developing South and the industrialized North, and the disparate economic, social, and political climates of each – constitutes a central problem of international relations and a central challenge for the UN. Development aid can only be effective 'when it is conceptualized and organized as a cross-cutting task, and bound up with foreign and human rights policy, trade and international finance policy, and environmental and agricultural policy in a coherent politics of the whole' (Nuscheler, 2002a, p. 7). From Nuscheler's perspective, external assistance is just one of many strategies for effective development.

Political science presents a number of different and competing ideas about the causes of underdevelopment, and also presents a range of different strategies for addressing them. Old arguments were based on 'modernization theories' (the belief that development will catch up with modernization and economic growth) and 'dependence theories' (the belief in independent development through disengagement from the world market), but these have been outgrown. Today, the argument focuses on a different key question, one that is also of essential importance to the conceptualization of development politics at the UN: are free trade and the promotion of market structures an appropriate path to the dismantling of developmental differences, or do these only serve those who are already more capable?

A number of different concepts are used in the discussion on development policy to describe the problem that cannot be discussed in full here. Along with the current transition from the concept of 'development aid' to 'development co-operation', the term 'Third World' has come under increasing criticism. Born of the decolonization processes of the 1960s, the term 'Third World' came from the analytical division of the world into three groups of states: the 'first' world (the industrialized states), the 'second' world (the socialist states); and the 'third' world' (the developing countries). The end of the Cold War, and the subsequent collapse of the bipolar world order, meant that the analytical basis of the world's three groups became out-dated, and the increasing heterogeneity among developing countries provides a further reason why a new conceptual differentiation is necessary. What remains contested, however, is the often-described phenomenon of the 'end of the Third World'. In particular, there exists a controversial debate concerning the use of the term: is it about encouraging states to reach a western standard and the strong internal differentiation among developing countries, or is it simply a cover for the still extremely unequal levels of development on a global scale? The controversial terminologies in development politics are further reflected in the different understandings of what is a 'developing country' (see Thomas, 2008). One common characteristic is that developing countries cannot satisfy the basic needs of existence for large portions of their populations. The following criteria can also be found in differing levels in most developing countries, although how these criteria are to be weighted has still found no consensus in the academic literature:

- *Economic characteristics*: very low average per capita income together with extremely unequal income distribution, low saving and investment rates, low productivity, insufficient infrastructure, a dominant traditional sector partly orientated on providing for itself, export dependence on a few products aimed primarily at industrialized countries – predominantly raw materials – and a high level of debt.
- *Socio-demographic characteristics*: comparatively low life expectancy against a background of a broad absence of overall good health and very bad medical care, a high illiteracy rate and low levels of education, very high population growth, and a large transitory element in areas surrounding urban centres.
- *Ecological characteristics*: ecological over-exploitation because of poverty, and the destruction of particularly delicate ecosystems.
- *Socio-cultural and political characteristics*: an orientation on primary groups such as the extended family or ethnic group, together with a low level of loyalty to institutional structures (such as the state), low mobility, authoritarian (but weak) states, weak political legitimization for the leadership, inadequate protection of human rights, a lack of practicable political programmes, high rates of corruption, and a tendency to violent resolution of both internal and external disputes.

The different levels of development in evidence have led the UN and other various associated institutions to use different criteria for sub-grouping developing countries. For example, the World Bank categorizes based on per capita income, thus distinguishing countries with middle income levels (MICs) from those with low income levels (LICs), but it also differentiates into further sub-groups based on a wide range of criteria such as the level of a country's external debt. The UNDP produces an annual *Human Development Index* (HDI) based on a combination of life expectancy, literacy rates, and buying power, and produces a three-way grouping of countries with very high, high, medium and low human development as well as group of 'other counties and territories' of which the programme was not able to collect reliable data. In the year 2010, there were forty-two states in the very high human development category, including Norway, Australia, Canada, the USA, Sweden, Belgium, Japan, Germany, Spain, Singapore, Israel, Poland, Bahrain, Estonia and Barbados. In the second group, there were forty-three states with high human development, such as Bahamas, Chile, Argentina, Croatia, Mexico, Russia, Brazil, Peru, Turkey and Tonga. Countries like Fiji, China, Tunisia, Morocco, South Africa Cambodia or Pakistan belonged to the forty-two medium-developed countries. Another forty-two countries formed the category of low development countries to which the report counts inter alia Kenya, Lesotho, Sierra Leone, Haiti or Afghanistan. The 'other countries and territories' encompasses states with radically different socio-economic backgrounds – such as Monaco, Oman and San Marino (which are extremely affluent) and Cuba, Eritrea, and Somalia (which are extremely poor) – whose only common attribute is the unavailability of development indicator data (see UNDP, 2010, p. 143 *et seq.*).

The so-called least developed countries (LDCs; see Table 7.1) form a distinct category in the UN. Members of the LDC group share several common criteria: low income levels (less than US$905 per annum based on a three-year average estimate of the gross national income (GNI) per capita); low human capital status criterion development (a Human Assets Index (HAI) based on indicators including but not limited to percentage of population undernourished, mortality rate for children aged five years or under, gross secondary school enrolment ratio, and adult illiteracy rate); and economic vulnerability criterion (a composite Economic Vulnerability Index (EVI) based on indicators including but not limited to population size, remoteness, share of agriculture, forestry and fisheries in gross domestic product; homelessness owing to natural disasters; or instability of agricultural production). States that match all three criteria may be included on the list of LDCs and are eligible for special conditions for development aid and forgiveness of debt. When the General Assembly first used the LDC classification in the early 1970s there were twenty-five states on the list. In 2001 the General Assembly and the Secretariat established the UN Office of the High Representative for Least Developed Countries (LDCs), Landlocked Developing Countries and Small Islands Developing Countries (UNOHRLLS) for the purpose of providing a better and co-ordinated support to LDCs. According to UNOHRLLS in 2011 the number of LDC states had increased to forty-nine, comprising more than 815 million people or more than one-tenth of the world's population, with a rapid annual population growth rate of 2.37 per cent.

TABLE 7.1
Least developed countries (LDC) (2011)

Africa (33)		Asia (15)	
Angola	Madagascar	Afghanistan #	Myanmar
Benin	Malawi #	Bangladesh	Nepal #
Burkina Faso #	Mali #	Bhutan #	Samoa *
Burundi #	Mauritania	Cambodia	Solomon Islands *
Central African	Mozambique	Kiribati *	Timor-Leste *
Republic #	Niger #	Lao People's	Tuvalu *
Chad #	Rwanda #	Democratic	Vanuatu *
Comoros #	Sao Tomé and	Republic #	Yemen
Democratic Republic	Príncipe *	Maldives *	
of the Congo	Senegal		
Djibouti	Sierra Leone	**Latin America and the Caribbean (1)**	
Equatorial Guinea	Somalia	Haiti *	
Eritrea	Sudan		
Ethiopia #	Togo		
Gambia	Uganda #	**Total: 49 states**	
Guinea	United Republic		
Guinea Bissau *	of Tanzania		
Lesotho #	Zambia*		
Liberia			

* Also SIDS (Small Island Developing States)   # Also LLDCs (Landlocked Developing Countries)

Source: UNOHRLLS.

In 1945, then-Secretary of State for the USA, Edward Stettinius, noted poignantly that 'the fight for peace must be waged on two fronts. On one front, it is about security, and on the other, it is about the economy and social justice. Only a victory on both fronts will present the world with a lasting peace' (cited by French, 1995, p. 6 *et seq.*). The terrorist attacks of 9/11 did not merely show up the vulnerability of the global infrastructure, they also removed 'from the islands of prosperity the illusion that the world's crises brew on at a safe distance' (Nuscheler, 2002a, p. 2). In countless documents and declarations, the UN has stated the connection between peace, development and the environment. In the June 1992 'Agenda for Peace', for example, it was stated that problems such as uncontrolled population growth, crushing debt, barriers to trade, and the ever-increasing disparity between rich and poor can each trigger conflict as well as they can be the consequences of conflict, and they each require unflagging UN attention and prioritization. 'Agenda 21' – as agreed in June 1992 at the Conference for Environmental Protection and Development – calls for a global partnership for sustainable development that would find its expression in meeting the development and environmental needs of present and future generations. In the 'Agenda for Development' of June 1997 it is claimed that a prerequisite for an effective multilateral system of development is the recognition and support of the unique role of the UN: its universality, its global network of relationships, and its ability to create consensus, to shape politics, and to aid in the rationalization of public and private development efforts (see Glanzer, 2001). The Millennium Declaration of 2000 and the World Summit Outcome Document of 2005, both adopted by the heads of state and government, also express this understanding of the organization's function in the area of global development efforts.

It has already been discussed that the UN, and in particular its numerous specialized agencies and subsidiary organs, are active in practically all sub-areas of this issue, with global implications. Commensurate with this, the organization has grown greatly: 'For years now, the recipe for solving new challenges seems to have been the founding of a new committee or body' (Dicke, 1994, p. 115). This brings with it, however, the problem of growing confusion and dwindling transparency, as well as decreasing manoeuvrability across the system as a whole: 'The more the UN in New York built up its own battalions, the less capable its policy bodies became of providing an interdisciplinary framework: it became even more difficult for the UN to put brakes on inter-agency rivalry when it was competing in the game itself (Righter, 1995, p. 49). Because of its institutional complexity, the UN system is often described as 'ungovernable'. Organizational expansion has been accompanied by an increase in substantive areas of responsibility – where peacekeeping initially held pride of place as a core responsibility of the UN, economic, development, and social responsibilities now constitute a central pillar of UN work and account for approximately 80 per cent of the organization's total spending.

This chapter is not intended to give a detailed structural description of all the activities of the entire UN system in economic, social, development, and environmental issues. Rather, select areas of activity will be analysed and particular problems examined.

Responsibilities and Fields of Action

The will of UN founders that socio-economic and development issues should constitute one of the UN's core responsibilities is first expressed in Article 1(3). The League of Nations failed to bring such issues to the fore, but the UN makes clear that international co-operation is necessary for 'solving international problems of an economic, social, cultural, or humanitarian character'. This notion is based on a broad concept of peace that expressly recognizes that particular conditions must be created under which peace and international security can be better, and more permanently, maintained. The Charter preamble lists some of these conditions as the promotion of social progress and better standards of life – the assumption being that there exists an indissoluble connection between the maintenance of international peace and security and international economic and social co-operation. Klaus Dicke (1994, p. 87 *et seq*.) points to the fact that this has become possible only against the backdrop of a particular understanding of politics and the state in which 'international organizations are allowed much more access to member states' societies than was imaginable at the time of the League of Nations'. Hüfner (1994, p. 101) even argues that a precondition for this ambitious catalogue of activities was that, in the place of the 'night-sentry state on the basis of a liberal laissez-faire conception', the social-political responsibility of the state in the form of the 'intervention-orientated welfare state' had assumed precedence. Whether such trust in state (respectively supra-state) action remains relevant in the age of globalization is a matter of controversy.

The mission of solving international problems of an economic, social, cultural, and humanitarian nature is regulated in UN Charter Chapter IX: International Economic and Social Co-operation. Here, the distinction between specialized agencies and subsidiary organs becomes particularly relevant (see Chapter I). It must also be noted that, over the years, the UN system has undergone substantive internal growth and expansion, and was less confusing in its original construction than it is now. Subsidiary organs are created by the General Assembly; some of them reporting directly to the General Assembly and some via other organs. The General Assembly, however (unlike the Security Council) does not have the competence to issue binding decisions; it can only give recommendations. The work of specialized agencies is thus somewhat more independent than that of the subsidiary organs, but these also are unable to act against the will of their members.

The first article in Chapter IX – Article 55 – establishes three areas of work for 'the creation of conditions of stability and well-being which are necessary for peaceful and friendly relations among nations based on respect for the principle of equal rights and self-determination of peoples' (Article 55). These three areas are:

(a) higher standards of living, full employment, and conditions of economic and social progress and development;
(b) solutions of international economic, social, health, and related problems; and international cultural and educational co-operation; and

(c)   universal respect for, and observance of, human rights and fundamental free-
      doms for all without distinction as to race, sex, language, or religion.

Article 56 contains an obligation for all states 'to take joint and separate action in
cooperation with the organization for the achievement of the purposes set forth in
Article 55'. Articles 57 to 59 deal with the specialized agencies (which have 'wide
international responsibilities, as defined in their basic instruments, in economic,
social, cultural, educational, health, and related fields') with Article 58 specifically stating that the UN is to 'make recommendations for the coordination of the
policies and activities of the specialized agencies'. Article 59 expressly authorizes
the creation of new specialized agencies as necessary (the work of the specialized
agencies goes back to Article 22, which gives the General Assembly the right to
create subsidiary organs in so far as it may see this as being necessary to the carrying out of its duties). Since 1997, administrative tasks for economic and development issues have been conducted by the Secretariat's Department of Economic
and Social Affairs under the leadership of an Under-Secretary-General; this does
not, however, affect the possibility of creating other independent secretariats for
individual programmes, commissions and subsidiary organs.

Chapter X (Articles 61–72) regulates the competencies of ECOSOC as the
principle organ responsible for co-ordinating the economic and social work of UN
specialized agencies and commissions. According to Article 62, ECOSOC may
'make or initiate studies and reports with respect to international economic, social,
cultural, educational, health, and related matters, and may make recommendations
with respect to any such matters to the General Assembly, to the Members of the
United Nations, and to the specialized agencies concerned'. Furthermore,
ECOSOC may make recommendations, draft conventions, and call international
conferences on matters within its jurisdiction. According to Article 63, it 'may
enter into agreements with [agencies]… subject to approval by the General
Assembly, and may co-ordinate the activities of the specialized agencies'. Subsequent articles give ECOSOC a broad mandate in social and economic tasks, and
Article 68 specifically enables it to set up commissions 'as may be required' – a
power that ECOSOC has used extensively. Thus, the subsidiary machinery of the
ECOSOC now consists of a completely incomprehensible web of thirty units and
a further sixty-one sub-units.

Among the most important of these sixty-one sub-units are the nine
Functional Commissions (on which states serve a maximum term of four years)
as follows:

- Statistical Commission
- Commission on Population and Development
- Commission for Social Development
- Commission the Status of Women
- Commission on Narcotic Drugs
- Commission on Crime Prevention and Criminal Justice
- Commission on Science and Technology for Development

- Commission on Sustainable Development
- United Nations Forum on Forests

ECOSOC also has five Regional Commissions, each of which have in turn established large numbers of functional subcommittees. The five Regional Commissions are:

- Economic Commission for Africa (ECA)
- Economic and Social Commission for Asia and the Pacific (ESCAP)
- Economic Commission for Europe (ECE)
- Economic Commission for Latin America and the Caribbean (ECLAC)
- Economic and Social Commission for Western Asia (ESCWA)

Regional Commissions were established as early as 1947 in order to provide help for states hit especially hard by the Second World War. The ECE and ESCAP were founded in 1947 in Geneva and Bangkok respectively in order to facilitate and support intra-continental co-operation on all levels in each region (since 1974, ESCAP has also included a statistical institute and a centre for the transferral of technology). ECLAC was founded in 1948 in Santiago de Chile; ECA was founded in 1958 in Addis Ababa; and ESCWA was founded in Beirut in 1973. Today, the work of the Regional Commissions has to some extent been taken over by other regional organizations (in Europe, for example, by the European Union and the European Council) and they tend to play only a secondary role. However, Regional Commissions continue to be significant insomuch as they continue to promote inter-regional exchange and to provide impetus for co-operation. Furthermore, it has been possible to conduct a number of macroeconomic studies and technical conventions within their frameworks. Not least, ECOSOC maintains a number of useful permanent committees and expert committees, some of which have their own secretariats.

The 'proliferation of sub- and subsidiary organs' (Boutros-Ghali, 1994, no. 227) has been the target of much criticism. In particular, ECOSOC has been accused of being barely able to reach coherent decisions, and questions remain as to whether or not the continual expansion of ECOSOC constitutes an over-stepping of its mandate and capabilities.

The United Nations and Multilateral Co-operation on Development

The UN and its specialized agencies constitute an important pillar of multilateral development co-operation having 'contributed substantially to making the development problematique [*sic*] visible and [to] letting the interests of the South influence their own definitions of "interest"' (Brock, 1995, p. 68). Two separate groups dominate these issue areas and constitute two largely separate systems of organizations:

- *The Bretton Woods Organizations/financial institutions:* The World Bank Group and the International Monetary Fund (IMF) – these two are not integral parts of the UN system and are not subject to its instructions, but they do exercise important functions in the politics of multilateral development.
- *Other UN agencies, programmes, and funds for development,* including but not limited to: the UN Conference on Trade and Development (UNCTAD), the UN Development Programme (UNDP), the World Food Programme (WFP) or the UN Children's Fund (UNICEF), as well as the specialized agencies, like the Food and Agriculture Organization (FAO), the International Fund for Agricultural Development (IFAD), the International Labour Organization (ILO), the Industrial Development Organization (UNIDO), or the World Health Organization (WHO).

The Bretton Woods Organizations (named after the 1944 international conference – held at Bretton Woods, New Hampshire, USA – on reordering the world economy and the global finance architecture) is comprised of the World Bank Group and the IMF, both of which offer technical and financial assistance to developing states. The Bretton Woods Organizations were born of the experiences of the global economic crises of the 1930s and are based on the idea that international economic issues should be rooted in an institutional framework and subjected to common rules. The Bretton Woods Organizations are dedicated to the principles of free trade, the convertibility of currencies, and an open market economy. The organizational relationship between the Bretton Woods Organizations and the UN is complicated – they formally and legally belong to the UN system – but in practice they occupy a special position, characterized by high independence, their own by-laws, budgets and structures, and a very rudimentary connection to the UN system.

    The World Bank is not a bank in the traditional sense, it is made up of two development institutions – the International Bank for Reconstruction and Development (IBRD) and the International Development Association (IDA). The purposes of the World Bank are the stabilization of economic development in its member states through capital investments and credit, the promotion of private international investment, the expansion of international trade, and the stabilization of the balance of payments. Recently added to the World Bank's list of goals is the promotion of growth in developing and transition states. The most important instrument of the World Bank is its ability to grant credit, primarily for the purposes of project financing. Additionally, so-called 'sector operations' are sometimes carried out for the stabilization of entire economic sectors. The primary targets of financing are investment projects, technical aid and programmes for economic reform (structural adaptation credit). The World Bank offers assistance on the basis of strict economic criteria, and the granting of credit is tied to very specific conditions that sometimes require drastic and sometimes controversial adaptation measures on the part of the receiving country. The IDA offers credit – primarily for the purposes of fighting poverty – under much less stringent conditions. The work of the World Bank is complemented by three other members of the

World Bank Group: the International Finance Corporation (IFC), the Multilateral Investments Guarantees Agency (MIGA), and the International Centre for the Settlement of Investment Disputes (ICSID). The institutions in the World Bank Group are owned by the governments of the member states in each institution   the highest membership is of the IBRD (187 member states). The other four World Bank Group institutions each have between 147 and 182 member states.

The IMF is comprised of 187 member states whose representation is based on their relative size in the global economy. The purposes of the International Monetary Fund (IMF) are closely related to those of the World Bank group (indeed, entry into the IMF is a formal pre-requisite for membership of the World Bank). The IMF promotes international co-operation in the area of currency politics, with the purpose of expanding trade and exchange stability; provides funds for individual states in balance of payments difficulty; and plays an important role in member states' decisions on exchange rates. The IMF's area of competence has grown markedly since the 1970s. On the one hand, the volume of credit has expanded enormously, and on the other, the IMF has developed into the guarantor – for both public and private actors – of the willingness of countries in crisis to adopt reforms. The concluding of a structural adaptation programme with the IMF symbolizes a seal of good faith, guaranteeing subsequent access to the international capital market (Metzger, 2002). Their sometimes considerable interference in the economic and social systems of the developing countries has made the Bretton Woods Organizations subject to the accusation that they are representatives of a 'radical market turbo-capitalism', and that they pay far too little attention to a country's social stability – but this book is not the place for that debate. The differences between the Bretton Woods Organizations and the rest of the UN system of development co-operation do however have consequences for the UN's work (see Table 7.2). In the Bretton Woods Organizations, voting rights are weighted according to financial contribution and economic capacity, which means that the western industrialized countries dominate not only *de facto* (as they do in much of the rest of the UN system), but also structurally.

Initially, the work of the UN agencies, programmes, and funds for development (those not part of the Bretton Woods Organizations) was restricted to the analysis of economic development, the collection of data, and the occasional giving of advice. Very quickly, however, the demand for some level of integration between the world trade order and development aid measures found its way onto the General Assembly's agenda. Even then, the conviction remained that the Bretton Woods Organizations would address the needs of the developing countries, and that special development institutions and organizations within the UN thus seemed superfluous (Ferdowsi, 2002, p. 156).

The processes of decolonization resulted in a rapid increase in the number of sovereign states and thus there was a rapid increase in the number of UN member states. Between 1945 and 1954, only nine new states joined the UN (a growth from fifty-one to sixty member states). In 1955 alone, sixteen new states joined the organization. From 1956 to 1959 a further seven were accepted, and in 1960 another sixteen states became members. The influx of new member states shifted

TABLE 7.2
Basic principles of the UN and the Bretton Woods Organizations

UN specialized agencies and programmes	Bretton Woods Organizations
Membership for all peace-loving states by a decision of the General Assembly	Membership depends on financial contributions, economic prerequisites and the consent of important states
Every member state has one vote	Voting rights weighted depending on economic strength and financial contributions
All member states treated as equals	Special treatment for poor members
Members subjected to punishment only if they violate provisions of the Charter	Members who fail to meet certain economic requirements are subjected to punishment
Programmes and measures apply to all members	Programmes and measures are tailored to particular states
Co-ordination with the main UN organization (in many cases only rudimentary)	Co-ordination with the main UN organization is largely neglected
No economic measures taken against members with the exception of sanctions in the case of a breach of the peace	Access to international capital markets depends on the evaluation of a state's credit-worthiness
Development aid funds either need not be repaid at all, or are levelled out by a long repayment period with very low interest rates	Development help conducted primarily according to the conditions of the market for capital

Source: Based on discussion in Childers and Urquhart (1994, p. 78).

the balance of UN membership and consequently shifted the General Assembly's priorities so that there was a significant lessening of western (particularly US) dominance. The majority of new member states believed that the world economic and financial status quo was not in their interests, and they fought for radical changes. Moreover, the differences in the prosperities of industrialized and developing countries made clear that increased global trade was required. The General Assembly and ECOSOC were considered the most appropriate forums for debating these issues. The founding of the UN Conference on Trade and Development (UNCTAD) in 1964 – the first important subsidiary organ in the area of development – was considered a milestone in this direction. UNCTAD was followed in 1965 by the UN Development Programme (UNDP) and in 1966 by the Industrial Development Organization (UNIDO). Additionally, the affairs of developing countries were beginning to receive a greater share of the attention in the General

Assembly, for example, the 1961 declaration of the 'UN Decade for Development' and the 1974 'Charter of Economic Rights and Duties of States'. The 1974 'Declaration for a New International Economic Order' (NIEO) claimed that the economic status quo stood in unmitigated contradiction to the development of international relations and was supported by a majority in the General Assembly, but that majority did not include the industrialized western countries. During this period, developing countries became a power that used their majority in the General Assembly to make their influence felt in all areas of international politics. This 'irreversible shifting of the world balance of power requires the active, unlimited, and equal participation of the developing countries in the formulation and implementation of all decisions affecting the international community.' As a consequence, the interests of developed countries could no longer be separated from those of developing countries, and the close relationship between the prosperity of the developed states and the growth and development of the developing countries could no longer be ignored.

The developing states' majority in the General Assembly resulted in a number of declarations for a new world economic order, including but not limited to: easier access to markets for goods from developing countries, full sovereignty over natural resources, fair conditions for trade, the granting of active aid to developing countries free of political or military conditions, and free access to technology. These declarations, however, remained largely without effect. Industrialized states did not respond with the required structural reforms, nor did they increase their engagement in multilateral development aid. As a result, developing states became more radical in their demands which were 'again met with criticism and rejection from western publics, and prejudiced them increasingly against the world organization' (Ferdowsi, 2002, p. 159). Quite simply, very little attention was paid to the countless well-intentioned declarations of the General Assembly, specialized agencies, and subsidiary organs. Furthermore, 'the great political debates have always led to stylization of reality, to self-delusion about the complexity of problems, to the suppression of uncomfortable realizations, and to the denial of [the General Assembly's] own responsibility' (Brock, 1995, p. 79). In October 1970, the General Assembly determined that the industrially developed states should provide an annual minimum contribution of 0.7 per cent of their gross national income (GNI) in the form of official development aid (ODA). By 2009 – a period of thirty-nine years –this decision had been enacted only by Denmark, Luxembourg, Norway, the Netherlands and Sweden. Japan, for example, provided only 0.18 per cent, whereas Germany fulfilled half of its obligation by donating 0.35 per cent. This largely missed target exemplifies the disparity between needs, non-binding declarations, and reality.

The inadequate financing of the UN's development activities is a constant topic of international discussion and concern. In the 1960s, one analyst wrote that 'in recent times, there has been an observable lessening in international efforts at development, and development aid is in a state of acute crisis' (cited in Martens, 2001, p. 52). From 1994 to 1998, contributions by western industrialized states to developing states in the form of public development aid sank by nearly US$10 billion. At the same time, however, private direct investment in many developing states rose rapidly and in March 2002 – after a ten-year preparation phase – a large-scale UN conference on the financing of development was held in Monterrey, Mexico. The goal of the Monterrey conference was the creation of new resources for fighting poverty and establishing sustainable development. Meeting such aims, however, requires more than mere financial resources, and the Monterrey conference aimed for the:

> (Re-)conceptualization of the role and responsibility of states and the private sector in the financing of development aid. In the end, the question that must be answered is: what, in view of the failure of the state- and market-centred ideas for development of the last few decades, the rather urgently needed new paradigm for development aid should be. (Martens, 2000, p. 103)

The resultant 2002 'Monterrey Consensus' had the following outcomes: (1) new partnerships in the fight against poverty should be the primary peacekeeping task of the twenty-first century; (2) industrialized states should make new and concrete obligations that should contain their levels of development aid; and (3) developing states should implement good governance practices. Despite upward trends in this direction, Secretary-General Kofi Annan noted in 2005 that: 'Expressed as a percentage of developed countries' gross national income, global ODA currently stands at 0.25 per cent – still well short of the 0.33 per cent reached in the late 1980s, let alone the long-standing (since 1970) target of 0.7 per cent that was reaffirmed in the Monterrey Consensus in 2002' (Annan , 2005, para. 48). However, in 2010 (according to the OECD), global funding for development totalled around US$126 billion – significantly more than the Secretary-General's expectation for US$100 billion in that year.

Beyond all the declarations and announcements, a large and tightly woven web of UN specialized agencies, subsidiary organs, funds, and programmes are actively engaged in development issues (on the right to development, see also Chapter 5). A limited selection will be examined in this chapter, but detailed information on each is available on the various organizations' websites – usually formed by the name of the organization with the addition of '.org', i.e. www.undp. org – or at www.un.org.

UN Conference on Trade and Development (UNCTAD)

During the early 1960s, developing states' dissatisfaction with the economic status quo and the dominance of industrialized states in the Bretton Woods Organizations led to demands by developing states that their numerical majority in the General Assembly should be reflected in the membership compositions of UN development agencies. In response to these concerns, ECOSOC called for a world trade conference for the purpose of improving the position of the developing countries in the world economy. The resultant UN Conference on Trade and Development (UNCTAD) has met every four years since 1964 (the last time in Accra,

Ghana in April 2008) as a subsidiary organ of the General Assembly and has grown to 193 members (as of October 2011). UNCTAD is based in Geneva, where it has a secretariat of approximately 400 personnel, and a Trade and Development Board (TDB) to oversee the activities of the organization (the TDB meets in regular session and up to three times a year in executive sessions to deal with urgent policy issues, as well as management and institutional matters). The basic function of UNCTAD is to promote the integration of developing countries into the world economy and the creation of a forum for the comprehensive treatment of trade and development issues. For example, UNCTAD organized the third LDC conference in May 2001. Additionally, UNCTAD publishes a yearly *Trade and Development Report* that promulgates important information for development politics. Although UNCTAD's focus is not in the operative realm it also co-ordinates around 300 projects for the purpose of strengthening political institutions in developing and transitioning states and educating such states' decision-makers in the areas of trade and finance politics.

Compared to UNCTAD's original – and extremely ambitious – goals (including but not limited to: raising the rate of economic growth in developing countries, raising their share of world trade, improving terms of trade, the abolition of all limitations on trade for developing countries, and the co-ordination of trade and development politics), UNCTAD's current agenda appears much more modest and is the result of a more realistic expectation concerning the limits of UNCTAD action. Opportunities are restricted because binding orders cannot be made, and decisions (even when commanded by a two-thirds majority) are merely recommendations. Furthermore, members have been unable to establish UNCTAD as the primary forum for North–South dialogue; the Bretton Woods Organizations (where power is weighted to the industrialized western states) remain the monopolizing force in development politics. It remains that case that:

> The policy of the developing countries fails for a number of reasons. First, they have attempted to bridge their differing interests simply by lengthening the list of their demands. Second, the self-critical discussion of those barriers to development which come from the developing countries themselves has been bracketed out of the whole conversation on a new world economic order. Third, the developing countries' bargaining position was worsened by falling prices for raw materials. (Brock, 1995, p. 72)

The UN Development Program (UNDP)

The UNDP was created in 1965 as the result of a merger of the Expanded Programme of Technical Assistance and the United Nations Special Fund, and was intended to be an independent instrument for the financing and co-ordination of technical aid. The UNDP has no formal membership, but it has more than 5,000 personnel worldwide who are responsible for planning, financing, and co-ordinating UN development projects that are then implemented by states or other organizations. UNDP is lead by an administrator (who also holds the rank of Under-Secretary-General) – a position held since 2005 by Helen Clark, the former Prime Minister of New Zealand) – and is headquartered in New York with field offices in more than 166 countries. At any given time, UNDP is involved in approximately 5000 projects. UNDP reports to the General Assembly through ECOSOC, and is supervised by an executive council of thirty-six member states, as follows:

- eight from Africa;
- seven from Asia;
- four from Eastern Europe;
- five from Latin America and the Caribbean; and
- twelve from Western Europe and Other States.

UNDP decisions are reached by consensus. UNDP is financed through the voluntary contributions of member states, institutional donors, and the private sector. In 2009, the UNDP total budget was approximately $5billion, with US4.1billion being used for its programme budget (see UNDP 2009/10, p. 8 *et seq.*).

UNDP focused primarily in four issue areas: poverty reduction and the Millennium Development Goals, democratic governance, crisis prevention and recovery, environment and energy. The Millennium Development Goals (MDGs) agreed upon by the heads of states and government at the 2000 Millennium Summit (see below) form the largest and most complex framework for co-ordinated and coherent UN action in the field of development. UNDP campaigns and mobilizes partners to support the MDSs, develops and shares strategies and practices for the realization of the MDGs, and gives operational assistance as required.

Additionally, the UNDP administrator is the convenor of the UN Development Group (UNDG), one of the four Executive Committees established by Secretary-General Kofi Annan in 1997. UNDG co-ordinates the work of the thirty-two UN programmes, funds, and agencies involved with development work. UNDP also administrates a number of UN funds and programmes such as the Capital Development Fund and the Development Fund for Women. UNDP is also the 'mother' organization of UN Volunteers (UNV), a worldwide network of people volunteering in the service of peace and development.

UNDP has sometimes been criticized for lack of focus and for spreading itself too thin over too many activities. Certainly the programme has not always been able to adequately fulfil its co-ordination and steering roles – neither at the strategic level in the UNDG nor at the operational level in the field of the Resident Co-ordinator System (in which UNDP representatives are responsible for the co-ordination of the various UN players in complex peace operations or peace-building missions). Despite these criticisms, UNDP continues to play a key role in UN development work. Since 1990 in particular, the UNDP's publication of the *Human Development Report* has won it specific esteem in the eyes of the global development community.

The Food and Agriculture Organization (FAO)

The Food and Agriculture Organization (FAO), founded in 1945, is the largest specialized agency in the UN system with 191 member states, one associate member (the Faroe Islands), and one member organization (the European Union). The FAO is headquartered in Rome, Italy, but also has five Regional Offices in Accra (Ghana), Bangkok (Thailand), Budapest (Hungary), Cairo (Egypt), and Santiago de Chile (Chile), and has eleven sub-regional offices and seventy-four country offices, many of which are responsible for multiple states. In total, the agency has approximately 3,700 staff in more than 130 states. The supreme governing body of FAO is the Conference of member states that meets every two years to determine the Organization's work and priorities and to adopt the programme budget. FAO's executive organ is the Council with forty-nine seats, in which seven regions are represented by states delegated by the regions themselves. The Council also forms a number of functional sub-committees and expert panels, while the Secretariat in Rome takes care of the day-to-day business.

FAO's work is focused on achieving global food security, raising nutrition levels and living standards, increasing agricultural productivity, improving rural living conditions, and contributing to the growth of the world economy. FAO conducts comprehensive research and has developed expertise in a number of agricultural issues (agriculture, forestry and fisheries) and also covers global issues such as biodiversity, climate change, avian flu, and the MDGs. FAO additionally provides strategies for securing food, and provides practical help to developing states through technical aid projects – all efforts are aimed at assisting states and societies to help themselves. FAO's work is funded by assessed and voluntary contributions from its member states (set at the biennial Conference) – in the fiscal year 2010–11 the regular FAO budget was US$1 billion and voluntary contributions totalled US$1.2 billion.

The International Fund for Agricultural Development (IFAD), founded in 1977, is an independent specialized agency that is not connected to the FAO. IFAD is financed by voluntary contributions from its 165 member states, and primarily supports projects and programmes for the improvement of the nutritional situation of rural populations in developing countries.

Other Specialized Agencies, Subsidiary Organs, Programmes and Initiatives

The UN Industrial Development Organization (UNIDO) – originally founded as a UN programme in 1966 – became the sixteenth UN specialized agency in 1985. UNIDO's mandate is to promote sustainable industrial development in developing and transitioning states. This it does by acting as a forum for the organization of dialogues between various public and private sectors. UNIDO's secretariat is located in Vienna, Austria, where it has approximately 700 staff. UNIDO's 173 member states meet every two years in a General Conference to determine the annual budget (approximately US$183 million in fiscal year 2010–11) and to set the agenda. It also chooses fifty-three member states (primarily developing states) to serve on the Industrial Development Board to oversee the implementation of programmes.

The UN International Children's Emergency Fund (UNICEF) was founded in 1946 for the purpose of supporting children suffering from the after-effects of the Second World War. UNICEF has been a subsidiary organ of the UN since 1953, reporting to the General Assembly through ECOSOC, but has since shifted its focus towards development issues. UNICEF acts as a general lobbyist for children's rights (it was a UNICEF initiative in 1989 that resulted in the General Assembly passing the Convention on the Rights of the Child), but also has specific programmes for the improvement of child health, nutrition, and education, as well as for the basic improvement of living conditions for children, young people, and mothers. UNICEF is politically active in the fight against the use of child soldiers and the protection of refugees. Additionally, UNICEF conducts emergency aid projects – and often longer-term projects – in cases of disaster, and in the wake of armed conflict. UNICEF is headquartered in New York but has activities in 190 states and runs a budget of approximately US\$3.25 billion (2009), of which 60 per cent comes from member state voluntary contributions, and the remaining 40 per cent comes from private fundraising by thirty-six national UNICEF committees, the private sector, and other activities. UNICEF programmes and activities are monitored by an administrative council of thirty-six government representatives.

During the 1990's a new milieu emerged – UN subsidiary organs, programmes, funds, and specialized agencies began to play an important role as a central space for dialogue. The decade was 'characterized by a heretofore unimagined level of international dialogue, in which the problems of developing countries were increasingly recognized as global problems for which all states and their peoples carry some responsibility' (Bundesministerium für Wirtschaftliche Zunammenarbeit und Entwicklung, 2001, p. xv). These dialogues often took place in the form of world conferences, and in these world conferences there come together several thousand representatives of governments, civil society, and private business.

The output of these world conferences, as measured by concrete results, varies from one to the next, but the 'historic United Nations conferences and summits

TABLE 7.3
Important UN World Conferences

1992	United Nations Conference on Environment and Development	Rio de Janeiro
1993	World Conference on Human Rights	Vienna
1994	International Conference on Population and Development	Cairo
1995	World Conference on Women	Beijing
1995	World Summit for Social Development	Copenhagen
1996	Habitat II Conference on Human Settlements	Istanbul
1996	World Food Summit	Rome
1997	Conference on Climate Change	Kyoto
2001	World Conference Against Racism	Durban
2002	International Conference on Financing for Development	Monterrey
2002	*World Summit* on Sustainable Development	Johannesburg
2009	Climate Change Conference	Copenhagen
2010	Climate Change Conference	Cancún

held in the 1990s helped build a comprehensive normative framework around these linkages for the first time by mapping out a broad vision of shared development priorities' (Annan 2005, para. 28). Without doubt, world conferences constitute an important forum for international communication and co-operation; they also ease learning processes – and thus also create the necessary prerequisites for a fair balancing of interests – and draw media attention to specific world problems. Furthermore, the history of the world conferences demonstrates that non-binding conference declarations constitute an important part of building normative strength, so that they can increase pressure on governments to observe non-binding self-imposed obligations. These summits belong to the 'theatrical direction of globalism'. Their weakness remains the actual implementation of their agreements, because if member states do not begin 'to implement their declarations and determinations from the world conferences of the 1990s, then these conferences are likely to appear to the backward-looking eye of history as nothing but a huge waste of money' (Zumach, 2001, p. 24).

Suggestions for reforming institutional weaknesses in UN development practices run like a scarlet thread through the organization's history (Hüfner and Martens, 2000). The high point so far has been the passing of the aforementioned 1997 'Agenda for Development' that sets ambitious goals for defining a new framework for international co-operation and the future role of the UN in development work. However, the road to the 'Agenda for Development', was anything but smooth. In December 1992, the General Assembly requested that the Secretary-General build upon the well-received 'Agenda for Peace' and create an 'Agenda for Development', but it took five years for the General Assembly to accept the document without a formal vote. Important progress was made in the first draft document of May 1994. In that draft, five closely interconnected main areas of development politics were differentiated from one another (a reflection of the international debate over development):

- without peace, there could be no development ('peace as a foundation');
- without economic growth, there could be no sustainable improvement of living conditions ('the economy as the motor of progress');
- without protection of the environment, no lasting development was conceivable ('the environment as the basis of existence'); and
- without social justice on a global scale (justice as a pillar of society') and free political participation ('democracy as good governance'), there could be no stable development.

The 1994 draft, however, was criticized for not being binding, and it proved impossible to reach a consensus concerning the draft's practical implications. It took another three years – and many more hurdles – before the final version of 'An Agenda for Development' was accepted.

The 'Agenda for Development' attempted a comprehensive stocktaking of development policies and the establishment of concrete development policy perspectives. In the first section ('Settings and Objectives'), the opportunities and risks of the globalization process are described, and the global political post-Cold-War situation – with particular attention to developing states – is analysed. It is suggested that more intensive international co-operation is urgently needed under a totally new concept of development policy where economic growth, social development, and protection of the environment are seen as inter-dependent goals. In the second section ('Policy Framework, including Means of implementation'), the various aspects of development issues are aligned with each other (*inter alia* economy, social development, strengthening of the rights of women and children, population development, migration and environment). In the third part ('Institutional Issues and Follow-ups'), the need for compromise is clearly articulated: the UN's uniqueness and its enormous potential for action in the realm of development is emphasized, but there is also insistence that the system of international development co-operation must have new life breathed into it. The new and comprehensive re-ordering that is required is not foreseen in the document itself, and 'aside from empty formulas about continuing necessities, this section merely says that according to the principle of hope, reform would be necessary, but there is no consensus over which reforms should be realized when or how' (Hüfner and Martens, 2000, p. 182). The *status quo* is not really called into question: there is no attempt to address the separation between the Bretton Woods Organizations and the UN system, the General Assembly is reaffirmed as the most important forum, ECOSOC is given the usual co-ordination tasks, and the competencies of the various funds and programmes are left, in principle, in their existing form. At most, the Agenda promotes better voting practices: '[B]etter inter-institutional coordination within the system is absolutely indispensable'. Finally, the Agenda advocates for improved financing, and the longstanding target of 0.7 per cent ODA contributions. However:

> [N]ew qualitative recognitions or extra obligations which go beyond the non-binding statements from the world conferences are not to be found in the Agenda. At its core, it remains a catalogue of platitudes as they are to be found in all the Action Programmes from Rio to Rome. (Martens, 1998, p. 52)

The Millennium Development Goals

The 2000 Millennium Summit saw UN member states solemnly declare their commitment to achieving specific development goals by 2015. Notably, the then 189 member states obligated themselves to 'making the right to development a reality for everyone and to freeing the entire human race from want' (Millennium Declaration, 2000, para. 11). Within one year the catalogue of aims and benchmarks contained in section III of the Millennium Declaration was transformed into a set of eight concrete Millennium Development Goals (MDGs) that have maintained a prominent place on the UN's agenda ever since, and have proven to be one of the most comprehensive and ambitious project ever pursued by the UN. The MDGs were broken down into twenty targets, shown in Table 7.4.

TABLE 7.4
The Millennium Development Goals

Goals	Target
Goal 1: Eradicate extreme poverty and hunger	1a: Halve, between 1990 and 2015, the proportion of people whose income is less than $1 a day 1b: Achieve full and productive employment and decent work for all, including women and young people 1c: Halve, between 1990 and 2015, the proportion of people who suffer from hunger
Goal 2: Achieve universal primary education	2a: Ensure that, by 2015, children everywhere, boys and girls alike, will be able to complete a full course of primary schooling
Goal 3: Promote gender equality and empower women	3a: Eliminate gender disparity in primary and secondary education, preferably by 2005, and in all levels of education no later than 2015
Goal 4: Reduce child mortality	4a: Reduce by two-thirds, between 1990 and 2015, the under-five mortality rate
Goal 5: Improve maternal health	5a: Reduce by three-quarters the maternal mortality ratio 5b: Achieve universal access to reproductive health
Goal 6: Halt and begin to reverse the spread of HIV/AIDS	6a: Have halted by 2015 and begun to reverse the spread of HIV/AIDS 6b: Achieve, by 2010, universal access to treatment for HIV/AIDS for all those who need it 6c: Have halted by 2015 and begun to reverse the incidence of malaria and other major diseases
Goal 7: Ensure environmental sustainability	7a: Integrate the principles of sustainable development into country policies and programmes and reverse the loss of environmental resources 7b: Reduce biodiversity loss, achieving, by 2010, a significant reduction in the rate of loss 7c: Halve, by 2015, the proportion of the population without sustainable access to safe drinking water and basic sanitation
Goal 8: Develop a global partnership for development	8a: Develop further an open, rule-based, predictable, non-discriminatory trading and financial system 8b: Address the special needs of least developed countries 8c: Address the special needs of landlocked developing countries and small island developing States 8d: Deal comprehensively with the debt problems of developing countries 8e: In co-operation with pharmaceutical companies, provide access to affordable essential drugs in developing countries 8f: In co-operation with the private sector, make available benefits of new technologies, especially information and communications

Source: www.un.org/millenniumgoals.

The MDGs swiftly became the benchmark for international development policy progress and have been reaffirmed in numerous declarations, including: the 'Monterrey Consensus' of the International Conference on Financing for Development (2002), the Johannesburg Implementation Plan of the World Summit on Sustainable Development (2002), the 2005 World Summit Outcome, and the Doha Declaration on Financing for Development (2008). The MDGs meant that the narrow and inadequate approaches to development that had previously been favoured by OECD states were replaced by a step-by-step programme for the eradication of global poverty, and the UN became the frontrunner in the programmatic orientation of international development efforts:

> [P]overty in the poorest countries can be dramatically reduced only if developing countries put well designed and well implemented plans in place to reduce poverty – and only if rich countries match their efforts with substantial increases in support . . . Under the auspices of the Goals, countries have agreed to hold each other to account, and citizens of both high-income and low-income countries are empowered to hold their own governments to clear standards. (UN Millennium Project, 2005, p. 4)

In practice, however, the implementation and monitoring of the MDGs has posed serious challenges for the UN and its member states. To a certain extent, this is the result of some of the goals looking like arbitrary normative exhortations rather than measurable parameters (i.e. target (1b) to 'Achieve full and productive employment and decent work for all, including women and young people'; (7a) to 'Integrate the principles of sustainable development into country policies and programmes and reverse the loss of environmental resources'; or (8a) to 'Develop further an open, rule-based, predictable, non-discriminatory trading and financial system'). The reason for most MDGs being behind schedule, however, is that most UN member states seem unwilling to take serious and focused action in favour of the goals and targets. So despite repeatedly confirmed commitments to the MDGs by practically all states and major international institutions, and despite considerable efforts taken by MDG campaigns, task forces, official and private actors, the balance of this largest UN project is mixed (see Tables 7.5 and 7.6).

Considerable progress has been made in a number of areas and regions, especially in east and south Asia where China and India contributed most to the overall reduction of extreme poverty. On the other hand, progress has been hampered on a number of fronts by the impacts of climate change and natural disasters. The prevalence of civil wars and destabilizing crises means that millions of refugees are not having their needs met, and inadequate provision of resources and funding by many member states is similarly slowing progress. Furthermore, progress was reversed in many states by the global food, economic, and financial crisis of 2008 and 2009 (see UNDESA, 2010, p. 4).

The achievement of the MDGs will, of course, require money and resources. In 2005, the G8 pledged to contribute US$50 billion per year (from 2010) to development funding. However, the UN Millennium Project panel estimated that industrialized states would have to provide an additional US$43 billion increase to ODA funding between 2010 and 2015 in order to meet the 2015 MDG (equivalent to industrialized states to meeting the longstanding target of 0.7 per cent ODA contribution; see Table 7.6). Whether or not the achievement of the MDGs can be met by industrialized states' monetary contributions is the subject of ongoing debate in politics and political science. Rather than perpetually increasing ODA budgets, some practitioners and scholars advocate for non-financial measures like liberalized trade relations or improved market access for developing states.

In September 2010 the General Assembly gathered a high-level plenary meeting to review MDG progress and to chart the way forward. The plenary found that despite some successes, progress had generally been uneven and greater effort would be required by the international community in general and the industrialized states in particular, for the MDGs to be met. The Summit Outcome document contained an agenda for how to better meet every MDG goal and target, and elaborate lists of commitments, recommendations, and encouragements on how to accelerate progress towards those targets by 2015. As in previous declarations, however, the Outcome Document lacks any sort of binding obligation and it remains the case that meeting the 2015 MDG goal does not seem very likely.

The UN's Balance Sheet on Development Policy

The end of the Cold War and the collapse of bipolarity resulted in a fundamental shift in the conditions for development policy. The instrumentalization of particular political arguments became less common, market economies and free trade established themselves as the central paradigms, and globalization brought with it a fundamental change in global economic relationships. As a result, the control of economic processes and the practicability of political intentions became more difficult. At the same time, however, the necessity for an active politics of development remained (and remains) as urgent as ever. In this regard, the 'United Nations comparative advantage in addressing economic and social threats is its unparalleled convening power, which allows it to formulate common development targets and rally the international community around a consensus for achieving them' (High-Level Panel, 2004, para. 57).

Many problems of development co-operation are not specific to the UN, but hold for all forms of multilateral action in the area. It is a 'fundamental error' to expect that development can be created 'through the external impetus of money, expertise, and personnel' (Nuscheler, 2001, p. 7) and the balance-sheet on development politics reflects the mixed results of this reality.

In terms of positive results, UN development work has played a vital role in ensuring no further escalation of the North–South conflict: 'This [attribution] appears particularly plausible as it was hardly to be expected that the international relations conflicts over development policies could have been handled in a comparably cooperative fashion without the global negotiating system of the UN' (Rittberger *et al.*, 1997, p. 80). Furthermore, the UN plays a vital role in public consciousness-building and in the promotion of internationally agreed-upon prin-

TABLE 7.5
Millennium Development Goals: 2010 progress chart

Goals and targets North	Africa/ Sub-Sahara	Africa/ east	Asia/ South	Asia/ East	Asia/ south	Asia/ west	Oceania America / Caribbean	Latin (CIS)	Europe (CIS)	Asia
Goal 1 *Eradicate extreme poverty and hunger*										
Productive and decent employment	-	-	++	O	O	-	-	O	++	+
Reduce hunger by half	++	O	+	+	-	-	m.d.	O	++	O
Goal 2 *Achieve universal primary education*										
Universal primary schooling	+	O	O	O	+	O	m.d.	O	+	-
Goal 3 *Promote gender equality and empower women*										
Equal girls enrolment in primary school	+	+	++	++	++	+	-	++	++	++
Women's equal representation in national parliaments	O	O	-	O	O	O	O	O	O	O
Goal 4 *Reduce child mortality*										
Reduce mortality of under-fives by two-thirds	+	O	O	O	O	O	O	+	O	O

TABLE 7.5 – continued

Goals and targets North	Africa/ Sub-Sahara	Africa/ east	Asia/ South	Asia/ East	Asia/ south	Asia/ west	Oceania America/ Caribbean	Latin (CIS)	Europe (CIS)	Asia
Goal 5 'Improve maternal health'										
Access to reproductive health	+	O	+	O	O	O	m.d.	O	m.d.	O
Reduce maternal mortality by three-quarters	+	-	+	O	O	O	O	O	+	+
Goal 6 'Combat HIV/AIDS, malaria and other diseases'										
Halt and begin to reverse the spread of HIV/AIDS	-	O	O	O	O	+	O	O	O	-
Goal 7 'Ensure environmental sustainability'										
Reverse loss of forests	+	O	+	-	-	+	-	O	++	-
Improve the lives of slum-dwellers	++	O	++	+	++	-	-	O	m.d.	m.d.
Goal 8 'Develop a global partnership for development'										
Internet users	+	O	++	O	O	+	O	++	++	O

Key:
++   Already met the target or very close to meeting target
+   Progress sufficient to reach the target if prevailing trends persist
O   Progress insufficient to reach the target if prevailing trends persist
-    No progress or deterioration
m.d. Missing or insufficient data

Source: Based on the 2010 Progress Chart by the UN Department of Economic and Social Affairs' Statistics Division.

TABLE 7.6
Plausible ODA needs to meet the Millennium Development Goals

	Estimated and projected ODA requirements			
	Estimated 2002	Projected 2006	Projected 2010	Projected 2015
Baseline ODA for the Goals in 2002	28	28	28	28
Incremental MDG investment needs	-	94	115	161
Adjustment for countries not qualifying due to inadequate governance	-	-21	-23	-25
Reprogramming of existing ODA	-	-6	-7	-9
Emergency and distress relief	4	4	5	6
Other ODA	34	36	34	35
Total indicative ODA needs for the Goals	**65**	**135**	**152**	**195**
Share of OECD/DAC countries' GNI (per cent)	**0.23**	**0.44**	**0.46**	**0.54**
ODA to Least Developed Countries (% of OECD/DAC countries' GNI)	0.06	0.12	0.15	0.22
Absolute increase in ODA required (compared with 2002)	-	70	87	130
Difference between total ODA needs and existing commitments	**-**	**48**	**50**	**74**

Source: UN Millennium Project (2005, p. 251).

ciples in the area of development politics. Its universality, its global presence, and its integrated mandate with respect to the interconnection of human rights, development, environment, and peace are widely recognized as indispensable in international relations. On the other hand, there is constant criticism of development implementation. Rosemary Righter, for example (1995, pp. 87–242), formulates doubts about a meaningful operative role for the UN and calls instead for the UN to remove itself largely from this area. She argues that in a world in which governments must compete as never before with other economic and social actors, it is imperative that the UN concentrates its energies on issues in which inter-state cooperation and the mediation of common institutions is absolutely necessary. Moreover, she raises a number of principled objections to the competency of the UN in these areas, and describes the goals articulated in the Charter as utopian and hardly practical. Institutional splintering in also an issue of concern, and it has been suggested that the countless development organizations should be gathered together under one roof, or at least better organized with respect to one another (on reforms, see Chapter 8).

These objections still do not alter the fact that the UN, on the basis of its singular universality and impartiality, as well as its presence in all parts of the world, takes on a central function among all these organizations. However, UN development capacities are still not being utilised to their full potential, and could be much improved upon.

Protection of Refugees, Humanitarian Aid and Population Issues

Human population movement – specifically flight and expulsion – constitute some of the core issues confronting the UN. The International Refugee Organization (IRO) began its work in 1947 as a specialized agency of the UN. The IRO was created amidst significant controversy and with a limited three-year mandate. In January 1951, the UN High Commissioner for Refugees (UNHCR) was established as a successor organization (with a renewable five-year mandate) to oversee the Geneva Refugee Convention, protecting refugees and providing humanitarian aid. UNHCR received an unlimited mandate from the General Assembly in December 2003.

At the beginning of the 1950s – concurrent with the debates on the organizational composition of protection for refugees – negotiations were taking place on the holding of a conference on the protection of refugees. The 1951 UN Conference of Plenipotentiaries on the Status of Refugees and Stateless Persons resulted in the Convention Relating to the Status of Refugees (the Geneva Refugee Convention), which came into force on 22 April 1954. The Convention establishes the rights and duties of refugees, as well as the duties of the signatory states with respect to refugees. A refugee is any person who, 'out of a well-founded fear of being persecuted for reasons of race, religion, nationality, membership of a particular social group or political opinion, is outside the country of his nationality' People who have fled or been driven out of their homes but have not left their own country (internally displaced persons) do not fall under the purview of international law. The right to asylum – contained in the 1948 Universal Declaration of Human Rights of 1948 – is not expressly mentioned in the Geneva Refugee Convention, but the prohibition on expulsion or deportation lies at its heart. Every signatory state assumes the responsibility that they will not force any refugee to cross a border into an area where their life or freedom would be threatened. The original limitation of this protection to people who had become refugees because of events happening before 1951 was removed by a protocol in 1967. As of October 2011, the Convention had 144 states-parties, and the protocol had 145 states-parties.

Currently, the UNHCR protects and supports more than 30 million people. At the beginning of 2011, there are 10.3 million refugees who have fled across state borders because of war, persecution, and massive human rights violations. An additional 4.7 million Palestinian refugees are under the care of the UN Relief and Work Agency (UNRWA). Refugees come from all over the world – around 50 per cent from Asia and 20 per cent from Africa. Internally displaced persons have become increasingly significant to the work of the UNHCR. In 2008, there were 14.4 million internally displaced persons under the care of the UNHCR, 11.3 million of which are in nineteen African states. In 2008, the states with the highest numbers of internally displaced persons were Sudan, Colombia, and Iraq (all data from UNHCR).

The present High Commissioner for Refugees is former Prime Minister of Portugal António Guterres (elected first in 2005, and re-elected in 2010 for another five-year term). The UNHCR is chosen by the General Assembly and heads a division of approximately 7,200 personnel – 700 of which work in the Geneva headquarters and 230 of which work in the Budapest-based Global Service Centre. Other staff serve in the 123 states where UNHCR is active, running 124 regional and branch offices, and 272 sub- or field offices. A small amount of the UNHCR budget comes from marginal allowances from the overall UN budget, but UNHCR is largely financed through voluntary contributions from UN member states and international agencies (overseen by an executive committee of seventy-nine states). The UNHCR reached a record budget of US$3.32 billion in 2011; the top five donors are the US, the European Commission, Sweden, Japan, and the Netherlands.

The UNHCR seeks to guarantee basic human rights standards in the treatment of refugees, and to investigate solutions to the refugee problem. In addition, UNHCR aid programmes help states to finance emergency help for refugees in the form of food, shelter and medical services under an oath of impartial humanitarianism. Despite an unchanged mandate, the UNHCR's activities have evolved since the 1950s. Along with new regional focuses (primarily in developing states), the persons eligible to receive UNHCR assistance has expanded beyond refugees to include asylum-seekers, refugees seeking to return home, internally displaced persons, and populations affected by armed conflict. Most recently, the UNHCR has assumed a role as the leading UN organization for humanitarian issues and has become active in unstable regions of conflict.

The UN relief and Works Agency for Palestinian Refugees in the Near East (UNRWA) has its own budget and structure, and deals exclusively with refugees from the 1948 Arab–Israeli conflict. UNRWA currently delivers assistance to approximately 4.7 million people living in approximately sixty refugee camps.

Humanitarian Aid in the Framework of the UN

The politics of humanitarian aid has become more and more complex since the 1950s, delivering multitudes of measures 'aimed at mitigating the acute need of any population group', and which 'are clearly separated from political, economic, or military aid in that they have a humanitarian motivation and pursue exclusively humanitarian goals' (Swamy Meier-Ewert 2010).

The Office for the Co-ordination of Humanitarian Affairs (OCHA) was established in 1997 to facilitate organizational co-ordination. The office is led by an Under-Secretary-General, since 2010 Valerie Amos of the United Kingdom, who also serves as the Organization's Emergency Relief Co-ordinator. In the event of an emergency situation, OCHA brings together and provides leadership to all relevant humanitarian actors and acts as the focal point for governmental, intergovernmental, and non-governmental relief activities. OCHA is funded primarily by voluntary contributions from member states and international agencies like the European Commission; in 2011 the administrative and programme budget totalled around US$242 million. OCHA has also established relief funds to allow for quick and flexible emergency responses measures. Sixteen Emergency Relief Funds – providing grants of up to US$500,000 – had been established by the end of 2010. Additionally, four Common Humanitarian Funds provide resources for larger projects in core activities. The funds for Sudan and the Democratic Republic of Congo each attracted more than US$100 million. The most important mechanism for rapid international responses at the onset of humanitarian operations is the Central Emergency response Fund (established at the 2005 World Summit) that has since collected more than US$1.6 billion from more than 100 public and private donors.

The World Food Programme (WFP) – founded in 1961 as a common programme of the General Assembly and the Food and Agriculture Organization (FAO) – also plays an important role in humanitarian aid. The primary goal of the WFP is the provision of foodstuffs for states whose populations suffer from widespread malnutrition, as well as emergency aid in cases of natural disaster like the earthquakes in Pakistan 2005 or Haiti 2010. This kind of emergency aid has been increasing steadily since the 1990s, and at the time of writing accounts for some 80 per cent of the stores given out. In 2009 – with around 10,000 personnel – the WFP provided 4.6 million metric tons of food aid for 101.8 million people in seventy-five states and is thus the largest food-aid organization in the world. On average, the WFP reaches 90 million people in more than seventy states every year. Contributions to the WFP's budget (approximately US$4 billion in 2009) are made on a voluntary basis, and can also be made in kind. An executive council of thirty-six states (chosen by the ECOSOC and the FAO, and answerable to those organs) controls the work of the WFP and usually meets four times a year. At the head of the permanent secretariat, based in Rome, is an executive director.

In its 2008 to 2013 Strategic Plan, the WFP focuses five overarching objectives: to save lives; to prevent hunger; to restore livelihood in post-conflict or post-disaster situations; to reduce chronic hunger and under-nutrition; and to strengthen countries' capacities to reduce hunger. The Programme is undergoing a transformation from a food-aid agency into an assistance agency that helps states and governments to find long-term solutions against hunger (see WFP 2008; Omamo *et al.*, 2010).

Population Issues in the United Nations

Population development is one of the most important issues for the future of the human race. The question of the ecological, social, economic and political consequences of population growth (quite simply, the question of how many people the Earth can support) is an extremely difficult one to answer. In general, the rate of population growth is considered too high 'when – even with a subsistence-oriented lifestyle for the affected people – there is over-exploitation of the available natural resources or the available capital is not sufficient to finance the investments necessary for an appropriate quality of life' (Leisinger, 2000, p. 57). It is extremely difficult to objectively identify when this over-exploitation has been reached, but the rapidly increasing global population suggests that it will be sooner rather than later. On 12 October 1999, the UN declared the birth of the six-billionth person on Earth – representing a significant population expansion in a relatively short period of time. It was not until the beginning of the nineteenth century that the world's population reached one billion: by 1925 it had doubled to two billion; by 1955 three billion had been reached; and by 1969 there were five billion people on Earth. What is clear, however, is that the resource-hungry lifestyle enjoyed in industrialized states could not be exported globally without forcing a collapse of the world's ecosystem. In fall 2011, the world population has reached seven billion (of which 1.35 billion are in China, and 1.1 billion are in India). The UN projects – granted the uncertainty of the underlying assumptions – that the world population will be anywhere from seven billion (low estimate), to nine billion (middle estimate), to eleven billion (high estimate) by the year 2050. Should population fall closest to the middle estimate it would mean that the world's population would grow in a period of under forty years by the same number of people that comprised the total world population in 1960. Regional distribution of population growth varies greatly – populations of industrialized states are shrinking (dramatically in some cases) and more than 90 per cent of population growth is taking place in developing and newly industrialized states. The uneven distribution of population growth means, of course, that the problems of population growth are also distributed unevenly. The UN serves as the switchboard for international population politics. In 1946, the UN Population Commission was created as a consultative sub-organ of ECOSOC, and in 1994 was renamed as the Population and Development Commission, a change in name that reflects the integration of population politics into the broader context of development politics. The UN's centre for population issues is the UN Fund for Population Activities (UNFPA), which has been a subsidiary organ reporting to the General Assembly since 1969 and is the world's largest and most important structure for population issues. UNFPA is based in New York with five regional offices in Panama City, Bratislava, Cairo, Bangkok, and Johannesburg. UNFPA also has five worldwide liaison offices and is represented in 150 states. UNFPA is funded by voluntary contributions from UN member states and private donors; in 2009 it had a total budget of approximately US$783 million. UNFPA has no formal membership of states; its mandate includes a number of activities in the areas of family planning and population politics, as well as the co-ordination of population issues within the UN system. Beyond that, UNFPA publishes a yearly report on world population and conducts large conferences on this theme (the most recent of which have been the Conference on Population and Development in Cairo in 1994 and the 1999 special session of the General Assembly on population issues in New York) – such conferences and events usually yield a significant number of concrete results.

Health Issues in the United Nations

The World Health Organization (WHO) has served as the UN's central organization for health issues (as a specialized agency) since 1948. Based in Geneva, WHO is not a development aid organization in the strict sense – although health is, of course, given high priority within the larger framework of development politics – but rather has the purpose of improving health conditions for all humans. The 1946 WHO Constitution defines health as 'a state of complete physical, psychological, and social wellness and not merely the absence of illness' (Preamble of the Constitution). Given the organization's very broad concept of health, the responsibilities derived from it are comprehensive. WHO's primary tasks (as defined in Chapter 2 of its constitution are:

- the co-ordination of international health policy;
- active co-operation with other UN organs, national health administrations, and professional groups on health issues;
- support for the fighting of epidemics, research on illnesses and the promotion of research, health education and standardization of diagnostic procedures; and
- improvement of the health systems of the member states and the elucidation of health issues.

The organization serves as both a co-ordination point for international health work as well as an instrument of technical support and advice for governments that may request such assistance. The 193 member states meet annually in Geneva at a World Health Assembly in order to make basic decisions and to agree to the budget for the forthcoming year (approximately US$4.54 billion for 2010–11). The executive council – comprised of thirty-four members – implements the World Health Assembly's decisions. A secretariat of approximately 8,000 staff – headed by Director-General Margaret Chan of the People's Republic of China/Hong Kong (since 2007) – work in WHO headquarters and across six largely independent regional offices – in Washington DC (USA), Brazzaville (Democratic Republic of Congo), Alexandria (Egypt), Copenhagen (Denmark), New Delhi (India), and Manila (Philippines), and also across 147 country offices.

The rapid spread of HIV/AIDS is one of the most serious challenges facing the global health community. In Sub-Saharan Africa, AIDS is already the number one cause of death, and is threatening to destroy entire social systems and to substantially damage political systems. In sixteen countries, more than 10 per cent of the adult population (between the ages of fifteen and forty-nine years) are infected; in seven states in southern Africa, one in every five adults is living with AIDS. The number of those infected worldwide is estimated to be over 30 million. UNAIDS was founded in 1986, and is now supported by eight organizations – UNICEF, UNDP, UNFPA, UNESCO, WHO, ILO, the World Bank and UNDCP. The Security Council met to discuss health issues (and the resultant implications for peace and security) for the first time at the beginning of 2000. In 2001, the topic was also discussed in the General Assembly. The main purpose of UNAIDS is to bundle the capacities of the various organizations within and external to the UN system and to use such capacities in a concentrated way in the fight against AIDS. Headquartered in Geneva, UNAIDS has seven regional offices and over eighty country offices, and it has an annual budget of approximately US$273 million (2009). In addition, the 'Global Fund to Fight Against AIDS, Tuberculosis and Malaria' was established in 2002, as a 'public–private partnership organization' and has raised approximately US$21.7 billion for more than 600 programmes in 150 countries.

Protection of the Global Environment as an International Challenge

At the founding of the UN in June 1945, it could not have been foreseen that a new challenge for the survival of humanity – unimaginable in its dimensions – would arise beyond the 'scourge of war' and force itself on to the international agenda. In fact, environmental concerns are not even mentioned in the Charter. Nonetheless, the protection of the global environment has become one of the most important issues confronting humanity and commanding a large portion of the UN's resources. Sustainable development – wherein the needs of the present could be satisfied in a way that the opportunity of future generations to meet their own needs is not destroyed – has become the central arena for addressing environmental issues at the UN. This particular expansion of UN jurisdiction goes back to the previously discussed broadening of the concept of security, and demonstrates the flexibility of the UN system to react to new challenges on the understanding of all member states without any need to change the Charter.

Issues such as the ozone layer, species diversity, or the global climate are known as global public goods: they cannot be divided, no one can be prevented from using them, and they cannot be protected through the individual actions of states (Kaul *et al.*, 1999a; Vogler, 2008). However, global public goods can be utilised by individual actors without their having to pay a particular price for them. This can lead to over-use, which can lead to lasting ill-effects for all the other users. Additionally there exists the problem of the 'free-rider phenomenon' in which an actor derives benefit from the behaviour of others without contributing to a solution for the problem. For example, if the majority of states were to agree to a drastic reduction of carbon dioxide emissions, thus stabilizing the world climate, the decision would also benefit the state or states that had not participated. Independent of the fact that some individual actors might in fact profit from global ecological crises:

[I]n the end they are all victims, and constitute a community of risk who are all sitting metaphorically in the same boat. The inmates of this boat, however, do not conduct themselves rationally in the collective sense, i.e. with respect to common survival, but in the individual sense, meaning that they try to win small advantages for themselves. The product of such individual activities is a catastrophe which no one wanted, but which after a certain point in time, no one could prevent from happening, either. (Wöhlcke, 1992, p. 8)

The institutional protection of collective global goods contains at least two problem areas, which are also fundamental problems for international co-operation:

(i) a responsibility vacuum is created by the discrepancy between an increasingly global set of problems and the decisional competencies and possibilities for action, which are still based primarily on the structure of the nation-state; and
(ii) under the current conditions of international environmental politics, there is a deficiency of motivation, in that actors are not sufficiently rewarded for behaviour that is to the benefit of all, and in some cases may even be punished for a politics of sustainability because it may cause them to suffer competitive disadvantages. (Kaul *et al.*, 1999b, pp. 466–98)

Global environmental concerns have developed into being a new scourge for humanity that demands a central position in the world's attention (for a more in-depth outline of the problem see Simonis, 1998; Oberthür and Ott, 2000; the *Global Environmental Outlook* published annually by the UNEP, and the reports of the Foundation for Development and Peace, the World Watch Institute, and the World Resources Institute). UN Secretary-General Kofi Annan expressed the problem succinctly in his Millennium Report to the General Assembly. At stake is:

> the freedom of future generations to sustain their lives on this planet. We are failing to provide that freedom. On the contrary, we have been plundering our children's future heritage to pay for environmentally unsustainable practices in the present... Nevertheless, we must face up to an inescapable reality: the challenges of sustainability simply overwhelm the adequacy of our responses. With some honourable exceptions, our responses are too few, too little and too late. (Annan, 2000, p. 42)

Whereas such a statement might previously have been regarded as an expression of apocalyptic fear of the end of the world, contemporary science and politics (with a few notable exceptions) are close to unanimous agreement the issue. In his 2005 'In Larger Freedom' report, Annan states that: 'Our efforts to defeat poverty and pursue sustainable development will be in vain if environmental degradation and natural resource depletion continue unabated' (Annan 2005, para. 57). In the same report Annan highlights three existential challenges that require urgent action:

- *Desertification*: The degradation of more than a billion hectares of land has had a devastating impact on development in many parts of the world.
- *Biodiversity*: The loss of biodiversity severely undermines health, livelihoods, food production and clean water, and increases the vulnerability of populations to natural disasters and climate change.
- *Climate change*: Since the advent of the industrial era in the mid-eighteenth century, the earth has warmed considerably and sea levels have risen measurably, resulting in the increase in the global mean surface temperature is likely

to trigger increased climate variability and greater incidence and intensity of extreme weather events, such as hurricanes and droughts.

Global climate change, in particular, has become one of the most pressing world problems. In January 2001 the Intergovernmental Panel on Climate Change (IPCC, set up in 1998 by the UN Environmental Programme and the World Meteorological Organization) reported that unless there is a drastic turnaround, the planet's temperature will rise by up to 5.8°C – an increase that would have formidable consequences such as weather extremes, soil erosion, desertification, and flooding. Developing states would bear the brunt of the suffering (Bangladesh, for example, would be existentially threatened by the predicted rise in sea level), but industrialized countries would not be immune to the negative effects.

If current global consumption of energy and resources were extrapolated and applied to future generations – taking into account the probable population growth to nine billion by 2050 and using the figures of energy use by people in industrialized countries as the basis for calculation – the world's resources would quickly be depleted. The western model of prosperity is not feasible for the whole world. Indeed, the world, as noted by former UNEP director Klaus Töpfer, is: '[O]n a course that cannot be sustained. The time for a rational, well-thought-through transition to a workable future is quickly running out' (1999, p. 87).

For example, industrialized states – constituting approximately 20 per cent of the world's population – account for approximately 60 per cent of the world's carbon dioxide emissions (also closely correlated with the economic performance of a country, and a primary cause of world climate change). India's emissions lie at around one tonne of carbon dioxide per person per year, while Japan's are nine times that, Germany's eleven times more, Russia's sixteen times, and the USA's twenty times that rate. That said, the rate of increase of emissions from developing countries is considerable. Should India or China – with populations of more than one billion each – reach Germany's level of per person emissions, the world climate would collapse irrevocably. It is still estimated, however, that global energy use is likely to double in the next few decades, possibly leading to conflicts and, under certain circumstances, to war over access to scarce resources. Similar calculations can be made for nearly all ecologically relevant criteria including industrial production, degree of mobility, and standard of consumption.

In order to prevent irreversible damage, or even the collapse, of the global ecosystem there needs to be:

(1)   an ecological restructuring of the economies of industrialized states; and
(2)   an ecologically sound type of development in the developing states.

Such goals will not be realizable without international regulations and implementation instruments. The necessity for the internationalization of environmental politics, however, comes not only from the increasing economic-ecological interdependencies, the complexity of physical–chemical cause-and-effect relationships, the long-term nature of the effects, and the possible irreversibility of the damage to the environment, but also and in particular from the large number of political actors, the contradictory nature of their interests, and the differences in their economic and technical capacities. Global or universal environmental problems require a politics that does not release the state from its responsibilities as the traditional primary political actor, but which is beyond its individual capabilities (Simonis, 2004, p. 570).

From Stockholm to Cancún

The UN's involvement with environmental issues can be seen as a classic case of international agenda-setting. As early as the 1960s – well before the urgency was recognized by most member states – the General Assembly was demanding greater attention be paid to environmental problems. The June 1972 'Declaration of the Conference on the Human Environment' – the result of a conference of the same title held in Stockholm, Sweden – included a large number of direction-setting environmental principles, including the establishment of UNEP (see Chapter 2). Stockholm can be seen as the beginning of an increasing environmental sensitivity in politics, the media, and business – not to suggest that any such sensitivities have always been on a par with the size of the problem, or on a par with proffered solutions. (On the development of UN environmental politics, see Birnie, 1993; Conca and Dabelko, 1998; Esty, 2002; French, 1995.) Twenty years after the Stockholm Declaration, the UN reached a new milestone with the UN Conference on Environment and Development (UNCED) held in Rio de Janeiro in 1992, which has become the reference point for the global political debate on environmental and development issues.

The Rio Conference – attended by 178 governments and 1,400 NGOs (with advisory status) – successfully initiated diverse institutional changes in international environmental politics, and passed (after two years of preparation) a large number of legally non-binding agreements as guidelines for future work. The 'Rio Declaration' articulated political principles in the interests of future, as well as present generations, and established fundamental environmental and development principles to this end. Thus the right to development was reinforced by treaty, the fight against poverty named as a necessary precondition for sustainable development, and the responsibility of the industrialized countries as the source of the main cause of the current environmental damage recognized. The 'UN Framework Convention on Climate Change' (UNFCCC) – signed by more than 150 states in Rio – set in process a motion that has since attempted to stabilize or reduce the concentration of greenhouse gases in the atmosphere (the sixteenth Conference of Parties met most recently in November 2010 in Cancun, Mexico for this purpose). Furthermore, conventions for the maintenance of biodiversity, for the prevention of desertification, and for the protection of forests were also set in motion. The central outcome document of the Rio Conference is 'Agenda 21', which consists of approximately 800 pages, in forty chapters, detailing more than 2,000 recommendations for action on the social, ecological, and economic problems and challenges of future global development. Agenda 21 'aspires to be seen as *the* list of duties for the road into the 21st century' (Waldmann, 1999, p. 73).

TABLE 7.7
Main outcomes of the 1992 Rio conference

Major principles adopted	• *Sovereign right of states to exploit their resources* • *Rights of states to develop* • *Priority of the needs of less developed states* • *Responsibility of developed states for global environmental problems* • *Implementation of Agenda 21 based on principles of universality, democracy, cost-effectiveness and accountability*
Main institutional outcomes	• *The adoption of the Convention on Climate Change and the Convention on Biological Diversity* • *Creation of the Commission on Sustainable Development* • *Charge to states to produce national reports and action plans for sustainable development* • *Integration of non-governmental organizations as partners in sustainable development efforts*
Main financial outcomes	• *Commitment by developed states to commit 0.07 per cent of their GNP ratio to foreign assistance by 2000* • *Agreement to strengthen the Global Environment Facility* • *Pledge of developed states for new financial assistance to less developed states at a rate of US\$607 billion per year to implement the conventions*

Source: Based on discussion in Mingst and Karns (2000, p. 151).

After the coming into effect of the Climate Framework Convention in 1994, the States-parties agreed in 1997 to the Kyoto Protocol, which obliged industrialized states to reduce their total emissions of the most important greenhouse gases by at least 5 per cent below their 1990 levels, between 2008 and 2012. Targets for the accomplishment of this goal by each participating state were based on a very complicated computation process known as the 'clean development mechanism', which made it possible for industrialized and developing states to carry out joint implementation of climate control projects wherein developed states finance emissions-reductions projects in developing states, and the resultant emissions reductions are then credited to the sponsoring industrialized state. Furthermore, a certain amount of 'emissions trade' is allowed between states. The Kyoto protocol came into force in February 2005 after fifty-five states, accounting for at least 55 per cent of the world's emissions, had ratified it (on climate control in general, see Oberthür and Ott, 2000).

Another important test for the UN's efforts was the 'World Summit on Sustainable Development' ('Rio Plus 10 Summit') held in Johannesburg in 2002 to take stock of the progress achieved in the ten years since Rio. The summit was the UN's

TABLE 7.8
The difficult road to climate control

Conference	Results
Rio de Janeiro 1992	At the World Summit for Environment and Development, the Framework Convention on Climate Control was created as a basis in international law basis for international climate control. It came into effect in 1994, and had been ratified by 186 states by 2001
Berlin and Geneva 1995 and 1996	The first two conferences of states-party try in vain to reach agreement on a binding timeline with concrete goals for reductions
Kyoto 1997	At the third conference of states-party, the industrialized states committed themselves to reducing their emissions by the year 2012 to 5 per cent below 1990 levels. Specific reduction goals for individual states were also laid down
Bonn 1999	At the fifth conference of states-party, a system for the review and monitoring of greenhouse gases was discussed
The Hague 2000	The sixth conference of states-party ended without agreement on the important questions, and the conference was postponed until 2001
New Delhi 2002	The eighth conference produced agreement on, among other things, rules for trade of CO_2 emissions among developing countries
Bali 2007	Roadmap for a negotiation process to be concluded in 2009 to feed into a post-Kyoto international agreement on climate change
Copenhagen 2009	Recognition that anthropogenic climate change is a global challenge; agreement on working towards keeping increase in global average temperature below 2 degrees Celsius; failure to achieve a legally binding Post-Kyoto instrument
Cancún 2010	Recognition of the two-degrees-criterion; financial support to developing states; establishment of the Green Climate Fund

Source: Data from conferences concluding communiqués.

largest to that point and included more than 21,000 representatives of 191 states, among them 104 heads of state and/or government, 9,000 official delegates, 8,000 NGO representatives and 4,000 journalists. The most important goal was the re-emphasis of the concept of sustainable development. On the agenda, among other things, were the maintenance of fish stocks, protection of the oceans, prohibition of the most dangerous environmental toxins, promotion of non-fossil-fuel sources of energy, and debt relief for the very poorest countries (see Table 7.4). For these purposes, two documents were passed: the 'Johannesburg Declaration', comprised thirty-seven guiding principles to be observed by member states when formulating policies on sustainable development; and the 'Johannesburg Plan of Action', comprising 153 sections devoted to the environment and development. In

TABLE 7.9
Selected time goals in the Johannesburg plan of action

Target date	Goal
2005	Development of integrated water resource management and water efficiency plans
2005	Reduction by a quarter of the occurrence of HIV in people between 15 and 24 years old
2005	Development of integrated water resource management and water efficiency plans
2005	Reduction by a quarter of the occurrence of HIV in people between 15 and 24 years old
2005	Progress in the formulation of national sustainability strategies and their implementation
2010	Improvement of developing countries' access to alternatives to ozone-damaging substances
2010	Reduction of the present rate of destruction of biological diversity
2012	Creation of protected ocean areas
2015	Reduction by one half the number of people in absolute poverty
2015	Reduction by one half the number of people suffering from hunger
2015	Reduction by one half the number of people with no access to clean drinking water
2015	Reduction by one half the number of people with no access to proper sewage and sanitation
2015	Reduction of the infant mortality rate by two-thirds and the maternal mortality rate by three-quarters
2015	Creation of an opportunity for all children to have a basic education
2020	Improvement of the living conditions for 100 million inhabitants of slums
2022	Access to energy sources for at least 35 per cent of the population of Africa

Source: Adapted from Martens and Sterk (2002, p. 12).

the concluding declaration, more than 180 states obligated themselves to implement the comprehensive programme of action passed at the summit and to engage themselves more actively with sustainable development, but once again, results concerning implementation have been mixed.

Whatever the lack of measurable implementation, such conferences have been successful in firmly establishing environmental and sustainable development issues in the world consciousness. (Sustainable Development had, in fact, been established in expert circles for significant time – in particular under the chairmanship of then-prime minister of Norway Gro Harlem Brundtland.) Despite the weaknesses stemming from the non-binding nature of the provisions and the insufficient realization of financial promises, Rio and Johannesburg mark a new phase in international environmental concerns to the extent that:

> [N]o nation-state and no national or international organization [can] deny the existence of the problems being discussed, and above all the relationships between them. Thus, in the future policies may be judged by their compatibility with the recommendations of the Agenda 21. (Waldmann, 1999, p. 80)

Any potential for success, however, must be measured against the experience that attractive-sounding agreements can sometimes command little attention in practice.

After a series of meetings the states-parties of UNFCCC convened their 2009 conference in Copenhagen to work on a follow-up agreement for the Kyoto Protocol. The results of the Copenhagen Summit, however, were sobering. Participating states accepted a formula that recognizes climate change as one of the worlds most pressing challenges and acknowledged that action should be taken to ensure temperature increases do not exceed two degrees Celsius. But the Copenhagen negotiations failed to agree on a new treaty, and also failed to set a future deadline for a new binding instrument.

After dramatic debates, a kind of last-minute breakthrough was achieved during the Climate Conference held in Cancún, Mexico, in November and December 2010 (16th Conference of Parties to the Convention (COP16) and the 6th Meeting of the Parties to the Protocol (CMP6)). Though the states-parties again did not agree on a legally binding instrument, the multilateral process was put back on track. In the COP16 Outcome document states-parties for the first time officially recognized that the increase in average global temperature has to be kept below two degrees Celsius (para. 4) and accepted action plans submitted by industrialized and developing countries to reduce greenhouse gas emissions. The Cancún Adaptation Framework (Section II) was also established to improve planning and implementation of projects in developing states through financial and technical support. In the crucial field of finance (Section IV) industrialized states committed themselves to providing an 'Fast-start Finance' amount of US$30 billion for the period of 2010–12, and confirmed their commitment to jointly mobilizing US$100 billion per year as a long-term obligation to the needs of developing states. The Green Climate Fund also aims to provide improved funding for climate protection undertaken by developing states. Finally, states agreed to periodically review the adequacy of the long-term two-degree goal (Section V).

The Functions of Relevant UN Bodies

Diverse agencies, functions, and commissions of the UN system are involved with environmental issues. The concept of sustainable development integrates environmental politics into a broad spectrum of international economic and development politics, and is not the exclusive task of any single institution or actor. This so-called 'sectoral approach', however, often means that the protection of the environment is secondary to the other politics of the various groups and their contradictory interests (French, 1995, p. 31).

UNEP has been the central UN organ in the area of environment politics since 1972. UNEP serves 'to provide leadership and encourage partnership in caring for the environment by inspiring, informing and enabling nations and peoples to improve their quality of life without compromising that of future generations', and often plays the role of driving force or catalyst for the environmental activities of other institutions. UNEP Executive Director Adam Steiner (since 2006, re-elected in 2010 for another four-year term, also serving in the rank of Under-Secretary-General) functions as the environmental co-ordinator for the entire UN system. UNEP is not a specialized agency in the sense of the UN Charter with its own legal personality and membership; it is a subsidiary organ of the General Assembly and ECOSOC. Headquartered in Nairobi, Kenya, UNEP employs approximately 1000 staff and is represented in twenty-five states – including a second major office in Paris, France, a liaison office to the UN in New York, and six regional offices. The Governing Council, consisting of fifty-eight states chosen for four-year terms according to a regional key by the General Assembly, is UNEP's highest decision-making organ. Administrative costs are paid out of the regular UN budget; but the programme budget is usually funded by voluntary contributions (approximately US$570 million for 2008–09). UNEP supports national activities in environmental protection, advises governments on global environmental issues and the development, evaluation, and supervision of global environmental law. One of UNEP's most important tasks is the review and registration of data and the publication of reports and books on environment issues.

The UN Commission on Sustainable Development (CSD) is the second central building block of UN environment policy. Founded at the conclusion of the Rio Conference in December 1992 (under Article 68 of the UN Charter) the CSD seeks to address the environmental and development tasks addressed in Agenda 21 – its treaty-defined purpose is to secure the process following from Rio in the sense of a cross-cutting undertaking, to push forward the integration of environmental and development politics, and to guarantee the implementation of Agenda 21 at national, regional, and international levels. Classified as a functional commission of ECOSOC, the CSD's administrative work is carried out by its Division for Sustainable Development in the Department of Economic and Social Issues, and its political agenda is set by a group of fifty-three high-ranking state representatives (chosen according to a regional key). There has been a certain amount of (much criticized) overlap between the work of the CSD and UNEP.

Along with UNEP, the CSD, and other relevant specialized agencies (especially the FAO, IMO, UNESCO, WMO and WHO), there are other subsidiary organs of the UN – including UNCTAD and UNDP – involved with monitoring environmental issues. Some regional commissions have also integrated environmental issues into their work, although without a global focus. Not least, the Bretton Woods Organizations have also begun to draw environmental concerns into their work, but that will not be addressed here.

Additionally, the UN framework also includes many conventions and programmes that have given rise to their own secretariats and offices. Every individual convention needs the ratification of the participating states, and the legal hurdles and regulations in the various conventions are each handled very differently. There are also regulations on dispute settlement to be made, implementation to be monitored, and compliance to be regulated. Furthermore, a differentiation must be made between framework agreements and protocols. While the former, as soft law, simply lay down general basic principles, concrete duties are usually laid down in the protocols (hard law). Since no enforcement measures are available in international environmental politics, a few guiding principles have been developed for the conventions:

- they should be conducted in a non-confrontational manner, and conflicts should be avoided to the furthest extent possible;
- decisions should be transparent, made by the states themselves, and documented by a reporting system; and
- the signatory states themselves should determine which concrete technical and financial measures should be considered necessary for implementation. (Loibl, 2001)

Among the most important conventions within the UN framework are the above-mentioned UN Framework Convention on Climate Change; the Protocol on the Reduction of Greenhouse Gases; the Convention on Biological Diversity; the Convention on International Trade of Endangered Species; the Law of the Sea Convention; the Vienna and Montreal Conventions on protection of the ozone layer; the Convention Against Desertification; and the Forest Agreement. The secretariats to these Conventions, some of which enjoy a well-developed administrative and scientific base, are located across the world. They administrate and monitor the conventions, and may also establish subsidiary organs for scientific advice and technical support. Furthermore, when necessary, they organize conferences of the signatory states, which take place at irregular intervals and are focused on a detailed reworking of the conventions as well as discussions on implementation problems.

International environmental politics is an area rife with failed attempts and missed opportunities, but there have also been positive developments. The model for difficult but finally successful environmental politics on a global level is the so-called 'ozone regime'. At the beginning of the 1970s, evidence was growing that the ozone layer was being damaged by the use of chlorofluorocarbons (CFCs), and that this constituted a serious health risk for human beings. Not least through the studies and conferences that took place under UN auspices, as well as the enduring lobbying of countless NGOs, the Montreal Protocol was signed in a 1987 UNEP conference. This contained a full prohibition – which has been further strengthened since that time – on the use of all the damaging substances. Although the UN has no direct ability to implement norms and is thus far dependent on the goodwill of the signatory states, the concentration of ozone-depleting substances was drastically reduced over the course of the 1990s and beyond, to such an extent that this problem can be considered to be largely solved. All the same, it was an important background condition of this successful agreement that viable alternatives to CFCs existed, and only one branch of industry was hit very hard by the prohibition.

Environmental Politics in the UN: The Balance Sheet

Despite almost 900 bilateral and multilateral environmental treaties, the global environmental situation continues to worsen. This is where the UN's work in environmental politics comes into play: it neither wants, nor has the capacities, to solve every environmental problem that exists, and the UN is not intended to replace bilateral or regional agreements, to say nothing of national efforts at environmental improvements. Rather, the UN is meant to concentrate on strategically important aspects with global significance, and to offer a forum for the handling of environmental issues.

As in other political areas, the balance sheet here comes out neither as uniformly positive nor entirely negative. This is in part because problems have become far more urgent in recent years, and the UN does not possess the means to rectify the environmental sins of its member states. If each of the declarations of principle and obligations of member states were observed and implemented, the global environmental situation would be much improved beyond its present condition. That this has clearly not been the case is part of the reason that there have been increasing calls to reform UN environmental politics. Just as in the area of protection of human rights, the problem is not a lack of norms and conventions, but rather a lack of effective instruments for their implementation. Indeed, there is 'a dilemma between the capacities and the duties undertaken' (Mingst and Karns, 2000, p. 153). Increasingly, UN conferences are also coming under criticism (Martens and Sterk, 2002, p. 11). The model of consensus-orientated multilateralism appears to have reached its limits at the Copenhagen summit, but as yet no alternative to this type of political co-operation has been developed.

In any case, the UN has performed an important service in linking the issues of environmental protection and development co-operation in the public consciousness. Global environmental problems require a global negotiating framework that can only be provided (at present) by the UN. At the same time, the institutional fragmentation and lack of co-ordination among the various UN bodies has been strongly criticized. If institutional and conceptual reform is required one possibility for improvement is to increase the efficiency and co-ordination of the already-existing bodies. Foremost, however, new approaches for a more balanced burden sharing between industrialized, transitioning and developing states must be found. In this regard, industrialized states carry a major responsibility to provide financial and technical assistance to developing states that implement green technologies and environmental protection strategies.

Whether such a minimalist strategy is sufficient to improve the effectiveness of the existing institutional system of international environmental and development politics remains to be seen. Proposals for the creation of a new specialized agency –the World Organization for Environment and Development, intended to bind existing agencies such as UNEP, the CSD and the various relevant convention secretariats under one institutional framework – remain at the discussion stage. Proposals for the founding of an environmental security council or of an international environmental remain mere conjecture.

Further Reading

Esty, Daniel (ed.) (2002) *Global Environmental Institutions: Perspectives on Reform,* London: Royal Institute of International Affairs.

Righter, Rosemary (1995) *Utopia Lost. The United Nations and World Order,* New York: Twentieth Century Fund Press.

United Nations Development Programme, *Human Development Report,* New York (published annually): Oxford University Press.

United Nations Environmental Programme, *UNEP Yearbook,* Nairobi (published annually): UNEP.

UN Millennium Project (2005) *Investing in Development. A Practical Plan to Achieve the Millennium development Goals,* London and Sterling, VA: Earthscan.

World Commission on Environment and Development (1987) *Our Common Future,* Oxford: Oxford University Press.

8

Reforms for the Twenty-First Century

The dramatic changes in international politics, along with the obvious weaknesses and insufficiencies of the UN itself, have given rise to the theme of UN reform. As noted by Secretary-General Kofi Annan in his Millennium Report: 'If the international community were to create a new United Nations tomorrow, its make-up would surely be different from the one we have' (Annan 2000, para. 352).

The key to UN reform – whether or not it will happen, what kind of reforms might be possible – must be addressed first and foremost by member states who have the sole power to implement large-scale reform. In that sense, the UN remains a classical inter-governmental organization, meaning that it can act only to the extent allowed by member states after they have weighed their own interests. At the same time, however, the world is increasingly looking to the UN to fill a political gap in the globalized world community, and it is precisely this contradiction – between an honest assessment of the UN's capabilities as a state-based organization and the ambitious political expectations placed upon it – that creates a climate of over-extension. This contradiction is reflected in the various theoretical understandings of the function and structure of international relations that were addressed in Chapter 2. For Realists, the UN is subordinate to the state sovereignty and attempts at reform will largely exhaust themselves in a negligible increase in organizational efficiency. Institutionalists and Idealists, however, see reform as a credible opportunity to create and stabilize an improved international system wherein conflicts are not resolved through force, and co-operation takes place according to rules made in the long-term interests of all participants.

In practice, efforts at reform appear modest, and a distinction must be made between internal reform of the organization's by-laws, which can be achieved without amending the Charter, and 'constitutional changes', which would require changes to the Charter. The hurdles in the way of the latter are extremely high – many of the reforms that have been under discussion for years have been postponed and put on the back burner because of these hurdles. As a result, some of the suggested reforms appear as regularly as clockwork on the agendas of diverse working groups of the General Assembly and Security Council, without any consensus ever being achieved (see Table 8.1).

TABLE 8.1
Typology of suggested reforms

Increased efficiency	Institutional reforms	Fundamental changes
Reforms aim at greater capability and more effectiveness in the classical central responsibility	Reforms aim at institutional remodelling and adjustment to new challenges	Reforms aim at basic and fundamental remodelling of the current principles on which the UN is founded and on which it operates
Example: rationalization/ streamlining in administrative or financial areas	Example: Security Council reform, empowerment of ECOSOC, upgrading the Human Rights Council to a principal organ	Examples: supra-nationalization of the UN; establishment of an effective responsibility to protect

Source: Based on discussion in Unser (2004, pp. 393–406).

In his 2005 report 'In Larger Freedom' – published in preparation for the 2005 World Summit – Secretary-General Kofi Annan argued that member states needed to reorganize the UN so that it could better meet the challenges of globalization. He specifically named three 'freedoms' that can be considered as the highest priority strategic goals of the UN:

- 'Freedom from Want' (a shared vision of development, including environmental issues).
- 'Freedom from Fear' (a vision of collective security).
- 'Freedom to Live in Dignity' (rule of law, human rights, democracy).

Secretary-General Annan also established a programme for reform entitled 'Strengthening the United Nations'. 'In Larger Freedom' became the backbone of the reform debate in the run-up to the World Summit, and some it its proposals were eventually endorsed at the Summit. Some reforms endorsed by the Summit have fared better than others: a number of projects have been realized since 2005, whilst others remain caught in the time-loop of continuing discussions (see below).

Reform as a Long and Difficult Process

The UN's history has been a process of constant change and reform. The organization has outlived both the beginning and the end of the Cold War, the beginning and the completion of the process of decolonization, and all of the associated membership increases, new challenges and organizational restructuring that has been necessary along the way. New global questions, such as the scarcity of natural resources, destruction of the environment, climate change, rapid population growth, weapons of mass destruction, and new threats to peace from internal conflict have crowded in upon the classical risks and problems that were recognized and anticipated at the UN's founding.

The UN has shown itself to be an integrative organization capable of development and adaptation. Along with the gradual realization of its claims to universality (as a result of increasing membership), the UN has also accrued enlarged competencies and capacities to deal with new challenges. However, the UN has generally limited its learning and reform processes to the expansion of existing panels and the creation of increasing numbers of subsidiary organs, programmes, and specialized agencies. The slow and steady increase in organizational bureaucracy has seen the organizational principles of the UN founders slowly slip out of control. The UN was meant to function as a sort of 'solar system', whose core organization was meant to co-ordinate a rather loose web of institutions and organizations in pursuit of effective co-operation. The core organization would have the aggregate wisdom of the entire system at its disposal, be able to formulate comprehensive strategies, and then to implement these in an agreed fashion (Childers and Urquhart, 1994, p. 14 *et seq.*). What this original concept underestimated was the centrifugal force of such a system, resulting from the divergent interests of individual states and groups of states, which led to extensive autonomy for the specialized agencies, as well as a growing consciousness of independence on the part of other subsidiary organs. The result was a UN system in which both vertical co-ordination and horizontal co-operation have been extremely difficult, and the potential of neither has been used to anything like its full extent. The impotence of the East–West conflict of the Cold War worked for a long time to conceal the underlying dysfunction of this inflationary organizational development, as well as strengthening the states and blocs in their own activities. The essential absence of the Security Council as the powerful, decision-making centre of the UN led to increased focus on the General Assembly, in which the developing states of the 'Third World' held a majority. For these newly independent states, the General Assembly was the decisive forum for an equal articulation of their interests and affairs. The creation of new institutions to deal with developing country-specific issues was supported by great powers and their blocs for a common purpose: the newly created panels were appropriate in a probationary capacity for the diversion of developing states' demands, but these panels could not threaten the basic global balance of power enshrined in the Security Council. Any reforms that had the potential to impact the fundamental structures and principles of the organization were simply not on the agenda. However, this *status quo* changed with the end of the Cold War and the end of the Security Council's Cold War-era impotence: the UN emerged from its status as a mere 'talking shop' to being an increasingly important, and powerful actor in international politics. In view of the Security Council's newly won capacity to act, and of the organization's emerging structural deficiencies, a debate emerged in which two different directions for suggested reform could be distinguished:

(i) The members of the Non-aligned Movement (NAM), more than a hundred states primarily drawn from the group of developing countries, were forced to recognize the weakening of their influence following the re-emergence of the Security Council in the post-Cold War years. Therefore, since the beginning of the 1990s, they have pushed harder than ever for greater opportunities to participate in the essential decision-making processes of the organization, as well as for more extensive consultation in the Bretton Woods Organizations, which are still completely dominated by the industrialized states (Saksena, 1993; South Centre, 1996).

(ii) The industrialized states, and above all the USA, continued to criticize the UN's lack of effectiveness, and to demand more streamlined, transparent, and cost-effective structures. The effectiveness argument was quickly indicted by developing countries as being nothing but a cover for the instrumentalization of the UN for the pursuit of the industrialized states' interests (Bourantonis, 1998).

The key-words 'participation' and 'effectiveness' have developed over the course of this discussion into mutually exclusive demands. During the 1990s the UN became the USA's 'whipping-boy of politics' and was the target of pointed criticism from the American political system. The UN was described as an institutional jungle, a ponderous apparatus with a personnel strength that was too big; it was described as incompetent and trapped in ossified structures and anachronistic working procedures, and vilified for throwing member states' money around in a totally irresponsible fashion. The USA's prescription for overcoming these problems was to concentrate on peacekeeping and to attempt to reduce the size of the entire UN apparatus; the US attempted to enforce such reforms by withholding its contributions to the regular budget and to peacekeeping budgets. Behind this institutional scolding, however, was the remaining superpower's unconcealed retreat from multilateralism as an organizing mechanism of international relations. The consensus at the heart of the UN – that global problems required global solutions – began to be questioned, and 'Wilsonian utterances' were confronted by a neo-realist renaissance of the ascendancy of the nation state (Eban, 1995, p. 50). Ives-Marie Laulan (1996, p. 51) compared the UN with the corpse of one who has died of an illness: it can no longer be healed, only reborn in some other form.

Reform by institutionally orientated experts – those who want to overcome the constructed contradiction between 'participation' and 'effectiveness' (Childers and Urquhart, 1994; Kennedy and Russett, 1995; Weizsäcker and Quereshi, 1995) – was not permitted at the forefront of the reform debate. Such proposals began from the assumption that member states had both the political will, and the endurance, to come to a conclusion on a systematic reform of the world organization. Such a procedure would begin with an analysis of the global challenges and the addressing of a few basic questions about the ordering of the international system (Russett, 1996, p. 261 *et seq.*):

- To what degree can the states be expected to allow the erosion of their sovereignty for the sake of collective mechanisms?
- How far do states hold themselves to commonly agreed-upon determinations, and what level of violation, non-observation, or lack of support is acceptable?
- How can power and law be brought into a balanced relationship, and how can conflicting interests be resolved in a constructive manner?
- What do global governance processes look like with states, international organizations, NGOs, and the global economy as central actors?

With these questions in mind, it would have been conceivable to produce a completely new institutional design for a 'world organization of the third generation' (Bertrand and Warner, 1996), and to give its organs the necessary competencies given the internal structures and modes of work. However, the international political environment of the 1990s was markedly different to that of 1945 when a significantly smaller community of states endured common suffering after the trauma of two consecutive world wars. However unwillingly, states recognized in 1945 that it would be both necessary and appropriate to give up some rights of sovereignty and accept the privileges of a small group of powers in order to avoid a third catastrophe. The global problems of the 1990s, in contrast, were far too abstract and multifaceted to provide the pressure necessary for unity on the questions of a new orientation for the organization and a new formulation for the Charter.

Why is there so little progress on UN reform, given that reform is so persistently urged by a large number of member states? Multilateralism means the continuous quest for compromise and consensus between actors, and requires a willingness on the part of member states to postpone individual interests in favour of common objectives. Despite public commitments to multilateralism, most governments and heads of states first and foremost pursue their individual national agendas resulting in a complex and highly complex UN structure with a large and diverse number of UN subsidiary organs, specialized agencies, funds, and programmes that reflects the disjointed wills of its member states. Furthermore, member state delegations to the UN receive their instruction from their foreign ministries. At the same time, delegations receive instructions from the various departments of the subsidiary bodies and specialized agencies to which they belong. As such, member states often find themselves on the receiving end of contradictory instructions and obligations. The system is highly fragmented and attempts at basic administrative reforms are motivated by a desire to lessen overlapping jurisdictions, redundancy and resource waste.

What is common to all reforms mentioned thus far is that measures for their implementation can only be agreed upon and implemented by the member states themselves. While operating and co-ordination procedures in the main bodies and subsidiary organs can easily be addressed by creating new provisions in the relevant by-laws or through resolutions, the majority of any substantive reforms would require a revision of the Charter. Articles 108 and 109 of the Charter deliberately set very high hurdles for any such amendment, requiring a two-thirds majority in the General Assembly, plus ratification by two-thirds of the member states including all five permanent members of the Security Council (essentially giving the Permanent Five a blocking minority). By the same criteria, however, the Permanent Five require the agreement of nearly 130 member states for any of their own projects to succeed. In view of this complicated criteria, and the uncertainty of its results, even completely uncontroversial changes such as the elimination of the enemy-state clauses have been left undone for prolonged periods. The overwhelming fear is that such initiatives might be linked to currently insoluble issues such as the veto privilege. In this continuing situation, prognoses on the chances of realizing central intentions such as reform of the Security Council are purely negative. The reform process has thus progressed only by smaller steps, and remained limited to measures that lie within the competence of the General Assembly or the Secretary-General.

Against this backdrop of fundamental disagreements on the future form and function of the UN, it is hardly surprising that ideas for comprehensive reform have remained somewhat vague.

The 2005 World Summit

If there was ever a window of opportunity in international politics it appeared wide open in 2005. At the UN's 60th anniversary in that year, it was acknowledged by most member states that the Charter – and the organization as a whole – was in need of a thorough overhaul:

- Many of the Charter's provisions have shown themselves to be impossible to implement (such as portions of Chapter VII, for example), or have become obsolete (such as the enemy state clauses).
- New areas of activity such as crisis prevention, environmental protection, and population issues are either addressed inadequately in the Charter or not mentioned at all.
- The composition of the Security Council with regard to the permanent members reflects the situation at the end of the Second World War, and with regard to the number of non-permanent members, the situation of the organization at the beginning of the 1960s.
- The veto is increasingly regarded as discriminatory and no longer justified in its function.
- One of the principal organs – the Trusteeship Council – has suspended its work because of a lack of areas needing supervision.
- The work of the General Assembly is complicated and labour-intensive, while the role of ECOSOC continues to lose importance.
- Effective co-ordination of the whole system, with its committees within committees and redundancy, is hardly possible.

As early as 2003, Secretary-General Kofi Annan pointed out in an address to the General Assembly that 'we have come to a fork in the road. This may be a moment no less decisive than 1945 itself, when the United Nations was founded' (Annan 2003). In his statement Annan also announced the establishment of a High-Level Panel (HLP) of eminent personalities, to which he assigned four tasks:

- to examine the current challenges to peace and security;
- to consider the contribution which collective action can make in addressing these challenges;
- to review the functioning of the major organs of the United Nations and the relationship between them; and
- to recommend ways of strengthening the United Nations, through reform of its institutions and processes.

The HLP – comprised of sixteen experts and chaired by former Prime Minister of Thailand Annand Panyarachun – published its landmark report in December of 2004. The report calls for a new security consensus that encompasses more than the prevention of inter-state wars: '[A]ny event or process that leads to large-scale death or lessening of life chances and undermines States as the basic unit of the international system is a threat to international security' (HLP, 2004). From this definition the HLP articulated six clusters of threats:

- economic and social threats, including poverty, infectious disease and environmental degradation;
- inter-state conflict;
- internal conflict, including civil war,
- genocide and other large-scale atrocities;
- nuclear, radiological, chemical and biological weapons; and
- terrorism, and transnational organized crime.

The HLP urged that contemporary threats must be regarded as interrelated, and requiring of a more comprehensive collective security system and framework for preventive action. Part III of the report examines collective security and the use of force, where the panel endorsed 'the emerging norm that there is a collective international responsibility to protect, exercisable by the Security Council authorizing military intervention as a last resort, in the event of genocide and other large-scale killing, ethnic cleansing or serious violations of international humanitarian law which sovereign Governments have proved powerless or unwilling to prevent' (ibid., para. 203). At the same time the HLP highlights the unique function of the Security Council with regard to the legitimization of coercive military measures and denies any new justification of the use of force beyond the Charter. Part IV of the HLP proposes institutional reforms concerning the main bodies as well as subsidiary organs. It puts up for discussion two models for the Reform of the Security Council, recommends the deletion of the enemy state clauses, the Trusteeship Council, and the Military Staff Committee from the Charter, and calls for a renewed Human Rights Commission and suggests the creation of a Peacebuilding Commission.

Following the HLP, Secretary-General Kofi Annan concentrated the panel's recommendations into 'an agenda of highest priorities' (ibid., para. 5) in his afore-mentioned report, 'In Larger Freedom'. Furthermore, during preparations for the 2005 World Summit Secretary-General Kofi Annan appealed to member states on countless occasions to consider fundamental and comprehensive reform of the institutions and mechanisms of the UN. A draft outcome to the 2005 World Summit was similarly based on the Secretary-General's paper.

During the summer of 2005, far-reaching UN reforms appeared to be within reach. The results of World Summit in September 2005, however, fell far short of the high expectations. In its 178 paragraphs, the World Summit Outcome (A/RES/60/1, 16 September 2005) largely refers to the array of preliminary papers while refusing to take substantial decisions. In the weeks before the Summit, member states – with the USA at the fore – started a complete revision of the draft outcome document to dilute the provisions that place further obligations or possible constraints of state sovereignty. Thus, commitments for enhanced efforts at development and the achievement of the MDGs were not corroborated by verifiable obligations (except the G8 promise to contribute US$50 billion from 2010); the acknowledgement of the 'responsibility to protect' was submitted to a number of preconditions; disarmament issues were excluded; and the question of Security Council reform was not seriously touched upon.

The 2005 World Summit was successful, however, on a number of alternative issues. It was agreed that the Human Rights Commission should be replaced by a Human Rights Council, and that a Peacebuilding Commission should be established – two projects that were realized within months of the World Summit Outcome document being adopted. Furthermore, the World Summit also agreed to the deletion of the enemy state clauses in the Charter, and to the dissolution of the Trusteeship Council – both of which required Charter amendments.

In the following sections, a number of completed and incomplete institutional reforms are addressed, and the various reform options and perspectives are examined.

Institutional Reforms

As mentioned above, reforms are most likely to be realized when they fall within the competence of the Secretary-General; decision-making in the General Assembly is often delayed by member states. However, there has been, and continues to be progress in those areas of reform that require member states' approval if those decisions remain below the threshold of Charter amendment.

Changes within the Secretariat

The UN's international civil service includes officers from more than 187 states (as of 2011), whose qualifications, mentalities, and understanding of public service are extremely different: 'To develop the streamlined management culture of a business undertaking [in such a] multicultural environment is a thing of pure impossibility' (Paschke, 1996, p. 42). Secretariat efficiency cannot be understood in a pure sense of economic rationality. Additionally, member states – through the General Assembly and the Security Council – often convey unclear and some-times contradictory mandates to the Secretariat and its subsidiary organs, and use the existing regulations to micromanage the Secretariat's various Departments (Paschke, 1999, p. 189 *et seq.*).

The reforms undertaken in the Department of Peacekeeping Operations and the Department of Field Support have already been discussed in Chapters 1 and 4. In addition to those reforms, the Secretariat has undergone considerable change in a number of different areas. Not least, the number of staff working in the Secretariat has been considerably reduced. A new Integrated Management Information System has been introduced in order to facilitate a network supported and computer-supported personnel for both issue-based and budget administration and the UN's long-neglected human resources management was reinvigorated with a new Perfor-mance Appraisal System (PAS) for the better evaluation of personnel. The rather opaque acquisitions body of the UN administration was reorganized and made more cost-conscious. Finally, in summer of 1994, at the instigation of the Secretary-General, the General Assembly created the Office of Internal Oversight Services (OIOS) with an Inspector-General at its head to facilitate an effective internal review UN (on these measures, see Paschke, 1996; Thant and Scott 2007, p. 88 *et seq.*).

Secretary-General Kofi Annan entered office under a great deal of pressure to reform and was able to effect change as early as March 1997. Annan articulated five core tasks of the UN – Peace and Security, Economic and Social Issues, Humanitarian Affairs, Development, and Human Rights – and designated the work of each UN Department and (some of) the subsidiary organs and programmes under Executive Committees for these tasks (the area of Human Rights Protection was designated to cut across – and thus touch upon – all of the other four areas). In his July 1997 programme for the UN reform renewal, Annan came up with a list of decisions that amounted to a 'quiet revolution' (Mingst and Karns, 2000, p. 208). Along with an abundance of suggestions for his own areas of competence, Annan gave recommendations to member states and suggested how the UN system as a whole might be better managed and directed. The only thing missing from Annan's programme was reform of the Security Council.

Annan proposals drew member states into a circle of responsibility for the real-ization of a more effective UN, a courageous move considering the fate of his predecessor who had not been elected for a second term after proving to be too controversial.

Steps for which the Secretary-General could take responsibility were quickly put into practice following General Assembly approval for administrative reform (Resolution 52/12A, 12 November 1997). A new Senior Management Group (SMG) – a sort-of cabinet chaired by the Secretary-General and composed of thirty-six members and one observer, among them the convenors of the Executive Committees, heads of departments, and other senior UN managers – was created as the basis of a new leadership and management culture. The Office of the High Commissioner for Human Rights (OHCHR) was strengthened by its integration into the UN Centre for Human Rights, and a new Department for Disarmament and Arms Control was formed in the Secretariat.

Of Annan's recommendations to the General Assembly, two were passed in full in Resolution 52/12B of 19 December 1997: first, the office of a Deputy Secretary-General was created (Louise Fréchette of Canada was the first to hold the office in Spring 1998, presently the position is held by Asha-Rose Migiro of Tanzania) to relieve the administrative burden on the Secretary-General; second, a Development Account was created, into which internal savings were to flow as a 'development dividend'. One suggestion the General Assembly did not choose to implement was the supplementary financing of the UN's running costs through a 'revolving credit fund'. The Secretary-General had envisioned this fund to be one where member states paid in voluntary contributions from which the UN could then borrow. Security for the fund would be based on the open requirements for contributions to the regular budget and to the peacekeeping missions. Annan's proposals to streamline the General Assembly's agenda through a concentration on yearly themes of global importance, to reduce the Secretariat's workload through the automatic expiration of mandates that had not been formally renewed (the 'sunset clause'), and to reintroduce the original division of labour among the main bodies, through which the General Assembly's accrual of influence over the daily work-order of the Secretariat would have been reduced, were equally unsuccessful.

The reforms accomplished – as well as those not accomplished or even attempted – at the end of the 1990s reveal a clear pattern: the Secretariat and its sub-bodies have shown themselves both ready for and capable of substantial reform in order to adjust their competencies and capacities to new challenges. Member states, in contrast, still lack the capacity to reach a consensus on those areas of reform for which their agreement is absolutely indispensable (Paschke, 1999, p. 190).

Finance Reform

A major reform success that member states can lay claim to is the reorganization of the contributions scale for the regular budget and for peacekeeping activities. In December 2000, after years of the most harrowing negotiations (Koschorreck, 2000) a solution was found that took into account both the USA's wish to reduce its contributions and a realistic assessment of the financial capacities of the poorest states. The resultant new scale of assessments encompasses a broad spectrum of contributions from 0.001 per cent of the programme budget (a total of US$23,506 in 2011) to 22 per cent of the budget (a total of US$517,133,507 in 2011, that the USA is obliged to provide) (see A/RES/64/248, 24 December 2009). Contributions must be paid on time, in full, and without preconditions.

The annual budget for the whole UN system is approximately US$31billion, including all voluntary contributions to funds and programmes as well as specialized agencies (as of 2011), but there is a gross disparity between the responsibilities that the UN is expected to meet, and the willingness of member states to adequately fund the organization so that it can meet its obligations. According to the Global Policy Forum, member states' arrears to the regular budget topped $348 million, of which the US owed 80 per cent (as of December 2010). The only sanctioning instrument offered by the Charter in this area is found in Article 19: that states which owe the UN more than two full years' worth of contributions lose their right to vote in the General Assembly. Since contributions to peacekeeping missions are not included in that provision, and the most notorious debtors tend to keep their debts just under the critical limit and make last-minute payments, this sanction has proved to be less than effective. In February 2011, seven of the poorest member states were in arrears under the terms of Article 19, of which six were nonetheless granted temporary voting rights by a General Assembly resolution.

The creation of new specialized funds – such as the Peacebuilding Fund that relies on voluntary contributions and provides monies quickly if needed – has been heralded as a way out of the UN's current financial difficulties. Other ideas tend in the direction of a kind of 'world tax' levied on the international arms spending, foreign exchange transactions, or the use of space or the oceans. The so-called Tobin Tax (after James Tobin, the Nobel Prize winner for Economics) on international currency transactions could – if levied at only 0.5 per cent on these primarily speculative transactions – result in an income of several billion dollars. The refusal of certain member states to co-operate in developing these ideas, however, means there is no real chance for their realization, as demonstrated by the fate of the Secretary-General's comparatively modest suggestion of a revolving credit fund in 1997. The UN must simply continue to appeal to member states to take their payment obligations seriously.

Member states' contributions for peacekeeping operations are in addition to their required contributions to the regular budget. Peacekeeping contributions are based on a roster of ten categories from which the poorest and very poor member states benefit from differentiated rebates of up to 90 per cent of their contributions (equivalent to their contributing 0.0001 per cent share of the cost of a UN peace mission; for details, see A/RES/55/235). The imbalance incurred from these rebates is carried by the permanent members of the Security Council.

Member states' – not least the USA's – readiness to reach an agreement on finance reform might suggest an overall readiness to engage with a wider UN reform agenda. However, finance reform has proven to be the exception rather than the rule, as a brief examination of Security Council reform will demonstrate.

Reforming the Security Council

Reform of the UN Security Council constitutes one of the organization's greatest challenges wherein all the difficulties and obstacles of wider institutional reform are collected together in microcosm. Article 23 of the Charter states that the Security Council shall consist of five (specifically named) permanent members and ten non-permanent members chosen according to the principle of equitable geographical distribution. The non-permanent members are elected by the General Assembly for a two-year term (and may not serve two consecutive terms). Security Council composition has changed once – in 1965 – on the recommendation of the 28th General Assembly that the number of non-permanent members be raised from six to ten. The Article 108 amendment process took a surprisingly short two years, it was recommended in 1963 and came into effect in 1965. The enlargement indicated that the size and composition of the Security Council should keep pace, at least to some extent, with the increasing total membership of the organization. Since 1965, UN membership has increased from 115 to 193, but there have been no further Security Council membership increases. Indeed, constant initiatives to further increase Security Council non-permanent membership have been sidelined continuously since the 1970s.

In addition to the 1965 expansion, there have been two changes to Security Council memberships. In October 1971, the People's Republic of China took over the permanent seat that had originally been assigned to the Republic of China, but had latterly been assumed by the exiled Republic of China government in Taiwan. Since 1971, the People's Republic of China has held both UN membership and the permanent seat on the Security Council. In December 1991, the permanent representative of the Russian Federation communicated to the Secretary-General that the Russian Federation would be replacing the dissolved Soviet Union in the General Assembly and the Security Council. Both the Republic of China and the Soviet Union remain named specifically in the Charter in Article 23 as permanent members, both the General Assembly and other permanent members of the Security Council have accepted the succession permanent memberships of the People's Republic of China and the Russian Federation.

The increase in non-permanent memberships and the succession of permanent memberships of the People's Republic of China and the Russian Federation represent the only significant changes to Security Council composition. Despite energetic noises for reform from certain UN membership blocs – both from important financial contributors (such as Japan and Germany) as well as the Non-aligned Movement (NAM) – Security Council composition, decisional mechanisms, and operating procedures have remained unchanged. The main difference between previously successful reforms and those aspired to by Japan, Germany, and NAM (among others) was that they were aiming for changes to the Security Council's permanent members' circle. The Charter-based veto privileges guaranteed to the five permanent members are largely considered to be out-dated and not reflective of contemporary global politics. What was once an understandable and sensible arrangement now seems less appropriate more than half a century later. The massive developments of the last few decades – the process of decolonization, the end of the Cold War and the birth of newly independent states – has created a new global order to which the traditional power distribution in the Security Council no longer corresponds. New political groupings have emerged, and new forms and centres of conflict have arisen. Despite these changes in the global political environment, the permanent membership of the Security Council remains as it was in the wake of the Second World War. Europe continues to dominate the permanent membership, and the entire Asiatic region remains represented by only one state.

Africa and Latin America continue to lack any representation among the permanent members.

At the 47th General Assembly, India proposed a resolution – passed the next year in November 1992 – that the General Assembly should concern itself with a comprehensive discussion of Security Council reform. Initially, in the summer of 1993, member states submitted (at the request of the Secretary-General) fifty more-or-less constructive proposals concerning the future size and composition, decision-making structures, and operational procedures of the Security Council. The fifty proposals from member states grew to be 140 proposals and eventually, in the autumn of 1993, the General Assembly delegated the negotiation of proposals to a committee open to all UN member states entitled the 'Open-ended Working Group on the Question of Equitable Representation on and Increase in the Membership of the Security Council and Other Matters related to the Security Council'.

The diversity and scope of member states' proposals is not under discussion here (see Kühne and Baumann, 1995), nor is the working group's reports (which essentially communicate the general helplessness to be expected when all possible arguments are put forward, but no decisions can be made). In March 1997, the president of the working group (then President of the 51st General Assembly Razali Ismail, of Malaysia) suggested that the Council should be expanded by a further five permanent and four non-permanent members, to reach a total strength of twenty-four. The five new permanent members should include two representatives from two industrialized states, and three representatives from three developing states in Africa, Asia, and Latin America and the Caribbean. The four new non-permanent member seats should be assigned to Africa (one seat), Asia (one seat), Latin America and the Caribbean (one seat) and Eastern Europe (one seat). The five new permanent members should be chosen as a group in order to avoid the possibility that only one or two new members make it through the process before it is abandoned (meaning that the publicly declared intent to elect five new members was only a front for getting one or two specific members onto the Council). With regard to the veto, the Razali Plan suggested that it should not be extended to new permanent members, and that the original Permanent Five should pledge to use it less and less frequently. The Razali Plan accorded with the discussions taking place in both UN bodies and among member states and made concession to the political and legal realities of what a reformed Security Council might look like. Especially, the Razali plan understood that the veto was a particularly sensitive and well-protected privilege that the five existing permanent members would be unlikely to give up, or have diluted by having to share it with new permanent members (ratification would be required by all five existing permanent members to amend the Charter). Furthermore, the Razali Plan understood that the admission of more veto players into the Security Council would make the already difficult process of interest-balancing into one of practical impossibility. Attempts to bring the Razali Plan onto the Agenda of the General Assembly ultimately failed because of strong resistance from an Italian-led bloc that opposed any reforms that would create new permanent seats.

Though never realized, the Razali Plan formed the basic model for subsequently proposed Security Council reforms. The 2004 HLP could not agree on a single common reform model, so offered two:

- Model A provides for six new permanent seats, with no veto being created, and three new two-year term non-permanent seats.
- Model B provides for no new permanent seats but creates a new category of eight four-year renewable-term seats and one new two-year non-permanent (and non-renewable) seat. (HLP, 2004, paras 252, 253)

Model A is based on the Razali Plan; Model B reflects the interests of member states that would probably not be selected for permanent membership (and might therefore try to prevent other member states from achieving this prestigious upgrade). The HLP models formed the basis of the campaigns put together by various groups of member states in the run-up to the 2005 World Summit. Brazil, Germany, India, and Japan – known as the Group of Four, or G4 – unified for four of the six permanent seats, and there were also campaigns from Egypt, Nigeria, and South Africa, and counter-campaigns by groups of member states such as Italy, Pakistan, Turkey, or Mexico. In the summer of 2005, three Security Council reform models were presented to the General Assembly:

- The G4 – together with twenty-three supporters – tabled a draft resolution based on Model A, comprising six permanent seats (two for Africa, two for Asia, one for Latin America, one for Western Europe) and four non-permanent seats (one each for Africa, Asia, Eastern Europe and Latin America). The G4 proposed that new permanent members should enjoy the same rights and privileges as the existing Permanent Five but that the right to veto should be withheld for fifteen years but be subject to review after such a period.
- The group 'Uniting for Consensus' (UFC); (Argentina, Canada, Colombia, Costa Rica, Italy, Malta, Mexico, Republic of Korea, San Marino, Spain, and Turkey) also proposed to increase Security Council membership to twenty-five, but by creating ten new non-permanent seats. The twenty non-permanent members (six from Africa, five from Asia, four from Latin America, three from Western and two from Eastern Europe) would be eligible for immediate re-election, subject to approval by their respective regional groups.
- Forty-three African states proposed to increase Security Council membership to twenty-six through the creation of six new permanent seats and four new non-permanent seats. In contrast to the G4 proposal, the African proposal insisted on equal rights for all permanent members, requiring that the existing Permanent Five give up their veto privilege or to share it with their new peers.

By the time of the 2005 World Summit, none of the three groups had garnered the support of the 128 member states required to achieve the two-thirds majority in the 59th General Assembly, and as a consequence the draft resolutions were not put to vote. The World Summit Outcome Document makes only short reference to Security Council reform, declaring that 'We support early reform of the Security Council – an essential element of our overall effort to reform the United Nations – in order to make it more broadly representative, efficient and transparent and thus to further enhance its effectiveness and the legitimacy and implementation of its decisions' (World Summit, 2005, para. 153).

Member states have continued to work towards Security Council reform – albeit in a much more low key manner – following the failure of the World Summit to make any meaningful progress (see Freiesleben 2008). Facing deadlocked discussions in the open-ended working group, member states decided in September 2008 to continue intergovernmental negotiations in an informal plenary open to all member states focusing on five key issues: categories of membership; the question of the veto; regional representation; size of an enlarged Security Council and working methods of the Council; and the relationship between the Council and the General Assembly (A/RES/62/557, 15 September 2008). In 2010, intergovernmental negotiations' Chairman Ambassador Zahir Tanin of Afghanistan provided member states, and invited them to comment on, a composite paper highlighting the key issues and major parameters of Security Council reform. The first results of this exchange were published in May 2010, and revealed continuing fundamental differences between the G4 and UFC – especially over the categories of membership. It was agreed however, that the Chair's approach of text-based and member state-driven procedures should be continued.

Security Council reform remains vital for the continued acceptance of Security Council authority and the legitimacy of its decisions. This was demonstrated during the Kosovo crisis of 1998–99, when Russian and Chinese threats to veto any Security Council decision led to NATO simply bypassing the Council altogether and taking independent – i.e. non-Security Council sanctioned – military action. Security Council wrangling in the run-up to the 2003 Iraq War similarly underscored the necessity for reform. In a rules-based system of international politics, and in a collective security system in which states make decisions with far-reaching consequences and existential significance for other states, it is essential that the exercise of power be limited and brought under control (Fassbender, 1998, 1998a). Even without the right to veto, member states with permanent representation on the Security Council can exercise more influence over decisions than non-permanent members, and can contribute to a broader basis of acceptance for Security Council decisions.

It is difficult to imagine the final outcome of any Security Council reforms. Given the strong and lasting resistance to the creation of new permanent seats by a considerable number of member states, the widespread discordance over possible candidates to take those seats, and the limited enthusiasm of the existing Permanent Five to share their veto privilege, it seems unlikely that any eventual reforms would be based on Model A. In the absence of any new permanent memberships, the creation of non-permanent, renewable seats might be more viable and a more realistic response to improving the *status quo*. In any case, significant flexibility is required from member states to bridge the gaps between the differing positions and to bring forward a successful reform agenda that can also serve as a litmus test for the organization's capacity for renewal.

Revitalisation of the General Assembly

In contrast to Security Council reform, improvements to the General Assembly exist somewhat on the sidelines of contemporary UN reform discussions. Although the General Assembly rose to considerable influence during the Cold War – extending its areas of responsibility to include issues such as development, health, human rights, social and economic issues, disarmament and environment – it still does not play a central role in world politics. As noted by Edward C. Luck (2007, p. 657) the core strength of the General Assembly – its universal membership – is also its major weakness. Diplomats often criticize the 193-member General Assembly as inefficient and capable only of producing non-legally-binding resolutions that cannot be forcibly implemented. Article 14 empowers the General Assembly to recommend measures for the peaceful resolution of any situation considered likely to have a negative impact on peaceful international co-existence provided that the Security Council is not seized with that matter according to Article 12[. Despite any prominence assumed by the General Assembly during the Cold War, however, the Security Council remains the main body for the consideration of all peace and security related activities. Following the end of the Cold War, deliberations started on how to recover some political weight to the General Assembly.

The 2005 World Summit reaffirmed 'the central position of the General Assembly as the chief deliberative, policymaking and representative organ of the United Nations, as well as the role of the Assembly in the process of standard-setting and the codification of international law' (World Summit, 2005, para. 149). Member states called for 'full and speedy implementation' (ibid., para. 150) of measures to strengthen the General Assembly. To this end, an *ad hoc* working group on General Assembly revitalization was established wherein member states focused reform proposals on three major clusters (see Swart, 2008, p. 21):

- enhancing the role and authority of the General Assembly; e.g. *vis-à-vis* the Security Council or with regard to the implementation of its resolutions;
- the role of the General Assembly in the election of the Secretary-General, e.g. by reviewing the election procedures; and
- improving the working methods of the General Assembly, e.g. by streamlining the agenda or improved proceedings.

General Assembly revitalisation has been slow, however, due to the 'inherent inertia' (Luck, 2007, p. 659) of the Assembly's political machinery (not to mention the political polarization of its member states). Indeed, the consensus-based procedures of the General Assembly make it difficult to even evaluate the effectiveness of its committees or its countless subsidiary organs. General Assembly revitalisation continues to be a long-term project.

Reforms in the Area of International Law

The 2003 Iraq War constituted a fundamental break with established international law. The USA justified its actions – undertaken without a Security Council mandate – as pre-emptive self-defence against the threat of Iraq's development of weapons of mass destruction and to free a country from a cruelly repressive regime. If one were to interpret the action as 'regime change' (which was the eventual outcome) instead of self-defence, one would also have to question the legality of the action – self-defence is permitted under international law, but 'regime change' is not (see Chapter 3). According to Michael Glennon (2003), the action in Iraq made clear once again that states in general – and not just the USA – are primarily interested in serving their national interests before any consideration of international legality. Critics have suggested that international law – designed to regulate and limit war – were proven ineffective by the Iraq action and that international law needs to be reformed to match contemporary realities.

Before examining the debate on reforming international law provisions on war and peace, a few general remarks on international law are necessary. The most important sources of international law – as laid down in Article 38 of the ICJ Statute – are international conventions, customary international law, the general principles of law and judicial decisions. Customary international law in particular is based on the idea that states observe it in their practice – in the case of non-observation, however, there is no effective and fair instrument available that is equivalent to a national criminal law system. The most important difference between national and international law is that there is no effective authority that can implement international law. International law as a whole is obviously not perfect, but over the twentieth century and, in particular since the catastrophe of the Second World War, it has undergone dynamic development. The leading international law paradigm is no longer that of unlimited state sovereignty weakened only in isolated and individual instances – in that sense the Westphalian order has been shot with many holes, and there are many international law treaties concerning international trade, economic exchange and the protection of human rights. Without a doubt, 'the vast majority of international law regulations are followed without difficulty by the states affected by them, and that they thus constitute, just like national law, a secure framework for worldwide activities' (Frowein, 2003). However, international law is also inherently political insomuch that its observation is dependent on governments subjecting their behaviour to those legal provisions. A 'supra-nationalization of international law' (Wiesbrock, 2002) may be desirable, but is unlikely to be achieved considering the past and present realities of world politics.

Reform of international law does not mean that the entire system of international law has failed or is being brought into question. The reform discussion relates primarily to the question of how to deal with future risks without compromising the UN Charter. The debate is concerned with 'how normative–legal principles on the one hand and political interests and problems on the other can in the future be brought into harmony with one another in a dramatically changed world environment with new crisis scenarios' (Rechkemmer, 2003, p. 2 *et seq.*).

The Debate Over Pre-emptive Security Politics

Under what conditions, and in which cases, military intervention should be allowed are controversial questions, and are bound up in the debate over so-called pre-emptive security politics. For example, the 2002 US National Security Strategy argued that today's threats must be met in a different way from those of the past. The concept of 'immediate threat' must be aligned with the capabilities and goals of today's opponents. This debate is taking place in a significantly altered strategic landscape where terrorism and weapons of mass destruction play a central role. Cold War-era concepts – such as deterrence – are not applicable in current conditions. In individual cases, 'deterrence by punishment' must progress to 'deterrence by denial'. Should military intervention be understood only as the *ultima ratio,* the most favourable moment for intervention – when involvement in a conflict occurs with the lowest expenditure of resources and with the lowest possible credible threat to create the maximal political effect – might be lost. The most auspicious time for intervention rarely occurs at the same time as when public support for such an intervention is highest. Public and political attention tends happen only after the conflict has escalated, but in the age of weapons of mass destruction and terrorism, the risks of inaction are significantly increased:

> [T]he more compelling the case for taking anticipatory action to defend ourselves, even if uncertainty remains as to the time and place of the enemy's attack. To forestall or prevent such hostile acts by our adversaries, the United States will, if necessary, act pre-emptively. (White House, 2002, sec. v)

The distinction between prevention and pre-emption is in need of a more detailed explanation. A pre-emptive attack is one that takes place in the face of an imminent aggressive action from the opposing side. A preventive attack is an act of war based on the belief that an opponent intends to engage in aggressive actions as soon as their capabilities are sufficient, and is aimed at destroying those capabilities before they can reach a threatening level. As discussed in Chapter 3, the UN Charter articulates self-defence as a classical and legitimate right of states (Article 51) – but in the age terrorism and weapons of mass destruction, the meaning of self-defence must be thoroughly re-examined. Under what conditions can self-defence now legitimately be claimed? As previously discussed, pre-emptive self-defence is built on the so-called 'Caroline Criteria' of 1837 (see Chapter 3). A state does not have to wait for an armed attack to occur, but is entitled to take measures of self-defence if the necessity is 'instant, overwhelming, leaving no choice of means, and no moment of deliberation' and the action is not 'unreasonable or excessive'. The postulate for pre-emption articulated in the 2002 US Security Strategy, however, far exceeds those identified under customary international law criteria: it claims the right of action even in cases of suspicion and potential threat. In 1980, the USA supported a Security Council resolution condemning Israel's strike against the Iraq nuclear power plant 'Osirak' as an illegal preventive attack. Israel claimed that Iraq might have the intention of developing an offensive nuclear programme directed against it, but a lack of evidence and agreed-upon criteria for judgement prevented a Security Council resolution. Clearly, there is an urgent need to examine the use and applicability of this customary international law in the current era.

The boundaries of the right to self-defence have always been somewhat blurred, but since 9/11, those boundaries have become even more blurred and it has become clear that states may perceive threat from scenarios that look nothing like the classical armed attack by State A on State B. The Security Council made it clear in Resolution 1368 of 12 September 2001 that the USA had the right to take measures of self-defence against the perpetrators of the 9/11 terrorist attacks, demonstrating that international law is capable of adjusting to respond to new dangers. The precondition for legitimate action remains, however, that dangers are not simply asserted, but that their existence is shown to be highly plausible. While military pre-emption might be considered legitimate in individual cases, preventive actions fundamentally challenge the international order. This is because it remains undetermined as to who decides how appropriate such military actions are, on which international legal grounds they are to be conducted, and what relationship they bear to the general prohibition on the use of force. Kofi Annan expressed his concerns thus:

> Now, some say this understanding is no longer tenable, since an 'armed attack' with weapons of mass destruction could be launched at any time, without warning, or by a clandestine group. Rather than wait for that to happen, they argue, States have the right and obligation to use force pre-emptively, even on the territory of other States, and even while weapons systems that might be used to attack them are still being developed. According to this argument, States are not obliged to wait until there is agreement in the Security Council. Instead, they reserve the right to act unilaterally, or in ad hoc coalitions. This logic represents a fundamental challenge to the principles on which, however imperfectly, world peace and stability have rested for the last fifty-eight years. My concern is that, if it were to be adopted, it could set precedents that resulted in a proliferation of the unilateral and lawless use of force, with or without justification. (Annan, 2003)

The consequences of requiring any and every use of force to be sanctioned by the Security Council must also be considered. Situations can certainly be imagined in which the Security Council might be blocked by veto threats – not necessarily on rational grounds – when there is a clear and urgent need for action. In order not to leave the definition of what does or does not constitute a threat to security to the arbitrary will or interest of individual member states, a discussion for the progressive development of international law in the light of new threats has emerged (Roberts, 2003).

It might be conceivable to have a debate over the level of tolerance that should apply to the proliferation of weapons of mass destruction, the support of international terrorism, or the systematic violation of human rights. A comprehensible catalogue of criteria for legitimate intervention would have to be developed, but there are likely to be numerous difficulties in accomplishing such a catalogue, not least the differing opinions of 193 member states. The alternative, however, is to maintain the *status quo*, which is equally unsatisfying. Agreement might be most likely on the issue of weapons of mass destruction because of the all-encompassing nature of the threat posed by such materials. It should be possible for the permanent members of the Security Council to agree with each other on when – and under what conditions and possessed by which actors – the capacity to use such weapons should constitute an immediate threat. The HLP proposes that 'in deciding whether or not to authorize the use of force, the Council should adopt and systematically address a set of agreed guidelines, going directly not to whether force *can* legally be used but whether, as a matter of good conscience and good sense, it *should* be' (HLP, 2004, para. 205). The HLP offers five basic criteria of legitimacy:

(a)   *Seriousness of threat.* Is the threatened harm to state or human security of a kind, and sufficiently clear and serious, to justify *prima facie* the use of military force? In the case of internal threats, does it involve genocide and other large-scale killing, ethnic cleansing or serious violations of international humanitarian law, actual or imminently apprehended?

(b)   *Proper purpose.* Is it clear that the primary purpose of the proposed military action is to halt or avert the threat in question, whatever other purposes or motives may be involved?

(c)   *Last resort.* Has every non-military option for meeting the threat in question been explored, with reasonable grounds for believing that other measures will not succeed?

(d)   *Proportional means.* Are the scale, duration and intensity of the proposed military action the minimum necessary to meet the threat in question?

(e)   *Balance of consequences.* Is there a reasonable chance of the military action being successful in meeting the threat in question, with the consequences of action not likely to be worse than the consequences of inaction? (Ibid., para. 207)

Terrorist organizations and failed states are obvious cases; the cases of dictators and totalitarian regimes might need a more intensive discussion. The most difficult discussion would concern whether states' behaviour in the research and production or acquisition of such weapons could itself constitute a threat. In the case of massive violations of human rights, on the other hand, there is very little chance for the development of a binding catalogue of criteria. The selectivity with which humanitarian interventions have been undertaken so far, and the arbitrary, self-interest-determined involvement of the western states suggests that the already familiar contestable *ad hoc* decisions will likely remain the *status quo*.

The UN and the current international legal order were not destroyed by the intense confrontations in the Security Council in the run-up to the 2003 Iraq War, but they faced – and continue to face – a serious crisis. Whether or not these issues can now be resolved lies in the hands of the same member states that initiated the crisis. The Security Council remains a decisive partner for member states, and also serves to initiate new standards of reaction that will become increasingly necessary in the future as the world faces more and more complex risks. The Security Council – at least from the perspective of most states – continues to offer valuable strategic commodity: legitimacy.

Reforms in the Area of Peace Maintenance

In keeping with the dramatically shifting geo-political landscape, UN peacekeeping has similarly found itself in a process of permanent change and adjustment since its renaissance in 1988. Under pressure from international political events, peacekeeping has had to develop a new task profile and operational form – distinctly dissimilar to the first generation – within the space of only a few years. However, as is usual with the UN, this process of adjustment was not the result of forward-looking conceptual considerations and planning, but rather a collection of reactive measures, to meet the need of the moment, and often hesitatingly implemented. Additionally, the UN has been entrusted with peace missions whose complexity goes far beyond that of the classical type since the middle of the 1990s. Military peacekeeping and civilian post-conflict peacebuilding are inextricably bound together in current missions to the extent that they might justifiably be referred to as 'fourth-generation peace missions' (see Chapter 4). With these new missions come new responsibilities and difficulties in planning, set-up, and execution. Most of the peacekeeping reform measures that have been undertaken since the 1990s have already been discussed in Chapter 4: the 2000 Brahimi Report on UN peace missions was a landmark document in catalysing echelons of peacekeeping reforms. The report calls for more realistic assessments of the situation 'on the ground' and for tailored mandates to meet assessments, robust rules of engagement to deter spoilers and an increased engagement by member states in meeting their responsibilities in supporting UN missions. Some recommendations of the Brahimi Report have been realized; others are still on the agenda. In 2004 the HLP proposed the creation of a peacebuilding commission – a proposal that was agreed upon at the 2005 World Summit and subsequently realized by member states. The new Peacebuilding Commission (PBC) was created in 2006 has resulted in significant progress in the area of peace maintenance, but challenges continue to exist.

New Horizon Initiative

The UN is increasingly tasked with the preparation and the conduct of complex missions to make, keep and build peace. Peacekeeping is a 'unique global partnership' (DPKO/DFS, 2009, ii) wherein the UN provides the legal, political, and organizational framework for missions; member states provide personnel, equipment and finances. In the face of new geo-political challenges there has been a shrinking willingness among richer member states to support UN peacekeeping. In 2009, a 'non-paper' (jointly produced by the DPKO and the DFS) created a 'New Partnership Agenda' to create a common vision and a mutual accountability of all actors involved in UN peacekeeping. The paper outlines three major fields of partnership:

- *Partnership in Purpose*, focusing on issues like political strategy, direction, mission planning and management to foster unity and cohesion among the relevant stakeholders.
- *Partnership in Action*, calling for faster deployment, the delivery of critical roles (e.g. in the security sector), and advanced capabilities in crisis management.
- *Partnership for the Future*, aiming to build-up UN peacekeeping capacities to serve as a peace and security instrument by defining future need, recruiting and retaining military and civilian specialists, and the creation of a new field support strategy that improves logistics and management on all mission levels.

In a short progress report published in October 2010 the heads of both departments sketched a common priority agenda comprised of four focus areas: policy development, capability development, global field support strategy and planning and oversight (DPKO/DFS, 2010, 9), thus marking a starting point for intensified process of consultation and debate. Some tangible progress has been achieved with regard to the concept and the financing of the Global Field Support Strategy (presented by Secretary Ban Ki-Moon in January 2010) (see A/64/633). In any case, the New Horizon Initiative serves as a long-term project that will require the UN and the various governmental and non-governmental partners to undertake serious efforts in further developing UN peacekeeping as a crucial tool of international peace and security

Peacebuilding Commission

The necessities of shared vision and unified action that are anchored in the New Horizon Initiative are also reflected in the work of the PBC. The PBC works to support peace efforts in post-conflict states by: bringing together all of the relevant actors; marshalling resources; and advising on and proposing integrated strategies for post-conflict peacebuilding and recovery (see www.un.org/peace/peacebuilding/) – and has done so with mixed results to date. The PBC has had significant success in Sierra Leone and in Burundi, but is confronted with stagnation or even backlashes in Guinea-Bissau or the Central-African Republic. Three facilitators reviewed the PBC and concluded that the Commission suffers from a lack of clear identity (the Commission is neither a technical nor an implementing body but a political actor) and that it still has to find its role (see Anderson *et al.*, 2010, p.38). In order to increase its political weight within the UN system and in the international community, and to improve the effectiveness of its work in the field, the PBC and the Peacebuilding Support Office (PBSO) are in need of better capacity building and mobilization of resources. A crucial factor is to enhance relationship with key players within the UN System – the Security Council, the General Assembly, ECOSOC and beyond (financial institutions, donors, contributors of personnel and resources). The PBC also requires enhanced communication strategies to maintain global attention on the peacebuilding processes. As in most UN reform efforts, the success or failure of an improved PBC depends largely on member states' political will to support it – not only through contributions of staff and finance but also through an enhanced appreciation of multilateral bodies and the opportunities they offer.

Human Rights and the Responsibility to Protect

The 2005 World Summit identified human rights as an important – but not a central – concern (see World Summit, 2005, section IV). The after-effects of 9/11 saw human rights protections being largely subordinated to national security requirements and the 2005 World Summit was a significant turning point for the return of human rights to a more prominent position on the global agenda. The 2004 HLP had already highlighted the close interrelation between human rights and international peace by requesting the Security Council actively involve the Office of the High Commissioner for Human Rights into its deliberations (HLP, 2004, para. 289) and the 2005 'In Larger Freedom' report articulated:

> Human rights are as fundamental to the poor as to the rich, and their protection is as important to the security and prosperity of the developed world as it is to that of the developing world. It would be a mistake to treat human rights as though there were a trade-off to be made between human rights and such goals as security or development. (Annan, 2005, para. 140)

On the contrary: security cannot be achieved without fundamental human rights being protected. The 2005 World Summit Outcome emphasized a renewed commitment to universal human rights and adopted a number of provisions to improve human rights protection in and through the UN, including:

- the 'further mainstreaming of human rights throughout the United Nations system, as well as closer co-operation between the Office of the United Nations High Commissioner for Human Rights and all relevant United Nations bodies' (para. 126);
- the upgrading and strengthening of the role the High Commissioner (para. 124);
- the establishment of a Human Rights Council (para. 157 *et seq.*); and
- the endorsement of the responsibility to protect (paras 138 and 139).

Many of the reform initiatives announced at the 2005 World Summit have been implemented, the most visible being the creation of the Human Rights Council.

The inclusion and subsequent prominence of the 'responsibility to protect' or 'R2P' is the success of norm entrepreneurs such as former Australian Foreign Minister and chair of the International Commission on Intervention and State Sovereignty (ICISS) Gareth Evans, The ICISS – created by the Canadian Government in 2000 at the request of Secretary-General Kofi Annan – was intended to examine viable ways for the international community to react to massive human rights violations that happen within the borders of a state such as those that happened in Rwanda, Bosnia, and Kosovo. The mandate of the ICISS was:

> [G]enerally to build a broader understanding of the problem of reconciling intervention for human protection purposes and sovereignty; more specifically, it was to try to develop a global political consensus on how to move from polemics – and often paralysis – towards action within the international system, particularly through the United Nations. (ICISS, 2001, p. 2)

The debate on R2P highlights the inherent problem of tensions between the principle of sovereign equality of all member states and the limitations of this sovereignty in favour of superior values like 'peace' or 'humanity' that has characterized the UN since its birth.

In its 2001 report, the ICISS emphasized that state sovereignty implies responsibility and that the primary responsibility for the protection of its people lies with state itself, but also that: 'Where a population is suffering serious harm, as a result of internal war, insurgency, repression or state failure, and the state in question is unwilling or unable to halt or avert it, the principle of non-interventions yields to the international responsibility to protect' (ICISS, 2001, p. XI). R2P, however, is not simply an attempt at legitimizing external (military) intervention. R2P envisions a tripartite concept of responsibility: to prevent, to react, and to rebuild with a focus on the prevention of humanitarian tragedies by international assistance to states on the edge of catastrophe. Intervention shall only be possible in situations of compelling need and the ICISS proposes a number of guiding principles for intervention:

- just cause (massive loss of life, ethnic cleansing);
- right intention;
- last resort;
- proportionality;
- reasonable prospect; and
- right authority.

The similarities between the principles of R2P and those of just war (see Chapter 3) caused considerable concern that international law would backslide to the pre-Westphalian era. Can R2P be abused as a pretext for crusaders? The question of authority is crucial in that debate. The ICISS confirms the Security Council's primary role in the authorization of the use of force – but at the same time reminds the Security Council of its responsibility in 'conscience-shocking situations crying for action' (ibid., p. 55). It is possible to envisage situations where *ad hoc* coalitions or individual member states may have to decide which evil is worse: to bypass a blocked Security Council or to let happen serious crimes against humanity. The 2005 World Summit gave clear answer to this question by accepting only a very narrow interpretation of the responsibility to protect: in paragraphs 138 and 139 they denied a comprehensive international responsibility for the prohibition of large-scale human rights violations and acknowledged R2P in only four cases: genocide, war crimes, ethnic cleansing and crimes against humanity. The 2005 World Summit reinforced that primary responsibility for the protection of citizens lies with the state and summoned the international community to encourage and help states in the exercise of this responsibility. In the case of states manifestly failing to protect their populations from genocide, war crimes, ethnic cleansing and crimes against humanity, member states declared themselves prepared to take collective action through the Security Council – as permitted in Chapter VII – on a case-by-case basis and in co-operation with relevant regional organizations (para. 139).

The World Summit's limited endorsement of R2P invites questions as to the doctrine's legal and political weight. Is R2P a newly emerging norm of international law or is it just 'the Emperor's New Clothes?' (Strauss, 2009). R2P establishes no new authority for the use of force beyond the existing rules articulated in the Charter. In political practice, very little reference has been made by the Security Council or other bodies to this new norm. However, member states have explicitly accepted the practice of Security Council involvement in internal conflicts and civil wars, qualifying them as a threat to world peace. Essentially, a state's treatment of its citizenry is no longer a sacrosanct matter of domestic jurisdiction, or as noted by Gareth Evans: '[S]overeignty is not a license to kill' (Evans, 2008, p. 11). R2P represented substantial progress even if there is yet no new justification for interventions to halt severe human rights violations.

Reforms in the Areas of Economics, Development and the Environment

Despite many improvements in areas of socio-economics and development following Secretary-General Kofi Annan's 1997 reforms, the UN's work in this area suffers particularly badly from overlapping competencies and a lack of co-ordination. ECOSOC especially – with its huge number of subsidiary bodies – is a central target of criticism and it is demanded that the entire system undergo a fundamental examination. ECOSOC's system of countless specialized agencies, subsidiary organs and programmes with similar task profiles can lead to mutually contradictory mandates. Another especially difficult problem is the lack of co-ordination between the UN panels and the increasingly significant Bretton Woods Organizations. As it is presently structured, ECOSOC is simply unable to efficiently co-ordinate its functions and bureaucracies to the extent that the complete dissolution has been suggested. Others, however, would prefer to improve its efficiency with stronger directive authority. Suggestions range all the way from the creation of a new Economic Council with competencies analogous to the Security Council (that is, the right to make binding determinations), all the way to the creation of a dovetailed triple-council system, with three Councils, one each being responsible for Security, Economics, and Social Affairs and Development. Such suggestions have yet to be officially suggested by any UN panel so as of yet remain mere conjecture. The 2005 World Summit requested the Secretary-General to produce a set of reform proposals aiming to overcome the fragmentation of ECOSOC. In 2006, a High-Level Panel on System-wide Coherence presented a pragmatic report, arguing that the UN system

> [N]eeds to deliver as one at the country level. To focus on outcomes and improve its effectiveness, the United Nations should accelerate and deepen reforms to establish unified United Nations country teams – with one leader, one programme, one budgetary framework and, where appropriate, one office. (High-Level Panel on System-wide Coherence, 2006, p. 2.)

To date, the 'Delivering as One' approach has been realized in eight pilot countries.

Reform of the International Trade and Finance Architecture

The increasing divergence between developed and developing states has resulted in calls for the reform of the international trade and finance – but in this area too, no real effective regulations have been developed.

Dating as far back as the 1994 Mexico crisis, architectural reform of the leading financial bodies – the G8, the IMF, the World Bank, national governments, the private finance economy, the sciences, and countless NGOs – has been the subject of constant discussion. Among the various suggestions for reform are a separation of the tasks in the IMF and the World Bank, and a refocusing of the IMF on its original purpose; the reduction of IMF credit and a less-automatic guaranteeing of credit; the introduction of pre-qualification measures whereby only countries that have actually implemented certain reforms should receive emergency credit; a departure from the one-size-fits-all approach and a stronger consideration of national conditions; and heightened transparency in the international finance markets. The creation of a World Central Bank or an international bankruptcy court, the creation of target zones for the most important exchange rates in order to reduce fluctuations on the foreign exchange markets, or the introduction of taxes on foreign exchange transactions (such as the previously discussed Tobin Tax) have all been discussed as possible solutions.

The Debate over an Umbrella Organization for the Environment and Development

A particularly intense debate has taken place concerning the idea for an umbrella organization for the environment and development – a 'World Organization for

Environment and Development' (Biermann and Simonis, 1998, 2000) that could incorporate existing institutions into a new, overarching structure, and amalgamate the UNEP, CSD, and other relevant environmental convention secretariats into a single organization. Were this to take place, the new organization would have to work closely with the Bretton Woods Organizations, the WTO, and the related UN specialized agencies. Such an organization would serve to lead national governments, IGOs, and private actors in according a higher value to environmental and development needs, and to give greater prominence to such concerns on their own agendas, in turn creating better political conditions for the successful implementation of solutions. Supporters of basic institutional reforms are looking to the 'Rio Plus 20 Summit' (scheduled for 2012) for solutions – though it is not clear yet what kind of substantial reform steps will be realizable. The central hurdle for such an organization would be the achievement of both administrative effectiveness and political acceptability. Proponents argue that 'North' and 'South' would have to be given equal status, constituting something of a middle road between the 'South'-orientated procedure of the UN General Assembly and the 'North'-dominated Bretton Woods Organizations. Additionally, NGOs could be allowed to participate, as in the ILO. With respect to financing, combining the budgets of UNEP and UNDP and an integration of all the existing programmes would save a huge amount in expenditures; another possibility might be a tax on aircraft fuel or a tax on financial or stock market transactions. Critics of the idea of an umbrella organization (Gehring and Oberthür, 2000) argue that they see no specific contribution to the improvement of global environmental problems from the creation of such an institution and there could in fact be good reason why no such organization exists as yet. Effective international organizations tend to be characterized by specialization and simplified decision-making processes, thus being capable of independent action. It is unclear as to why states would surrender sovereignty to a new organization and make it any more capable of action than all the organizations that already exist and it is not likely that an international environmental politics would emerge in the framework of a world environmental organization. However, in considering models for a world environmental organization, three suggest themselves:

- *The 'UN model'*: An overarching framework organization, under which the various existing international conventions and organizations could remain essentially independent of one another, but collected together under one roof. This sort of model would, however, possess very little problem-solving capability, and would seem to offer no decisive additional advantages beyond what already exists.
- *The 'WTO model'*: A central decision-making panel to be responsible for discussing all environmental problems. This model presents the danger of linking problems to one another that should not be linked. Along with the danger of over-complexity, there is the risk of a politics that could use the non-solution of one problem to block the solution of problems in other areas.

- *The 'EU model'* would involve the preparation of decisions in individual panels and not the connection of different problem areas as in the WTO model. This would be effective, but hardly realistic, as decisions made by strict majority would still have to be implemented by all members – implying a far more extensive transferral of sovereignty rights to such an organization than is at all likely.

The potential of each model varies a great deal: while the UN model would contribute little and the WTO model might in fact produce negative effects, the more effective EU model is simply impossible. Furthermore, in order to establish an institution with some promise of success, there would have to be considerable resources made available. Such resources, however, might very well produce better effects if they were invested in the existing structures rather than used to make a new one. Other suggested reforms in this area relate to the creation of an Environmental Security Council, the conversion of the Trusteeship Council into an Environmental Trusteeship Council, or the founding of a World Environmental Court. Practitioners of international environmental politics are particularly keen to point out that all this planning cannot simply remain on the drawing board: the realities of the situation must be kept in mind – states are still unwilling to surrender sovereignty except in very limited ways. Mere declaration of environmental, economic, or social councils or organizations achieves nothing: in the end their usefulness depends on the competencies and the type of legitimacy given to them, and this is fundamentally related to the issue of sovereignty, and the political will of the member states to create effective institutions and to then abide by their underlying norms and procedures. Thus it becomes necessary to ask whether it might not be overextending and asking too much of the UN to assign it the task of solving all the problems of humanity.

A Negative Balance Sheet for Reform in the Social and Economic Areas

Klaus Hüfner and Jens Martens (2000, p. 226 *et seq.*) – in their broad evaluation of the proposed and implemented reforms of recent years – concluded that apart from a number of administrative and organizational changes and certain structural improvements, the reform picture is overwhelmingly negative. Proposals for reform lead to success only when they are 'compatible with the knowledge and self-interests of a sufficient number of relevant decision-makers'. Influence in the UN system results from the factors of financial power and voting power, and in view of the power differences and the enormous heterogeneity of interests among the 193 member states, reform proposals will be realizable only in isolated cases (such as the 1972 founding of the UN Environmental Programme, when exogenous factors created a pressure for action that the main actors could not escape). Aside from such exceptional situations, proposals for reform could succeed only if the power differential among the states were less, or if their interests were to converge.

Since it is unlikely that the power structures will change significantly at any time in the near future, and the heterogeneity of interests is also unlikely to disappear, the fundamental question arises of whether the UN can be reformed at all. Hüfner and Martens (2000) suggest that efforts would be better concentrated on longer-term attempts to increase the knowledge of the decision-makers, which is a key factor in the formation of self-interest, and thus also in the alteration of the UN:

> It is only when the knowledge of the concrete advantages and opportunities to be gained from a more intensive world-wide cooperation in the framework of the UN has spread itself through the respective populations that the pressure on national decision-makers will grow, and with it the chance for a change in state politics with respect to the UN. Only thus is a long-term deconstruction of the existing heterogeneity of interests among UN member states possible. (p. 234)

The efficacy of UN world conferences has also come under fire: their function as a platform for global communication and interaction is uncontested but their limited role in concluding unanimous declarations and formal compromises is perhaps limited:

> If one were in the future at such summits on environmental and development themes to be freed from the pressure of unanimity and use such summits instead as global forum to work towards coalitions of the willing in important issues, the interests of those people affected most by the destruction of the environment and by underdevelopment would be far better served. (Rechkemmer, 2002, p. 4)

Further Reading

Annan, Kofi (2005) 'In Larger Freedom: Towards Development, Security and Human Rights for All', Report of the Secretary-General (UN document A/59/2005).

Center for UN Reform Education (ed.) (2008) *Managing Change at the United Nations*, New York: Center for UN Reform Education.

High-Level Panel on Threats Challenges and Change (2004), 'A More Secure World: Our Shared Responsibility', New York (UN document A/59/565).

Mueller, Joachim W. (ed.) (2006) *Reforming the United Nations: The Struggle for Legitimacy and Effectiveness,* Leiden/Boston: Marinus Nijhoff Publishers.

9

Conclusions

Since 1945, the UN has become – and remains – an important centre of multilateral politics. However, as was discussed at the very beginning of this book, there is no such thing as 'the' UN. Instead, the UN system comprises a complex range of activities aimed at different goals, each equipped with various tools, and demonstrating different levels of effectiveness. In a best-case scenario, the 'three United Nations' (Russett *et al.*, 2000, p. 282) develop mutually supporting and strengthening synergy effects. For example, human security concerns the survival and well-being of people living in states – not just the survival of the state itself. The emergence of human security as a core concern of the UN, however, does not mean that traditional state security has become less important. In fact, the two are seen as mutually conditioned. Such inter-connectedness of issues within the framework of a universal organization presents tremendous opportunities, but also presents significant limitations. The UN was tailored to an inter-*national* world, but we now live in a *global* world – and the organization's ability to react and remain effective in this changing environment is the fundamental institutional challenge of this century.

Multilateralism and Global Governance: Opportunities and Limitations of a Political Concept

An effective UN requires member states' willingness to engage in multilateral approaches to tackling global challenges. Multilateralism can be understood as a style of politics in which the relationships between three or more states function on the basis of certain generally accepted principles and rules of behaviour (Ruggie, 1993, p. 11). Multilateralism is the counter-concept to unilateralism in which individual states behave according to their own national interests even when that means acting alone or in opposition to other states. In political practice, large and powerful states tend to prefer unilateral behaviour because it promises a maximization of self-interest. Even if powerful states behaved according to the principle of 'as much multilateralism as possible, as much unilateralism as necessary' (that is, to act unilaterally only in 'emergencies') an important precondition for international co-operation would be damaged, since they who are prepared to act alone and against the will of their potential partners can hardly, even in isolated cases, be surprised if other states act in the same way. In other words, only those who are prepared to subject themselves to the norms of international co-operation can expect and demand the same of others. According to Ernst-Otto Czempiel (1999, p. 238), multilateralism is the recognition that the states, because of their interdependence, are 'no longer isolated, but relate to each other in a common context, which [understanding] must be made visible in the exercise of power'. Common interests are essential for the success of multilateral politics, just as a basic pattern of interdependence makes unilateral politics more likely. The principles of multilateral politics include an unlimited prohibition on the use of force in the pursuit of political goals, and the recognition that national interests can be better realized through co-operation than through competition between states (Brenner, 1995, p. 9 *et seq.*). These very different concepts reflect basic theoretical assumptions about the composition of the international system (see Chapter 2, and a schematic representation in Table 9.1). Multilateralism is the international influence that arises from competent handling of the circumstances of interdependence. While multilateralism relies on a broadly conceived rationality on the part of the various actors, unilateralism focuses on the anarchical nature of the international system. From a multilateral perspective, international processes can be best explained by the motives and behaviour of international organizations. From a unilateral perspective, states are the central actors in the international arena and international organizations play a secondary role.

The maximization of self-interest – even if it means a violation of the rules – generally trumps co-operative multilateralism in the event of a crisis. In extreme cases, unilateralism is the only kind of behaviour that can accomplish results. Knowing this ironclad rule, it cannot be expected that international politics is capable of evolving into being norm-guided, peaceful, and interdependence- and consensus-orientated. Even if one or two actors confined themselves to multilateral rules of play, it would by no means indicate that they could count on anyone else to do the same.

Whether unilateralism or multilateralism dominates is dependent on which theoretical paradigms are dominant in the relevant states. The extent of the role that can be assumed by the UN is entirely dependent on the will of member states. In other words, the success of the UN is highly conditional, and conditions cannot be counted on.

If the UN is to play an important role in international relations, the vast majority of its member states must abide by multilateral norms and principles even when common interests are at stake. The experience to date, however, is that the traditional understanding of 'sovereign' foreign policy is most often prioritized.

The United Nations and Global Governance

Global governance is a particularly far-reaching form of multilateralism. As already discussed, the creation of inter-state binding commitments – and their long-term viability – is one of the great challenges of political science. There is consensus, however, that some type of international governance, extending

TABLE 9.1
The unilateralism–multilateralism debate

Unilateral premises	Multilateral premises
Anarchy is the reigning basic pattern and structural principle of international relations	Interdependence is the reigning basic pattern and structural principle of international relations
States are the only meaningful actors of international politics; other actors take on meaning only in their functions as means or agents of states	Many international processes can be explained only with reference to the motives and behaviour of IGOs and NGOs
International politics are the result of the interactions of individual states, which have as their goal the retention of power in the sense of classical national security	International relations are the result of the border-crossing activities of countless international actors, which (who) have comprehensive security as their goal
International relations are a zero-sum game; that is, an increase in one actor's power can only mean a decrease in another's. Standard mode of interaction is conflictual	International relations are not a zero-sum game; that is, the advantage of any given actor results from the increased overall sum of the good(s) to be distributed. Standard mode of interaction is co-operative
International influence results from the use or threat of force, defined as actual or potential military and/or economic capability	International influence arises from the competent handling of the circumstances of international interdependence; the ability to persuade others is an aid to influence
International politics is like a game among self-contained, independent billiard balls constantly moving and running into each other on the world stage (the 'billiard-ball model').	International relations are a web-like network of various interwoven decisions, which overlayer successively the world of states.

Source: Adapted from Meyers (2004, p. 472).

beyond the traditional limits of borders, is absolutely necessary. The classical perception of the state as the only source of governance is increasingly being challenged by the notion that not only 'hierarchical governance through states, but also horizontal governance with states as equal partners, or even governance without any states at all, is possible' (Zürn, 1998, p. 25; see also Rittberger, 2000, pp. 198–209). According to Michael Zürn, three possible forms of governance – through states, with states, and without states – creates the possibility of a 'project of complex global governance'. Franz Nuscheler claims that global governance is the result of even powerful states being overtaxed by the increasing quantity and density of cross-border transactions, the decreasing significance of the borders of territorial states, and the growing challenges of global risks. But the forms of inter-national governance that have been adopted thus far are no longer up to the task. Nuscheler (2002a, p. 182) argues that global governance 'is not a romantic project aimed at a safe and tidy global neighbourhood, but a realistic response to the chal-lenge of globalization and global risks. It is an evolutionary project, developing step by step'. ˙

Positive governance beyond the traditional parameters of the state – which need not indicate the *end* of the sovereign statehood – is theoretically possible but hindered by countless practical problems. There is in particular a lack of collective binding effect in international governance. Classical state governance is based on the idea that there is a fundamental correspondence between those affected by something and the space within which the actions to be regulated are taking place, and that decisions once taken (at least theoretically) are also capable of being implemented in practice. In contrast, international governance requires a great deal of time and effort to replicate this correspondence. The primary structural characteristic of the international system is anarchy; the state recognizes no authority higher than itself for the making and realization of decisions. As a result, global governance models suffer from the double problem of practicability and legitimacy:

- How is a voluntary process of self-co-ordination to take place in a system of overlapping and inter-penetrating partial sovereignties?
- How can it be guaranteed that any such process of co-operation would corre-spond to democratic principles if co-ordination does not happen voluntarily?

It therefore appears downright audacious when advocates of multilateralism claim that only multilateralism can provide solutions to the challenges of globalization. Our world will always be plural, and for this reason our world – with over six billion inhabitants – will need a UN capable of real action (Fischer, 1999, p. 109). That said, the world is going through a process of tension and transformation wherein the trends of globalization and fragmentation struggle against each other, and movement is taking place on many different levels (Kühne, 2000, p. 447 *et seq.*). Unfortunately, no global 'domestic politics' has emerged as a result of this tension, only 'small islands of developments similar to domestic politics' which must be stabilized and expanded.

Despite the conceptual and practical, difficulties associated with such a perspective, it is still necessary to conceive of a political model that can stand up to the attractions of the nation state-based world of the past; what is needed now is 'institutional imagination projecting beyond the nation-state' (Zürn, 1998, p. 28).

Under the chairmanship of former German Chancellor Willy Brandt, and in the much different global conditions of the early 1980s, the Independent Commission on International Development Issues – the so-called 'North–South Commission' – noted the main points of a debate that is increasingly becoming relevant again today. According to the Commission's concluding report, humanity increasingly sees itself as being confronted with problems that concern humanity as a whole, leading to the logical conclusion that the solutions to these problems must also be increasingly internationalized. The globalization of dangers and challenges requires a global domestic politics that looks far into the future, and far beyond state borders. Conclusions drawn from the report, however, vary considerably. Global governance is but one attempt to meet the challenges of a globalised world.

The Commission on Global Governance (also instigated by Willy Brandt) attempted to give the concept some content. The Commission on Global Governance (1995, p. 4 *et seq.*) defined global governance as 'the sum-total of the many ways in which individuals as well as public and private institutions regulate their common concerns'. The concept includes formal institutions and systems of government with implementational competence as well as informal arrangements. The basic mantra remains that the globalization of problems requires a globalization of politics. This means not only more classical inter-state co-operation, but also the development of a new model of politics that goes beyond simple demands for 'more' multilateralism and global thinking. Such a model would have to make it possible for state and non-state actors to work together in new ways and on many different levels.

The concept of Global Governance has roused many academics to make attempts to define it more precisely and to clarify its content (see Muldoon, 2004). The primary outcome of all such attempts at a definition have in common is that they all stop short of a federalist vision of world government. According to Commission Co-chair Shridath Rampha, the world possesses no government in the sense of a central supra-national authority, 'and only a very few consider such a world government either necessary or desirable' (Ramphal, 1998, p. 3). The idea of such a monolith ruling the world is frightening rather than confronting, yet at the same time 'the world needs governance: formal and informal agreements to regulate common affairs, promote common interests, and pursue common goals'. Thus global governance means:

- The redefinition of state sovereignty and its basic principles – inviolability of borders, prohibition on interference in 'internal' affairs, the state's sole authority over social behaviour.
- The 'thickening' and legalization of international relations through international organizations and regimes, understood as institutionalized forms of norm- and rule-guided behaviour in the political handling of conflicts that build on common principles, norms, rules, and decision-making processes.
- A focus on the expansion of the circle of actors beyond the state and classical international organizations, and the development of a new style of politics.

The UN system stands at the centre of these global strategy concepts – alongside other international organizations such as the WTO, international regimes such as those for nuclear non-proliferation or climate control, regional arrangements such as the European Union (which could conceivably function as the seeds of the desired development) and various global networks. The main actors in such global networks are the NGOs of the so-called international civil society. The insight of the insufficiency of pure inter-state co-operation – and the often modest results of the politics of classical international organizations – should form the foundation for the emergence of new forms of co-operation between public and private actors: the beginnings of a global public policy. The UN should, as has been demanded of it, work more closely with these international political networks, support their creation, and promote the participation of state and non-state actors (Reinicke and Deng, 2000).

The UN's relationship with organizations of the so-called international civil society is not new, indeed, it has been the status quo for decades in the realms of humanitarian and development work. NGOs play a key role in the UN system to the extent that some authors see an impending 'privatization of international politics' (Brühl *et al.,* 2001). There are approximately 3,000 NGOs accredited with consultative status for ECOSOC, each of which can influence outcome by attending international conferences and negotiations, and some of which and have become indispensable in development, environment, and other operative fields. Co-operation with private undertakings – the so-called 'business international non-governmental organizations' (BINGOs) – is also becoming increasingly common. One example is the Secretary-General's initiative calling for a 'global compact' in which multinational corporations would co-operate with the UN to promote just labour norms, the observation of human rights and the protection of the environment.

These initiatives show that such international processes are gaining a level of significance that 'cannot be classified unambiguously as taking place in an inter-state milieu in the sense of the [traditional] models of international politics' (Kaiser, 1969, p. 80; that this idea came in the late 1960s, and that the concept of 'transnational politics' associated with Kaiser also comes from the late 1960s, shows that not all ideas packaged and sold as new really are what they claim to be). It also demonstrates, however, that the idea of strengthening international civil society still has an unbroken power to attract adherents. Whether it is the case – as argued by Jessica Mathews (1997) and Ulrich Beck (2003) – that there has already been a fundamental power shift away from states toward a transnationally networked civil society, remains unclear. At the very least, such a statement must be qualified by differentiation among regions of the world and among political fields; even the globalized world does not allow itself to be painted with a single brush.

Outlook: The United Nations in the Twenty-First Century

What role will the UN play in the twenty-first century? The first – and most obvious problem to be overcome – is the tension between the goals and principles of the organization, and the political reality of its functions (see Table 9.2), because in the meantime, the rules of the Charter are constantly becoming relativized, changed or simply systematically ignored (see also Chapter 1).

What does all this mean for the UN? Are there possible alternative arrangements that could replace the UN in its function for international peace and secu-

TABLE 9.2
Purposes and principles of the UN versus political reality

Purposes and principles of the Charter	Political reality
Sovereign equality of all member states (Articles 2 and 1)	Marked power differential among states and regions; dominance of the Permanent Five
Fulfilment of the obligations foreseen in the Charter (Articles 2 and 2)	Withholding of contributions and refusal or failure to fulfil obligations based on the dictates of national interests
Obligation to the peaceful resolution of disputes (Articles 2 and 3)	Persistent lack of political will to use mediation, international justice or diplomatic efforts to prevent the outbreak of violence
General prohibition on the use of force (Articles 2 and 4)	Repeated unilateral use of force by many states
World peace and international security as a collective task of all member states (Articles 2, 5 and 6)	Dominance of the interests of industrialized countries, and a wilful blindness towards conflicts in developing countries; refusal to support the UN in complex peace missions
Prohibition on interference in the internal affairs of other states (Articles 2 and 7)	The globalization of fundamental problems forces an erosion of state sovereignty

rity? (The UN's time-consuming and often enough inefficient decision-making processes, combined with its dependence on authoritarian states like China or Russia have galvanized many western developed states, especially the US, to deliberate new political mechanisms that might be more efficient and effective.) If a new organization were to be created its representatives should possess a *sui generis* legitimization to take measures in favour of the maintenance of peace, including forceful action. Since the 1990s US–American think tanks and intellectual circles have propagated ideas of a 'league of democracies' (see Kagan, 2008) as a better alternative to a UN that is hijacked by a majority of at least dubious regimes (an idea prominently heralded by Republican presidential candidate John McCain in 2008; a 'global NATO' also continuously appears on some agendas). In the course of the global financial and economic crisis (2008 to 2011) the G20 was considered as a possible nucleus of new global governance architecture. All thinkable alternatives to the UN do little to extend legitimacy beyond its current reach and they continue to perpetuate the disparities between the poor and the rich, the strong and the weak. Alternative arrangements do little to overcome the UN's birth defect – that of the privileges of the Permanent Five. On the contrary, problems would be aggravated by a lack of even basic formal approval and legitimization by the vast majority of states. From that perspective, the question remains open as to why the international community should accept a global leadership by a self-appointed elite. The UN is still the sole universal organization equipped to tackle global challenges.

This book has tried to make clear that differentiation is necessary, and that there is no such thing as 'the' UN. In conclusion, however, the argument should be focused even more. Based on the structures, processes, and actors in the UN and in international politics, three possible scenarios for the UN's further development emerge. These are not meant to be predictions, but are intended rather to demonstrate what kinds of future development are possible, under which conditions they are likely to obtain, and what their implications are. These scenarios are summarized in Table 9.3.

The first scenario (marginalisation) assumes a substantial weakening or even a mid- to long-term downfall of the UN. If important member states cease to engage with the UN and instead look to other forums for problem-solving – either on an ad hoc basis, on the basis of 'coalitions of the willing', or in the framework of other international organizations or regimes – other member states would eventually do likewise and a gradual collapse of the UN would result. Possible starting points for such a development could be spectacular failures in peacekeeping, or a systematic avoidance of the Security Council mechanism by important state actors. Such failures would be sure to have effects on the willingness of member states to grant the UN competencies in other areas of activity. In the field of protection of human rights, the various existing pacts and conventions would remain but there would no longer be a global forum available for debate and monitoring. In the areas of economics, development and environment, there would be issue-specific bodies – perhaps some of the specialized agencies and subsidiary organs (for example, UNICEF) would remain in existence – but they would be completely separate from the UN system and the UN would cease to play any further role. The most likely consequences of such a development would be an increase in the frequency of war and an intensification of the security dilemma. The likelihood that this scenario will take place is low, but it is certainly not impossible.

The second scenario supposes that the UN could establish itself in the long term as a sort of world government. As the central actor of a federalized world republic, the UN would have the power to co-ordinate and sanction behaviour that could be exercised through civil, police or military measures. The organization would form the central co-ordinating hub of the global governance process, and would broaden its competencies successively, to the detriment of those of member states. Such a UN might levy taxes, it might develop and implement a worldwide legal order, and it might create a form of global citizenship rights. In the area of human rights, conventions and agreements would be codified and supported by effective enforcement mechanisms. Where peace maintenance is concerned, the UN would exercise a monopoly on the use of force as well as the functioning of an effective collective security system. In economics, development, and the environment, the UN would be at the centre of the global system. A world government would most

TABLE 9.3
Future scenarios for UN development

	'Marginalization'	'World government'	'Muddling through'
Peace-maintenance	The UN plays no role, the prohibition on force erodes, and the frequency of war increases	The UN plays a central role, maintains the monopoly on the use of force, and a functioning collective security system emerges	The UN is used or ignored according to whether it has demonstrated competence and usefulness in particular task areas
Protection of human rights	Individual conventions remain, but there is no longer a global forum for debate, norm development, and monitoring	The numerous codified agreements are not only developed further, but also endowed with effective implementation mechanisms	The presumption must remain that there is a gap between the codification and implementation of norms, and that the politics of human rights remains subject to interest-guided selectivity
Economics, development, and environment	Issue-specific organizations besides the UN emerge with no central governing instance	The UN is the institutional centre of global structural politics with direct regulatory competence for fields previously reserved to the nation-state	The UN is only one actor among many and only inadequately equipped to reach its ambitious goals
In international politics, the UN plays . . .	No role	The role of central actor	Sometimes the role of actor, sometimes as instrument, and sometimes as an arena

probably involve a power concentration that would prove highly problematic from the perspective of democratic monitoring mechanisms and the likelihood of this scenario coming to pass is extremely low.

The third scenario is essentially that the UN remains what it is now: an imperfect instrument in need of reform, but also an extremely important international organization. Within this scenario, it remains an open question as to whether continued development will be in the direction of the organization being used as an instrument of member state diplomacy with little independence external to its member states, as an arena for different levels of co-operation in different political fields, or as an actor in its own right. If the UN can prove its ability to take meaningful action, and member states allow it to do so, the UN could yet play an important role – or it will simply be pushed to the sidelines. In practice, the UN would have no monopoly on the use of force, but the Security Council's monopoly on the *legitimization* of the use of force might be strengthened. As for the protection of human rights, it must simply be accepted that there will continue to be a gap between the codification and the realization of norms. In economy, development, and environment, the UN would continue to be one actor among many and would have very limited chances of achieving ambitious goals. In general, member states would be unlikely to invest more resources in the system and would increasingly rely on bilateral measures.

Of these three scenarios, the third is the most likely. The eventual shape of the UN will depend largely on the general international political attitude towards multilateral arrangements, which can, of course, be subject to rapid changes. Without doubt, twenty-first-century international politics will continue to be governed by states – despite their shrinking influence. The obvious insufficiencies of mere intergovernmental co-operation have already led to the increasing significance of transnational networks encompassing a broad variety of non-state actors. New forms of governance are emerging within a framework of a global public policy, with the UN as one major focal point. In practice, however, the tensions between the goals and principles of the UN Charter and the *realpolitik* of member states is still evident and practically all essential postulates of the Charter (with regards to multilateral co-operation and collective mechanisms) have been relativised, altered, or simply disregarded by member states. The principle of sovereign equality is challenged by the imbalance of power between member states, that the obligation to the peaceful settlement of disputes is frequently disregarded, and member states again and again resort to the unilateral use of force.

The UN is in the hands of its member states – the same member states that often prefer a weak organization (where they don't have to surrender too much of their sovereignty) to an effective collective institution. The hesitating steps to reform taken at the 2005 World Summit demonstrate that most agreements are still only reached by the lowest common denominator, and the organization's prospects for becoming a central player in global governance looks modest.

Nevertheless the UN continues to be a unique and indispensable forum for the shaping of international relations providing a framework that enables member states to mutually monitor resolutions and to call for the observation of common legal norms and political procedures. In fact, a milieu has appeared over the last two decades in which the norms and provisions of the Charter have become the reference-point for member states' international behaviour. They are not always respected, but the pressure for justification in cases of norm violation has increased tremendously and even great powers cannot escape this pressure, (strengthened as it is by international public opinion) but further work is needed to limit the arbitrary use of force by single states or groups of states, and to reduce the risks of new regional or worldwide arms races.

The UN must carry on persuading governmental and non-governmental actors to comply the goals and principles anchored in the Charter. Problems that have exhausted all possibilities of state-based solutions must have the opportunity for a collective attempt at solutions.

In sum, the organization's shortfalls and its continuing need for reform should not distract from the fact that the UN is absolutely essential to the stability of the international system. Political practice very seldom keeps pace with an ever-more-complex list of international problems, and sound answers to the central troubles facing the human race in the twenty-first century will have to be multilateral. In the warp and woof of multilateral regimes and organizations, the UN plays a unique role. A new and improved organization would certainly still find itself discharging the fundamental goals and principles established in the Charter. If member states refuse to support the UN more than they have done thus far, success will remain permanently elusive. If member states comply more consistently with the obligations they imposed on themselves by signing the UN Charter the world may yet become a more peaceful place to live.

Bibliography

Abiew, Francis K. (1999) *The Evolution of the Doctrine and Practice of Humanitarian Intervention*, The Hague/London/Boston.

Ackerman, Bruce (2002) 'But What's the Legal Case for Preemption?' Yale Law School www.law.yale.edu/news/4340.htm.

Afoaku, Osita G. and Okechukwu Ukaga, (2001) 'United Nations Security Council Reform: A Critical Analysis of Enlargement Opinions', *Journal of Third World Studies* (2) 2001, pp. 149–71.

Africa Banjul Charter on Human and Peoples' Rights – 27.06.1981, CAB/LEG/67/3.

AKUF (Arbeitsgemeinschaft Kriegsursachenforschung) (ed.) (2000), *Das Kriegsgeschehen. Daten und Tendenzen der Kriege und bewaffneten Konflikte*, Opladen (published annually).

Alagappa, Muthiah and Takashi Inoguchi (eds) (1999) *International Security Management and the United Nations*, Tokyo.

Albright, Madeleine K. (2003) 'United Nations', *Foreign Policy* (138) pp. 16–26.

Alger, Chadwick F. (ed.) (1998) *The Future of the United Nations System. Potential for the Twenty-First Century,* Tokyo.

Alger, Chadwick F., Gene M. Lyons and John E. Trent (eds) (1995) *The United Nations System. The Policies of Member States*, Tokyo/New York/Paris.

Alston, Philip (1994) 'Appraising the United Nations Human Rights Regime', in Philip Alston (ed.), *The United Nations and Human Rights*, Oxford.

Alston, Philip (ed.) (2000) *The Future of UN Human Rights Treaty Monitoring*, Cambridge.

Alston, Philip (ed.) (2004) *The United Nations and Human Rights: A Critical Appraisal*, Oxford.

Amnesty International, Annual Report, London (published annually).

Amr, Mohamed Sameh M. (2003) *The Role of the International Court of Justice as the Principal Judicial Organ of the United Nations*, The Hague.

Anderson, Anne, Claude Heller and Baso Sangqu (2010) 'Review of the United Nations Peacebuilding Architecture' (UN document S/2010/393).

Annan, Kofi (1997) 'Renewing the United Nations: A Programme for Reform', Report of the Secretary-General (UN document A/51/950).

Annan, Kofi (2000) 'We the Peoples: The Role of the United Nations in the Twenty-First Century', Report of the Secretary-General (UN document A/54/2000).

Annan, Kofi (2000a) 'Report of the Secretary-General on the Implementation of the Report of the Panel on United Nations Peace Operations' (UN document A/55/502).

Annan, Kofi (2001) 'Implementation of the Recommendations of the Special Committee on Peacekeeping Operations and the Panel on United Nations Peace Operations (UN document A/55/977).

Annan, Kofi (2001a) 'Prevention of Armed Conflicts' (UN document S/2001/574).

Annan, Kofi (2002) 'Strengthening of the United Nations: An Agenda for Further Change', Report of the Secretary General (UN document A/57/387).

Annan, Kofi (2003) Statement in the general assembly, 23 september: online at www.un.org/news/ossg/sg/stories.

Annan, Kofi (2005) 'In Larger Freedom: Towards Development, Security and Human Rights for all', Report of the Secretary-General (UN document A/59/2005).

Annan, Kofi (2005a) 'In Larger Freedom: Towards Development, Security and Human Rights for all', Report of the Secretary-General. Addendum Human Rights Council (UN document A/59/2005, Add.1).

Annan, Kofi (2005a) 'In Larger Freedom: Towards Development, Security and Human Rights for all', Report of the Secretary-General. Addendum Peacebuilding Commission. Explanatory note by the Secretary General (UN document A/59/2005, Add.2).

Annan, Kofi (2006) 'Investing in the United Nations: For a Stronger Organisation Worldwide', Report of the Secretary General (UN document A/60692).

Annan, Kofi (2006a) 'Progress Report on the Prevention of Armed Conflict', Report of the Secretary-General (UN document A/60/891).

Annan, Kofi (2006c) 'Uniting Against Terrorism. Recommendations for a Global Counterterrorism Strategy'. Report of the Secretary-General (UN document A/60/825).

Anthonson, Mette (2003) *Decisions on Participation in UN Operations: Do Media Matter? Danish and Swedish Response to Intra State Conflicts in the 1990s*, Goteborg.

Arangio-Ruiz, Gaetano (1979) *The UN Declaration on Friendly Relations and the System of the Sources of International Law,* Alphen.

Archer, Clive (2001) *International Organizations*, London.

Armstrong, David, Lorna Lloyd and John Redmond (eds) (1996) *From Versailles to Maastricht. International Organisation in the Twentieth Century*, Basingstoke and New York.

Armstrong, David, Lorna Lloyd and John Redmond (2004) *International Organisation in World Politics*, Basingstoke and New York.

Arnim, Gabriele von (ed.) (2002) *Menschenrechte 2003*, Frankfurt-am-Main.

Arquilla, John and Douglas A. Borer (eds) (2007) *Information Strategy and Warfare. A Guide to Theory and Practice* , New York and London.

Art, Robert J. and Kenneth N. Waltz (eds) (1999) *The Use of Force. Military Power and International Politics*, Lanham, MD.

Atlantic Charter (1941) Avalon Project at Yale Law School. www.yale.edu/lawweb/avalon.

Baehr, Peter R. and Leon Gordenker (2001) *The United Nations at the End of the 1990s*, New York.

Bailey, Sydney D. and Sam Daws (eds) (1995) *The United Nations. A Concise Political Guide*, Lanham, MD.

Bailey, Sydney D. and Sam Daws (1998) *The Procedure of the UN Security Council*, Oxford.

Ban, Ki Moon (2007) 'Comprehensive Report on Strengthening the Capacity of the United Nations to Manage and Sustain Peace Operations', Report of the Secretary-General (UN document A/61/858).

Ban, Ki-Moon (2009) 'Implementing the Responsibility to Protect', Report of the Secretary-General (UN document A/63/677).

Ban, Ki-Moon (2010) 'Composition of the Secretariat: Staff Demographics', Report of the Secretary General (UN document A/65/350).

Bah, A. Sarjoh (ed.) (2009) Annual Review of Global Peace Operations 2009. A Project of the Center on International Cooperation. Boulder and London

Baratta, Joseph P. (1995) *United Nations System, Bibliography*, Oxford.

Barker, Enno (1990) 'Rüstungskontrolle in den Vereinten Nationen', *Vereinte Nationen* (5) pp. 183–5.

Bartl, Jürgen (1999) *Die humanitäre Intervention durch den Sicherheitsrat der Vereinten Nationen im 'Failed State'*, Frankfurt-am-Main.

Baum, Gerhart (1999) 'Die Menschenrechtskommission der Vereinten Nationen', in: Gabriele von Arnim *et al.* (eds), *Jahrbuch Menschenrechte 2000*, Frankfurt-am-Main, pp. 241–8.

Baum, Gerhart, Eibe Riedel and Michael Schäfer (eds) (1998) *Menschenrechtsschutz in den Vereinten Nationen*, Baden-Baden.

Baylis, John and Steve Smith (eds) (2008) *The Globalization of World Politics. An Introduction to International Relations*, 4th edition, Oxford.

Beck, Ulrich (2003) 'Kosmopolitische Globalisierung', *Internationale Politik* (7) pp. 9–13.

Bellamy, Alex, J. (2009), *Responsibility to Protect*, Cambridge.

Bellamy, Alex J., Paul Williams and Stuart Griffin (eds) (2010) *Understanding Peace-keeping*, 2nd edn, Cambridge.

Benner, Thorsten and Jan Martin Witte (2001) 'Brücken im globalen System', *Internationale Politik* (5) 2001, pp. 1–8.

Berdal, Mats (2000) 'Lessons Not Learned: The Use of Force in Peace Operations in the 1990s', *International Peacekeeping* (4) pp. 54–74.

Berdal, Mats (2003) 'Ineffective but Indispensable', *Survival* (2) pp. 7–30.

Bertrand, Maurice and Daniel Warner (eds) (1996) *A New Charter for a Worldwide Organization*, The Hague.

Bhatta, Ghambir (2000) *Reforms at the UN: Contextualising the Annan Agenda*, Singapore.

BICC (Bonn International Center for Conversion) , *Conversion Survey*, Baden-Baden (published annually).

Biermann, Frank and Udo Ernst Simonis (1998) *Eine Weltorganisation für Umwelt und Entwicklung. Funktionen, Chancen, Probleme*, Bonn.

Biermann, Frank and Udo Ernst Simonis (2000) ,Institutionelle Reform der Weltumweltpolitik? Zur politischen Debatte um die Gründung einer Weltumweltorganisation', *Zeitschrift für Internationale Beziehungen* (1) pp. 163–83.

Biggs, David (2000) 'United Nations Contributions to the Process', *Disarmament Forum* (2) pp. 25–39.

Birnie, Patricia (1993) 'The UN and the Environment', in: Roberts and Kingsbury 1993, pp. 327–38.

Blumenwitz, Dieter (1994) 'Die humanitäre Intervention', *Aus Politik und Zeitgeschichte* (47) pp. 3–10.

Boekle, Henning (1998) 'Die Vereinten Nationen und der Schutz der Menschenrechte', *Aus Politik und Zeitgeschichte* (46–7) pp. 3–17.

Bothe, Michael (2002) 'Peace-keeping', in: Simma (2002) pp. 648–700.

Bothe, Michael and Thomas Dörschel (eds) (1999) *UN Peacekeeping: A Documentary Introduction*, The Hague.

Boulden, Jane (2001) *Peace Enforcement. The United Nations Experience in Congo, Somalia and Bosnia*, Westport, CT.

Boulden, Jane (ed.) (2003) *Dealing with Conflict in Africa: The United Nations and Regional Organizations*, Basingstoke.

Bourantonis, Dimitris (1998) 'Reform of the UN Security Council and the Non-Aligned States', *International Peacekeeping* (1) pp. 89–109.

Boutros-Ghali, Boutros (1992) *An Agenda for Peace: Preventive Diplomacy, Peacemaking and Peacekeeping*, New York: United Nations Press ,.

Boutros-Ghali, Boutros (1994) 'An Agenda for Development', Secretary-General's Report, 6.5.1994, A/48/935.

Boutros-Ghali, Boutros (1995) 'Introduction', *United Nations, The United Nations and Human Rights 1945–1995*, New York, pp. 3–125.

Brahimi, Lakhdar (2000) 'Report of the Panel on United Nations Peace Operations of 23 August 2000', UN documents A/55/305 and S/2000/809.

Brauch, Hans Günter (2010) 'Disarmament', in: Volger (2010) pp. 115–35.

Brayton, Steve (2002) 'Outsourcing War: Mercenaries and the Privatization of Peacekeeping', *Journal of International Affairs* (2) pp. 303–29.

Brenner, Michael (1995) 'The Multilateral Moment', in Michael Brenner (ed.) *Multilateralism and Western Strategy*, New York, pp. 1–41.

Brock, Lothar (1995) 'UNO und Dritte Welt. Fünf verlorene Jahrzehnte?', *Jahrbuch Dritte Welt*, Munich, pp. 62–80.

Browne, Marjorie Ann (compiler) (2003) *Iraq-Kuwait: United Nations Security Council Resolution Texts, 1992–2002*, New York.

Brühl, Tanja, Debiel, Tobias, Hamm, Brigitte, Hummel, Hartwig, and Martens, Fens (eds) (2001) *Die Privatisierung der Weltpolitik. Entsstaatlichung und Kommerzialisierung im Globalisierungsprozess*, Bonn.

Bundesministerium für Wirtschaftliche Zusammenarbeit und Entwicklung (2001) *Elfter Bericht zur Entwicklungspolitik der Bundesregierung*, Berlin.

Burgess, Stephen F. (2001) *The United Nations under Boutros Boutros-Ghali, 1992–1997*, Lanham, MD.

Butfoy, Andrew (1993) 'Themes Within the Collective Security Idea', *Journal of Strategic Studies* (4) pp. 490–510.

Cable, Vincent (1999) *Globalization and Global Governance*, London.

Call, Charles T. and Vanessa Wyeth (eds) (2008) *Building States to Build Peace*, Boulder and London.

Callaway, Rhonda L. and Julie Harrelson-Stephens (eds) (2007) *Exploring International Human Rights. Essential Readings*, Boulder, CO.

Camilleri, Joseph A. (ed.) (2000) *Reimagining the Future: Towards Democratic Governance: A Report of the Global Governance Reform Project*, Bundoora, Victoria.

Caplan, Richard (2002) *A New Trusteeship? The International Administration of War-Torn Territories*, Oxford.

Cardenas, Sonia (2003) 'Emerging Global Actors: The United Nations and National Human Rights Institutions', *Global Governance* (9) pp. 23–42.

Carle, Christophe (1999) 'Disarmament: The Next Ten Years', *Disarmament Forum* (1) pp. 13–18.

Carlsnaes, Walter, Thomas Risse and Beth A. Simmons (eds) (2002) *Handbook of International Relations*, London.

Carlsson, Ingvar, Sung-Joo Han and Rufus Kupolati (1999) *Report of the Independent Inquiry into the Actions of the United Nations during the 1994 Genocide in Rwanda*, New York.

Carnegie Commission on Preventing Deadly Conflicts (ed.) (1998) *Preventing Deadly Conflicts*, New York.

Cede, Franz (2001) 'The Purpose and Principles of the United Nations', in: Cede and Sucharipa-Behrmann (2001), pp. 11–24.

Cede, Franz and Lilly Sucharipa-Behrmann (eds) (2001) *The United Nations: Law and Practice*, The Hague.

Center for UN Reform Education (ed.) (2008) *Managing Change at the United Nations*, New York.

Chesterman, Simon (2001) *Just War or Just Peace. Humanitarian Intervention and International Law*, New York.

Chesterman, Simon (2004) *You, the People. The United Nations, Transitional Administration and State-Building*, Oxford.

Chesterman, Simon (ed.) (2007) *Secretary or General? The UN Secretary-General in World Politics*, Cambridge.

Childers, Erskine and Brian Urquhart (1994) *Renewing the United Nations System*, New York.

Clark, Grenville and Louis B. Sohn (1960) *World Peace Through World Law*, Cambridge.

Clark, Wesley K. (2001) *Waging Modern War. Bosnia, Kosovo and the Future of Combat*, Washington, DC.

Claude, Inis L. (1966) *Power and International Relations*, New York.

Claude, Inis L. (1970) *Swords into Plowshares. The Problems and Progress of International Organizations*, New York.

Coleman, David (2003) 'The United Nations and Transnational Corporations: From an Internation to a "Beyond-state" Model of Engagement', *Global Society* (4) pp. 339–59.

Commission on Global Governance (1995) *Our Global Neighborhood*, New York.

Conca, Ken and Geoffrey D. Dabelko (1998) *Green Planet Blues: Environmental Politics from Stockholm to Kyoto*, Boulder, CO.

Conforti, Benedetto (2000) *The Law and Practice of the United Nations*, The Hague.

Cordesman, Anthony H. (2003) *The Iraq War*, Washington, DC.

Cortright, David and George Lopez (eds) (1995) *Economic Sanctions – Panacea or Peace-building in a Post-Cold War World,* Oxford.
Cortright, David and George Lopez (2000) *The Sanctions Decade. Assessing UN Strategies in the 1990s,* Boulder, CO, and London.
Cortright, David, George A. Lopez and Linda Gerber-Stellingwerf (2007) 'Sanctions', Weiss and Daws (2007), pp. 349–69.
Counter-Terrorism Committee (2010) 'Survey of the Implementation of Resolution 1373 (2001) by Member States' (UN document S/2009/620).
Creveld, Martin (1991) *The Transformation of War,* New York.
Czempiel, Ernst-Otto (1993) *Weltpolitik im Umbruch. Das internationale System nach dem Ende des Ost-West-Konfliktes,* Munich.
Czempiel, Ernst-Otto (1994) *Die Reform der UNO. Möglichkeiten und Missverständnisse,* Frankfurt am Main.
Czempiel, Ernst-Otto (1995) 'Aktivieren, reformieren, negieren? Zum 50-jährigen Bestehen der Vereinten Nationen', *Aus Politik und Zeitgeschichte* (42) pp. 36–45.
Czempiel, Ernst-Otto (1998) *Friedensstrategien. Eine systematische Darstellung außenpolitischer Theorien von Machiavelli bis Madariaga,* Opladen.
Czempiel, Ernst-Otto (1999) *Kluge Macht: Außenpolitik für das 21. Jahrhundert,* Munich.
Czempiel, Ernst-Otto (2002) *Weltpolitik im Umbruch. Die Pax Americana, der Terrorismus und die Zukunft der internationalen Beziehungen,* Frankfurt am Main.
Datan, Merav (2002) 'The United Nations and Civil Society', *Disarmament Forum* (1) pp. 41–5.
Daws, Sam (ed.) (2000) *The United Nations,* Aldershot.
De Wet, Erika (2004) *The Chapter VII powers of the United Nations Security Council,* Oxford.
Debiel, Tobias (2003) *UN-Friedensoperationen in Afrika. Weltinnenpolitik und die Realität von Bürgerkriegen,* Bonn.
Debiel, Tobias and Franz Nuscheler (1996) *Der neue Interventionismus. Humanitäre Einmischung zwischen Anspruch und Wirklichkeit,* Bonn.
Degener, Theresia (1995) 'Disabled Persons and Human Rights: The Legal Framework', Degener/Koster-Dreese (1995), pp. 9–39.
Degener, Theresia and Yolan Koster-Dreese (eds) (1995) *Human Rights and Disbaled Persons: Essays and Relevant Human Rights Instruments,* Dordrecht.
Deiseroth, Dieter (1999) 'Humanitäre Intervention und Völkerrecht', *Neue Juristische Wochenschrift* (42) pp. 3084–8.
Deutsches Übersee-Institut (ed.) *Jahrbuch Dritte Welt,* Munich (published annually).
Dicke, Detlev Christian and Hans-Werner Rengeling (1975) *Die Sicherung des Weltfriedens durch die Vereinten Nationen,* Baden-Baden.
Dicke, Klaus (1994) *Effizienz und Effektivität internationaler Organisationen. Darstellung und kritische Analyse eines Topos im Reformprozesse der Vereinten Nationen,* Berlin.
Diehl, Paul F. (ed.) (1997) *The Politics of Global Governance. International Organizations in an Interdependent World,* Boulder, CO.
Dobson, Hugo (2003) *Japan and United Nations Peacekeeping: New Pressures, New Responses,* London.
Doyle, Michael W., Ian Johnstone and Robert C. Orr (eds) (1997) *Keeping the Peace: Lessons from Multidimensional UN-Operations in Cambodia and El Salvador,* Cambridge.
DPKO (Department of Peacekeeping Operations/Department of Field Support) (2008) *United Nations Peacekeeping Operations. Principles and Guidelines,* New York.
DPKO (Department of Peacekeeping Operations/Department of Field Support) (2009) *A New Partnership Agenda. Charting a New Horizon for UN Peacekeeping,* New York.
DPKO (Department of Peacekeeping Operations/Department of Field Support) (2010) *The New Horizon Initiative: Progress Report No 1,* New York.
Dunne, Michael (2003) 'The United States, the United Nations and Iraq: "Multilateralism of a Kind"', *International Affairs* (2) pp. 257–79.

Durch, W. (1993) *The Evolution of UN Peacekeeping*, New York.
Dwan, Renata (ed.) (2002) *Executive Policing: Enforcing the Law in Peace Operations*, Oxford.
Eban, Abba (1995) 'The U.N. Idea Revisited', *Foreign Affairs* (5) pp. 39–55.
Eböck, Kerstin (2000) *Der Schutz grundlegender Menschenrechte durch kollektive Zwangsmaßnahmen der Staatengemeinschaft*, Frankfurt-am-Main.
Eide, Espen Bart, Anja Therese Kaspersen, Randolph Kent and Karin von Hippel (2005) *Report on Integrated Missions. Practical Perspectives and Recommendations*. Independent Study for the Expanded UN ECHA Core Group, New York.
Elliot, Lorraine M. (2001) *Global Governance: A Report Card for the United Nations*, Manchester.
Esquivel, Adolfo Perez (ed.) (1989) *Das Recht auf Entwicklung als Menschenrecht*, Munich/Zurich.
Esty, Daniel (ed.) (2002) *Global Environmental Institutions. Perspectives on Reform*, London.
Evans, Gareth (2008) *The Responsibility to Protect. Ending Mass Atrocity Crimes Once and For All*, Washington, DC.
Fassbender, Bardo (1998a) *UN Security Council and the Right of Veto. A Constitutional Perspective*, The Hague.
Fassbender, Bardo (1998b) 'Reforming the United Nations', *Die Friedenswarte* (4), pp. 427–42.
Ferdowsi, Mir A. (2002) 'Die Vereinten Nationen und die wirtschaftliche Entwicklung der Länder des "Südens", *in Opitz* (2002), pp. 155–77.
Ferencz, Benjamin B. (2001) 'The Evolution of International Criminal Law: A Bird's Eye View of the Past Century', in Hasse *et al.* (2001) pp. 354–64.
Fetherston, Anthony (1994) *Towards a Theory of United Nations Peacekeeping*, New York.
Findlay, Trevor (2002) *The Use of Force in UN Peace Operations*, Oxford.
Fink, Udo (1999) *Kollektive Friedenssicherung: Kapitel VII UN-Charta in der Praxis des Sicherheitsrates der Vereinten Nationen*, 2 vols, Frankfurt-am-Main.
Fischer, Joseph (1999) 'Rede des deutschen Außenministers vor der 54. Generalversammlung der Vereinten Nationen', *Internationale Politik* (12) pp. 103–09.
Fischer, Joseph (2002) 'Rede vor der Generalversammlung der Vereinten Nationen am 14. September 2002', *Internationale Politik* (11) pp. 126–30.
Fleitz, Frederick H. (2002) *Peacekeeping Fiascos of the 1990s: Causes, Solutions, and Interests*, Westport, CT.
Forschungsinstitut der Deutschen Gesellschaft für Auswärtige Politik (ed.), *Jahrbuch Internationale Politik*, Munich (published annually).
Forsythe, David P. (1997) 'The United Nations, Human Rights and Development', *Human Rights Quarterly* (2) pp. 334–49.
Freedom House, *Freedom in the World. The Annual Survey of Political and Civil Liberties*, New York (published annually).
Freiesleben, Jonas von (2008) 'Security Council Reform', Center for UN Reform Education (2008), pp. 1–19.
French, Hilary F. (1995) *Partnership for the Planet. An Environmental Agenda for the United Nations*, Washington, DC.
Frowein, Jochen (2002) 'Ist das Völkerrecht tot?' *Frankfurter Allgemeine Zeitung*, 23 July.
Frowein, Jochen Abraham (2003) 'Issues of Legitimacy around the United Nations Security Council', *Verhandeln für den Frieden*, pp. 121–40.
Galtung, Johan (1975) *Strukturelle Gewalt. Beiträge zur Friedens- und Konfliktforschung*, Reinbek.
Gareis, Sven Bernhard (2009) 'Sechzig Jahre Allgemeine Erklärung der Menschenrechte – Herausforderungen und Chancen des Internationalen Menschenrechtsschutzes', in: Gareis and Geiger (2009), pp. 19–39.

Gareis, Sven Bernhard and Gunter Geiger (eds) (2009) *Internationaler Schutz der Menschenrechte. Stand und Perspektiven im 21. Jahrhundert*, Opladen.

Gehring, Thomas and Sebastian Oberthür (2000) 'Was bringt eine Weltumweltorganisation? Kooperationstheoretische Anmerkungen zur institutionellen Neuordnung der internationalen Umweltpolitik', *Zeitschrift für internationale Beziehungen* (1) pp. 185–211.

Glanzer, Hans-Peter (2001) 'An Agenda for Development', in: Cede and Sucharipa-Behrmann (2001), pp. 215–30.

Glen, Carol M. and Richard C. Murgo (2003) 'United Nations Human Rights Conventions: Obligations and Compliance', *Politics and Policy* (4) pp. 596–620.

Glennon, Michael (2003) 'Why the Security Council Failed', *Foreign Affairs* (3) pp. 16–35.

Goldstone, Richard (2007) 'International Criminal Court and Ad Hoc Tribunals', in: Weiss and Daws 2007, pp. 463–78.

Gorman, Robert F. (2001) *Great Debates at the United Nations: An Encyclopaedia of Fifty Key Issues 1945–2000*, Westport, CT.

Gottstein, Margit (1998) 'Frauenrechte – Menschenrechte?', *Amnesty International*, pp. 75–86.

Gowlland-Debbas, Vera (ed.) (2001) *United Nations sanctions and International Law*, The Hague.

Grewe, Wilhelm G. and Daniel-Erasmus Khan (2002) 'Drafting History', in: Simma (2002) pp 1–12.

Griffiths, Martin (1999) *Fifty Key Thinkers in International Relations*, London and New York.

Grove, Eric (1993) 'U.N. Armed Forces and the Military Staff Committee: A Look Back', *International Security*, XVII (2) pp. 172–82.

Grunberg, Isabelle (ed.) (2000) *The United Nations Development Dialogue; Finance Trade, Poverty, Peace-building*, Tokyo.

Guggenheim, Paul (1932) *Der Völkerbund in seiner politischen und rechtlichen Wirklichkeit*, Leipzig and Berlin.

Guicherd, Catherine (1999) 'International Law and the War in Kosovo', *Survival* (2) pp. 19–33.

Haftendorn, Helga (1990) 'Zur Theorie außenpolitischer Entscheidungsprozesse', in Volker Rittberger (ed.), *Theorie der Internationalen Beziehungen*, Opladen, pp. 401–23.

Hasenclever, Andreas, Peter Mayer and Volker Rittberger (1997) *Theories of International Regimes*, Cambridge.

Hasse, Jana (2000) 'Resolutionen des UN-Sicherheitsrates contra Menschenrechte?' *Sicherheit und Frieden* (2), pp. 158–63.

Hasse, Jana, Erwin Muller and Patricia Schneider (eds) (2001) *Humanitäres Völkerrecht. Politische, rechtliche und strafgerichtliche Dimensionen*, Baden-Baden.

Heidelberg Institute of International Conflict Research (ed.), *The Conflict Barometer* (published annually).

Heinrich-Böll-Stiftung (ed.) (2001) *Entwicklungspolitik als globale Strukturpolitik*, Berlin.

Herz, Dietmar (2002) Das Weltwirtschaftssystem, in: Opitz 2002, pp. 131–54.

Herz, Dietmar, Christian Jetzlsperger and Marc Schattenmann (eds) (2002) *Die Vereinten Nationen. Entwicklung, Aktivitäten, Perspektiven*, Frankfurt-am-Main.

Herz, John (1961) *Weltpolitik im Atomzeitalter*, Stuttgart.

Hilderbrand, Robert C. (1990) *Dumbarton Oaks. The Origins of the United Nations and the Search for Postwar Security*, London.

Hill, Christopher (2003) *The Changing Politics of Foreign Policy*, Basingstoke.

Hill, Ronald P. and Dhanda, Kanwalroop K. (2003) 'Technological Achievement and Human Development: A View from the United Nations Development Program', *Human Rights Quarterly* (4) pp. 1020–34.

Hill, Stephen M. (2002) *United Nations Disarmament in Intrastate Conflict*, Basingstoke.

Hinic, Dejan (2001) 'The International Tribunal for the Former Yugoslavia: A Serbian View', in: Hasse, Milner and Schneider (2001), pp. 420–05.

HLP (High-Level Panel on Threats Challenges and Change) (2004) 'A More Secure World: Our Shared Responsibility', New York (UN document A/59/565).

HLP (High-Level Panel on System-wide Coherence) (2006), Report, New York (UN document A/51/583).

Hoch, Martin (2001) 'Krieg und Politik im 21. Jahrhundert', *Aus Politik und Zeitgeschichte* (20), pp. 17–25.

Hoffman, Stanley (1981) *Duties Beyond Borders: On the Limits and Possibilities of Ethical International Politics,* Syracuse, NY.

Howard, Rhoda (1997/8) 'Human Rights and the Culture Wars. Globalization and the Universality of Human Rights', *International Journal* (1), pp. 94–112.

Hüfner, Klaus (ed.) (1995) *Agenda for Change. New Task for the United Nations,* Opladen.

Hüfner, Klaus (2010) 'UN-System', in: Volger (2010) , pp. 827–32.

Hüfner, Klaus and Jens Martens (2000) *UNO-Reform zwischen Utopie und Realität. Vorschläge zum Wirtschafts- und Sozialbereich der Vereinten Nationen,* Frankfurt-am-Main.

Hüfner, Klaus and Wolfgang Spröte (1994) 'Zur Reform des Wirtschafts – und Sozialbereichs der Vereinten Nationen', in: Hüfner (1994), pp. 99–118.

Hurrell, Andrew (1992) 'Collective Security and International Order Revisited', *International Relations* (1), pp. 37–55.

IBRD (International Bank for Reconstruction and Development), *World Development Report,* New York (published annually).

ICISS (International Commission on Intervention and State Sovereignty) (2001) *The Responsibility to Protect,* Ottawa.

IISS (International Institute for Strategic Studies) *The Military Balance,* London (published annually).

IMF (International Monetary Fund) *World Economic Outlook,* Washington, DC (published twice a year).

Jäger, Thomas/Kümmel, Gerhard (eds) (2007) *Private Military and Security Companies: Chances, Problems, Pitfalls and Prospects*, Wiesbaden.

Jakobsen, Peter Viggo (1998) 'The Danish Approach to UN Peacekeeping Operations after the Cold War: A New Model in the Making?', *International Peacekeeping* (3), pp. 106–23.

James, Alan (1990) *Peacekeeping in International Politics,* New York.

Jett, Dennis C. (2000) *Why Peacekeeping Fails,* New York.

Joint Four Nations Declaration (1943) *The Moscow Conference; October 1943.* Avalon Project at Yale Law School www.yale.edu/lawweb/avalon.

Kagan, Robert (2003) *Of Power and Paradise. America and Europe in the New World Order,* New York.

Kagan, Robert (2008) 'The Case for a League of Democracies', in *Financial Times* of 13 May 2008.

Kaiser, Karl (1969) 'Transnationale Politik. Zu einer Theorie der multinationalen Politik', in: Ernst-Otto Czempiel (ed.), *Die anachronistische Souveränität. Zum Verhältnis von Innen-und Außenpolitik,* Opladen.

Kaiser, Karl and Hans- Peter Schwarz (eds) (2000) *Weltpolitik im neuen Jahrhundert,* Bonn.

Kaldor, Mary (2007) *New and Old Wars. Organised Violence in a Global Era,* 2nd edition, Cambridge.

Kälin, Walter (1998) 'Die Allgemeine Erklärung der Menschenrechte: Eine Kopernikanische Wende im Völkerrecht?', *Amnesty International* pp. 5–17.

Katayanagi, Mari (2002) *Human Rights Functions of United Nations Peacekeeping Operations,* The Hague.

Kaul, Hans-Peter (1998) 'Durchbruch in Rom. Der Vertrag über den Internationalen Strafgerichtshof', *Vereinte Nationen* (4) pp. 125–30.

Kaul, Inge (2010) 'Development Concepts, Development Research', in: Volger (2010) pp. 74–82.

Kaul, Inge, Isabelle Grunberg and Marc A. Stern (eds) (1999a) *Global Public Goods. International Cooperation in the 21st Century,* New York.

Kaul, Inge, Isabelle Grunberg and Marc Stern (1999b) *Global Public Goods. Concepts, Policies and Strategies,* in Kaul, Grunberg and Stern (1999) pp. 450–507.

Keeley, James F. and Rob Huebert (eds) (2004) *Commercial Satellite Imagery and United Nations Peacekeeping: A View From Above,* Aldershot.

Kellogg-Briand Pact (1928) Avalon Project at Yale Law School www.yale.edu/lawweb/avalon.

Kennedy, Paul (2006) *The Parliament of Man. The United Nations and the Quest for World Government.* London.

Kennedy, Paul and Bruce Russett (1995) 'Reforming the United Nations', *Foreign Affairs* (5) pp. 56–71.

Keohane, Robert O. (1989) *International Institutions and State Power,* Boulder, CO.

Kimminich, Otto (1997) *Einführung in das Völkerrecht,* Tubingen and Basle.

Kinloch, Stephen P. (1996) 'Utopian or pragmatic? A UN Permanent Military Volunteer Force', *International Peacekeeping* (4) pp. 166–90.

Knight, W. Andy (2000) *A Changing United Nations: Multilateral Evolution and the Quest for Global Governance,* Basingstoke.

Knight, W. Andy (ed.) (2001) *Adapting the United Nations to a post-modern era: Lesson Learned*, Basingstoke.

Knipping, Franz, Volker Rittberger and Hans von Mangoldt (eds) (1995) *,Das System der Vereinten Nationen und seine Vorläufer/The United Nations System and its Predecessors* vol. 1/1: *Vereinte Nationen ',* in Hans von Mangoldt (ed.) vol. 1/2: *Sonderorganisationen und andere Institutionen*, Munich.

Koops, Joachim (2007) 'UN SHIRBRIG and EU Battlegroups. Recommendation to the European Union and the United Nations, The Oxford Council on Good Governance Security Recommendations', no. 6, Oxford.

Koschorreck, Wilfried (1997) 'Zahlungsfähigkeit versus Zahlungsbereitschaft. Die Debatte urn die Beiträge zu den Vereinten Nationen', in *Vereinte Nationen* (5) pp. 161–7.

Koschorreck, Wilfried (1998) 'Beitragsfestsetzung weder gerecht noch transparent', *Vereinte Nationen* (1) pp. 33–5.

Koschorreck, Wilfried (2000) 'Noch mehr Rabatt für die Reichsten?', *Vereinte Nationen* (4) pp. 142–4.

Krasno, Jean E. (ed.) (2004) *The United Nations: Confronting the Challenges of a Global Society,* Boulder, CO.

Kratochwil, Friedrich and Edward D. Mansfield (eds) (1994) *International Organizations. A Reader,* New York.

Kreuzer, Christine (2001) 'Kinder in bewaffneten Konflikten', in: Hasse, Muller and Schneider (2001) pp. 304–20.

Kubbig, Bernd W. (ed.) (2003) *Brandherd Irak. US-Hegemonieanspruch, die UNO und die Rolle Europas,* Frankfurt-am-Main.

Kühne, Winrich (1993) 'Völkerrecht und Friedenssicherung in einer turbulenten Welt: Eine analytische Zusammenfassung der Grundprobleme und Entwicklungsperspektiven', in: Winrich Kühne (ed.), *Blauhelme in einer turbulenten Welt,* Baden-Baden, pp. 17–100.

Kühne, Winrich (2000) 'Die Vereinten Nationen an der Schwelle zum nächsten Jahrtausend', in: Kaiser and Schwarz (2000), pp. 442–57.

Kühne, Winrich (2000b) 'Zukunft der UN-Friedenseinsätze. Lehren aus dem Brahimi-Report', *Blätter für deutsche und internationale Politik* (11) pp. 1355–64.

Kühne, Winrich and Katja Baumann (1995) *Reform des Sicherheitsrates zum 50-jährigen Jubiläum. Auswertung und Analyse der Stellungnahmen der Mitgliedstaaten im Überblick,* Ebenhausen.

Kühnhardt, Ludger (1991) *Die Universalität der Menschenrechte,* Bonn.

Kulessa, Manfred (1998) 'Stumpfes Friedensinstrument? Zur Problematik der UN-Sanktionen', *Aus Politik und Zeitgeschichte* (16–17) pp. 31–8.

Kulessa, Manfred and Dorothee Starck (1997) *Frieden durch Sanktionen?,* (SEF Policy Paper no. 7), Bonn.

Kupchan, Charles A. and Clifford A. Kupchan (1995) 'The Promise of Collective Security', *International Security* (1) pp. 52–61.

Lagoni, Rainer (1995) 'ECOSOC', in: Wolfrum (1995), pp. 461–9.

Lang, Winfried and Andreas Kumin (2001) 'Disarmament Issues', in: Cede and Sucharipa-Behrmann (2001), pp. 127–42.

Laulan, Ives-Marie (1996) 'Il faut réformer l'ONU', *Défense Nationale* (12) pp. 45–53.

Le Monde Diplomatique (ed.) (2003) *Atlas der Globalisierung,* Berlin.

Lehmkuhl, Ursula (1996) *Theorien Internationaler Politik. Einführung und Texte,* Munich and Vienna.

Leisinger, Klaus M. (2000) *Die sechste Milliarde. Weltbevölkerung und nachhaltige Entwicklung,* Bonn.

Lewis, Patricia (2001) 'From "UNSCOM" to "UNMOVIC": The United Nations and Iraq', *Disarmament Forum* (2) pp. 63–9.

Lie, Trygve (1954) *In the Cause of Peace,* New York.

Liese, Andrea (1998) 'Menschenrechtsschutz durch Nichtregierungsorganisationen', *Aus Politik und Zeitgeschichte* (46–7) pp. 36–42.

Link, Werner (1998) *Die Neuordnung der Weltpolitik. Grundprobleme globaler Politik an der Schwelle zum 21. Jahrhundert,* Munich.

Loibl, Gerhard (2001) 'Environmental Protection and Sustainable Development', in: Cede and Sucharipa-Behrmann (2001), pp. 195–214.

Luard, Evan (1982) *A History of the United Nations. Vol. 1: The Years of Western Domination 1945–1955; Vol. 11: The Age of Decolonization 1955–1965,* Basingstoke.

Luard, Evan (1995) *The United Nations. How It Works and What It Does,* New York.

Luck, Edward C. (2007) 'Principal Organs', in: Weiss and Daws (2007), pp. 653–74.

Luttwak, Edward N. (1999) 'Give War a Chance', *Foreign Affairs* (4) pp. 36–44.

MacDermott, Anthony (1999) *The New Politics of Financing the UN,* Basingstoke.

MacWhinney, Edward (2000) *The United Nations and a New World Order for a New Millenium: Self-Determination, State Succession, and Humanitarian Intervention,* The Hague.

Malone, David M. and Lotta Hagman (2002) 'The North–South Divide at the United Nations: Fading at Last?, *Security Dialogue* (4) pp. 399–415.

Malone, David M. and Karin Wermester (2000) 'Boom and Bust? The Changing Nature of UN Peacekeeping', *International Peacekeeping* (4) pp. 37–54.

Mani, Rama (2007) 'Peaceful Settlement of Disputes and Conflict Prevention', in: Weiss and Daws (2007) pp. 300–22.

Martens, Jens (1998) 'Kompendium der Gemeinplätze. Die Agenda für die Entwicklung: Chronologie eines gescheiterten Verhandlungsprozesses', *Vereinte Nationen* (2) pp. 47–52.

Martens, Jens (2000) 'Globale Entwicklungspartnerschaft: Zielvorgabe für 2001', *Vereinte Nationen* (3) pp. 99–104.

Martens, Jens (2001) ,Möglichkeiten und Probleme in der Zukunft der Entwicklungsfinanzierung', in: Heinrich-Böll-Stiftung (2001), pp. 52–63.

Martens, Jens and Wolfgang Sterk (2002) *Multilateralismus zwischen Blockadepolitik und Partnerschaftsrhetorik,* Bonn.

Massimino, Elisa (2007) 'Leading by Example? U.S. Interrogation of Prisoners in the War on Terror', in: Callaway and Harrelson-Stephens (2007) pp. 280–86.

Mathews, Jessica T. (1997) 'Power Shift', *Foreign Affairs* (1) pp. 50-66.

Mathson, Michael J. (2001) 'United Nations Governance of Postconflict Societies', *American Journal of International Law* (1) pp. 76–86.

May, Ernest and Angeliki E. Laiou (eds) (1998) *The Dumbarton Oaks Conversations and the United Nations 1944–1994,* Washington, DC.

Mayall, James (ed.) (1999) *The New Interventionism 1991–1994: United Nations Experience in Cambodia, Former Yugoslavia and Somalia,* Cambridge.

McDermott, Anthony (1998) 'The UN and NGOs: Humanitarian Interventions in Future Conflicts', *Contemporary Security Policy* (3) 1998, pp. 1–26.

Mearsheimer, John (1994) 'The False Promise of International Institutions', *International Security* (3) pp. 5–49.

Menzel, Ulrich (ed.) (2000) *Vom Ewigen Frieden und vom Wohlstand der Nationen,* Frankfurt-am-Main.

Menzel, Ulrich (2001) *Zwischen Idealismus und Realismus. Die Lehre von den internationalen Beziehungen,* Frankfurt am Main.

Mertus, Julie and Tazreena Sajjad (2007) 'Human Rights Post-September 11', in: Callaway and Harrelson-Stephens (2007) pp. 287–95.

Messner, Dirk and Franz Nuscheler (eds) (1996) 'Die Weltkonferenzen der 90er Jahre. Eine Gipfelei ohne neue Perspektiven?', in: Messner and Nuscheler (1996) , pp. 160–09.

Messner, Dirk and Franz Nuscheler (1996a) (eds) *Weltkonferenzen und Weltberichte. Ein Wegweiser durch die internationale Diskussion,* Bonn.

Messner, Dirk and Franz Nuscheler (1996c) 'Global Governance. Organisationselemente und Säulen einer Weltordnungspolitik', in: Messner and Nuscheler (1996) , pp. 12–36.

Metzger, Martina (2002) 'IMF', in: Volger (2002) , pp. 300–07.

Meyers, Reinhard (1981) *Die Lehre von den Internationalen Beziehungen. Ein entwicklungsgeschichtlicher Überblick,* Dusseldorf.

Meyers, Reinhard (2004) Theorien der Internationalen Beziehungen' in: Woyke (2004) , pp. 450–81.

Michie, Jonathan (ed.) (2003) *The Handbook of Globalization,* Cheltenham.

Millennium Declaration (2000) Resolution adopted by the General Assembly, UN Document A/RES/55/2.

Mingst, Karen A. and Margaret P. Karns (2000) *The United Nations in the Post-Cold War Era,* Boulder, CO.

Moore, John Allphin (2002) *Encyclopedia of the United Nations,* New York.

Moore, John Norton and Morrison, Alex (eds) (2000) *Strengthening the United Nations and Enhancing War Prevention,* Durham, NC.

Morgan, Patrick M. (2000) 'The Impact of the Revolution in Military Affairs', *Journal of Strategic Studies,* March, pp. 132–62.

Morris, Virginia and Michael Scharf (1995) *An Insider's Guide to the International Criminal Tribunal for the Former Yugoslavia,* Irvington-on-Hudson.

Morsink, Johannes (1999) *The Universal Declaration of Human Rights. Origins, Drafting and Intent,* Philadelphia.

Morton, Jeffrey S. (2000) *The International Law Commission of the United Nations,* Columbia, SC.

Mueller, Joachim W. (ed.) (2001) *Reforming the United Nations: The Quiet Revolution,* The Hague.

Mueller, Joachim (ed.) (2006) *Reforming the United Nations. The Struggle for Legitimacy and Effectiveness*, Leiden and Boston

Muldoon, James P. (2004) *The Architecture of Global Governance. An Introduction to the Study of International Organizations,* Boulder, CO.

Münkler, Herfried (2004) *The New Wars,* Cambridge and Malden.

Neack, Laura, Jeanne Hey and Patrick Haney (eds) (1995) *Foreign Policy Analysis. Continuity and Change in its Second Generation,* Englewood Cliffs, NJ.

Nelson, Jane (2002) *Building Partnership: Cooperation between the United Nations System and the Private Sector,* New York.

New Zealand Ministry of Foreign Affairs and Trade, *United Nations Handbook,* Wellington (published annually).

Newman, Edward (ed.) (2001) *The United Nations and Human Security,* Basingstoke.

Nordquist, Myron H. (1997) *What Color Helmet? Reforming Security Council Peacekeeping Mandates,* Newport Paper no. 12, Newport, Rl.

Nowak, Manfred (2002) 'Civil and Political Rights, Including Questions of: Disappearance and Summary Executions', Report to the ECOSOC (UN document E/CN.4/2002/71 of 8 January 2002).

Nullmeier, Frank (1997) 'Interpretative Ansätze in der Politikwissenschaft', in: Artur Benz and Wolfgang Seibel (eds), *Theorieentwicklung in der Politikwissenschaft – eine Zwischenbilanz,* Baden-Baden, pp. 101–44.

Nuscheler, Franz (1996) *Das Recht auf Entwicklung. Blaue Reihe der Deutschen Gesellschaft für die Vereinten Nationen,* no. 67, Bonn.

Nuscheler, Franz (ed.) (2000) *Entwicklung und Frieden im Zeichen der Globalisierung,* Bonn.

Nuscheler, Franz (2001) 'Halbierung der absoluten Armut: die entwicklungspolitische Nagelprobe', *Aus Politik und Zeitgeschichte* (18–19) pp. 6–12.

Nuscheler, Franz (2002a) 'Überforderte Entwicklungspolitik. Veränderungen nach dem 11. September', *Internationale Politik* (1) pp. 1–8.

Nuscheler, Franz (2002b) 'Global Governance, Development, and Peace', in: Paul Kennedy, Dirk Messner and Franz Nuscheler (eds), *Global Trends and Global Governance,* London, pp. 156–82.

Nye, Joseph (1999) 'Redefining the National Interest', *Foreign Affairs* (4) pp. 22–35.

Nye, Joseph (2002) *The Paradox of American Power. Why the World's Only Superpower Can't Go It Alone,* Oxford.

Nyc, Robert S. (2000) *Understanding International Conflicts. An Introduction to Theory and History,* New York.

Oberleitner, Gerd (2007) *Global Human Rights Institutions,* Cambridge.

Oberthür, Sebastian and Hermann E. Ott (2000) *Das Kyoto-Protokoll. Internationale Klimapolitik für das 21. Jahrhundert,* Opladen.

OHCHR (Office of the High Commissioner for Human Rights) (2005) 'The International Convention on Migrant Workers and its Committee', Fact Sheet no. 24 (Rev 1), Geneva.

OHCHR (Office of the High Commissioner for Human Rights) (2008) *Rule-of-Law Tools for Post-conflict States. Maximizing the legacy of hybrid courts,* New York and Geneva.

OHCHR (Office of the High Commissioner for Human Rights) (2011a) *United Nations Special Procedures. Facts and Figures 2010,* New York and Geneva.

OHCHR (Office of the High Commissioner for Human Rights) (2011b) *OHCHR Report 2010,* Geneva.

Olsen, Mancur and Richard Zeckhauser (1966) 'An Economic Theory of Alliances', *Review of Economics and Statistics* (3) pp. 266–79.

Omamo, Steven Were, Ugo Gentilini and Susanna Sandström (eds) (2010) *Revolution: From Food Aid to Food Assistance. Innovations in Overcoming Hunger,* New York.

Opitz, Peter J. (2010) 'Collective Security', in: Volger (2010) pp. 33–41.

Orakhelashvili, Alexander (2011) *Collective Security,* Oxford: Oxford University Press.

Osman, Mohamed Awad (2003) *The United Nations and Peace Enforcement: Wars, Terrorism and Democracy,* Aldershot.

Osmanczyk, Edmund Jan and Anthony Mango (eds) (2003) *Encyclopaedia of the United Nations and International Agreements,* 4 vols, New York and London.

Otto, Dianne (1996) 'Nongovernmental Organizations in the United Nations System. The Emerging Role of International Civil Society', *Human Rights Quarterly* (1) pp. 107–41.

Otunnu, Olara A. and Michael W. Doyle (eds) (1998) *Peacemaking and Peacekeeping for the New Century,* Lanham, MD.

Paolini, Albert J. (ed.) (2003) *Between Sovereignty and Global Governance: The United Nations, The State and Civil Society,* Basingstoke.

Pape, Matthias (1997) *Humanitäre Intervention. Zur Bedeutung der Menschenrechte in den Vereinten Nationen,* Baden-Baden.

Paris, Roland (2001) 'Human Security: Paradigm Shift or Hot Air?', *International Security* (4) pp. 87–102.

Paris, Roland (2004) *At War's End. Building Peace after Civil Conflict*, Cambridge.

Paris, Roland (2007) 'Post-conflict Peace Building', in: Weiss and Daws (2007), pp. 404–26.

Paris, Roland and Timothy D. Sisk (eds) (2009) *The Dilemmas of Statebuilding: Confronting the Contradictions of Postwar Peace Operations*, London and New York.

Parsons, Anthony (1995) *From Cold War to Hot Peace: UN Interventions 1947–1995*, London.

Partsch, Karl Josef (1995) 'Human Rights, Petitions and Individual Complaints', in: Wolfrum (1995), pp. 619–27.

Paschke, Karl Theodor (1996) 'Innenrevision in den Vereinten Nationen – eine neue Erfahrung', *Vereinte Nationen* (2) pp. 41–5.

Paschke, Karl Theodor (1999) 'Kein hoffnungsloser Fall. Fünf Jahre UN-Inspektorat: Versuch einer Bilanz', *Vereinte Nationen* (6) pp. 187–91.

Patil, Anjali V. (1992) *The UN Veto in World Affairs 1946–1990*, London.

Peck, Connie (1998) *Sustainable Peace. The Role of the UN and Regional Organizations in Preventing Conflict*, Lanham, MD.

Petterson, Thorleif (2002) 'Individual Values and Global Governance: A Comparative Analysis of Orientations Towards the United Nations', *Comparative Sociology* (3–4) pp. 439–65.

Pfetsch, Frank R. (ed.) (1991) *Konflikte seit 1945. Daten – Fakten – Hintergründe*, 5 vols, Freiburg.

Pfetsch, Frank R. and Christoph Rohloff (2000) *National and International Conflicts 1945–1995. New Empirical and Theoretical Approaches*, London.

Prittwitz, Volker von (ed.) (2000) *Institutionelle Arrangements in der Umweltpolitik*, Opladen.

Pugh, Michael (ed.) (2001) *The UN, Peace, and Force*, London.

Quinn, Gerard and Theresia Degener (2002) *Human Rights and Disability. The Current Use and Future Potential of United Nations Human Rights Instruments in The Context of Disability*. New York and Geneva.

Rahman, Mahfuzur (2002) *World Economic Issues at the United Nations: Half a Century of Debate*, Boston, Mass.

Ramcharan, Bertrand G. (2002) *The United Nations High Commissioner for Human Rights: The Challenges of International Protection*, The Hague.

Ramcharan, Bertrand G. (2007) 'Norms and Machinery', in: Weiss and Daws (2007) pp.439–62.

Ramphal, Shridath (1998) 'Global Governance', *Internationale Politik* (11), 1998, pp. 2–10.

Randelzhofer, Albrecht (2002) 'Art 2' (4), in: Simma (2002) pp. 112–35.

Rao, Vinayak (2001) *International Negotiation: The United Nations in Afghanistan and Cambodia*, New Delhi.

Rathgeber, Theodor (2010) *Reviewing the UN Human Rights Council. Perspectives from Civil Society*, Berlin.

Ratsimbaharison, Adrien M. (2004) *The Failure of the United Nations development programs for Africa*, Lanham, MD.

Rechkemmer, Andreas (2002) *Globale Umwelt- und Entwicklungspolitik in der Krise?* Berlin (SWP-Aktuell 44).

Rechkemmer, Andreas (2003) *Die Zukunft der Vereinten Nationen. Weltorganisation am Scheideweg – eine deutsche Perspektive*, Berlin.

Reinicke, Wolfgang and Francis Deng (2000) *Critical Choices. The United Nations, Networks, and the Future of Global Governance*, Ottawa.

Ress, Georg (2002) 'The Interpretation of the Charter', in: Simma (2002) pp. 13–32.

Review Conference (2010) RC/Res.6 'The Crime of Aggression'. See Depositary Notification C.N.651.2010 Treaties-8, dated 29 November 2010, available at www.treaties.un.org.

Rice, Condoleezza (2000) 'Promoting the National Interest', *Foreign Affairs* (1) pp. 45–63.
Riedel, Eibe (1998) 'Universeller Menschenrechtsschutz. Vom Anspruch zur Durchsetzung', in Baum *et al.* (1998), pp. 25–55.
Riedel, Eibe (2004) 'Einleitung', in Bundeszentrale für Politische Bildung (2004) *Menschenrechte. Dokumente und Deklarationen,* Bonn, pp. 11–36.
Riedel, Eibe (2002) 'Artikel 55 (c)', in: Simma (2002) pp. 918–40
Righter, Rosemary (1995) *Utopia Lost. The United Nations and World Order,* New York.
Risse, Thomas, Stephen C. Ropp and Kathryn Sikkink (1999) *The Power of Human Rights,* Cambridge.
Rittberger, Volker (ed.) (2002) *Global Governance and the United Nations System,* New York.
Rittberger, Volker (1994) 'Vereinte Nationen', in Dieter Nohlen (ed.), *Lexikon der Politik, vol. 6: Internationale Beziehungen,* ed. Andreas Boeckh, Munich, pp. 561–81.
Rittberger, Volker (1995) *International Organizations, Theory of,* in: Wolfrum (1995), pp. 760–70.
Rittberger, Volker (1996) 'Die Vereinten Nationen zwischen weltstaatlicher Autorität und hegemonialer Machtpolitik', in Berthold Meier (ed.), *Eine Welt oder Chaos,* Frankfurt-am-Main, pp. 301–36.
Rittberger, Volker (2000) 'Globalisierung und der Wandel der Staatenwelt. Die Welt regieren ohne Weltstaat?', in: Menzel (2000), pp. 188–218.
Rittberger, Volker and Bernhard Zangl (2003) *Internationale Organisationen – Politik und Geschichte,* Opladen.
Rittberger, Volker, Martin Mogler and Bernhard Zangl (1997) *Vereinte Nationen und Weltordnung. Zivilisierung der internationalen Politik?,* Opladen.
Ritter, Scott (2005) *Iraq Confidential: The Untold Story of America's Intelligence Conspiracy,* London and New York.
Roberts, Adam (1993) 'The United Nations and International Security', *Survival* (2) 1993, pp. 3–30.
Roberts, Adam (2003) 'Law and the Use of Force after Iraq', *Survival* (2) pp. 21–56.
Roberts, Adam and Benedict Kingsbury (eds) (1993) *United Nations, Divided World. The UN's Roles in International Relations,* Oxford.
Robinson, Mary (2002) 'Menschenrechte im Schatten des 11. September', in: Arnim *et al.* (2002) pp. 25–36.
Rochester, Martin J. (1993) *Waiting for the Millennium. The United Nations and the Future of World Order,* Columbia.
Rodley, Nigel (2003) 'United Nations Human Rights Treaty Bodies and Special Procedures of the Commission on Human Rights', *Human Rights Quarterly* (4), pp. 882–909.
Rosenau, James N. (1992) *The United Nations in a Turbulent World,* Boulder, CO, and London.
Rosenau, James N. (1994) 'New Dimensions of Security – The Interaction of Globalizing and Localizing Dynamics', *Security Dialogue* (3) pp. 255–81.
Rosenau, James N. and Ernst-Otto Czempiel (eds) (1992) *Governance Without Government: Order and Change in World Politics,* Cambridge.
Ruggie, John Gerald (1993) *Multilateralism Matters,* New York.
Rumsfeld, Donald H. (2001) 'America's New Kind of War', *New York Times,* 27 September.
Russell, Ruth (1958) *The History of the United Nations Charter,* Washington, DC.
Russett, Bruce (1996) 'Ten Balances for Weighing UN-Reform Proposals', *Political Science Quarterly* (2), pp. 259–69.
Russett, Bruce, Harvey Starr and David Kinsella (eds) (2000) *World Politics. The Menu for Choice,* Boston, MA, and New York.
Ryan, Stephen (2000) *The United Nations and International Politics,* Basingstoke.
Saksena, Krishan P. (1993) *Reforming the United Nations. The Challenge of Relevance,* New Delhi.

Salmon, Trevor C. (ed.) (2000) *Issues in International Relations,* London.

Santiso, Carlos (2002) 'Promoting Democratic Governance and Preventing the Recurrence of Conflict: The Role of the United Nations Development Programme in Post-conflict Peace-building, *Journal of Latin American Studies* (3) pp. 555–86

Sarooshi, Danesh (2000) *The United Nations and the Development of Collective Security: The Delegation by the UN Security Council of Its Chapter VII Powers,* Oxford.

Schabas, William A (2007), *An Introduction to the International Criminal Court,* 3rd edition, Cambridge.

Scharpf, Fritz W. (1999) *Regieren in Europa. Effektiv und demokratisch?,* Frankfurt and New York.

Schechter, Michael G. (2001) *United Nations-sponsored World Conferences: Focus on Impact and Follow-up,* Tokyo.

Schellinski, Kristina (1998) *Ausbeutung von Kindern – Herausforderung für das gesamte UN-System,* in Baum (1998), pp. 139–54.

Schlesinger, Stephen C. (2003) *Act of Creation: The Founding of the United Nations; a Story of Superpowers, Secret Agents, Wartime Allies and Enemies, and Their Quest for a Peaceful World,* Boulder, CO.

Schlesinger, Thomas (2001) 'Financing and Financial Crises', in: Cede and Sucharipa-Behrmann (2001), pp. 289–302.

Schoepp-Schilling, Beate and Cees Flinterman (eds.) *The Circle of Empowerment. Twenty-five Years of the CEDAW Committee,* New York.

Scholte, Jan Art (1997) 'The Globalization of World Politics', in Baylis and Smith, pp. 13–30.

Schorlemer, Sabine von (ed.) (2002) *Praxis-Handbuch UNO. Die Vereinten Nationen im Lichte globaler Herausforderungen,* Heidelberg.

Schreiber, Wolfgang (2010) *Kriege und bewaffnete Konflikte 2010.* AKUF Analysen Nr. 9, Hamburg.

Schücking, Walther and Hans Wehberg (1924) *Die Satzung des Völkerbundes,* 2nd edition, Berlin.

Semb, Anne Julie (2000) 'The New Practices of UN-Authorized Interventions. A Slippery Slope or an Forcible Interference?', *Journal of Peace Research* (4) pp. 469–88.

Siedschlag, Alexander (1997) *Neorealismus, Neoliberalismus und Postinternationale Politik. Beispiel internationale Sicherheit – Theoretische Bestandsaufnahme und Evaluation,* Opladen.

Simma, Bruno (ed.) (2002) *The Charter of the United Nations: A Commentary,* Oxford.

Simmons, Beth A. and Lisa L. Martin (2002) 'International Organizations and Institutions', in: Carlsnaes *et al.* (2002), pp. 192–211.

Simonis, Udo-Ernst (2008) 'Weltumweltpolitik', in Woyke (2005) pp. 569–82.

Singer, Peter W. (2003) *Corporate Warriors: The Rise of the Privatized Military Industry,* Ithaca, NY.

Singh, Swarna (2000) *United Nations and Geopolitical Reality,* New Delhi.

SIPRI (Stockholm International Peace Research Institute), Yearbook Armaments, Disarmament and International Security, London (published annually).

Smith, Michael J. (1998) 'Humanitarian Intervention: An Overview on the Ethical Issues', *Ethics and International Affairs* (12) pp. 63–79.

Smith, Rhona K.M. (2007) *Textbook on International Human Rights,* 3rd edition, Oxford.

Sondhi, Sunil (2000) *United Nations in a Changing World,* New Delhi.

South Centre (ed.) (1996) *For a Strong and Democratic United Nations: A South Perspective on UN Reform,* Geneva.

Stares, Paul B. (ed.) (1998) *The New Security Agenda. A Global Survey,* Tokyo and New York.

Stein, Torsten (2000) 'Einsatzarten der Streitkräfte außer zur Verteidigung', *Neue Zeitschrift für Wehrrecht* (1) pp. 1–15.

Stiftung Entwicklung und Frieden (ed.) *Globale Trends. Fakten, Analysen, Prognosen,* Frankfurt-am-Main (published frequently).

Stoecker, Felix (2000) *NGOs und die UNO. Die Einbindung von Nichtergierungsorgani- sationen (NGOs) in die Strukturen der Vereinten Nationen,* Frankfurt-am-Main.

Strauss, Ekkehard (2009) *The Emperor's New Clothes? The United Nations and the Imple- mentation of the Responsibility to Protect,* Baden-Baden.

Stremlau, John (1998) *Sharpening International Sanctions,* New York.

Strohal, Christian (2001) 'The Development of the International Human Rights System', in: Cede and Sucharipa-Behrmann (2001), pp. 157–76.

Strunz, Johann (1930) *Der Völkerbund.* Leipzig.

Sucharipa, Ernst (2001) 'The United Nations Today: Its Current Status, Reforms and Perspectives for the Future', in: Cede and Sucharipa-Behrmann (2001), pp. 313–31.

Sucharipa-Behrmann, Lilly (2001) 'Peace-Keeping Operations of the United Nations', in: Cede and Sucharipa-Behrmann (2001), pp. 89–104.

Swamy Meier-Ewert, Gita (2010) 'Humanitarian Assistance', in: Volger (2010), pp. 337-46.

Swart, Lydia (2008) 'Revitalisation of the General Assembly', Center for UN Reform Education (2008), pp. 21–36.

Tangredi, Sam J. (2000) *All Possible Wars? Towards a Consensus View of the Future Secu- rity Environment 2001–2025,* McNair Paper 63, Washington, DC.

Thant, Myint-U and Amy Scott (2007) *The UN Secretariat. A Brief History (1945–2006),* New York.

Taylor, Ian (2003) 'The United Nations Conference on Trade and Development', *New Political Economy* (3) pp. 409–19.

Taylor, Paul and A.J.R. Groom (eds) 2000: *The United Nations at the Millennium: The Principal Organs,* London.

Teixeira, Pascal (2003) *The Security Council at the Dawn of the Twenty-First Century,* Geneva.

Thakur, Ramesh (ed.) (2000) *New Millennium, New Perspectives: The United Nations, Security, and Governance,* Tokyo.

Thakur, Ramesh (ed.) (2001) *United Nations Peacekeeping Operations: ad hoc Missions, Permanent Engagement,* Tokyo.

Thakur, Ramesh (2006), The United Nations, Peace and Security, Cambridge.

Thomas, Caroline (2008) 'Poverty, development and hunger', in: Baylis and Smith (2008), pp. 468–89.

Thomsen, Bernd (1998) 'Rechtliche Grundlagen für einen wirksamen Menschenrechts- schutz', *Amnesty International,* pp. 19–30.

Tomuschat, Christian (1983) 'Neuformulierung der Grundregeln des Völkerrechts durch die Vereinten Nationen: Bewegung, Stillstand oder Rückschritt?', *Europa-Archiv* (23) pp. 729–38.

Tomuschat, Christian (ed.) (1992) *Menschenrechte. Eine Sammlung internationaler Doku- mente zum Menschenrechtschutz,* Bonn.

Tomuschat, Christian (1995a) 'Human Rights, Petitions and Individual Complaints', in: Wolfrum (1995), pp. 619–27.

Tomuschat, Christian (ed.) (1995b) *The United Nations at Age Fifty. A Legal Perspective,* The Hague.

Tomuschat, Christian (1995c) 'Human Rights, States Reports', in: Wolfrum (1995) pp. 638-45.

Tomuschat, Christian (2000) 'Globale Menschenrechtspolitik', in: Kaiser and Schwarz (2000) pp. 431–41.

Tomuschat, Christian (2003) 'Völkerrecht ist kein Zweiklassenrecht. Der Irak-Krieg und seine Folgen', *Vereinte Nationen* (2) pp. 41–6.

Tomuschat, Christian (2008) *Human Rights. Between Idealism and Realism.* 2nd revised edition, Oxford

Töpfer, Klaus (1999) 'Rede des Exekutivdirektors des Umweltprogramms der Vereinten Nationen am 15.9.1999 in London', *Internationale Politik* (12) pp. 85–8.

Touval, Saadia (1994) 'Why the U.N. Fails', *Foreign Affairs* (5) pp. 44–57.
Trauttmansdorff, Ferdinand (2001) 'The Organs of the United Nations', in: Cede and Sucharipa-Behrmann (2001) pp. 25–56.
Ul Haq, Mahbub, Richard Jolly, Paul Streeten and Khadija Haq (eds) (1995) *The UN and the Bretton Woods Institutions*, New York.
Unabhängige Kommission für internationale Entwicklungsfragen (1980) *Das Überleben sichern. Gemeinsame Interessen der Industrie- und Entwicklungsländer*, Cologne.
UNCTAD *Trade and Development Report*, Geneva (published annually).
UNCTAD (2000) *The Least Developed Countries Report 2000*, New York.
UNCTAD (2000) *World Investment Report 2000*, Geneva.
UNDESA (2010) *The Millennium Development Report 2010*, New York
UNDP, *Human Development Report*, New York (published annually).
UNEP, *Global Environmental Outlook*, London (published annually).
Union of International Associations (UIA) (ed.) (2010–11), *Yearbook of International Organizations*, 4 vols, Munich.
Union of International Organizations (UIO) (2008–09) *Yearbook of International Organizations*, Munich.
United Nations (ed.) (1995) *UN Fiftieth Anniversary 1945–1995*, Dordrecht.
United Nations (2002) 'Report of the International Conference on Financing Development', New York (A/Conf. 198/11).
United Nations (ed.) (2004) 'International Instruments Related to the Prevention and Suppression of International Terrorism', New York.
United Nations Association of the USA (ed.), *Global Agenda. Issues before the General Assembly of the United Nations* (published annually).
United Nations Department of Public Information (ed.) (1996) *The Blue Helmets. A Review of the United Nations Peace-keeping*, New York.
United Nations Department of Public Information, *Basic Facts About the United Nations*, New York (published frequently).
United Nations Department of Public Information, *Yearbook of the United Nations*, New York (published annually).
United Nations Development Program (2009/10) delivering on Commitments. UNDP in Action 2009/10, New York.
United Nations Development Program (2010) 'The Real Wealth of Nations: Pathways to Human Development', Human Development Report 2010, Basingstoke and New York.
United Nations Library, *Monthly Bibliography*, Geneva (published monthly).
United Nations Non-governmental Liaison Service (ed.) (1999) *Economic and Social Development in the United Nations System. A Guide for NGOs*, Geneva.
United Nations Non-governmental Liaison Service (2000) *The Handbook of UN Agencies, Programmes, Funds and Conventions Working for Sustainable Economic and Social Development*, Geneva.
UN Millennium Project (2005) *Investing in Development. A Practical Plan to Achieve the Millennium Development Goals*, London and Sterling, VA.
Universal Declaration of Human Rights, 10 December 1948, A/Res/217 (t11).
Unser, Günter (2003), *Die UNO*, Munich.
Urquhart, Brian (1972) *Hammarskjöld*, New York.
Urquhart, Brian (2000) 'Between Sovereignty and Globalization – Where Does the United Nations Fit In?', *Development Dialogue* (1–2), pp. 5–14.
Van Krieken, Peter J. (ed.) (2002) *Terrorism and the International Legal Order: With Special Reference to the UN, the EU and Cross-border Aspects*, The Hague.
Varwick, Johannes (2003) 'Preventing War, Securing Peace', *Transatlantic International Politics* (1) pp. 11–16.
Vasak, Karel (1974) 'Le droit international des droits de l'homme', *Recueil des Cours de L'Académie de Droit International*, vol. IV, pp. 333–415.

Vassilakis, Adamantios (2006) *Report of the Informal Working Group of the Security Council on General Issues of Sanctions* (UN document S/2006/997).
Verdross, Alfred and Bruno Simma (1984) *Universelles Völkerrecht*, Berlin.
Victor, David G. (2001) *The Collapse of the Kyoto Protocol and the Struggle to Slow Global Warming*, Princeton, NJ.
Vienna Declaration and Programme of Action (1993) (UN document A/Conf.157/23 of 12 July 1993).
Viotti, Paul R. and Mark V. Kauppi (2001) *International Relations Theory*, Boston, MA.
Voeten, Erik (2000) 'Clashes in the Assembly', *International Organization* (2) pp. 185–215.
Vogler, John (2008) 'Environmental Issues', in: Baylis and Smith (2008) pp. 350–69.
Voigtländer, René (2001) *Notwehrrecht und kollektive Verantwortung*, Frankfurt-am-Main.
Volger, Helmut (ed.) (2010) *A Concise Encyclopedia of the United Nations*, 2nd revised edition, Leiden and Boston.
Völkerbundssatzung (1919), in: Knipping *et al.* (1995) pp. 401–25.
Wagner, Teresa and Leslie Carbone (eds) (2001) *Fifty Years after the Declaration: The United Nations' Record on Human Rights*, Lanham, MD.
Waldmann, Jörg (1999) 'Agenda 21 – ein neuer Ansatz zur Lösung internationaler Probleme?', *Politische Bildung* (1) pp. 73–87.
Wallensteen, Peter (2002) *Understanding Conflicts. War, Peace and the Global System*, London.
Weber, Hermann (1995) 'League of Nations', in: Wolfrum (1995), pp. 848–53.
Wehberg, Hans (1927) *Das Genfer Protokoll betreffend die friedliche Erledigung internationaler Streitigkeiten*, Berlin.
Weiss, Thomas G. (1996) 'Humanitäre Intervention. Lehren aus der Vergangenheit, Konsequenzen für die Zukunft', in: Debiel and Nuscheler (1996), pp. 53–75.
Weiss, Thomas G., David P. Forsythe and Roger A. Coate (2000) *The United Nations and Changing World Politics*, Boulder, CO.
Weiss, Thomas G and Sam Daws (eds) (2007) *The Oxford Handbook on the United Nations*, Oxford.
Weizsäcker, Richard von and Moeen Quereshi (1995) *The United Nations in its Second Half Century. A Report of the Independent Working Group on the Future of the United Nations*, New York.
Wellens, Karel (ed.) (2001) *Resolutions and Statements of the United Nations Security Council (1946–2000)*, The Hague.
White House (2002) *The National Security Strategy of the United States of America*, Washington, DC.
White, Nigel D. (2002) *The United Nations System: Toward International Justice*, Boulder, CO.
WHO (World Health Organization), *World Health Report*, Geneva (published annually).
Wieczorek-Zeul, Heidemarie (2000) 'Deutsche Entwicklungspolitik', in: Nuscheler (2000), pp. 131–43.
Wiesbrock, Katja (2002) 'Die Supranationalisierung des Völkerrechts', *Sicherheit und Frieden* (3), pp. 157–62.
Wilenski, Peter (1993) 'The Structure of the UN in the Post-Cold-War Period', in: Roberts and Kingsbury (1993) pp. 437–67.
Wilson, Woodrow (1918) 'Rede des Präsidenten der Vereinigten Staaten vor beiden Häusern des Kongresses', in: Knipping *et al.* (1995) pp. 360–07.
Wissenschaftlicher Beirat der Bundesregierung Globale Umweltgefahren (ed.) (2001) *Welt im Wandel: Neue Strukturen globaler Umweltpolitik*, Berlin.
Witte, Jan Martin, Charlotte Streck and Thorsten Benner (eds) (2003) *Progress or Peril? Partnership and Networks in Global Environmental Governance*, Washington, DC.

Wöhlcke, Manfred (1992) *Der ökologische Nord-Süd-Konflikt. Interessen, Argumente und Verantwortlichkeiten in der internationalen Umweltpolitik,* Ebenhausen (SWP-Studie 380).

Wolfrum, Hildegard (1995) 'Woman's Rights', in: Wolfrum with Philipp (1995) pp. 1450–59.

Wolfrum, Rüdiger (2002) 'Preamble', in: Simma (2002) pp. 33–7.

Wolfrum, Rüdiger with Christiane Philipp (eds) (1995) *United Nations: Law, Policies and Practice,* 2 vols, Munich.

World Bank, *World Development Report,* Washington, DC (published annually).

World Bank (2000) *Global Statistics,* New York.

World Food Program (2008) *Strategic Plan*, New York.

World Resources Institute, *World Resources,* New York (published annually).

World Summit (2005) '2005 World Summit Outcome' (UN document A/RES/60/1).

Woyke, Wichard (ed.) (2004) *Handwörterbuch Internationale Politik,* 9th edition, Wiesbaden.

WTO (World Trade Organization), *International Trade,* Geneva (published annually).

Yoder, Amos (1997) *The Evolution of the United Nations System,* Washington, DC.

Zangl, Bernhard and Michael Zürn (2003) *Frieden and Krieg. Sicherheit in der nationalen und postnationalen Konstellation,* Frankfurt-am-Main.

Ziring, Lawrence, Robert E. Riggs and Jack C. Plano, (2000) *The United Nations: International Organization and World Politics,* South Melbourne.

Zumach, Andreas (2001) 'Globale Zukunftssicherung oder Geldverschwendung? Was die UN-Weltkonferenzen bewirken könne', *Internationale Politik* (5) pp. 21–4.

Zürn, Michael (1998) *Regieren jenseits des Nationalstaates. Globalisierung and Denationalisierung als Chance,* Frankfurt-am-Main.

Index